2ND EDITION

INFORMATION SYSTEMS

a business approach

Steve Benson
EDITH COWAN UNIVERSITY

Craig Standing
EDITH COWAN UNIVERSITY

WILEY
John Wiley & Sons Australia, Ltd

Second edition published 2005 by
John Wiley & Sons Australia, Ltd
42 McDougall Street, Milton, Qld 4064

Typeset in 10/11.5 pt Giovanni Light

National Library of Australia
Cataloguing-in-Publication data

Benson, Steve.
Information systems: a business approach.

2nd ed. Includes index.
For tertiary students.
ISBN 978 0 470 80467 4.

1. Management information systems.
2. Information resources management.
I. Standing, Craig. II. Title.

658.40380285

Printed in Singapore by
Kyodo Printing Co (S'pore) Pte Ltd

10 9 8 7 6 5 4

Contents

CHAPTER 6

Systems integration: information systems at work 149

CHAPTER 7

Introduction to systems development 178

Preface

Information Systems: A Business Approach second edition has been developed and organised for:

- students, professionals, managers, accountants and other professional groups who require a foundation in information systems with a business emphasis
- undergraduate courses where there is an information systems component of study
- undergraduate courses in computer science where a business approach to information systems is required
- postgraduate courses in which there is a foundation-level unit in information systems
- Master of Business Administration (MBA) courses where there is an information systems component
- professional-level courses in information systems and information technology.

This text forms the basis for lecture, seminar and tutorial materials and can be used in standard, online and flexible delivery modes.

Why we wrote the book

There are many foundation-level textbooks on information systems and information technology, so why have we written another? We argue that our book is different. It provides a business perspective of information systems and emphasises how information systems can be used to improve the strategic, tactical and operational performance of business.

It is important to realise that information systems are not merely supporting technology for business operations, but are major competitive forces in their own right and drivers for organisational change. These themes recur throughout the text and are examined in depth in our coverage of e-commerce.

Another major difference is our emphasis on principles. Our text highlights core principles of business and information systems and illustrates them using regional and global examples. In a world in which technology and business environments change rapidly, it is important to focus on developing transferable skills which can be applied to new problems and situations as they arise. In all our dealings with IS consultants and employers, we found this to be a constant theme: a sound knowledge of business and information systems principles, adaptability and flexibility, and good communication skills are prerequisites for success.

What is different in the second edition of this book? As with the first edition, we consulted extensively with students, academics, businesses, professional bodies and information systems practitioners. In response to their input we have updated content throughout, most notably in chapters which cover hardware, networking and e-commerce. New sections have been added on wireless networking and security. Requests to provide an extra chapter on ethics were considered carefully, but rather than depart from the 12-chapter format which was such an attractive feature of the first edition, we decided to provide an online supplement to meet this need.

Our target audience has not changed since we wrote the first edition. However, we have been pleased to note that the book has found its way into businesses and consulting houses in different parts of the world, confirming its relevance to professional practice.

The first edition of this text was designed for effective learning. The second edition has built on this and has additional resources for the lecturer.

Key features of the book

Before writing this book we undertook an extensive review of information systems curricula in universities and colleges in Australia, Europe and the United States. Each of the resulting 12 chapters was developed and modified in close consultation with academics and students. Our intention was to produce a book which was applicable and adaptable to a wide variety of course structures. The book incorporates the following useful features:

- *Principles*: The key principles of the information systems discipline are highlighted throughout. These provide a solid foundation for new students so that they can gain an understanding of the concept and the principle behind it, as well as examples of it in practice, i.e. teach through principles — support by examples.
- *Reflection questions*: In accordance with the principles of good cognitive design, each chapter includes questions closely associated with their related concepts. These often relate to the reader's personal observations or extra options not covered in the text. These questions can form the basis of research exercises or be used as rhetorical questions to stimulate the reader's thought processes for a few seconds. Accordingly, the book actively engages readers in learning.
- *IS in action*: The 'IS in Action' boxes provide up-to-date illustrations of how real-world organisations are using information systems to increase productivity, reduce costs or gain competitive advantage. They serve as a mechanism to show the concepts in practice in the business environment, and allow students to look through a window to the professional world of information systems. The companies and situations chosen reflect the global nature of information systems and information technology and highlight best practice on a world scale. Once information systems skills and knowledge have been gained, those same skills are in demand internationally.
- *Info bytes*: Each chapter includes a number of 'Info Bytes' — concise, up-to-date examples of the latest technologies and developments related to the information systems profession.
- *Key concepts:* These short statements are embedded into each chapter and provide insight and advice from a practitioner's perspective.
- *Case studies*: At the end of each chapter there is a case study which focuses on the concepts and principles emphasised in that chapter. The case studies can be used as individual exercises or as the basis of tutorial sessions using group work to discuss the various issues which arise from the material. Each case has a number of key questions which can be used to start the analysis. The case studies encourage the development of metacognition and communication skills in students.
- *Questions*: Each chapter has a number of questions designed to help revise the chapter's material. These can be used to test students' knowledge and understanding of each chapter.
- *Exercises*: Exercises provide tasks to be completed by students to consolidate understanding of the principles or to gather and analyse additional information. The exercises can form the basis of a tutorial or laboratory session.

Other resources for lecturers

An instructor's resource guide provides:

- an overview of the authors' teaching philosophies and strategies with suggestions for small and large groups and course organisations
- a set of PowerPoint slides for each lecture with accompanying notes, supporting examples and further references and sources where indicated
- model answers for the questions, exercises and cases studies
- examples of assignments and examinations with marking schemes

- a collection of test questions.
- acts as a portal, providing lists of useful sites, sources of information and case studies
- provides access to 'hot' news items and technology briefings
- provides a set of additional exercises and case studies to allow for several runs of a course without repetition.

The web site (www.johnwiley.com.au/highered/IS2e) will be maintained and updated on an ongoing basis.

A web chapter devoted to business and professional ethics gives an introduction to ethical theory and practice. It provides numerous ethical vignettes and cases suitable for class discussion or individual consideration.

In support of the PowerPoint slides, a second collection of PowerPoint slides will contain video mini-lectures. These were first developed for students using the text in distance mode, but provided a useful resource for academics. Adopters of the text should contact their Wiley sales representative for the PowerPoint slides with videos.

Organisation of the book

The text divides into two sections. The first six chapters introduce students to the various components of information systems within a business context, including hardware, software, networking, systems integration, enterprise resource planning and knowledge management.

The second half of the text covers the development and management issues related to information systems and e-business. A major feature of the book is its coverage of e-business strategy and development. These are given considerable emphasis since they are such an important part of the many organisational transformations that are taking place.

The last chapter examines the topic of personal information management, which is relevant to students and practitioners alike. While organisational information systems have made great progress, the individuals in organisations are often drowning in a sea of information. This chapter examines the tools, methods and techniques that can be used to operate effectively on a personal level in business.

We are confident that you will find this text readable and relevant.

Steve Benson and Craig Standing
August 2004

About the authors

Steve Benson

Dr Steve Benson is currently a senior lecturer in Management and Information Systems at Edith Cowan University in Western Australia. He holds a first-class honours degree in computer science and geology and a Master of Science in systems design from the University of Manchester. He completed a Doctor of Philosophy at Curtin University in Western Australia where he researched teaching excellence in information systems.

Steve has worked as an analyst and software developer in real time and business systems and has over 20 years experience in tertiary education, including periods as head of department and school. His background also includes motor vehicle engineering, management, geology and computer science. He has published at international conferences and in international journals. Steve maintains a small but active consultancy providing specialist services to education and industry in Australia and Canada, and is a member of both the Internet Society and the IEEE.

Craig Standing

Craig Standing is currently Professor in Strategic Information Systems in the School of Management and Information Systems at Edith Cowan University in Western Australia. He completed a Master of Science in computation at the University of Manchester Institute of Science and Technology, and a Doctor of Philosophy at the University of Western Australia. He is a member of the British Computer Society and the Australian Computer Society.

Craig has an international reputation in the field of management information systems, has published widely in leading journals, and has presented his work at conferences worldwide. He is a consultant to local and international companies in the private and public sectors, specialising in information systems strategy and knowledge management.

Acknowledgements

The authors and the publisher would like to thank the following copyright holders, organisations and individuals for their assistance and permission to reproduce copyright material in this book.

Images

Fig 1.1: © Richard T. Watson • p. 15 (Prof. Kevin Warwick): Copyright iCube Solutions • fig 3.1: Screenshots reprinted by permission from Microsoft Corporation • fig. 3.3: Bootstrap Institute/Douglas Engelbart • fig. 7.3, 7.4, 7.9: © Knowledge Base • fig. 9.4: Special permission to reproduce 'Capability Maturity Model', © 2000 by Carnegie Mellon University, is granted by the Software Engineering Institute • fig. 10.5: © EBAY INC. All rights reserved • fig 10.8: © Ariba. www.ariba.com • fig. 11.1: © Nokia/Hausmann Communications • fig. 11.2: © IBM • fig. 11.5: © iSelect Pty Ltd • fig 12.2: Newspix/Troy Bendeich.

Text

Extracts from British Computer Society Code of Conduct. © The British Computer Society: pp. 331–2 • Excerpt from 'What is CRM?', © David Sims, CRM writer, david@davidsims.com: p. 215.

Chapter 1

Setting the scene

LEARNING OBJECTIVES

After reading this chapter, you should be able to:

- understand the three waves of knowledge
- understand what an information system is, how information systems are developed, and the nature of the discipline
- understand the distinctions between data, information and knowledge
- understand what is meant by the term 'system'
- understand the relationship between information systems and other disciplines such as computer science, information technology and management
- understand the three main functions that information systems serve
- understand the effects of information systems on business
- understand the benefits of information systems from a business perspective
- understand the role played by information systems in business process re-engineering (BPR) and enterprise resource planning (ERP).

1

Introduction

Since the publication of the first edition of this book there have been huge advances in technology and communication. These are best regarded as 'enabling mechanisms' or opportunities to transform and improve the way in which businesses operate and compete. The principles that underpin effective business operations have not altered significantly in the last hundred years or so. However, economic, social and technical trends have become shaping forces in the way in which businesses organise and operate. Information systems (IS) as a discipline has an intimate relationship with business. Businesses define their own information systems, and information systems constantly redefine business. In seeking to define information systems for the purposes of this text, we found two visions that seem to prevail in academia and industry. The first is that information systems is about 'developing a business philosophy of technology', and the second is that information systems is about 'using technology to gain tactical and strategic advantages in business'. The second view is the one that comes closest to what we believe: information systems is so much more than 'business computing'.

The aim of this chapter is to define a context for the study of information systems as a business discipline. It will help you to realise that it does not exist in a vacuum — it relates to every other business discipline. These disciplines in their turn operate in broader social and economic contexts. In order to be effective in the workplace you will need to appreciate these contexts because they will dictate what you do, the way you do it and why you do it. Information systems are social systems (at the very least they are systems with social implications). Although information systems make extensive use of technology, most consultants will tell you that they work in a 'people business' and that human factors are often more important than technical ones in successful systems. Understanding this will give a much better chance of success with information systems projects compared with those who take a narrower, technical view. Remember, 'Everything is connected to everything else' (attributed to Lenin; see Lyn & Jay 1989).

In order to understand where information systems are taking us, it is necessary to understand the nature of competition and the trends that influence business. To understand trends we need to examine the past. The Industrial Revolution transformed the way in which societies were structured and operated. It tends to be taught in schools as matter of factual history, i.e. something that happened at some time in the past and is now over. The truth is that the Industrial Revolution is still on a roll; however, we are in a position to examine its major effects. First, population centres developed around areas that had the right sort of resources (iron, coal, clay) and were fairly easily accessible by water or road. Other transport issues would be considered later. This led to the development of areas of expertise or 'clusters'. The economies were those of scale since transport costs were relatively low compared to manufacturing costs. With maturity, the centres of expertise were so well established that it was cheaper to take raw materials to manufacturing centres than to move people to the source of the raw material. Peter Drucker, in his book *Post Capitalist Society*, describes this period as the first wave of knowledge creation: the application of knowledge to industrial tools and technologies.

Drucker describes the second wave as the application of knowledge to human endeavour. This culminated in the development of scientific management by Taylor and Henry Ford, but the foundations had been laid more than a century earlier by Eli Whitney whose manufacturing systems allowed unskilled labour to mass produce goods and armaments. The development of the production line, attributed to Henry Ford, was merely an extension of the worker specialisation that was seen in the Chicago meat-packing factories in the 1860s. This second wave still represents the state of the art for most of the world. However, this wave peaked in the 1960s when computer technology began to be applied to engineering and business in a truly commercial sense. Again the economies are those of scale, being mass manufacture and, by implication, mass standardisation (the importance of standards is something we will return to time and again in this text).

Drucker's third wave concerns the application of knowledge to knowledge and hence the creation of wealth. It is here where businesses will differentiate themselves in the 'knowledge economy'. Here change is constant, and organisations must learn, adapt and manage their knowledge resources in order to survive. The fundamentals of competition (innovation, quality, speed to market and price) will still be significant business drivers, but the environments in which we operate are in a state of flux. As an example consider the establishment of large economic trading blocs such as the European Community and negotiations for free trade zones. This wave represents a real challenge for information systems professionals, but it also offers wonderful career and consulting opportunities. This text is intended to help you position yourself to take advantage of those opportunities.

Understanding information systems involves considering the key concepts and components, the nature of the IS **paradigm**/discipline and its relationship to other business disciplines. Our aim is to help you to develop a useful understanding of a vital business sector and the context in which it operates by presenting different but complementary perspectives of information systems with an emphasis on principles and IS in practice. We recommend that you keep that goal in mind as you read through this book.

Data, information and knowledge

To understand what information systems are we need to introduce some terms and establish a context for study. Different kinds of information systems and how they process data are considered in chapter 4, but for now it is enough to distinguish between data, information and knowledge.

- Data (singular form *datum*) are the raw inputs of information systems. For example, data might be the customer, order and payment details that are gathered in day-to-day business activities.
- Information is processed or value-added data. From an input/output perspective, data are input, processed in some way and then output. This view is rooted in the data processing thinking of the 1950s and 1960s which tends to focus on processes rather than on outcomes. Information is data which have been manipulated or summarised to highlight trends or features.
- Knowledge is understanding what the information means or implies. Knowledge is a human thing — it is based on experience and is subjective in nature.

As an example of the differences between data, information and knowledge, think about a spreadsheet which gives the raw sales figures for each product line for each financial quarter over a full year. These raw figures are data that require a great deal of processing — producing a graph or chart summarising the data would yield information. Managers request information and apply their knowledge to make decisions or plans. Figure 1.1 shows the relationship between data, information and knowledge.

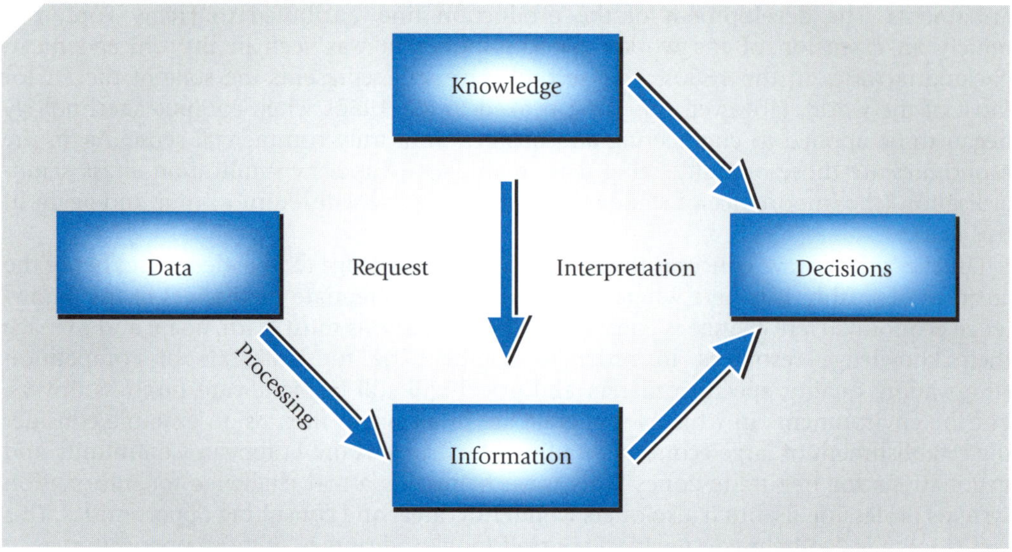

Figure 1.1 The relationship between data, information and knowledge
Source: Watson (1999, p. 27)

Information systems is about generating and managing information. Think of information as an asset or strategic resource. The more up to date and accurate your information is, the greater the advantage you possess. The business environment is now far more volatile than in the past. A short time frame can make the difference between profit and loss on the stock market. Knowing the asset and share value of your business can enable decisions to be made regarding takeovers. **Chief information officers (CIOs)** manage corporate information. Their view of information varies between resource, asset and commodity, allowing a dollar value to be placed on corporate information.

■ **Reflection question 1:** How would you go about classifying information for business purposes?

IS in action

Working smarter — not harder

Few business sectors have been changed by the Internet as much as the travel and hospitality sector. Internet users from all over the world are able to deal directly with airlines and hotels and save money in the process. For many travel companies prospects look bleak. For Trailfinders the solution is simple — use technology to enhance its existing business operation and realise its intellectual capital. Every Trailfinders consultant is required to have travelled extensively and to undergo a rigorous training program. Knowledge about booking systems, flights, hotels, geography, local customs and regulations all contribute to making the travel experience trouble free. But competing on cost, quality and convenience is only part of the Trailfinders business model. The Trailfinders web site allows customers and browsers to make routine enquiries, check on itineraries, etc. and also carries adverts for products, services and jobs. This not only saves costs but also allows staff to spend more time providing personalised, friendly service. The lesson is simple: to survive and thrive businesses must adapt to change.

Source: Information from www.trailfinders.com.au (accessed 23 July 2003).

It is more difficult to define knowledge than it is to define data or information. In fact, there is much controversy over the definition. Data and information can be measured in bytes, but what are the units of knowledge? Although some people contend that knowledge is meta-information, i.e. information about information, a more constructivist perspective is taken here. Knowledge is understanding the meaning and importance of information. Given that people interpret information on the basis of their own experience, knowledge must be subjective and internally (and personally) constructed. There is a naive realist assumption among many managers that information and knowledge are the same thing (Benson & Standing 2000). As the 'knowledge economy' grows in importance, managers need to shift their focus from information to knowledge. Since information and knowledge are different, trying to manage them in the same way is a recipe for failure. Drucker (1993) equates knowledge with power; thus the challenge faced by most businesses is how to encourage employees to share knowledge rather than keep it to themselves.

What is a system?

A system is 'a collection of parts that work together to achieve some purpose', according to Dr Alfred Howarth, a retired British computing academic. For a person with two degrees in mathematics and many years experience in using computers to model real-world phenomena, the above answer is surprisingly accessible. However, the way in which people define things largely depends on their life experiences, i.e. there is an element of subjectivity. To reach a more widely applicable definition a few more viewpoints must be examined. Dr Howarth's view was influenced by his work — the word 'parts' implies a physical nature to the systems he was modelling. Others regard a system as a set of related ideas or constructs which are organised in some way. In this context the system is purely abstract, perhaps a set of defined terms or an entire philosophical paradigm.

A distinction can be made between natural and human-made systems — the solar system is natural, the social security system is human-made. Some systems might be a combination of physical, abstract, natural and human-made subsystems. Here are some generalisations about systems:

- A system has a purpose or function.
- A system has a context or environment in which it has applicability.
- A system has a boundary which marks the limits of its environment.
- The removal of a single component of a system will cause that system to fail.
- A system usually has inputs and outputs.
- Complex systems usually consist of subsystems which in turn may have subsystems of their own.
- A component may belong to more than one system.

Looking at this list you can now understand the quotation 'Everything is connected to everything else'. It is the interconnectedness of systems, subsystems and components that makes life so difficult for system developers. Where to draw the boundary of a system is one of the most difficult questions that has to be considered in designing any system. Fortunately, there are methods, tools, techniques and even systems for thinking about systems, as you'll see in chapter 7.

What is an information system?

Over the years, the reliability of the underlying technology improved and there was a realisation that information systems had a social dimension, as many of the problems were identified as being people-related. The definition of an information system became broader, and the components of an information system were generally accepted as:

- people
- data/information
- procedures
- software
- hardware
- communications.

These components and their interactions are explained in some detail throughout this book and provide a basic structure not only for developing information systems but also for the discipline as a whole.

The history of information systems

Information systems have been around for at least 6000 years. Early information systems gave rise to the development of written language, accountancy, taxation and banking (Davies 1996).

The application of computing technology to information processing occurred at the end of the 1950s. In the 1960s, computer systems began to be used for truly commercial purposes. Before that time they had been used in science and engineering in the first phase of the information revolution. Just as the Industrial Revolution extended physical capabilities, so the information revolution extended mental capabilities, initially in the area of calculation, as problems which could take a human a lifetime to solve could be handled by a computer on a time scale that was almost immediate (e.g. finite element analysis calculations for the design of a modern skyscraper). From there it was a short step to using computers to access, process and filter huge quantities of data. This did not produce knowledge or give insight, but simply allowed mundane tasks to be automated and interesting questions to be raised and (potentially) answered. Many of the scientists and engineers who had worked in computer science fields moved into information-related activities, bringing with them a mindset that was rigorous, logical and grounded in mathematical notation. This exerted a huge influence over the development of the discipline for many years to come.

By the early 1970s, 'information systems' was appearing in the curricula of American universities. A question that needs to be asked is whether the mere inclusion of a subject in university curricula qualifies it as a discipline. The prevailing view seems to be that information systems as a field was insufficiently mature to be considered a discipline in its own right at that time. It seemed to be dependent on computer science and management for its existence.

There are two kinds of disciplines that are relevant in this context: scientific and engineering. People who work in scientific disciplines are concerned with classifying phenomena and developing and testing theories. In contrast, those who work in engineering disciplines are concerned with constructing and testing artefacts. Weber (1997) notes that both scientific and engineering disciplines were represented in the emerging information systems field. This led to the somewhat schizophrenic nature of information systems, as practitioners wondered whether they belonged to a scientific or engineering discipline.

A discipline has a paradigm (system of working) and an infrastructure (journals, committees and so on) that provide coherence. The more mature the paradigm, the higher the level of coherence and the better defined the discipline, i.e. an orthodoxy of terminology, philosophy and **methodology** emerges.

For pure sciences the paradigms are well established and reasonably easy to articulate. For social sciences (education, psychology and so on) the paradigms are not well defined — indeed part of the paradigm is to seek to define the paradigm. Such a high level of self-reference actively prevents a high degree of coherence resulting in divergence and differentiation, i.e. schools of thought within the discipline.

In the mid-1970s another school of information systems thinking emerged, which considered information systems to be a social system. Management had also been involved in the information systems area, since it was business-related. With four main constituents, the emerging information systems discipline was lacking coherence. Additionally the academic publishing system encouraged authors to produce highly specialised papers, focusing on the differences between authors rather than searching for common ground. When one considers the range of jobs within the industry and the huge number of specialist journals on information systems, it would appear that the discipline is fragmented. However, when talking to practitioners and academics there seems to be broad agreement on the core concepts.

During the formative period of information systems as a subject, however, there was little agreement as to what constituted information systems. In 1972, John Dearden of the Harvard Business School wrote, 'Management Information Systems is embedded in a mish-mash of fuzzy thinking and incomprehensible jargon' (Weber 1997, p. 2). Dearden's comments provoked an outcry from academia and industry. The most notable reaction was a sudden quest for respectability as journals, professional bodies and conferences promoted credible research and scholarship began to emerge. At the first International Conference on Information Systems, Keen (1980) argued that information systems researchers should borrow from other (more developed) disciplines, such as economics and behavioural sciences. It is possible that research methods became more important than research subjects for a time. However, this tended to emphasise the multidisciplinary nature of information systems.

Any discipline which is rapidly evolving and growing and which is partly based on rapidly developing technology is unlikely to be stable. With increasing maturity, higher-level (and less divisive) views of the nature of information systems have emerged. Unlike other philosophies, there is no great search for eternal truths or answers to the big questions. Real-world constraints mean that the perfect system will never be built; instead the search is directed towards finding the best compromise.

What is an information system for?

According to McKeown (2001), an information system exists to fulfil three basic functions:

- remembering the past
- handling the present
- preparing for the future.

Consider a motorcycle dealership. The level of stock on hand is variable. The owners do not want to tie up too much capital in components; equally, they do not want to lose business and let their customers down. They know there are seasonal variations in purchasing behaviour — many customers put their motorcycles off the road in winter and go into maintenance mode, but when summer comes, those customers take to the road, and demand for service items such as air filters and brake pads increases.

Table 1.1 shows the three basic information systems functions and associated tasks. The information needs of businesses will vary as will the technology deployed to achieve the tasks. However, the three basic functions apply to any information system.

TABLE 1.1 Three information systems functions with example tasks

Information systems function	Information systems task
Remembering the past	Analysing past transaction and purchasing patterns
Handling the present	Recording current transaction patterns, automating payment and ordering mechanisms, effecting stock control
Preparing for the future	Planning future inventory on the basis of statistical forecasts

The relationship of information systems to other disciplines

Earlier in this chapter, the multidisciplinary nature of information systems was alluded to. Given that 'everything is connected to everything else', it would be useful to see exactly where the field of information systems sits in relation to other disciplines.

Information systems or information technology?

There is a tendency on the part of some managers to regard information technology and information systems as being the same thing. This is not the case — information systems rely on technology and on other things such as people and procedures. Put simply, information technology is about the 'what?' questions of systems (e.g. what provides the processing power?). Information systems are about the 'how?' and 'why?' of systems (e.g. how do we manage the system? why are we doing this?).

Information technology is the hardware, software and communications that support information systems. There is a degree of overlap between the two. An understanding of the principles of information technology is needed for a person to be effective in information systems, but access to technical expertise when it is needed is important. To establish a context for how the different technical disciplines relate, refer to figure 1.2, which shows a framework for relating business and computing disciplines. Progressing from left to right in the figure, the trend is to move away from detailed, concrete, machine-oriented areas to more abstract, human-oriented areas, i.e. from technical skills to transferable skills. Note that working in a technical discipline requires a considerable amount of effort in order to keep up to date with the changes in technology. Although this makes for an interesting life, it makes it harder to develop a career path (hence the popularity of MBA courses). Information systems depend on technology but places a much greater emphasis on transferable skills; in short, it is easier to maintain skills in the information systems area than it is in the computer science area. Moving from electrical engineering to management, the trend is to move from highly structured activities to loosely structured activities.

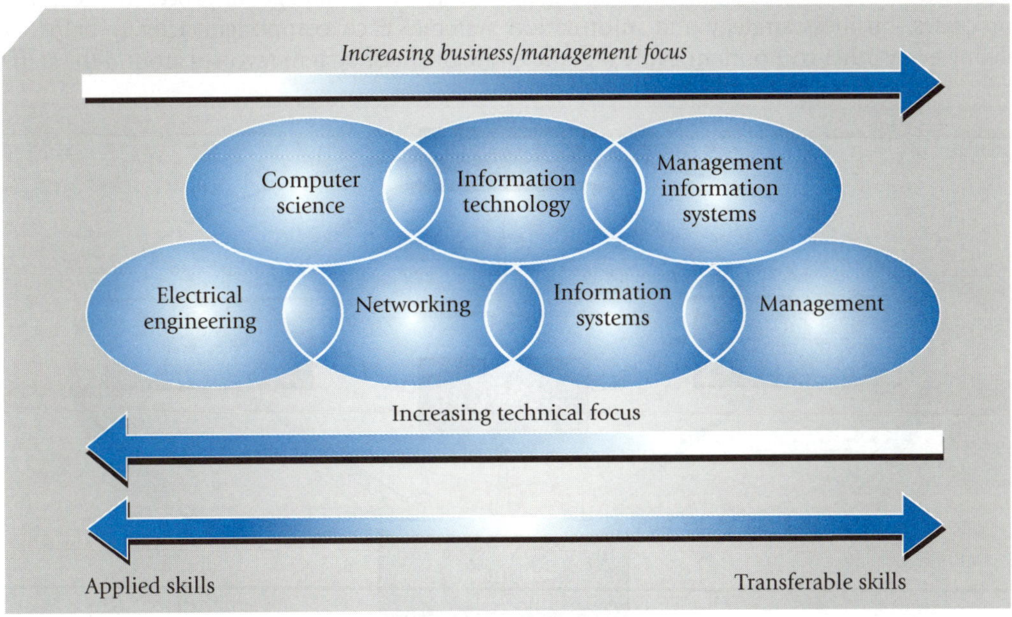

Figure 1.2 The relationship between information systems and other disciplines

Is information systems management a subset of management?

The information systems area has always had an ongoing need for high capital expenditure and a greater degree of complexity than other management functions. Additionally, there are problems associated with security and ethics. Being effective in this area requires an unusual blend of attributes. Information systems management draws on financial, human resource, operations and strategic management disciplines but could not easily be classified as any one of these. There is a reluctance on the part of many organisations to accept information systems management as a school of management in its own right. In many cases, there is a prevailing culture that says 'if you are a manager, you can manage anything'. This is somewhat contentious. Many projects fail because of overconfidence on the part of management. Some managers fail to realise the limitations of their staff and the supporting technology. Yourdon (1997) refers to these projects as 'death march' projects in which management pursues mission-critical systems with insufficient funds, insufficient staff and insufficient time. System development and project management will be examined later in this text. If anything needs to be emphasised it is that the human aspects of information systems management are vital. After all, any technical problem has a technical solution, provided staff have sufficient motivation. Motivating staff is the real problem.

The multidisciplinary nature of information systems means that information systems management cannot be regarded as a proper subset of any other school of management. For at least a quarter of a century there have been professional journals, conferences and associations for information systems management. It could therefore be argued that information systems management is sufficiently distinct to be regarded as a discipline in its own right. It affects every other business discipline, as discussed in the following sections. Figure 1.3 shows that an information system is usually part of a business system, which in turn may be regarded as the interaction of five main constituents: staff, managerial processes, business processes, business strategy and information systems. Each component actively helps to define every other component. Note that the entire business system revolves around the staff.

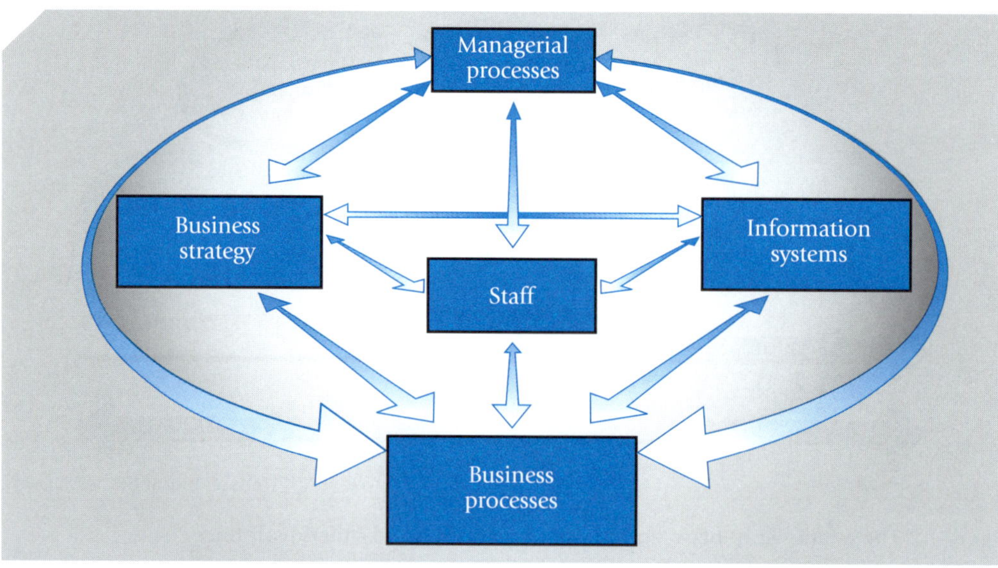

Figure 1.3 Five components of a business system

Technology and business trends

Any work of art, building or artefact is a product of its time and culture and is best appreciated when something is known of its time and culture. Information systems, technology and management philosophies are also products of their time and culture. To appreciate them, the trends that have led to their creation and shaped their development must be examined. Overwhelmingly, these trends have been economic.

In 1994 John Naisbit wrote one of a series of books on megatrends. His insightful analysis was wide-ranging, but only a few of his themes will be covered here. First, Naisbit argues that economic trading blocks are getting bigger. Next he suggests that companies are getting smaller on average, which comes about from the application of intelligence and technology. The evidence for this may be found by examining the decline in the contribution of the Fortune 500 to the gross domestic product (GDP) of the United States over a 20-year period, during which time it virtually halved. (The Fortune 500 is an annual list of the 500 largest industrial corporations in the United States, published by *Fortune* magazine; the corporations are ranked on such things as revenue, profits and market value.) At the time Naisbit was writing, just over 55% of the GDP of the United States came from **small–medium enterprises** (SMEs), many of them true multinationals. These trends continue (Audretsch et al. 2000): personal wealth is increasing, and downsizing is an ongoing corporate phenomenon. Naturally there are exceptions. Some megacorporations — most notably those in the communications and media sectors — continue to grow, but on average companies are getting smaller.

What circumstances brought about this state of affairs? Advances in manufacturing technology account for some of this shift. A traditional large corporation relies on economies of scale, reducing the unit cost of manufacture by bulk purchases, mass manufacture and substantial investment in infrastructure. It was this massive investment requirement that was the barrier to market entry for manufacturing 'wannabes'. The advent of microprocessors and **flexible manufacturing systems (FMS)** has allowed many smaller companies to enter the market, since the entry costs have been reduced by the new technology. (Flexible manufacturing systems are computer-operated manufacturing tools which can carry out a wide range of processes as compared with the older, highly specialised, single-function machinery.)

The new machinery is capable of performing many tasks rather than a small number of highly specialised tasks. This allows production lines to be much smaller and makes it economical to set up for small production runs since FMS do not need to retool when switching between production runs. Additionally, manufacturing instructions and designs can now be accepted in electronic form, thus eliminating several steps in the old-fashioned process. This technology-driven shift means that geographic proximity is a more important advantage than sheer size. Since only 5% of manufacturing time is spent in adding value to the product, purchasing materials in bulk to obtain discounts does not yield a significant advantage. Bulk handling requires storage facilities and often leads to overcapitalisation in stock. Small companies are able to accept and make small deliveries frequently and quickly, allowing **just-in-time (JIT) delivery** and manufacturing strategies to be used. Coupled with fast payment mechanisms, this shortens timelines and speeds cash flow, thus improving the competitive edge. Some areas of the UK car industry have used this and made use of many small suppliers, not only giving greater flexibility and reducing stock on hand levels but also spreading risk. A strike from a major supplier would have crippled production previously, but now a car manufacturer can simply increase orders to other suppliers. Some manufacturers have taken the concept a little further. In some of the Volkswagen factories, the people who make the doors actually fit the doors; thus Volkswagen is able to reduce labour costs and stock on hand. This suggests two things: first, that the car manufacturing industry is in a process of transition to becoming a car manufacturing community; second, that intellectual capital is of increasing importance in the new industrial paradigm.

IS in action

Applying intelligence to inventory

In 2003 Harley-Davidson celebrated a hundred years of motorcycle manufacture and almost 20 years of profitable operation. Yet in 1981 the American icon was on the verge of extinction. Sales had dropped to a third of their usual level, and its US home market was in the grip of a recession. Reduced cash flow meant that the company was in default on its loans and needed to generate money to make its loan payments. Additionally, the home market had been flooded by Japanese motorcycles. Harley-Davidson's manufacturing processes were outdated, and it was impossible to leverage the capital required for new technology.

Its only road to survival lay in cutting costs. It was not possible to generate money from sales to repay loans so the company looked at work-in-progress inventory management to fund its payments. Introducing a variant of JIT called **materials as needed (MAN)**, Harley-Davidson was able to save more than $50 million from their work-in-progress inventory in a two-year period (Reid 1990). Although the company was not making any profit, cash flow was positive.

A quarter of a century later MAN is still a fundamental part of Harley-Davidson's continuing success.

Source: Information from www.harley-davidson.com (accessed 31 March 2004)

[**Key concept:** The secret of success is to work smarter — not harder.]

The prevalence of microprinting shops also emphasises the advantage of geography over size, i.e. the costs of distribution become the most significant factor in competition. Another factor to consider is the volatility of the business environment: things change quickly. The critical elements of competition are innovation, quality and speed to market. It is usually easier for small organisations to achieve in these areas than it is for large organisations. Many larger companies are restructuring along clustered lines to try to obtain the benefits of both large and small business organisational management.

Reducing market entry costs

The major barrier costs to market entry are usually advertising and business promotion. Many new companies have a very high dollar-turnover-to-staff ratio when compared with traditional manufacturing concerns. One reason for this is that they tend to make products which have a high level of intellectual content, such as software. Once the initial design and concepts are verified, the major costs are advertising and shipping, since there are few raw materials involved in the process.

In a traditional mass-marketing operation, businesses make use of broadcast advertising. The cost of TV advertising for a small–medium enterprise (SME) in start-up phase is usually prohibitive. However, depending on the nature of the business, Internet styles of operation may be ideal. Here the consumer has taken on the bulk of the costs: a computer, Internet service provider (ISP) fees and communications costs. A large corporation can have only one web site in a meaningful sense, i.e. the name www.largecorp.com is unique, just as www.smallbiz.com is. As far as the consumer is concerned, both large and small companies are on the same footing when it comes to searching the World Wide Web. Unless a company pays to register with an intermediary such as a search engine, then a user search will find both large and small companies competing to provide similar products and services. This competition can be global in nature.

Infobyte

Snap Printing Australia — local to global, defeating distance

Being close to your market can be a great advantage in business, as can the ability to operate globally. Snap Printing has managed to do both. Local premises with cutting-edge digital reproduction technology produce long and short printing runs with equal cost-effectiveness and can provide document design expertise if needed. The ability to submit printing jobs electronically (for example, via email) for collection or courier service anywhere in Australia or in any of 28 different countries allows customers to shorten timelines and save money. A strategic alliance with Sir Speedy (North America's leading business printer) adds the global dimension to the business. Technology, expertise, communication and strategic alliances exemplify modern business methods. However, the main driver here is technology: for Snap Printing the economies of scope are much more important than the economies of scale.

Source: Information from www.snapprinting.com (accessed 23 July 2003).

The shift in costs from business to customer has been accompanied by a corresponding shift in power. Note that the World Wide Web is not a broadcast system; it is not even a one-on-one communication. The user-to-web site relationship is in the nature of 1:*n*, i.e. the consumer has a greater choice of companies and web sites. This means more competition and hence reduced prices. This theme will be elaborated later in the text. The proliferation of media such as TV channels has made advertising a hit-and-miss affair. Consumers 'channel hop' to avoid advertisements, so much of advertising expenditure is wasted. However, it is obvious that traditional marketing models do not lend themselves to new styles of operation.

■ **Reflection question 2:** What strategies would you use to ensure that mass advertising hits its target market?

Tactical and strategic links

Improvements in technology and communication allow companies to make their suppliers and dealerships partners in their own enterprise. For example, Harley-Davidson uses an extranet (a private network which allows companies to interconnect their systems in selected areas) to facilitate the distribution of product information to and from its dealers. This allows the turnaround time on warranty claims to be shortened. The system also allows parts to be supplied worldwide in a short space of time, which means that dealers can spend less on inventory and more on customer service and marketing. Cash flow is improved for Harley-Davidson and its dealer network — a win–win scenario.

[**Key concept:** Use technology to create umbilical cords — make your suppliers and resellers full partners in your enterprise.]

Changing the way people work

Currently, smaller organisations are able to enjoy the benefits of technology previously enjoyed only by large companies. All these business transformations were made possible by providing information for business operations and decision making.

■ **Reflection question 3:** In times past a company would specialise in certain areas and product lines. Is specialisation still a viable business strategy?

Often (but not always) a **database** is at the heart of the business. Information is only one part of the equation. Communication systems allow business to reduce the effects of distance. There is a trend in information systems to create systems which are modular in nature — communications may be thought of as the 'glue' which binds systems together. The bland statement that 'geography is history' is contentious, but it is worth noting that many people now telecommute, i.e. use a computer and modem to work from home. It may be that these people are marginally less efficient, but the company does not need to provide an office. **Telecommuters** also provide their own heat and light, and so company infrastructure costs may be offloaded on to the employee. Thus businesses can become smaller in a physical sense while continuing to grow. Direct and indirect overheads can be reduced and cost savings can be high.

Business process re-engineering (BPR)

Many of the computer systems in current use date from a time when the technology was relatively primitive. Staff had to change their work patterns to suit the computer. Contemporary technology is much more capable and gives users greater freedom and more control over their day-to-day work. Improvements in technology allow businesses to examine their core processes and see how they can be improved, such as shortening timelines, speeding cash flow and eliminating intermediaries where possible, with the object of achieving greater effectiveness (doing the right thing) and efficiency (doing it well and economically). This analysis and improvement of operations is termed **business process re-engineering (BPR)**. BPR is often undertaken as part of an enterprise-wide planning exercise — it should be regarded as an ongoing exercise.

[**Key concept:** New technology creates new opportunities — be prepared to take advantage of them.]

Infobyte

Think honk if you are a telepath

Computers double their processing speed every 18 months — humans don't. Kevin Warwick, Professor of Cybernetics at Reading University in the UK, has been wondering since childhood about how to upgrade humans and has few qualms about being his own guinea pig. In 2002 he had a micro-electrode array implanted into the median nerve fibres of his left arm and was able to control an electric wheelchair and an artificial hand. The array provided sensory feedback and also allowed him to receive inputs from a similar array. Warwick predicts that enhanced humans will interact with technology and each other using the power of thought alone.

Source: information from www.kevinwarwick.com/ (accessed 23 July 2003).

Technology convergence

As touched on in the discussion of manufacturing, technology has tended to be developed in specialised areas. Integrating various incompatible technologies into a cohesive whole is very difficult and usually not possible. Current trends show various, previously separate, technologies are now melding, e.g. cable TV can be used to deliver Internet services and telephone communications.

Mobile phones provide photo and video service, send and receive email and faxes and allow web browsing. Mobile phones can be used instead of credit cards and can be used to control smart household devices. The trend appears to be one of fewer devices but with greater functionality, mirroring the trend seen in the emergence of FMS. On a larger scale, this seems to promise powerful new synergies with profound implications for business.

Infobyte

Imbuing traditional products with intelligence

Music lovers often dismiss electronic keyboards as 'cheating'. Yamaha set out to overcome that prejudice. The Disklavier pro series combines traditional grand piano sound and feel with computer technology at a fraction of the cost of a traditional grand piano. The Disklavier can play prerecorded performances, and the sensors and servos (electromechanical devices that reproduce the key movements) are so sensitive that every nuance can be recreated. Computer tuition systems are available and owners can record their own disks and play duets with themselves using multitrack recording. A silent feature is provided for practice. The Disklavier can also deliver 700 electronic voices. This provides an excellent example of clever marketing, technology convergence and new technology imbuing products with intelligence.

Electronic commerce

Despite the enormous hype that surrounds e-commerce, not all retail is suited to electronic commerce. Bob Seeman, state sales manager for Frasers (a large Australian motorcycle importer), which specialises in road bikes such as Harley-Davidson, says, 'Buying a Harley-Davidson bike is a complete experience; it is emotional, and although some customers will purchase a motorcycle online, most prefer to do business personally, and trying to do it on the Internet goes against the nature of our business.' Frasers promotes products and services via its web site and, although some customers will purchase a motorcycle online, most prefer to do business personally. In contrast, other businesses are moving into e-commerce at a high rate.

Some see e-commerce as supplementing their current business operations; others see their business models being totally transformed. A third category encompasses those companies that have never operated in traditional modes. The nature of the relationships between customers and businesses and between businesses and businesses is changing drastically. Information systems allow every aspect of the supply chain to be managed efficiently and effectively.

Proliferation of technology and communication

Most information systems were fairly centralised 30 years ago. The technical knowledge required to use them was restricted to an educated elite. Now the technology is widespread, and there is an entire generation who cannot remember life without the PC. The development of the Internet enabled new relationships and patterns of business to be formed. The impact is said to be akin to that of the printing press in Gutenberg's day. The Internet is still in its infancy, and its full impact has yet to be realised. However, the true value of the Internet is not vested in what can be owned and controlled but in what can be shared and extended.

Infobyte

Knowledge is power

'Knowledge is power, which is why people who had it in the past often tried to make a secret of it. In post-capitalism, power comes from transmitting information to make it productive, not from hiding it.' Peter Drucker, professor of social science and management at Claremont Graduate University (quoted by Harris 1993)

Moving to a knowledge economy

Many newer businesses do not manufacture anything; they make a profit by leveraging intellectual capital. They operate in a 3S model: synergise, synthesise, specialise. For example, consider the establishment of a web-based business which arranges romantic weekends. The proprietor would need to know about airlines, hotels and suppliers of limousines, champagne, flowers and chocolates. Getting all these people to work together yields the synergy which gives a marketable service which no single company could supply individually. Deciding what services and products to include in the package is synthesis. Finally, tailoring the promotional marketing to sell the same product to different groups is where the specialisation comes in. The collected fees are returned to the suppliers less the proprietor's percentage. Start-up fees would be quite low and the Internet would enable a global market to be reached. Obviously, better promotional marketing would improve profits, but enough should be made to be going on with and to prove the concept before a business development loan is sought. The main input would have been the idea.

Modern information systems allow many ideas that were previously impracticable to be realised. They also allow older business models to be revisited and improved. The knowledge economy relies on the application of knowledge-to-knowledge-related activities in order to produce wealth. Information systems are an integral part of this.

Business pressures and responses

The business environment is in a constant state of flux, i.e. the only constant is change. When an environmental pressure increases, a business must respond if it is to survive and maintain its competitive position. Figure 1.4 shows the major business pressures.

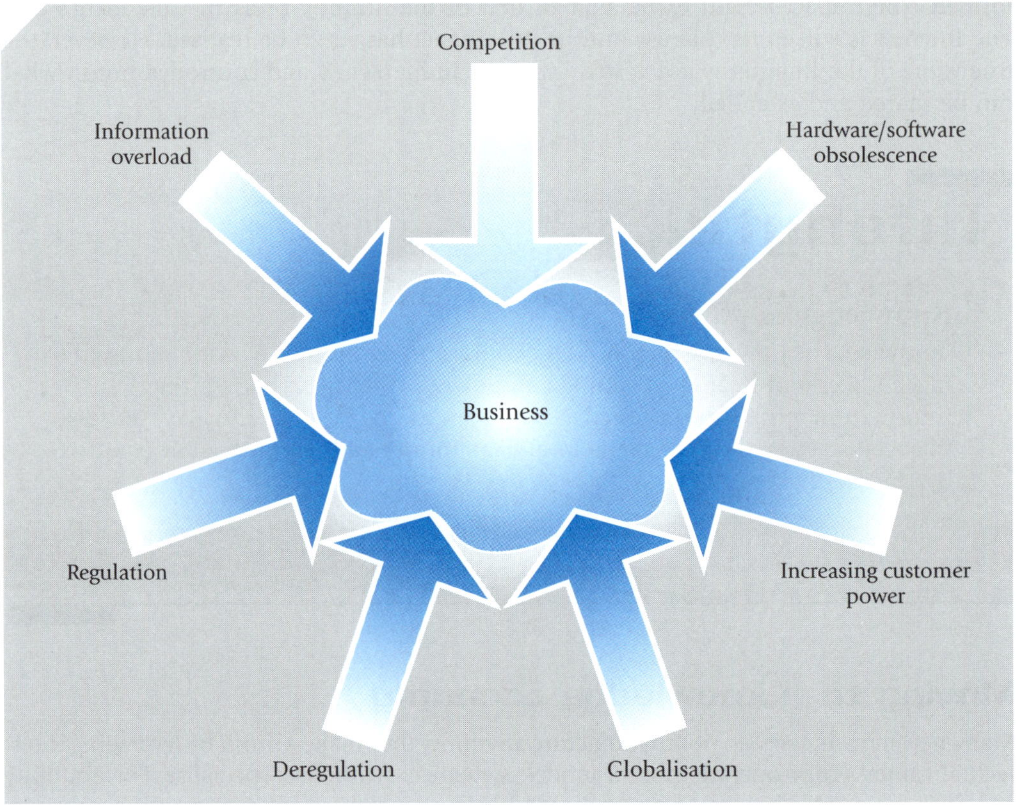

Figure 1.4 Seven major business pressures

Responses to pressures may take many forms, but almost all reduce to three main aspects: quality, innovation and speed. Figure 1.5 (opposite) shows seven major responses to business pressures.

As may be imagined, the behaviour of a business over a period of time is marked by the interaction of pressures and responses in a dynamic fashion. The difficulty most businesses have is in anticipating the pressures and taking evasive action.

Direct and indirect benefits of information systems

Part of your job as an information systems professional will be to present solutions to clients. As with any other form of marketing, you should never sell the product — you should sell the benefits. This requires you to do some research or engage in careful thought and prediction. Benefits may be direct (tangible) or indirect (intangible). Indirect benefits can only be estimated, but direct benefits can be predicted with a high degree of certainty.

For example, consider the introduction of computerised stock control to a motor vehicle dealership. The direct benefit is to improve response times to queries and hence make more sales — which can be quantified. Staff in the parts department now have more time to devote to relationship marketing of parts and service, which is an indirect

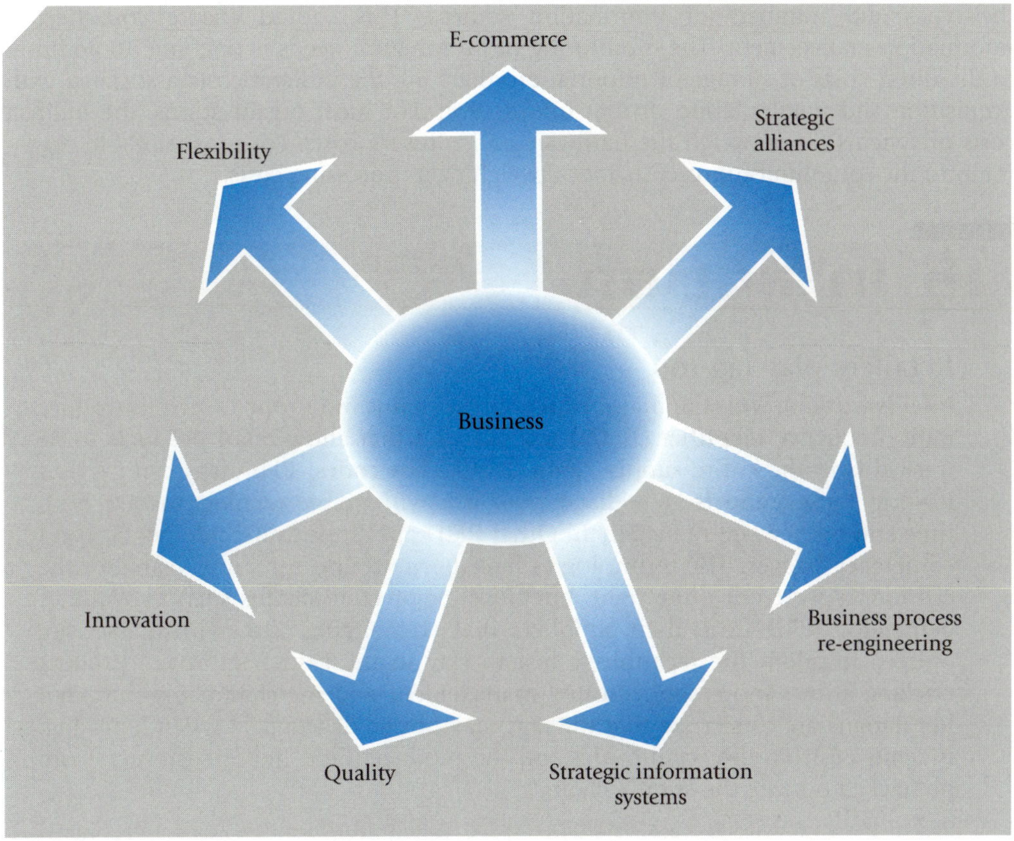

Figure 1.5 Seven major business responses

benefit, as is the enhanced image the company enjoys as a result of using new technology. Indirect benefits are harder to quantify but are no less real. The real benefits accrue by changing the nature of competition. When Volkswagen (VW) discovered that many of its dealers were failing to retain post-warranty service work on Volkswagen cars, it developed automated engine analysers and fitted each new car with a diagnostic plug. This new technology allowed VW dealers to complete engine tuning and diagnosis in a matter of moments and reduce their service charges to retain customers. Non-VW workshops were still able to carry out work on VW cars but were no longer able to compete on time and cost.

[**Key concept:** Technology can be used to create barriers to competition.]

If obvious benefits are discernible within a single organisation, then greater benefits should accrue when computer networking/communication is added. Being able to access other sources of information increases the overall amount of information available for decision-making purposes. The difficulty now is that there is too much information. Much of this information is not relevant and may be contradictory, but establishing that fact requires detailed sifting and analysis. The enemies of managers are diversity and complexity — careful assessment of information needs is required followed by a restriction on the types and numbers of information sources. This should ensure cost-effective information management. The monitoring of information needs is ongoing. In addition to the direct costs of storage of information, there are the indirect costs associated with acquisition and manipulation of that information. For most organisations, the indirect costs of systems far outweigh the hardware and software costs. For most sizeable organisations, the communications costs far outweigh data-processing costs.

IS in action

Retailers play tag too

Intel is working with the major supermarket chains in Europe to help introduce radio frequency identifier (RFID) technologies that allow retail products to be tracked over the entire supply chain. Unlike bar codes, RFID tags can be read from any angle and from a distance — this will enable retailers to save both time and money and reduce theft. Other RFID applications include pet tags and conference badges. The technologies have been around for some years but the economics were not quite right, but since major retail chains such as Walmart demanded RFID from their suppliers that is changing. Other businesses are obliged to adopt the technology just to stay in the game. Improved product tracking allows more sophisticated management and merchandising, but civil libertarians are concerned that the tags may not be deactivated when a product is removed from the retail outlet and the products (and hence customers) can be tracked outside the supply chain.

Source: www.infoworld.com/article/04/01/12/HNintelrfid_1.html (accessed 20 February 2004).

Why study information systems?

There is an apocryphal story about a bank robber. On sentencing, the judge asked the man why he had taken to robbing banks. The man replied, 'Because that's where the money is.' The job opportunities in information systems are wide-ranging, international and well paid. Best of all, the work is usually interesting, varied and satisfying. A useful thing about information systems is that the skills which one develops are transferable skills, i.e. they have broad applicability. The skills also have a long shelf-life, which makes it easier to pursue a career.

This text is written for students who are pursuing a business qualification. This may be the only information systems unit that some students will complete as part of the course, whereas others may go on to major in the subject. Information systems exist to serve business. As information systems practitioners, it is important to speak the same language as the client, and invariably this is the language of business couched in such terms as cash flow and return on investment. Equally, there is an onus on businesspeople to be able to converse with information systems specialists on an equal footing. The relationship of information systems to other disciplines was covered earlier in this chapter. Now it is useful to examine the relationship of information systems to other business disciplines which are studied as part of a business degree.

Information systems and the marketing major

Traditional 4P models of marketing (product, promotion, place and price) still have relevance in a world in which relationship marketing is in the ascendancy. Market research is about collecting information on customers, prospects, sales patterns and so on. Promotional marketing includes advertising, distribution and delivery. It is hard to imagine any sizeable company not using software for analysis, budgeting and forecasting.

Marketing also makes use of temporary information systems. Think about organising a large convention or trade fair over a two-week period. In addition to all the usual behind-the-scenes management that takes place, networked multimedia displays to guide visitors around the display centres are needed. Competitions and other promotions are used to gather potential customer information for later analysis. At the end of the two weeks, the entire system is dismantled and much of the equipment returned to the leasing company.

Hospitality and tourism is often considered to be a subset of marketing. Hotel management systems include complex food inventory systems, accounting systems and modelling software intended to improve occupancy rates and profit.

Information systems and the accounting and finance majors

Much of basic accounting is repetitious in nature. The automation of those mundane processes has produced a shift in the nature of accounting from bookkeeping to managerial decision-making. Data must be captured, manipulated, stored and audited. Increasingly, accountants are involved in policy formulation and system security. Much of accounting is about reducing complexity and diversity by standardising and automating procedures.

Many accountants rise to become senior managers. They understand the business as a series of cash flows. Information systems is complementary to this since it enables the business to be considered as a series of information flows. Accountancy is about recording the past for legal and planning purposes.

Finance concerns itself with the present and the future, answering such questions as 'What is our profit this year to date?' and 'What is our predicted return on this investment?' Most business decisions are based on financial considerations — it is hard to imagine any business being able to reach a decision quickly without the aid of information systems to retrieve, analyse and model data. Information systems security is vital for most organisations, and it is increasingly important to the accounting profession.

Information systems and management

Human resource managers are beset by large amounts of legislation which must be strictly adhered to. Additionally, attracting, retaining and developing staff are major tasks. The real challenge is to match the staffing capability to the current and future needs of the business in a cost-effective manner. This entails salary forecasting and skills requirement analysis, as there is a fine line between under- and over-staffing. Each employee must have his or her own set of records. The most mundane part of the operation is payroll. Information systems are an integral part of human resource management and, properly used, they can allow a manager to spend more time out of the office networking with staff.

Operations managers are concerned with balancing inventory against cash flow. All manufacturing requires processes and products to be monitored for quality and waste reduction. Reordering can be automated using **materials requirements planning (MRP)** systems. Information systems allow several perspectives of manufacturing to be obtained, so that individual processes and overall pictures may both be examined.

Both human resource managers and operations managers are extensive users of information systems.

Enterprise resource planning (ERP)

As the modelling and forecasting capabilities of information systems applied to manufacturing became apparent, the question arose about whether these techniques and thinking styles could be applied to other areas of business. The answer was 'yes'. The techniques used in production management were extended to total supply chain management, human resource management, accounting, finance and marketing. Integrating all these functions into a single enterprise-wide system in order to shorten timelines and yield inherent synergies became known as **enterprise resource planning (ERP)**.

The best known ERP software, comprising large modular integrated subsystems, is the German product SAP (the company name is System Anwedung Produkte). This supports multi-site, concurrent business processes.

Converting from a traditional style of operation to ERP is not without risk, since the transition process has teething problems and if the analysis and planning have not been thorough, the systems will not function as required. ERP tends to be the province of large, wealthy organisations because of the costs involved and the scale of the conversion. Most analysts would recommend undertaking BPR at the same time as implementing ERP.

Making technology manageable

Technology is wonderfully seductive, and it is easy to become too involved. Technical problems are very satisfying to deal with because there is usually a single problem and results are always forthcoming. Business and management problems are not so easy to deal with, as there is a degree of uncertainty and several problems tend to be handled concurrently. Some management and business problems are insoluble, so the best that can be hoped for is to improve the situation. Although technology can create opportunities, the business plan should be business-driven, not technology-driven. You need to balance being ignorant of technical issues and being too knowledgeable. As a guideline, consider your VCR — you do not need to have detailed technical knowledge in order to use the device effectively. The same applies to information systems technology — you need to focus on what you can do with the technology rather than the details of how it works.

[**Key concept:** Business first, then technology.]

Keeping up to date

The natural environment for information systems is business. By reviewing the changes and trends that are taking place in business and society, the effects that information systems are having may be seen and it is possible to estimate the effects that they might have in the future. Information systems professionals need to be good at understanding the big picture. A substantial portion of this chapter was devoted to a review of the nature and history of information systems. The onus is now on you to make the connections between academic coverage of business and information systems and the real world. As you work through this text, this task should become easier. However, we strongly suggest that you make use of the World Wide Web and some of the more popular journals and magazines to keep your awareness up to date. Should you eventually work in information systems, membership of professional bodies and attendance at meetings and seminars provide a cost-effective way to keep up to date.

Summary

This chapter introduced you to the background and nature of information systems and the issues surrounding the discipline. Most important is the relationship between information systems and other business disciplines. The key points in this chapter are:

- Data, information and knowledge are different things but they need to be considered holistically.
- Information systems is a business discipline in its own right but it relates to and supports every other business discipline.
- To be effective in information systems, it is necessary to know something of other business disciplines in order to develop a shared understanding with clients.
- Information systems is not about technology; rather, it is a framework for thinking about and managing technology.
- Information systems and communications have been instrumental in the huge growth of the small–medium business sector by lowering market entry and operating costs.
- As the mundane aspects of business have been automated, there has been a tendency to move towards a knowledge economy in which intellectual capital is vital.
- Information systems permit business processes to be transformed and integrated, allowing new forms of management and competition.

Questions

1. How difficult is it to use online information sources with confidence? What would you do to improve the situation?
2. In the modern business paradigm, it is said that it is possible to increase the value of a product by infusing it with expertise and information. Give three examples of such products and explain how their value has been increased.
3. Over the past 30 years, huge sums of money have been invested in information systems and information technology. Somehow, improvements in knowledge worker productivity have failed to keep pace with this investment. Do you think there is a

rule of diminishing returns here and, if so, how do you account for the lack of increase of knowledge worker productivity?

4. Modern communication systems have meant the death of distance. Will modern banking systems mean the death of money?
5. A major emphasis in the development of technology over the last hundred years has been the breaking down of barriers: the telephone started to break down the tyranny of distance; aeroplanes and more efficient transport have broken down national barriers. Do you think that technology has broken down the barriers between people? Explain your answer.
6. Consider the phenomena of outsourcing and flexible manufacturing systems. What are the implications for manufacturing if these trends are pursued to their logical extreme? Is this likely to happen?
7. It has been said that the critical elements of competition are innovation, quality and speed to market. In the light of technical advances, is this view still sufficient? Explain your answer.
8. Think about a supermarket chain operating a computerised checkout system (point of sales system). What advantages (immediate and potential) does the business obtain from its system? (Hint: think about integrating different aspects of business operation.)
9. Think about your web surfing and online purchasing experiences (if any) and suggest assessment criteria for judging the quality of web sites and web-based systems. What do you think are the three most important aspects and why?
10. The World Wide Web has levelled the playing field between large and small companies in terms of establishing a web presence, but what advantages does a larger company get from its web site that a smaller business does not?

Exercises

1. Imagine that you have been retained to produce a list of the function requirements for the next-generation Rolex watch. What features should it include? Should it be electronic or mechanical? Justify your suggestions.
2. Form a small discussion group and establish the information needs for a sizeable piggery (7000 pigs). The point of this exercise is to demonstrate that it is possible to define much of the information needs for an organisation at a fairly abstract level, leaving the detail for later. (Hint: look at the problem from at least two perspectives: (a) what purpose does the information serve? and (b) what information is it possible to collect/deduce and from what source?)
3. If Kevin Warwick's vision of technologically enhanced humans interacting with each other and technology via the power of thought were to come true, how would you see society and business changing? On a personal basis, how do you imagine what the interaction would be like? As an example, how would everyday business transactions be carried out?
4. Web sites such as cheathouse.com provide copies of graded student assignments for sale at very low prices. What does this do for the quality of education, and how should universities and colleges respond? Would you access material from this site and, if so, under what circumstances?

CASE STUDY Kewl Cookies

Kewl Cookies is an Australian company which operates in the main population centres of every state and territory. You have been retained by Kewl Cookies to produce an outline plan which describes the basic means of operation of the marketing and delivery side of the business and to identify the basic technology and strategies that are required to improve competitiveness. The following is information you need to know about Kewl Cookies before you can begin.

- Kewl Cookies makes preservative-free cookies. The shelf-life of these cookies is no longer than seven days. Old stock is removed when the delivery drivers replenish the shelves. Delivering more than can be sold to an outlet means waste since they operate on a sale-or-return basis. Delivering insufficient stock will result in lost sales.
- The shopkeeper receives an invoice within 14 days and has 28 days to pay.
- Sales are good, the company is profitable and Kewl Cookies makes a high-quality organic product.
- The Kewl Cookies fleet of trucks delivers to each shop twice a week on average.
- Kewl Cookies currently operates manual systems for delivery and marketing. Drivers come into the bakeries, collect their loads and then plan their own delivery routes.
- Kewl Cookies operates more than 700 outlets.
- Strategically, Kewl Cookies would like to be able to market more effectively at the individual outlet level.
- Ideally, the new operating plan should save money and time and help the company become more efficient.

Consider the problem from a number of different perspectives: the driver's, the shopkeeper's and the marketer's. Do not get bogged down in technical detail; a high-level view is what is required here.

QUESTIONS

1. What is the main difficulty that Kewl Cookies faces in managing the operation?
2. What information does the company need to be more effective in what it does? In other words, what are the information needs of the new system and how is that information to be gathered?
3. Is there a need to incorporate external information into the system? If so, what information is required and what advantages are there in using it?
4. How would you go about shortening timelines in this case?
5. What can be done to improve cash flow and what are the practical implications of this?
6. Is there anything you have devised which could be used elsewhere?
7. Are there any system refinements that would not form part of this brief but which might be useful to Kewl Cookies at a later date?

References

Audretsch, D.B., Carrie, M.A., van Stel, A.J. & Thurik, A.R. 2000, 'Impeded industrial restructuring: The growth penalty', Tinbergen Institute Discussion paper, www.tinbergen.nl/discussionpapers/00095.pdf (accessed 24 February 2004).

Benson, S. & Standing C. 2000, 'Synergising the personal–corporate knowledge nexus', in *Proceedings of the 5th UK Academy of Information Systems*, eds P. Benyon-Davies, M.D. Williams and I. Beeson, McGraw-Hill, Maidenhead, pp. 139–47.

Davies, G. 1996, *A History of Money from Ancient Times to the Present Day*, rev. edn, University of Wales Press, Cardiff.

Drucker, P.F. 1993, *Post Capitalist Society*, Harper Business, New York.

Harris T.G. 1993, 'The post-capitalist executive: An interview with Peter F. Drucker', *Harvard Business Review*, May–June, pp. 115–22.

Keen, P. 1980, 'Reference disciplines and a cumulative tradition', in *Proceedings of the First International Conference on Information Systems*, ed. E.R. McLean, Philadelphia, pp. 9–18.

Lyn, J. & Jay, A. 1989, *The Complete Yes Minister*, BBC Books, London, p. 457.

McKeown, P.G. 2001, *Information Technology and the Networked Economy*, Harcourt College Publishers, Orlando.

Naisbit, J. 1994, *Global Paradox: The Bigger the World Economy, the More Powerful Its Smallest Players*, William Morrow & Co., New York.

Reid, P.C. 1990, *Well Made in America: Lessons from Harley-Davidson on Being the Best*, McGraw-Hill/Harley-Davidson, Milwaukee.

Watson, R.T. 1999, *Organizational Memory*, John Wiley & Sons, New York, p. 27.

Weber, R. 1997, *The Ontological Foundations of Information Systems*, Accounting Research Methodology Monograph no. 4, Coopers & Lybrand, Melbourne.

Yourdon, E. 1997, *Death March: The Complete Software Developer's Guide to Surviving 'Mission Impossible' Projects* (Yourdon Computing Series), Prentice Hall, New York.

Chapter 2

Hardware fundamentals and trends

LEARNING OBJECTIVES

After reading this chapter, you should be able to:

- understand and use the basic units of processor speed and storage capacity
- explain basic computer history and the four generations of computer, appreciating the impact that each generation had
- explain the main types of computer in current use
- understand basic computer architecture and operation and the components used in a typical PC configuration
- appreciate the trends of microprocessor development
- purchase a suitable computer for personal use
- understand the acquisition process as it applies to larger organisations
- appreciate the importance of hardware standards from a management and business perspective.

2

Introduction

It is not realistic to study information systems without some consideration of the technology that forms the basis of the discipline. However, the coverage of the purely technical is restricted to a minimum, since you should always have access to people and resources for technical support and advice. The main focus is the business issues and implications that arise from technological developments. Information systems is about deploying technology for tactical and strategic advantage in business. Remember, the work is not the business.

In order to present a strong business focus it is necessary to provide some background in the history of the computer business. Although this chapter presents four generations of hardware, it is important to note that these generations overlap in space and time, e.g. generations 2 and 3 coexisted for as many as eight years. This chapter briefly introduces the main types of computer hardware and software in common use in business today. The development of computers and, hence, information systems changed the pattern of competition within business at large and the computer industry itself. An appreciation of this competition is vital to an understanding of contemporary information systems. Technology specifics are covered a little later, but for now accept that the more memory a computer has, the faster it performs.

Measuring memory capacity and processor speeds

Computers store and manipulate data in binary form, and an executable program code needs to be in memory before it can be run. Hence, memory capacity is an indicator of computer performance. Table 2.1 gives the names of commonly used computer memory capacities and concrete examples.

TABLE 2.1 Computer memory capacity

Memory capacity and name	Amount of data
1 **bit** (binary digit)	a '0' or a '1'
1 **byte** (8 binary digits)	1 alphanumeric character
1 **kilobyte** (Kb), 1024 bytes (2^{10})	Half a double-spaced page of A4
1 **megabyte** (Mb), 1 048 576 bytes (2^{20})	500 pages of A4
1 **gigabyte** (Gb), 1 073 741 824 (2^{30})	Half a million pages of A4

Note: Most people in the industry think about capacity in powers of 10, so a kilobyte is usually approximated to 1000 bytes, a megabyte to 1 000 000 bytes etc.

Computer speeds are defined in two ways: (1) the speed of the system clock usually quoted in **megahertz** (cycles per second) and (2) the number of machine instructions processed in a second (a more meaningful measure). Modern computer speeds demand that speeds are quoted in **millions of instructions per second (MIPS)**. The problem is that clock speed does not necessarily equate to instruction process rate. To give an idea of the number-crunching ability of a processor, a third speed — **floating point operations per second (FLOPS)** — is used.

[**Key concept:** Most business applications do not require vast amounts of number-crunching. Instead, they are input/output focused. Accordingly, disk access speeds and internal transfer rates are more important than raw processor power.]

A brief history of the computer

There have been four generations of computer technology, and each generation brought about large-scale change in a different way. The end of a generation is defined in this book as the point at which replacement technology started to be used. Many computers were made and used after the end of their generation so there was and is a great deal of coexistence of technologies. Try to appreciate the significant contribution each generation of computer made to modern business methods.

Generation 1: Valves (1946–59) — transforming business processes

Although mechanical and electromechanical computation devices have existed for many years, most people accept that the birth of the modern computer age occurred in the late 1940s when a research team at Manchester University in the United Kingdom produced the first electrical stored-program computer. Although primitive by today's standards, it extended people's mental abilities in the same way that pulleys and levers had extended the lifting capacity of their ancestors. The essence of modern digital computing is to reduce complex operations to a series of binary operations. Operation at its lowest level really consists of switching. By the end of the 1950s, vacuum tubes (valves) were the main switching devices in computers, and by 1960 valve-based computers were in use in many sectors of industry and government in the developed world.

The programs which these machines ran were specific to particular makes and models of computer and were in no way 'portable' as modern software is. Nor were they particularly sophisticated or flexible. However, even with their inherent unreliabilities, they were faster and more accurate than humans. A single computer or **mainframe** served an entire organisation.

The business environment at that time was fairly stable, and the rate at which information and markets changed was fairly modest by modern standards. Businesses tended to be fairly hierarchical in structure — a pyramid with senior management at the top. People's work patterns were changed so as to maximise the return on the investment in computers. Work tended to be well ordered and structured in larger corporations. The competitive advantage gained by deploying computer technology was to shorten the timelines of monotonous processes, i.e. the processes were automated. However, the organisation and management remained pretty much as they had been in previous decades. Valve-based computers usually had no more than 2 Kb of memory and operating speeds of 1000–10 000 instructions per second.

■ **Reflection question 1:** It is sometimes said that the old highly centralised mainframe systems were more reliable than modern distributed systems. Are people justified in saying this?

Infobyte

Back to the future

Although microprocessors are widely used, it seems that old-fashioned vacuum triode tubes still have their place. Superior resistance to heat, power surges and RF interference — plus an ability to deal with high frequencies — ensure their continuing use in avionics, military communications and RADAR (Wolverton 2002). Many satellites have vacuum tubes working side by side with the latest silicon chips. The problem has been that vacuum tubes are large. However, nanotechnologists have produced working nanotriodes that are 1/500th the size of transistors on microchips (less than 100 nm), which could offer all the advantages of vacuum tubes in a much smaller package.

Generation 2: Transistors (1959–64) — transforming organisations

The development of the transistor in 1947 by William Shockley, Walter Brattain and John Bardeen in the Bell laboratories opened up a new era in electronics and computer science. Vacuum tubes were large and slow, consumed lots of power and needed replacing at fairly regular intervals. Large computer installations of the late 1950s and early 1960s filled large rooms and sometimes entire floors of buildings. Transistors could do the same job but required a fraction of the size and power to operate. They were also more reliable. Circuit boards could be prefabricated and mass-produced, simplifying production and maintenance. Computer costs plummeted and the take-up rate in business increased dramatically. Profit margins for manufacturers were excellent.

In order to allow the technology to be more widely used, high-level portable computer languages were needed. Up to this time, computer programs were inextricably entwined with a single make and model of computer. Languages such as COBOL, FORTRAN, BASIC and LISP allowed programmers to write programs that could run on any machine. The trick was to have a translator program called a compiler that could translate the high-level code into a form that the local computer could handle. The software and the hardware were now independent of each other, and development of each would proceed at a much higher rate. The development of high-level languages allowed organisations to produce specialised, in-house software much more easily than before and to buy in software from specialised software developers at reduced cost. This simple step was to transform business irrevocably. The use of single transistors on circuit boards allowed memory to be extended to 32 Kb and processing speeds around 300 000 instructions per second.

The first generation of computers merely transformed individual business processes. This second generation allowed a higher degree of intelligence in the software/programs which in turn allowed business to restructure. Software was now capable of rendering complex analyses and forecasts on the basis of stored data with much greater speed than a human analyst could. Many routine management functions could also be computerised. The result was that businesses were able to shed several layers of middle management. They moved away from the older hierarchical structures and became flatter, leaner and more efficient. By shortening the lines of communication and the chains of command, businesses were able to respond to situations and opportunities much more quickly and so enjoy advantages over businesses that did not have the benefit of technology. Work flows revolved around the computer's processes because the advantages of the new age demanded sacrifices in terms of job satisfaction and true flexibility.

Generation 3: Integrated circuits (1965–71) — transforming markets

The trend towards smaller, faster and cheaper machines established in the second generation of computers was continued in the third generation at an exponential rate. These machines relied heavily on **integrated circuits (ICs)** — chips with many thousands of transistors printed onto a very small piece of silicon. The technology favoured mass production and while performance increased, prices continued to plummet and the technology penetrated many aspects of business. This proliferation also had implications for the development of software and, in particular, system software. Average memory sizes were in the order of 2 Mb and processing speeds increased to 5 million instructions per second. Perhaps the most significant thing to arise from this time was that computers became capable of running several programs concurrently. Previously, computer systems tended to operate as batch systems with little or no direct interaction with users. Improvements in technology in the early part of this computer generation provided real-time operation and interaction on a much larger scale. Applications software also became more sophisticated during this time. The demand for computing power outstripped the supply of skilled software developers and so software had to become easier to use.

Generation 4: Very large scale integration (VLSI) (1971–present) — transforming society

The **very large scale integration (VLSI)** period began with the invention of the microchip by Marcian (Ted) Hoff in 1971, codenamed the Intel 4004. For the first time it was theoretically possible to place millions of transistors on the same piece of silicon. This revolutionised the design of mainframes and led to the development of the 8080 chip. The 8080 was used to produce the world's first PC, the 1974 Altair (named after a planet in the TV series *Star Trek*), and its successor, the 8088, powered the first IBM PC. For the first time, mass-produced computers became affordable to small businesses and the general public. The advances in hardware were accompanied by advances in software, which became much easier to use and to develop. Current performance figures vary from 10 MIPS to 3 million MIPS, and computer memory can be anything from 128 Mb to 8000 Mb or more, depending on the type of computer.

■ **Reflection question 2:** What are the main developmental trends that you see when reading about the four generations of hardware? Are these trends still applicable? Explain your view.

Types of computers in current use

The following is intended as a 'field guide' only. The distinctions between the types of computers tend to be a little indistinct; for example, when does a high-end mainframe computer qualify as a supercomputer? You should also appreciate that these classifications are subject to change as technology continues to improve. Today's mainframe is tomorrow's desktop.

Supercomputers

Supercomputers are the most powerful, most expensive and rarest of the computers in use today. Their main uses have been in military and scientific work for such diverse applications as weather modelling, nuclear explosion simulations and aircraft design. They have also been used by the film industry to create graphic-intensive special effects. They are usually 5 to 10 times faster than mainframes with typical speeds around 10 000 MIPS, with speeds up to 8 million MIPS being state-of-the-art. Costs vary from $A4 million to $A8 million, and memory size is measured in gigabytes with 8 Gb a convenient minimum. Supercomputers are about the same size as a family car.

Mainframes

Mainframe computers were the first type of modern computer. Highly centralised, they provide services for a large community of users. With the centralisation of function there is a centralisation of power and control. With the increasing power of smaller computers and the availability of networks, the mainframe market has diminished and consolidated in recent years. Because there are relatively few mainframes, mainframe software is very expensive and limited in choice compared with PC software. Typical mainframe speeds are between 1000 and 5000 MIPS with 4 to 16 Gb of memory. Costs range from $A0.5 million to $A4 million. Mainframes are about the size of a large fridge, and many IS professionals refer to their mainframe as the 'big iron'. Mainframes usually require specially controlled environments in dust-free rooms.

Minicomputers

Minicomputers are almost cut-down versions of mainframes. Still relatively expensive, they provide services to a small–medium community of users. Because there are many more minis than mainframes, there is a much greater variety of software to choose from. This larger market attracts more software developers than the relatively restricted supercomputer and mainframe market. Minicomputers are filing cabinet size; speeds vary from 200 to 500 MIPS and memory size is typically 2 to 4 Gb. The cost of a minicomputer is usually in the range of $A40 000 to $A200 000.

Workstations

A workstation is really a cut-down minicomputer catering to the needs of a single user. Although the distinction between a high-end PC and a workstation has become blurred recently, most professionals regard a workstation as having much greater performance and functionality than a PC — a Silicon Graphics workstation, used to produce special effects for films, is a good example. Workstations frequently make use of a special type of microchip which has a RISC architecture (reduced instruction-set chip). These desktop machines cost between $A5000 and $A80 000, with speeds in the range of 100 to 200 MIPS and with 2 to 4 Gb of memory.

Microcomputers/PCs

Microcomputers/PCs are desktop or portable computers for single users. Most of the software processing is localised, although communications software and hardware allows PCs to access other computers and services. PCs transformed business operations and structures by allowing many activities to be decentralised. The advent of the PC contributed to the contraction and consolidation of the mainframe market.

Technology moves very quickly, and technical specifications for desktop machines change every few months. However, it is possible to generalise to some extent. Physical sizes vary, and it is assumed that readers are familiar with basic desktop, tower, mini-tower and laptop configurations. Clock speeds are usually in excess of 2 GHz for desktop machines whereas high-end machines can be two or three times faster. Internal memory (RAM) is usually around 1 Gb, tending to a maximum of 2 Gb, whereas typical hard disk sizes are in excess of 120 Gb. The increasing use of PCs as multimedia suites and gaming machines has been a major factor in increasing disk and memory capacity in PCs. It should be noted that a fast clock speed does not translate directly into high performance since some computers do more in one 'tick of the clock' than others. Workstations might have a slower clock speed than PCs but usually perform more instructions per second. The term 'PC' is generally taken to mean devices derived from IBM's original PC architecture; however, strictly speaking the term also includes other kinds of desktop computer, such as Apple Macintosh.

PCs are often configured as servers (shared computers on a network, which are dedicated to particular tasks such as email or web services). Although their architecture is PC based, they usually have much higher performance and storage specification (mainframes, minicomputers and supercomputers often operate as servers). Desktop machines that are networked and access servers are referred to as clients; hence the terms 'client–server applications' and 'networks'.

IS in action

Fat or thin?

By increasing server power and network capacity, businesses can make use of 'thin' clients (desktop PCs that are stripped-down versions of ordinary PCs). These have a longer service life and are cheaper to buy and to manage than ordinary PCs. However, this comes at the cost of reduced processing power at the desktop. The breakeven point for thin-client installations is 10–12 users. However, for intensive applications such as design work or publishing a desktop machine needs its own processing power. The interest in thin clients for business comes about in part owing to the rate at which PCs become

(*continued*)

obsolete. With thin clients, upgrades are carried out to the server and can often be managed without stopping any applications. Servers often have many processors and are designed with upgrading in mind. In addition to saving on initial purchase costs by 30–40%, thin clients reduce management costs substantially. Many organisations have both thick and thin clients depending on the needs of users.

The terms 'network computer' and 'thin client' are used interchangeably. Thin clients are well suited to 'front-end' banking and travel systems since the main data and processing facilities are highly centralised.

Handheld and wearable computers

Handheld and wearable computers are the smallest computing devices and include personal organisers and products such as Palm Pilot. The trend towards miniaturisation has led to the development of computer wristwatches incorporating video-conferencing hardware and other wearable devices, which are considered in chapter 5. Handheld and wearable devices are already used by warehousing and distribution operations, but the development trend seems to be towards wearable and hands-free operation. When combined with mobile communications, these have the potential to transform business processes. Sometimes these devices are mere extensions of and access points to a larger system. More usually, they are for use as **personal data assistants (PDAs)** and organisers. It is not certain whether PDAs will survive in their own right or be subsumed into mobile telephone technologies. Cost, performance and communications coverage are the limiting factors in the take-up rates for PDAs.

The architecture of the modern computer

In order to use computers effectively and make good purchasing decisions, it is necessary to have an understanding of the basic architecture and operation of the modern (classical) computer. With the possible exception of the supercomputer group, most computers use the same architecture and operate in the same manner. This architecture is called the **von Neumann machine**. What made the von Neumann architecture special was that it advanced the idea of storing the program in the computer instead of relying on punched tape. This gave a huge increase in performance over other architectures since accessing memory is many times faster than accessing an external storage device.

It is very easy to be impressed by technical terms, but it doesn't hurt to remember that the most complex computer system still performs the same basic functions: input, processing, output, communication and storage. This should help to keep things in perspective when talking to technical specialists and consultants. Input, processing, output and storage devices are covered in detail later.

Figure 2.1 shows a typical PC configuration and **motherboard** (also known as **systemboard**). This chapter is PC-focused because it is the architecture you are most likely to encounter and its operating principles are no different from most mainframe computers and workstations.

It is important to note the distinction between the main 'box', or **system unit**, and the attached devices which are referred to as peripherals. Figure 2.2 shows a conceptual view of the motherboard, processor, random access memory, bus, expansion slots and cards. The next sections shows how these basic components operate, interact and run programs.

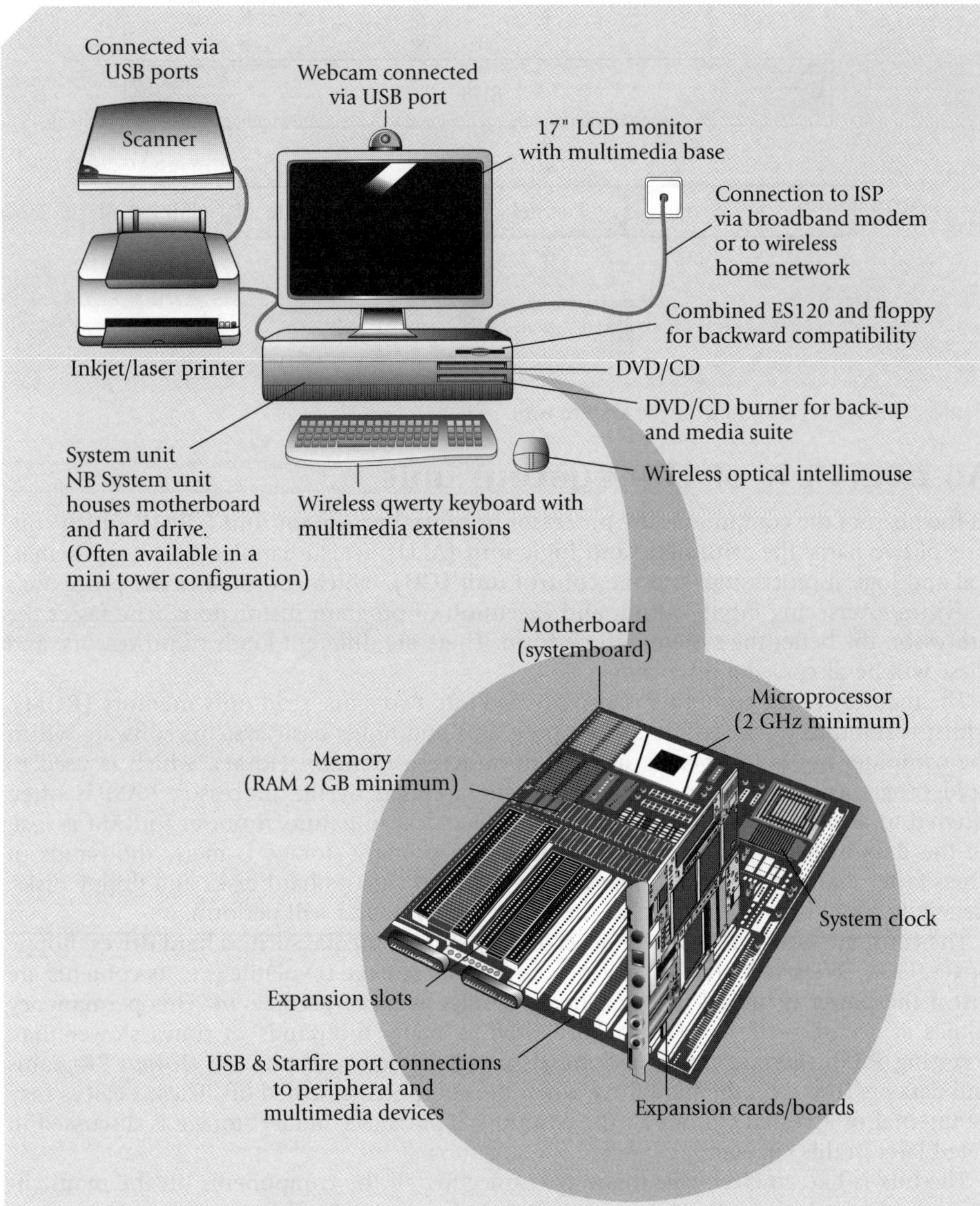

Figure 2.1 A typical PC configuration and motherboard

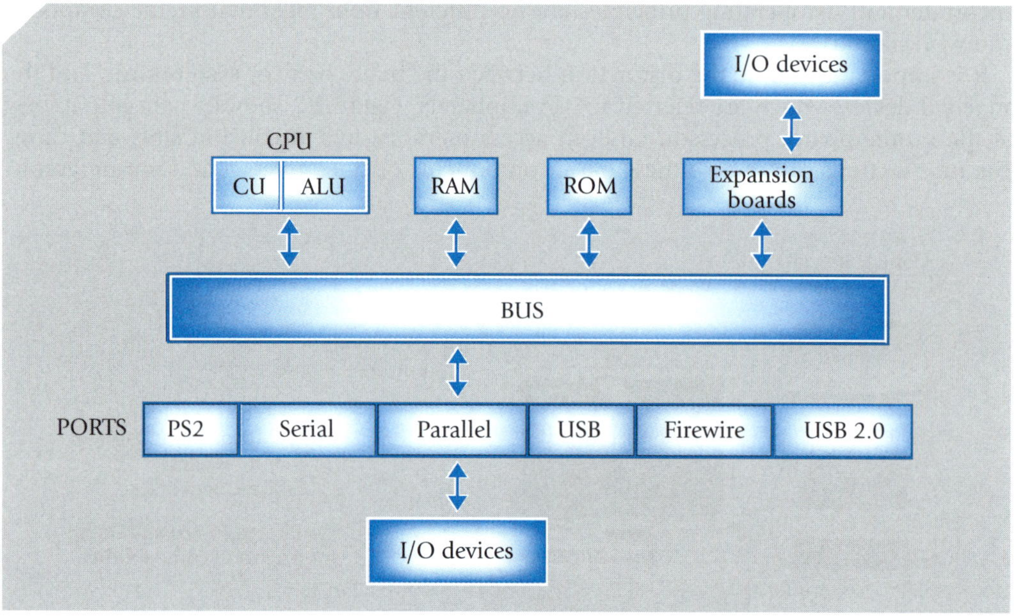

Figure 2.2 A conceptual view of the system unit

An overview of the system unit

At the heart of the computer is the processor or **central processor unit (CPU)**, which consists of two parts: the **arithmetic and logic unit (ALU)**, which handles all the mathematical and logical processing; and the **control unit (CU)**, which coordinates the processor's activities, overseeing input, output and execution of program instructions. The faster the processor, the better the system will perform. There are different kinds of processors, and these will be discussed a little later.

The memory of the computer is also divided into two parts: **read-only memory (ROM)**, which is not directly accessible to user programs and holds basic systems software which the computer needs to operate; and **random access memory (RAM)**, which is used to hold programs and data so that they can be accessed by the processor. RAM is often referred to as primary storage, and since it is electrical in nature, if power to RAM is lost, all the data in RAM will also be lost. Accessing primary storage is many thousands of times faster than accessing secondary storage devices such as hard disks and floppy disks. Generally speaking, the more RAM, the better the computer will perform.

The computer also has a variety of secondary storage media, such as hard drives, floppy drives, CDs, DVDs and ZIP drives. Whereas primary storage is volatile (i.e. its contents are lost if the power is turned off), secondary storage is more permanent. This permanency comes at a cost — if accessing a hard drive is many thousands of times slower than accessing RAM, then accessing peripheral storage devices will be even slower. Programs and data are stored on the hard drive when the computer is turned off. These devices may be internal or accessed via one of the computer's ports. Secondary storage is discussed in detail later in this chapter.

The **bus** is like an electronic highway connecting all the components on the main circuit board (motherboard). There are various industry standards for buses, and you need to check which is appropriate for your needs.

The motherboard houses the processor, memory and bus, plus a number of dedicated device handlers. The motherboard has **expansion slots**, which allow various special functions to be added to the computer, such as sound cards, fax/modem cards and video cards.

In order to improve performance, most PCs have an area of RAM set aside as a **cache**. Since accessing the RAM is much faster than accessing a hard drive, the system preloads data related to the first lot of data accessed into RAM. The next time a disk access is required, the first place the processor looks is in the cache. If the information is already there, then it needs to look no further; if not, it will access the hard drive as before with minimal increase in access time. Cache statistics are quoted as hit rates (i.e. the number of times the processor looked in the cache successfully). The bigger the cache, the better the performance of the PC.

Input usually takes place via the keyboard and the mouse and output via the monitor. Although many cathode-ray tube monitors are still in use, they are being superseded by flat panel screens. These are not affected by glare and flicker, and have a much smaller footprint. Ergonomically a 17-inch (43-cm) screen is about optimum. It should be positioned at eye height about an arm's length from the user.

Communication with peripheral devices takes place via the ports, which are affixed to the motherboard or expansion cards. Historically these were slow serial and parallel ports, which have now all but given way to faster **universal serial bus (USB)** ports, which operate at 12 Mbps. These have the advantage of being able to connect up to 127 devices via the same port and are used for web cameras, flash memory and networked devices. USB ports in their turn are giving way to even faster **FireWire** ports, which support the higher data transfer speeds that modern multimedia applications require. Current FireWire ports operate at 800 Mbps, but versions running at twice this speed will soon be available. Like USB ports, FireWire ports allow 'hot swapping' (connecting and disconnecting devices while the computer is switched on).

How programs run

Although you do not need to know processor-specific information regarding the fine details of program execution, you do need to know the basic principles if you are to make informed purchasing decisions and configure systems that perform well. Figure 2.3 shows the simplified processor operating cycle.

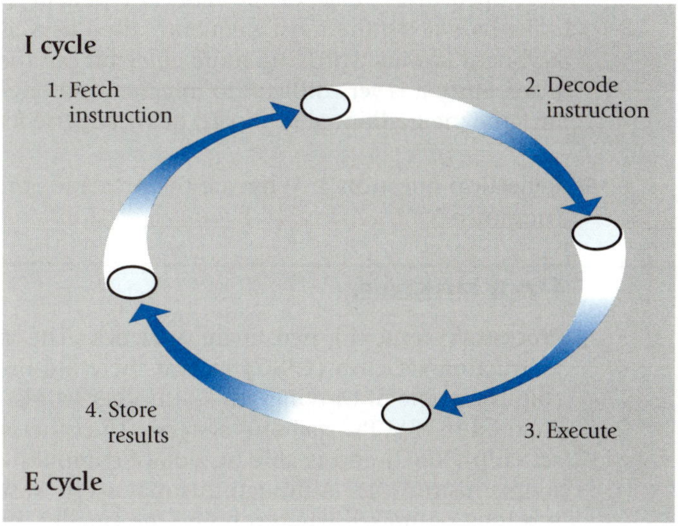

Figure 2.3 The simplified machine cycle

The **machine cycle** consists of two subcycles, the **I cycle** for instruction and the **E cycle** for execution. Instructions and data are retrieved from RAM and loaded into registers on the processor. Things are a little more complicated than the simple cycle implies; to ensure that the processor does not sit idle, instructions are preloaded. However, the basic principle remains unaltered.

Problems with the von Neumann architecture

As you will appreciate from the brief discussion above, all the data and every program instruction have to pass through the processor. Although modern processors are very fast compared with their predecessors, the processor imposes a physical bottleneck on computer performance. Equally significant is the fact that software developers need to consider the 'fetch, next, execute' cycle as they produce programs. In other words, the programs are not truly independent of the underlying hardware, and the von Neumann architecture represents a mental as well as physical bottleneck.

■ **Reflection question 3:** The processing speed of human consciousness is estimated to be 16 bits per second, and supercomputers are 50 billion times faster than this. Why are humans regarded as being superior to computers in terms of processing ability?

More on PC system components

Our coverage above was intended to help you understand how the basic components work together to run programs. Now we consider the operating principles and underlying technology of the system unit and peripheral devices.

Input devices

In addition to the usual mouse and keyboard, there are a few specialised input devices. Bar code and magnetic code readers may be used in conjunction with a PC provided that the necessary interfaces are in place. These are sometimes termed 'direct entry devices' since no human input is needed. Many handheld computers use a stylus for input rather than a keyboard due to their small size. Most PCs can interface with peripheral input devices such as web cameras and scanners via ports. The standard QWERTY keyboard was developed in the days of mechanical typewriters and was intended to prevent key jamming by placing the most frequently used keys as far apart as possible. There are several keyboard layouts which are more efficient, but these are under-represented in the marketplace. Since it is very difficult to migrate from one keyboard layout to another, it is hard to imagine the traditional keyboard being superseded.

■ **Reflection question 4:** What are the pros and cons of direct voice instruction for computers?

Processors

Processors come in two main varieties. The most widely used type is a **complex instruction-set chip (CISC)** in that there are literally hundreds of instructions that the chip is capable of carrying out — in other words, the chip is general-purpose. CISC chips are used in IBM PC standard systems. The other variety of chip is a **reduced instruction-set chip (RISC)** and is able to replace complicated instructions in terms of a number of simple instructions. Although this may seem wasteful, the design of the chip is such that it is fully optimised when running the smaller instructions set; i.e. despite the fact that it is running a larger number of instructions, it usually outperforms CISC processors. RISC chips tend to be used in workstations and Apple Macintosh computers.

Faster computers

Making the computer go faster has always been an obsession, and attention has usually focused on the processor. However, there are a number of ways in which performance can be achieved, e.g. reduce the distance between components on the same chip or simply fit more components into the same space.

Many people believe that the limits of silicon-based technology have now been reached and that the speed of light and the physical wavelength of light used to etch the chips are the limiting factors in technology development. Therefore using materials for chip manufacture that will conduct electricity more quickly would be a good move. Gallium arsenide is faster than silicon but the technology is taking a long time to develop.

Alternatively, manufacturers are exploring new computer architectures which use more than one microprocessor — so-called parallel architectures. Multiprocessor systems have been around for some time (although their main applications area was in fault-tolerant computing), but highly specialised, massively parallel architectures have been finding their way into supercomputers. Here the difficulty is to divide a task up into subtasks that may be executed simultaneously.

It seems likely that advances in performance will involve any or all of the above.

Infobyte

460 trillion calculations per second and counting

As with Formula 1 racing, speed is vital in computing, and building the fastest computer provides huge returns — not least for marketing. ASCI Purple and Blue Gene/L are supercomputers that have been developed by IBM for the US Department of Energy. Their combined processing power of 460 teraflops approaches that of the human mind. ASCI Purple achieves its great speed by making use of more than 12 000 processors and is used to carry out nuclear weapons research via simulation rather than via direct testing.

Source: information from www.ibm.com (accessed 24 July 2003).

Output devices

Output devices are hard copy or soft copy. Hard copy involves a printing process. Soft copy devices are display screens and monitors.

Hard copy

Laser printers are now the preferred option for most organisations, and good-quality colour options are available for a few thousand dollars. Although laser printers cost more initially, their operating costs are significantly less than ink jet printers, which are better suited to low-volume, personal-use systems. Neither laser nor ink jet printers actually make contact with the paper. Older dot matrix and daisy-wheel printers relied on impact methods to make an inked impression on the paper. These printers are now obsolete and cannot match the high throughput rates of modern laser printers.

When low-volume printers are used with personal systems, the PC does most of the printer control, i.e. the service is dedicated. With networked printers, the printer normally has a significant amount of RAM to enable it to store files. Additionally, files for printing are saved on the disk of a print server whose job it is to ensure that documents are printed and that users are informed of the success (or otherwise) of the operation.

Soft copy

Soft copy devices are basically computer screens. These use either cathode-ray tube technology (CRT), as is the case with most desktop machines, or **liquid crystal displays (LCDs)** which are used in portable computers. CRTs use more power than LCDs but are usually only a quarter of the cost of an LCD screen of the same size. LCDs are better ergonomically since they do not emit radiation or flicker in the same way that CRTs do. LCD screens may have a passive matrix, which has less speed and brightness than the active matrix variety.

Screen clarity, **resolution** and **refresh** rates are very important. The points on the screen which make up the display are called **pixels**. The more pixels the screen has, the better its resolution (clarity). The distance between the pixels also matters — the greater the pixel density, the better the picture. The refresh rate is the number of times per second the display is updated — the higher the refresh rate, the less the image appears to flicker. (A combination of fluorescent lighting and CRT displays can result in a stroboscopic effect in which displays with high refresh rates appear to flicker. This is very tiring for users.)

The entire display is generated by the PC and so it is important to have a large-capacity video card installed to ensure good performance when running graphic-intensive applications.

Infobyte

Organic displays

Organic light-emitting diodes (OLEDs) can be used to provide full-colour high-definition output and will probably replace the cathode-ray tubes and liquid crystal displays used on laptop and desktop computers (Forrest, Burrows & Thompson 2000). OLED displays are less than 2 mm in thickness and use less power than conventional displays, allowing longer operation of portable equipment. The display is very flexible and can easily be bent around a narrow tube. Eastman Kodak and Sony have produced an active matrix full-colour display for use in digital cameras. OLEDs are already in use in mobile phone displays, and prototype monitor screens have been developed. Problems with device lifetimes have yet to be fully overcome, but high-performance video screens should be commercially available in late 2005.

Source: www.kodak.com/US/en/corp/display/NUVUE.jhtml (accessed 25 February 2004)

Primary storage

The von Neumann architecture revolves around the stored-program concept. Put simply, this means that the program (or as many parts of it as are required for now) has to be in the computer's **primary storage** (memory). Memory is divided into read-only memory and random access memory.

Read-only memory

Read-only memory chips are non-erasable hardware modules that usually come with the programs installed. As their name implies, ROM chips can be read but not altered by the user and programs. These chips hold their contents even when the power is cut off, i.e. they are non-volatile. In mobile telephones, ROM chips contain all the software the device requires to operate. In computers, ROM chips are not big enough to hold all the software the system needs to run; instead, ROM chips hold the basic instructions for starting the PC, carrying out basic diagnostic tests and loading the operating system into random access memory.

ROM chips are called **firmware**. Additionally, there are **programmable ROM (PROM)** chips without any software installed for which the buyer then writes the program to be installed. These require special equipment **('PROM blasters')**. **Eraseable programmable read-only memory (EPROM)** chips work in the same way as PROM chips but the programs can be erased. PROMs and EPROMs can be used to add functionality to a computer or to enforce strict licensing conditions for certain software products.

Random access memory

Random access memory is referred to as main memory since it stores the data and programs on which the computer is working. Unlike ROM, it is volatile in that its contents are lost if power to the chip is cut. ROM chips are mounted on to boards and then packaged as **single inline memory modules (SIMMs)**, which can be plugged into the motherboard. Hardware designers place RAM as close to the processor as possible in order to guarantee good performance. Since accessing RAM is many times faster than accessing any secondary storage device, a PC with RAM to spare will run programs quickly.

RAM chips come in two main flavours, DDR and SDRAM. Although the differences are technical in nature, SDRAM is much faster than DDR for a marginal increase in cost.

Secondary storage devices and media

Secondary storage media operate using three basic types of technology: (1) magnetic, using tapes and disks, (2) optical, using writeable CDs and DVDs, and (3) electronic, using microchips. The information may be stored for use in two modes: serial access (e.g. tapes, which are slow) and random access (e.g. disks, which are much faster).

Magnetic tape

Magnetic tape provides serial access and although the technology is very old it is extremely cost-effective to store large data archives in this way. Older systems use large tape reels and smaller contemporary ones tend to use **digital audio tape (DAT)** or larger cassette formats. Magnetic tape is still used for older transaction processing systems which operate on a **batch** basis, i.e. the transactions are stored on tape for later processing. It is not possible to jump directly to a record on the tape in a short space of time and so the operating speed of serial media make it useless for modern, real-time interactive systems apart from data back-ups. DVD and CD writers are superceding many (but not all) tape back-up systems.

Magnetic disks

In contrast, random access media allow records to be accessed very quickly by jumping to their location on the storage medium. Random access systems normally use disks or diskettes, but drums are still used in parts of the industry. Floppy drives are intended to store small amounts of information and access speeds are very slow. Most PCs have them for backward compatibility. Internal hard drives are much faster than peripheral devices but are still many times slower than accessing RAM. However, there is a fundamental trade-off here between performance and reliability. Secondary storage is non-volatile so that in the event of a system crash the hard drive should hold enough information to allow transactions to be completed or properly abandoned. Because all disk drives have mechanical as well as electrical components, they are subject to wear and tear, and accordingly it is very important to make sure that all data are safely backed up. One method used by many companies is to have several disk drives on the same machine or scattered over a network. This allows data to be replicated, lessening the impact of disk failure. It also allows for swift retrieval of archived data. This strategy is referred to as **redundant arrays of inexpensive disks (RAIDs)**. In many cases the performance of database products such as Oracle is improved by using several disks.

Increasingly online or network-based storage such as Apple's iDisk is employed. Generally the retrieval speeds are too slow for demanding applications, but they allow important files and directories to be mirrored automatically, giving readily accessible back-ups in the event of systems problems.

The overwhelming trends for hard drives (and flash memory) are that they are becoming faster and cheaper with much greater storage capacities.

Optical disks

Optical storage media such as CDs and DVDs are significantly slower than their magnetic counterparts when it comes to data retrieval and very much slower when it comes to writing data. Many PC owners use CDs to back up their data; they cost around $1 and can hold a lot of data (650+ Mb). For single-user systems, performance is adequate. The CD has revolutionised the software industry, enabling large software suites to be sent anywhere in the world for a few dollars. Rewriteable CDs allow a CD to be reused up to 1000 times, but the cost of the technology is such that many PC owners prefer to stay with conventional CD burners. DVD burners cost round $200 but most home users do not find them cost-effective when compared to CD burners.

Protecting your data

If your data matter to you, make sure that you have another copy or back-up. All magnetic media are badly affected by lightning strikes or magnetism from motors, and just about every storage medium in existence will be wiped out by fire. Back-ups should be stored in a different place from the live system so that both aren't lost in the same accident.

Flash memory

Flash memory provides random access and is a sort of hybrid of primary and secondary storage. This technology uses microchips to store data in a stable format. A flash memory card is a little thicker than a credit card and is designed to fit a computer's PCMCIA slot or a USB port via a suitable adapter. (PCMCIA stands for Personal Computer Memory Card International Association, a standard for expansion slots in laptop computers, PDAs and other small devices. There are three types, with speeds in the order of 8 Mbps.) There are adapters that allow the floppy disk drive to access the flash memory and these give much better performance than the original floppy drive. At the time of writing, flash memory cards offer 256 Mb capacity for around $200. The fact that they have no mechanical components makes them potentially faster than a hard drive. Advances in chip circuit density may allow CDs and disks to be replaced by flash technology. Certainly, many digital cameras use flash cards in preference to disks. Flash memory is widely used in handheld and portable computing devices. Although the cost is much higher than conventional disk storage, they use only 10% of the power and hence prolong time between battery recharges.

Infobyte

Thanks for the memory

Backpackers and high-level business executives appear to have little in common, but the need to access email systems and bank accounts securely unites them. Taking a laptop computer everywhere is an inconvenience and invites theft. Using 'public' computers is a security risk since information is stored on the PC's hard drive. A simple solution is to use a USB flash drive. Costing less than $100 for 128 Mb, these can be attached to a key chain, and allow email and web browser settings to be moved between systems, guaranteeing security and privacy. Nothing is ever stored on the host computer.

Source: www.imaginelan.com/winboot/index.html (accessed 24 July 2003).

Moore's law

In 1965, Gordon Moore, one of the cofounders of Intel, noted that the amount of information storable on a square inch of silicon would double about every 18 months. This is called **Moore's law** (Gordon & Gordon 1999, p. 108). In general terms this means that the processing power effectively doubles every three to four years, although the actual figure is nearer a 20% increase per year for mainframes and roughly 25% per year for PCs. Although the cost of processors does not seem to change on the same scale, the real cost of one million instructions per second has decreased by approximately 20% per year. In short, people are buying more sophisticated and proportionately cheaper hardware each year. To appreciate the scale of the improvement, consider the following: if a $1000 investment made in 1977 had shown the same improvement as microchip technology, it would now be worth $3.5 million. If the same improvement rate applied to a car purchased in 1977 with a top speed of 150 km/h, it would now be capable of 260 000 km/h.

Accordingly, if you are working on the design and implementation of a large system, it is advisable to delay purchasing hardware until it is actually needed.

Reflection question 5: Extending the car analogy above, are there things that are routinely tolerated in a computer that would not be acceptable in a car?

[**Key concept:** ABC — Accept nothing, Believe nothing, Check everything.]

How to buy a PC

You will make some very important purchases in life, such as a house and a car. It is suggested that you treat buying a PC in the same vein — it is a serious affair. The following procedure will be useful.

- Analyse your needs. What do you need the computer to do for you?
- Choose software that will support your needs. Which applications do you require? (Software evaluation and acquisition are covered in detail in chapters 3 and 4.)
- Identify potential hardware configurations that will support your software.
- Produce a shortlist (about five) of possible computers. This will normally entail visiting retail outlets. Do not be pressured into buying. If the sales staff cannot answer your questions adequately, do not waste your time there. Do not be afraid of getting advice from different sources.
- Decide on your preferred platform — at the PC level this will normally mean choosing between an Apple Macintosh and a standard PC. Apple machines are generally better appointed but tend to be more expensive and have fewer choices for software. Now decide whether you need portability, i.e. do you need a laptop or a desktop? Laptops are much more expensive and more difficult to upgrade than an equivalent desktop machine.
- Review your options. Will the computer meet your needs? Check the processor and memory requirements for the software which you need to run. Remember that processor speed and memory size requirements quoted in software tend to be minimal. Technology changes very quickly but at the time of writing it is hard to imagine purchasing any PC with less than 256 Mb RAM, 20 Gb hard drive and a 1.7 GHz processor.
- Select manufacturers/suppliers and obtain quotations for your chosen platform. Try to avoid little-known companies. Adherence to widely adopted standards reduces risk and enhances upgradability. Most IS professionals change their PCs every 18–24 months or 36–42 months with an upgrade.
- Select one or two suppliers and negotiate the price. Under no circumstances believe that the marked price or package is the best deal that they can offer. Remember that you have the option of buying from well-established companies such as Dell and Gateway online. Online companies tend to offer better prices but are almost impossible to negotiate with, and user support can be an issue, too. Online purchasing requires good technical knowledge since you will have to provide input to the configuration of the finished product.
- In making your final decision, remember to take into account warranties and user support.

- Do not be influenced by 'bundling' (the practice of putting together a total package of hardware, software, games, desk, printer and scanner). Often much of the 'bundle' is of limited use to the buyer and only serves to increase the overall price.
- Be aware of consumer law, and don't sign any document that asks you to relinquish any rights.
- Beware of dealer-arranged financing — this comes at a cost.
- In some countries the law makes a distinction between hire purchase and a credit sale. In such countries the credit provider may be jointly responsible for the condition and suitability of the goods. It may pay you to use your credit card (if only for the frequent flyer points).

Certain employees, such as company directors, may be reimbursed for the purchase of one laptop computer per year, avoiding fringe benefits tax and maximising personal tax advantages (this does not apply to ordinary desktop machines). This can make a laptop a more cost-effective option despite the more expensive upgrade path. However, the rules are complex, and it is sensible to seek professional guidance.

IS in action

Overcoming unthemely delays

US-based Time Warner (now part of AOL) manages Sea World, Warner Bros. Movie World and Wet 'n' Wild theme parks. With a turnover of $175 million, more than 3 000 000 visitors per year and 3000 employees at peak times, swift access to operational data is needed to manage the parks' diverse and complex business affairs and identify non-performing areas. The existing system was US-developed but was not supported well in Australia and lacked the functionality required for compliance with Australian tax requirements. Reports and audit trials were taking months to produce, and the system was not reliable. Following consultations with its IT services provider, Dialog Information Technology (Australia's largest privately owned IT company), a decision was made to develop a new system using Microsoft's Navision Financials. This locally supported global technology allows the sort of flexible access that is required for performance management, and developments are in train to integrate customer relations management systems (CRM) and e-commerce with the new system. The lessons are simple: if your systems aren't helping, change them; use a tried and tested product that is well supported by local expertise, and integrate core business systems to fully leverage your investment.

Source: www.navision.com/sea/View.asp?Categoryid=504&Documentid=773 (accessed 24 July 2003)

[**Key concept:** There are advantages to being first.]

Infobyte

Making light work of keyboards

Few executives would doubt the usefulness of their PDA, but typing-intensive activities such as email are slow when using styli or pocket-sized keyboards. Canesta developed the world's first projection keyboard with this problem in mind. A special keyboard pattern projector displays a keyboard on any convenient flat surface, and a special chip set converts the user's finger movements into data entry. With this keyboard, people can obtain laptop functionality with PDA size and weight. The same sensing technology also provides a basis for new generation security systems, which can handle 3D facial recognition.

Source: www.canesta.com (accessed 24 July 2003).

Buying hardware for business systems

The basic principles outlined for PCs apply here. But since the consequences of making mistakes are much greater, care must be exercised in the selection process. Management has responsibilities to companies, shareholders and, in the case of government, taxpayers. The decision-makers need to choose whether to buy the equipment and build the system themselves or organise supply and installation from a third party. For a small quantity, of course, the process of evaluating bids for supply and negotiating contracts would probably exceed the value of the contract. Assuming that hardware and software needs have been carefully analysed and there is a commitment to proceed, then proceed as for PC selection, with the addition of the following.

Expression of interest

When working for public institutions it is important to make the tendering process as open as possible to avoid accusations of favouritism and corruption. Advertisements can be placed in newspapers asking for expressions of interest in tendering for the supply of goods and services, or companies may apply to join the list of government-approved suppliers. In industry, management can either advertise or simply write to potential suppliers with a tender or offer document, also known as a **request for proposal (RFP)**.

Potential suppliers need to be briefed as to your exact needs. Usually this involves preparing an information pack, giving background information on your organisation, its plans and needs, the timeline required for the project and some indication of the funding available. For large projects it is often a good idea to engage a consultant, especially if the area is outside your field of expertise. The RFP often forms the basis of a legal contract so it is very important to ensure that all the technical details are correct. It is also advisable to involve your legal team in the preparation of the RFP. The more work that you put into this document, the more likely it is that unsuitable suppliers will not respond. A business would normally give some indication as to the type of company that it is prepared to deal with, e.g. it must meet quality standard ISO9002, it must have been trading for five years, it must have a track record for supply in this area. This reduces risk and the amount of work involved in the evaluation and validation of bids. The information pack must give the criteria for assessment — although price is important, user support and warranties could be very significant. The exact format, content and timing of the bids/tenders are also specified, to make the resulting bids easier to compare. It also makes it much easier to eliminate unsuitable suppliers, since if they cannot deliver a document in the required format, they are unlikely to deliver a system as required.

When all the responses have been received, unacceptable bids/tenders should be eliminated from the process. This means anything that is late, in the wrong format, does not cover the criteria or contains errors of spelling and grammar. Write to these companies to inform them that their bids have been unsuccessful. Acceptable bids/tenders can now be ranked.

From this point, the highest ranked bids should be selected and validated. Validation means that every claim that the company makes for itself, its products and services is checked. This can be a lengthy, painstaking procedure and so the number of bids that are validated should be kept to a minimum — five or fewer is a rough guideline. It is not ethical to change the terms of reference, but it may be appropriate to seek clarification from suppliers on certain points.

[**Key concept:** Never assume anything.]

From childhood experience you may have memories of Christmas mornings spent with non-functioning toys because optimistic parents assumed that the toys came with batteries included. The IS industry is not exactly a toy shop, but the onus is on you to check the precise wording and specifications that companies give. Several companies have had their business affected by server failures, or have failed to notice that the standard manufacturer's warranty did not include a timeframe for response — they assumed that engineers would turn up as soon as the fault was reported. Same-day service and/or on-site replacement is a requirement for mission-critical systems. Suppliers do not usually have time to educate potential clients, so it is taken for granted that you actually want what you ask for. This is one area where being a member of a professional body is very useful. Many professional bodies publish technology reviews and hold breakfast meetings with industry speakers. If you network within the organisation effectively, it is usually possible to find someone who has detailed knowledge of a particular topic.

[**Key concept:** If you use technical terms, make sure that you understand what they mean and that others do, too.]

When the process of validation is complete, it is usually easy to select the final supplier. Remember that the solution should reduce complexity and diversity. Single-supplier solutions do this, and also eliminate many of the compatibility problems that are often found in multi-vendor systems. Next comes the process of negotiating and overseeing the contract. If the RFP has been prepared well, the contract is virtually written, subject to minor clarifications.

For simpler systems, it is possible to obtain quotations from online suppliers. These provide either online catalogues, pricing and shipping information, or a confidential guaranteed response to a written request. The assumption here is that you know exactly what you want and that it can be met from a standard package, i.e. unless it is a large contract, there is little room for negotiation.

Infobyte

A ray of hope in the race for speed?

As fast as modern computers are, they are still limited by the resistance of copper and semiconductor materials to the flow of electrons. Researchers at Intel have discovered how to use photons (light energy) to move vast amounts of data around inside computers. Previously the cost of the exotic materials needed made this impracticable, but the researchers have worked out how to use a more commonplace material. Initial experiments indicate that data-encoding rates in excess of 10 billion bits per second should be possible (Fordahl 2004). As the technology becomes available it seems likely to be used for links between servers in corporate data centres and to improve Internet performance. But it can only be a matter of time before it finds its way into servers and ultimately desktop machines. Besides allowing for high-definition Internet applications such as video-conferencing, the technology could support the biometric authentication systems needed for e-commerce and security systems.

Source: information from Fordahl, M. 2004, 'Intel photonics discovery could speed up servers, PCs', *eweek*, www.eweek.com/article2/0,4149,1525178,00.asp (accessed 25 February 2004).

Offloading problems

An important aspect of management is how problems are handled. The manager's survival guide says, 'Don't take ownership of any problem that is not rightfully yours'; we extend this to read, 'Don't take ownership of any problem that you do not need to'. When preparing RFPs and negotiating contracts, think ahead. If PCs are to be supplied with general-purpose software ready installed, have the supplier install your own software, configure the machines to be network-ready, or even let them do the final installation and configuration on your premises. This can save time, money and effort.

- **Reflection question 6:** Do you think suppliers can be trusted to deliver the right thing at the right time at the right price? What can you do to ensure that this happens?

[**Key concept:** Let others do the work.]

The importance of hardware standards

In order to manage effectively, we need to understand what we are trying to manage. So the more diverse and complex things are, the harder they are to manage. One way to reduce complexity and diversity is to standardise on hardware platforms (the hardware forms part of a standard operating environment or SOE). This also gives us better bargaining power since we are buying more machines of the same type and means that we have a high degree of interchangeability at a component level. In an ideal world a single hardware standard for desktop machines would be feasible, and indeed that is possible for many small or simple businesses. However, it is important to remember that the hardware is there to support business needs — in practice this means supporting business software. Many organisations use PCs, Unix Workstation and Macintosh computers in their everyday business and use the 'most appropriate tool for the job'. This does not mean that they have abandoned the notion of standards. Each type of hardware platform will be clearly defined. Other businesses have a variety of hardware platforms simply because they do not have the cash to replace older technology. Most IS/IT managers have a migration plan to reduce hardware diversity to a few manageable standards and hence simplify the task of management.

[**Key concept:** 'Business needs dictate the choice of software. Software dictates the choice of hardware. Everything else is about making it work efficiently and effectively.' Jane Barton-Grieg, senior IS consultant.]

■ **Reflection question 7:** If you developed a totally new computing concept, something which was a tenth the size and cost yet gave 100 times the power of a normal PC, would you make it PC compatible? Why or why not?

Summary

This chapter summarised the history of computers, explained the types of computers and peripheral devices in current use, and speculated on future developmental trends. The key points in this chapter are:

- There have been four main generations of computer, each more sophisticated than its predecessor. Each generation brought about a substantial amount of change.
- The four main types of computers in use today are supercomputer, mainframe, workstation and PC. The boundaries between these devices are sometimes indistinct.
- A typical PC configuration includes keyboard, mouse, monitor, webcam, hard drive, fax/modem, printer and system unit with ports for peripheral devices. Standard PC architecture has expansion slots to allow extra functionality to be added.
- The computer architecture that is most commonly used today is the von Neumann architecture, which imposes physical and mental bottlenecks on system development.
- Processors come in two main types: (1) general-purpose complex instruction-set chip (CISC) and (2) reduced instruction-set chip (RISC).
- There are two types of computer storage: (1) primary, which is onboard memory which loses its contents when the power is turned off, and (2) secondary, which is semi-permanent, cheaper and much slower. Primary storage may be subdivided into random access memory (RAM) for user programs and read-only memory (ROM) for specialised system programs.

- When making any computer purchase, take care to perform needs analysis, product evaluation and price negotiation. For larger systems it is advisable to employ a consultant and lawyer to help in this process.

Questions

1. Why is it important for an organisation to standardise its hardware platforms? What are the pros and cons of using several sets of hardware standards?
2. Given the advances in RAM and hard drive technology, do you think that CDs and DVDs have a long-term future?
3. Over the past twenty years the PC market has grown while the mainframe market has consolidated. Do you think this trend will continue? Explain your answer.
4. In your view, what will the primary input device for the next generation PC be like?
5. The quest for speed has driven computer development since its inception. Will the time come when computers will be fast enough?
6. Apple has always maintained that its machines make users more productive because they are easier to use and hence that Apple computers are more cost-effective. How valid do you think this view is, and why?
7. What are the practical implications of Moore's law when it comes to ordering hardware?
8. What do you think of the longer-term prospects for CDs when compared to DVDs?
9. Why would you carry out needs analysis and software selection before deciding on your hardware platform?
10. What are the relative merits of using flash memory compared with a traditional hard drive?

Exercises

1. You have recently assumed the position of IS manager of a large company. One of your first acts has been to specify standard operating environments and purchasing requirements. Unfortunately, the system of budgeting is decentralised and each business unit has control of its own purchases. All the managers have been cooperative with the exception of the head of marketing. He refuses to adopt your standards since he has a friend who builds PC clones and he gets a 'good deal'. You cannot afford to upset people so soon after joining the company, but equally you cannot afford to be undermined so soon in your career. How would you set about resolving the situation?
2. Form a small discussion group and establish how you would go about setting up a hardware purchasing policy for a larger company and deciding what its key features should be.
3. Your company is setting up a 350-user client-server network. The project has gone very well to date, and the network cabling, switching devices and servers have all been contracted out for supply and installation. The only remaining task is to decide on the client machines. Some users want Macintosh systems while the majority want PCs. The managing director is adamant that each manager will have a laptop. It would be possible to have desktop PCs built locally for a slightly lower cost than those supplied by a major, well-established manufacturer. At the moment tempers are running high, and you have been put in charge of PC procurement. How will you handle the task, and what would your recommendations be?

CASE STUDY Blue Books

Blue Books is a sizeable bookshop in Sydney. It occupies several floors of a prime high street location. In addition to selling books it also sells videos, DVDs and CDs and has a coffee shop on the fifth floor. Blue Books has a history of innovation: it was the first bookshop in Sydney with electronic point of sales systems, and the first to provide customers with PC-based catalogue browsing instore. Increased competition and declining profit margins led to the move into CDs and DVDs and, more recently, into select, upmarket stationery. A large amount of Blue Books' business is derived from overseas visitors to Sydney, but there is a substantial local customer base and repeat business from Australian visitors to the store.

There are 16 checkout positions, most of which have two electronic cash registers linked to a central database. The cash registers have limited processing power and cannot access the inventory system directly to answer customer queries. The system has worked very well for the past six years, but the hardware has started to show signs of failure. The software is efficient but limited, and it is very difficult to carry out data capture on customers or to carry out sophisticated queries on the database for marketing purposes. Blue Books is a good business, but in order to maintain its health it needs to market and merchandise more effectively, and this means replacing the exist hardware and software with something that is better aligned with the business plan. Consequently a replacement system has been commissioned.

Eric Kruger handles all IS/IT support for the Sydney store. He was closely involved in the development of the system that is now due for replacement. He was promoted to the position of IT manager two years ago. He started at Blue Books nine years ago, joining the company after graduating with first-class honours in computer science. He has since completed a Graduate Diploma in Business with a view to taking an MBA at a later date. The directors decided to put Eric in charge of the project to replace the older hardware and software, and he has been told to reduce costs where possible.

Eric has followed a traditional systems development approach and has taken the trouble to confirm the user requirements for an integrated software system that can handle sales, inventory, transaction processing and marketing. The software uses a single server and PCs with barcode readers to function. The company offered to provide a turnkey (ready to use) system for around $360 000 (including installation) with ongoing software and network licensing costs of $80 000 per year. Eric has taken the trouble to price everything that he would need to build the system and realises that he could save more than $60 000 by sourcing all the equipment locally and bringing in contract staff to handle the changeover. His procurement list includes a new network, PCs to use as both electronic tills and for handling customer enquiries, and a further 12 PCs placed on the shop floor to allow customers to browse the online catalogue and to place orders. The database server is a state-of-the-art dual processor model. Eric made sure that he specified conformance to the network and hardware standards

(continued)

specified by the software supplier in his purchase orders. Sensibly, he has arranged for the system to be installed over a weekend. Since the networking cabling was upgraded two years ago, it is quite capable of supporting the new systems and does not need to be replaced; however, the new system requires updated networking software.

Work began on dismantling the old system as soon as the store closed its doors on Saturday evening, and by midnight this part of the project was complete. By 9.00 a.m. on Sunday the new hardware is in place and the software has been installed. The project is well ahead of schedule. Eric tests the system by scanning a book — and finds that it fails to operate. Realising that he has only a short period of time in which to resolve the problems, he telephones the software company, the business that supplied the server, the PC supplier and the network software vendor in an effort to understand the problem. The network people blame the server company; the server company in turn point to problems with the PCs and networking. The PC company say that they manufacture to widely used, international standards and have never had any such problems before. The network software company points out that its product is used worldwide in many different applications.

Eric realises that he has less than 24 hours in which to sort out this problem or his future with the company looks bleak. It crosses his mind to walk off the job and tender his resignation. Right now he has six contract staff standing around waiting for instructions.

QUESTIONS

1. How did Eric manage to get himself into this mess?
2. Would walking off the job and resigning be a reasonable option? Why or why not?
3. What should Eric do immediately?
4. What should be done in the short term?
5. What should be done to resolve the problems on a permanent basis?
6. What revisions to policies and procedures should be made to prevent a recurrence?
7. Should Eric be allowed to keep his job? Why or why not?

References

Forrest, S., Burrows, P. & Thompson, M. 2000, 'The dawn of organic electronics', *IEEE Spectrum*, August, pp. 29–34.

Gordon, J.R. & Gordon, S.R. 1999, *Information Systems: A Management Approach*, 2nd edn, Harcourt Brace College Publishers, Orlando.

Wolverton, M. 2002, 'The tube is dead. Long live the tube', *American Heritage of Invention and Technology*, Fall 2002, vol. 18, no. 2. <www.americanheritage.com/it/2002/02/tube.shtml (accessed 24 July 2003).

Chapter 3

Business software

LEARNING OBJECTIVES

After reading this chapter, you should be able to:

- understand the nature, broad history and five generations of software
- understand the term 'software crisis' and what can be done to overcome its effects
- describe the types of software in current use
- understand the step–lock cycle and how communications alter the pattern of competition in the software industry
- distinguish between horizontal and vertical software
- distinguish between packaged, customisable and custom software, and explain their relative merits
- explain what is meant by the term 'intelligent agents' and give examples of their use
- understand the nature and importance of open source software.

3

Introduction

A detailed understanding of the underlying technology is not necessary to be an effective and visionary manager. However, you do need to understand the nature of what you manage. The actual process of producing software is covered later, but for now it is sufficient to examine the major categories of software in common use and the major trends in the software industry. As with hardware, reducing diversity and complexity simplifies management and reduces risk and cost in the process.

Consider the material in this chapter from the perspective of someone who is managing the information systems function for a sizeable organisation. Even though it has been clearly stated that business economics now favour smaller organisations, considering larger organisations will encourage you to develop a 'big picture' perspective which will be useful to you when managing the development of systems. The departments of many large organisations operate as quasi-independent business units — they are almost small–medium businesses in their own right. This allows a high degree of autonomy for the business units which, in turn, allows senior management to focus on outcomes rather than processes. Software plays a vital role in this process.

This chapter gives a brief selective coverage of the history of software, covering the main issues from a business perspective. Specific types of software application are discussed later in the book, but it is assumed that you are reasonably familiar with products that are available for desktop computers.

The history and nature of software

As might be expected, the development of software has closely paralleled that of hardware. Each generation of hardware has had its own generation of associated software. From earliest times there has always been a clear distinction between the tools and the intelligence which uses them. As technology has grown in complexity, it has become possible to automate some of the more routine tasks. It is now common to have tools that control other tools, as well as specialist tools and multipurpose tools. It may be seen that the same sort of distinctions have emerged in software. But when did software actually appear?

Vaucanson

Jacques de Vaucanson was (arguably) the earliest developer of software. Appointed as inspector of silk factories in France in 1741, he turned his attention to the problems of mechanising the industry (Britannica 2001). Celebrated as an inventor of mechanical automata, Vaucanson had produced a lifelike flute player in 1738 and a remarkable mechanical duck the year after. In developing his automata, the programmed behaviour was designed into the device. The mechanical duck's movements would eventually show repetition. Changing the behaviour of the duck required changing its design and internal workings. In 1745 he developed a fully automatic weaving loom which allowed intricate patterns to be produced, and chose to use punched cards as the medium of control. Although punched cards had been used before this time, they were used for generic settings only; a human operator was still required to provide the skilled input. Vaucanson's loom needed no skilled operator. The skill came in designing fabrics and transcribing those designs to punched cards. Once produced, the cards could be duplicated and reused on another Vaucanson loom. What prevented the take-up of the technology was that Vaucanson's cards could not be used on anything other than one of his looms. It would be comparable to someone nowadays producing a desktop software package that was not PC-compatible. The Vaucanson loom was largely ignored for the remainder of the eighteenth century.

Jacquard

Joseph Marie Jacquard discovered Vaucanson's loom and modified it in concept. Instead of a specialised loom, he produced a general-purpose attachment that could be fitted to any loom. The Jacquard attachment became available in 1804–05 and by 1812 there were more than 11 000 in use in France alone. An entire industry evolved to make and sell the cards ('software') that operated the looms.

Babbage

Charles Babbage first described his idea to make a 'computer' (actually a general-purpose analytical engine) in 1834 and had completed his first prototypes of elemental devices within two years. He had already designed a difference engine in 1822, a sophisticated mechanical calculator. Though the difference engine actually worked, the British government decided not to continue funding the project. Babbage improved the design and Georg Scheutz and his son, Edvard, successfully constructed a device based upon Babbage's design in 1853–54 (Babbage Institute 2001). The driving force behind its development was the need to improve military effectiveness and this entailed detailed calculations for accurate navigation and ballistics.

Sadly, Babbage was working in an area in which few people were interested. Babbage's thinking was surprisingly modern — his engine was divided into four units, each with its own function: input, processing ('mill' in Babbage's terminology), storage and output. Three types of punched card were used: constant cards for inputting a constant value, variable cards for variables and transporting values between the functional units, and control cards to control the way in which the mill operated (some IS professionals still use the term 'mill time').

Babbage spent his entire fortune in a fruitless quest to build his analytical engine (Bromley 1987). His reasons for failure were twofold — first, most Victorian engineering was insufficiently accurate for his needs (although it was theoretically possible to build the device with Victorian technology); second, he was a born tinkerer and kept trying to improve the design and trying out new ideas in the course of production. Little of Babbage's machinery remains, but in 1991, the Science Museum in South Kensington (UK) constructed a portion of his difference engine no. 2 using his design and Victorian technology. It functioned perfectly. Both Babbage and his assistant, Countess (Ada) Lovelace, had programming languages named after them.

Infobyte

Banana projects

This slang term is used to describe projects which never end because people can't resist the temptation to improve and tinker with the design. One apocryphal story claims the term evolved because a child once said, 'I know how to spell banana — I just don't know when to stop.' Many projects which fail to meet deadlines or criteria for success are 'banana projects'.

Hollerith

Herman Hollerith applied Babbage's punched card concept to data collection and processing in the US census in 1890. His technology allowed data capture over a wide range, enabling detailed demographic information to be obtained. Although his machinery carried out integration, its main function was counting and totalising. Nonetheless, it revolutionised the process, saving over $US5 million — the census takers compiled their results in just six weeks (Meyers 1999; Russo 2001). Hollerith founded the company that would later become IBM. His methods were in use until the 1960s over several generations of hardware.

[**Key concept:** Software outlives hardware.]

Summary of historical trends

With Vaucanson it may be seen that the information and data required to control a process are separate from the machinery which carries out that process. With Jacquard, the element of portability is added, increasing the applicability of the technology. Babbage provided the clear distinction between data and control codes (although he reverted to machine dependency). Finally, Hollerith showed that information has an existence which is independent of control codes and hardware. All these trends are still in evidence today.

First-generation languages

In the early days of modern computing, the data and control codes were input as a set of binary digits or **machine code**. Each machine was different, and the task of programming required intimate knowledge of the machine architecture. Although the task of programming was labour-intensive, the cost of manufacturing and maintaining the hardware was enormous by comparison. The number of programmers greatly exceeded the number of computers. Each machine had so many unique features that programs and even programming techniques were not portable from one machine to another. This period of software development belongs with the first generation of hardware as described in chapter 2.

Second-generation languages

With improvements in technology and an increased demand for programs, **assembly languages** began to emerge. These made use of mnemonic codes such as ADD and other instructions which were recognised by the processor. While these simplified the task of programming somewhat, they could not be described as user-friendly. They offered little in the way of portable software. Assembly codes emerged towards the end of the first generation of computer, and although it is still possible to program in assembly languages, most developers choose to use higher level languages for this purpose.

Third-generation languages

Towards the end of the 1950s, the demand for computer technology for business applications increased dramatically. Obviously, without software, hardware is useless. Two distinct directions emerged: (1) to simplify the task of programming so that the number of programmers could be increased and (2) to make the software that they produced portable so that it could be used on different computers irrespective of processor architecture. First- and second-generation programs were unsuited to this. New kinds of programming language were required, languages which were higher level, i.e. as similar as possible to natural language. These languages had to be as portable as possible so that programming effort need not be duplicated.

Three major **high-level languages** emerged at the end of the 1950s: FORTRAN (IBM's FORmula TRANslator), COBOL (COmmon Business Oriented Language) and LISP (LISt Processing language). These were remarkable for a number of reasons. All three languages incorporated the concept of substructures within programs, which allowed portions of programs to be reused. COBOL had separate descriptions for data and procedural code.

Each language relied on **compiler** technology for its implementation. A compiler is a program which translates all of a high-level language program into a form which the processor can handle, i.e. it translates high-level language into executable code for the processor. The high-level language is now independent of the underlying hardware (the compiler is, of course, still machine-dependent). A compiler translates all of a program at one and the same time. An alternative approach is to perform translation as required using an **interpreter**. Generally it is the case that interpreters are more flexible but slower than compiled software. In the 1950s and early 1960s, punched cards and tape were still the preferred medium for inputting code and data. In this way, one generation of software was able to outlive several generations of hardware and a program could be duplicated and run on many computers. The basis of the modern software industry had been established.

- **Reflection question 1:** Why is development usually faster in a high-level language than in a low-level language?

The software crisis

The success of third-generation languages transformed computing and led to the establishment of information systems as a practice in its own right. However, while the demand for software increased exponentially, the supply of computer programmers increased linearly. Improvements in technology had led to the mass production of computers and the cost of labour began to exceed hardware costs. The resulting shortfall was obvious in that companies could not build the systems they wanted due to lack of software. This shortfall was termed the **software crisis**. There were several solutions to this problem.

Simplifying programming

Sets of tools designed to help the developer produce good-quality code more quickly were developed but failed to produce the expected increase in programmer productivity. Although the task of programming was much easier, the relative complexity of the programs was much greater and so the two tended to cancel each other out. **Object-oriented programming (OOP)** is covered later in this text but note that OOP favours rapid development and prototyping and facilitates code reuse at a component rather than module level.

Reusing software

Instead of having each program tailored to a particular application, there was movement to produce code which was more modular in structure, enabling it to be reused in other systems. This in turn required the development of sophisticated design and management methodologies to ensure reusability and the adoption of internationally recognised language standards.

Developing new paradigms

If traditional programming methods were impeding progress, then moving to another method of working seemed logical. The development of large, customisable software packages which provided general solutions to business problems was one approach. The development of more specialised packages such as databases with their own inbuilt languages was another.

Fourth-generation languages

The first three generations of programming language were **procedural languages**. In other words, the software developer had to know what was required and how it should be performed. There were many users who knew exactly what they wanted from the system but who had no idea about how to write a program to perform the task. **Fourth-generation languages** (**4GLs**, or **non-procedural languages**) are query-oriented in that a user need only specify what is required and the underlying software will sort out the business of how it is to be obtained. Since databases were at the heart of most corporate information systems, it was there that the languages tended to evolve. SQL (Structured Query Language, a high-level database-oriented language for non-programmers) is the best known example of a 4GL. It is very high level and closer to natural language than third-generation languages.

It is not uncommon to see fourth-generation languages embedded into third-generation programs. The huge development effort expended in producing transaction processing systems had yielded fast and efficient (if primitive) programs which operated on files. Rather than redevelop everything, it was easier to embed the new database query language statements into the older third-generation code.

■ Reflection question 2: Is there still a software crisis?

Fifth-generation languages

With each generation of language, software developers have moved further away from the underlying hardware, i.e. the degree of abstraction has increased. There has been a distinct progression from machine level to human level, from syntax to semantics. The fifth generation, if it ever arrives, will use natural language. Although there are speech recognition systems and elementary dictation systems, they remain at a fairly primitive level. Dictation software usually has high correction requirements. There are systems which accept voice input, but these are restricted to single words or short phrases of known format. Parsing entire sentences and interpreting their meaning requires a high degree of intelligence and this problem is compounded by the diversity of sentence construction. It is very likely that these difficulties will be overcome in the next decade.

Contrasting hardware and software

Think about the nature of costs in the hardware industry. To a great extent it relies on a large market to justify its existence. There is substantial effort devoted to design, and the expense of putting together an assembly line is huge. In addition, there are the costs of components, labour, packaging, shipping and warranty.

Software also requires a substantial effort in design, simply because of the nature of the market. However, whereas the cost of fixing a design flaw in a microcomputer requires resetting the assembly line and recalling all affected units, often the only thing faulty software requires is the amendment/addition of a few lines of code. The bug fix can be downloaded from a web site instantly. With the exception of intelligence, no raw materials are required for the production of software and it can be sent to anywhere in the world on a CD for a few dollars. Compare that with hardware in which packing and shipping costs are a major cost item. The software industry has much higher turnover per employee than traditional manufacturing. But in an industry in which innovation is a major competitive edge, much of the income may be spent on research and development. This may hinder the growth of smaller companies. However, it is possible that a software futures market will emerge, and if so, it will provide a means of funding software development.

The software industry has grown to such an extent that it now exerts considerable influence on the direction that hardware development takes. Many computer manufacturers optimise their hardware so that it runs the most popular software more efficiently. This in turn causes market distortion and makes it hard for new and potentially better software to enter the market.

Like audio and video recordings, software is not usually purchased, but licensed. This imposes restrictions on users regarding unauthorised duplication and use. Licences may be for a single machine or for an entire site. Usually licences are restricted to a particular version of the software. To date, no software producer has promoted a licence which operates on a charge-for-use basis.

It is possible to change the entire look, feel and behaviour of software with relatively few additions/modifications of the code. Because of this, software packages contain fossil relics of previous systems. The economics of the situation mean that a lot of software has grown beyond its original specification. This, in turn, imposes technical and operational constraints on companies. The sheer development effort may mean that the software system can never be replaced, only modified or maintained. Many large corporate databases could represent more than 400 person years in development costs. It is easier to build a financial case for replacing a small system which is obsolete. Much of the software was designed and produced at a time when RAM was scarce and processors were slow; this limits the performance of many systems. Lastly, the nature of software means that it is relatively easy to steal and smuggle. Software piracy is a major problem for most developers, especially in some nations that do not recognise copyright laws. It is argued that piracy deprives the industry of the funds it needs to produce better products. Software pirates argue that the industry overcharges for its products anyway. Often the only way a company can promote a software product is to offer a cut-down version as shareware or freeware in the hope that the demand for extra functionality and services will make the product commercially viable. Such companies may turn a blind eye to a little piracy.

IS in action

The Free Software Foundation vs the Business Software Alliance

Stealing software is relatively easy, and up to 40% of proprietary software is believed to have been illegally copied (and these illegal copies could be further copied and distributed). If this figure were reduced by 10% it is estimated that 1.5 million jobs and $610 billion turnover would be added to the IS/IT industries. The Business Software Alliance (BSA) sees legislation as the best means to prevent copyright infringement. The software industry faces the kind of illegal copying that has beset the music and film industries for decades. The Free Software Foundation (FSF) does not condone the infringement of copyright but argues that proprietary software does not make sense in the Internet age. Instead the FSF encourages the development of open source software that anyone may use, modify and redistribute for commercial and non-commercial purposes. Large software corporations might now find themselves legally obliged to make information about their own products available to developers in the same way Microsoft is (Rosoff 2001). Whether this sounds the death knell for market domination by a few large software companies remains to be seen.

Source: information from www.wired.com/news/infostructure/0,1377,58306,00.html (accessed 21 July 2003); www.gnu.org/fsf/fsf.html (accessed 21 July 2003).

■ **Reflection question 3:** Are there any circumstances under which you would find software piracy to be ethical?

Types of software in current use

There are three main types of software:

- applications software
- systems software
- communications software.

Applications software

Applications software is something that does something useful for users. This may be specialised for some particular function in a company (**vertical software**), e.g. an in-house financial modelling package, or the software may be general-purpose software (**horizontal software**) which has been bought 'off the shelf' ready to use. The term 'horizontal' implies that the software package has the potential to be used right across the organisation — word processing and spreadsheet packages are good examples of this. Why reinvent the wheel? It makes far more sense in economic terms to buy general-purpose software off the shelf. After all, the development effort and costs of **custom software** are huge and are unlikely to be recovered. Often, the only software that should be developed or commissioned is specialised software (vertical software).

There is a category of software that comes between these two extremes — applications software environments that can be customised to meet the needs of a particular organisation (**customisable software**). Here, the software developer produces a high-quality package which is very flexible. Technical staff can then adapt the product to the needs of the organisation in such a way that it is convenient for all users to work with.

In buying off-the-shelf products, companies are taking advantage of the developer's economies of scale — they do not need to maintain a large technical staff with diverse skills, they have access to user support, and they can get the product quickly. Many large software projects may require more than 100 people years of development effort. Also, there is a greater choice and hence a greater likelihood of developing the best business solution.

Since much of system operating costs come from user support, it makes sense to standardise on applications software. Being 'state of the art' implies risk, since early versions of software may not be reliable. It also means that support staff need to maintain skills in several different products. The same argument for standardising applies to software, but which standards should be adopted? Choose the most appropriate package for the job, subject to the following conditions:

- The package is widely used and supported well — this means that there is a wealth of experience that can be drawn on and it should be easier to recruit people with skills in using the package.
- The supplier has a good track record and is financially sound — if the supplier goes broke, a business could lose access to user support and product development.
- The package is easy to use, and if it is part of a software suite the user interface and functions should be as consistent as possible.
- The package is compatible with existing packages and, to a lesser extent, existing hardware.

The last consideration is the most telling from a business perspective. The concern is to get the maximum **return on investment (ROI)** from hardware and software. IS managers are judged on a number of criteria, one of which is cost-effectiveness. Existing systems (legacy systems) often impose constraints on what is achievable. Information systems is about the art of the possible. No system is perfect — most people have seen compromises in performance, quality, user-friendliness and so on because of cost, time constraints or existing systems. The trick is to get the best compromise.

■ **Reflection question 4:** Why does vertical software usually cost more than horizontal software?

Stand-alone or integrated software?

In the past, most applications were independent, stand-alone packages. This approach led to 'islands' of information. For example, the effort involved in generating a report that contained spreadsheets, graphs and some simple illustrations was huge — synthesising all the elements using separate applications programs was often complicated because one package produced output that was not compatible with another.

These problems led to the development of software packages in which all common software is available in the same **software suite**, e.g. Microsoft Office — several pieces of compatible software are bundled together and licensed as a single package. Many software developers have argued that Microsoft's approach to bundling software products and shipping its Internet browser with the system software amounts to unfair competition, but a major advantage of this approach is that the interface, appearance and functions are consistent. Figure 3.1 shows the presentation graphics, web site creation and management, spreadsheet and word processing programs from Microsoft Office. Note the similarity in appearance and function. This improves personal productivity.

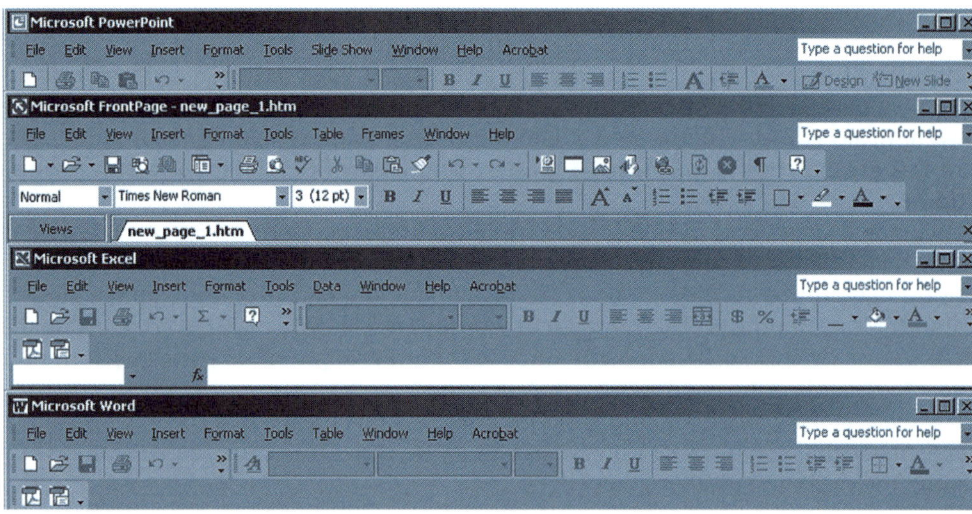

Figure 3.1 Microsoft Office software suite

Although it is true to say that there are other fully integrated office software suites, it must be acknowledged that Microsoft has more than 90% of this market (Glaser 2003) and that its nearest rivals have a very small slice of the action and hence reduced profits. The Canadian software company Corel has an excellent range of offerings, but Microsoft's market domination means that large corporate users tend to select and stay with Microsoft's products simply for transparency of use, even though files can be exchanged easily between the two products. Adobe has done much to standardise file exchange between programs and platforms, but the company is at the mercy of Microsoft. In 2004 the state of Massachusetts was investigating claims that Microsoft was stifling competition from unspecified Internet search engines and alleged that similar campaigns were planned against producers of other document software, such as Adobe Acrobat (Foss 2004).

The development costs of software are the same for a mainframe, mid-range system or PC. The mainframe market is much smaller in number and so to ensure cost recovery and profit, the cost of mainframe software licences is much greater than PC licences, e.g. $1 million to $2 million is not uncommon. Correspondingly, the range of software available for PCs far exceeds that available for mainframes. A rough survey indicates there are at least 15 000 commercial software packages for PCs as opposed to a few hundred for mainframes.

Giving it away — software for free

You are probably familiar with shareware and freeware. These are software that is available for download from the Internet or freely circulated on disk. Production values of shareware and freeware may be very low, and there is no guarantee of quality, user support or security. In fairness, the quality varies from very good to very poor. Naturally, most of the software is for PC or related platforms. Sometimes a company will allow a cut-down version of its software to be downloaded in order to sell the professional version. Some companies may trial software that is under development (beta versions). Sometimes a company may give its valuable program code away for nothing, as was the case with Netscape's Navigator software. However, you should realise that centring core business applications on shareware is potentially high risk.

There are other ways in which we obtain software 'free'. Original Equipment Manufacturers incorporates Microsoft's systems software into a computer that it then sells under its own brand name. Microsoft 'bundles' other products with the systems software, e.g. an Internet browser or a media player. The bundle might not be completed until after the purchase has been made. For example, Macintosh buyers can download entry-level media-editing software for free. Bundling has short-term advantages for the user but might stifle competition in the longer term.

Microsoft's Internet browser came free with the system software. Netscape's browser had to be purchased separately. As a result, Netscape's market share fell dramatically. Since a large portion of Netscape's business was in building private internets (intranets) for companies, the company took the view that if it gave away the software code for its browser, software developers would develop applications that would make use of its technology.

Despite this bold move, Netscape's fortunes continued to decline until the company was acquired by AOL in 1999, and use of the Netscape browser has declined to a few per cent. AOL's motives in acquiring Netscape might have been to prevent competition, but a popular (and — more importantly — free) browser would have been of enormous benefit to AOL. Although AOL's share of the domestic US market is considerable, it is a very small percentage of the total Internet user population. If direct competition is not possible, then a widely used vendor-independent browser might be a desirable option. In 2003 AOL opted to let the Netscape name disappear and donated start-up funding to the Mozilla Foundation. This is proving to be a shrewd move. Mozilla inherited all the source code from Netscape and has a commitment to open source code and documentation. Anyone can develop features for the Mozilla suite. All that is required is that developers adhere to Internet standards and that, if their code is meant for public distribution, then the source code and documentation are made freely available. When version 1.6 of Mozilla was released in 2004 it incorporated: an enterprise-grade email client that can synchronise with palm devices (Thunderbird); a web browser with security features built in (Firefox); Internet chat software; and a web page editor. Within the first few weeks of its release, more than a million downloads were recorded (www.mozilla.org 2004), indicating the demand for a vendor-neutral browser suite. Care was taken to ensure that both PC and Macintosh users were fully catered for.

It is hard to give a breakdown of browser use since many sites are not able to distinguish between browsers, but compiling information from different sources (http://dmoz.org/Computers/Internet/Statistics_and_Demographics/) gives a figure for Internet Explorer's share of the desktop of around 82 to 84%. It is even harder to tell the kind of machine from which a web search or request originates since this is often based on browser type. Estimates show that 94% of requests originate from Wintel machines, 4% come from Macintosh and the remaining 2% from various Unix systems (including PCs running LINUX). These figures should be taken as crude indicators only because Internet trends change rapidly and because many browsers are multiplatform. The figures are further distorted by the fact that different kinds of site attract a different user demographic. What may be said with confidence is that Mozilla's share of the browser market is small but growing. Only time will tell whether it will be a real contender. Mozilla is merely one alternative browser with a small market share among many; however, almost all of its peers conform to internationally agreed standards.

The 'browser war' is not merely about domination of the computer desktop but about controlling Internet standards and information channels. Since Microsoft's Internet Explorer has such a large share of the market, many web developers often ensure that their web site works best with that browser. From a purely pragmatic point of view this is not unreasonable. Other developers have a long-term commitment to open source code and international standards. They see an Internet that is free from domination by one or two mega-corporations as benefiting the majority of Internet users. We will discuss the nature of standards in our section on open source software later in this chapter.

Systems software

Systems software may be divided into two main categories — the operating system, and the user interface and its associated utilities.

The operating system manages the underlying resources of the computer such as the processor, RAM disks and file system transparently and handles communication with, and control of, peripheral devices. It is responsible for booting up (starting) the computer and carrying out diagnostic checks. It handles any errors that occur during the execution of programs.

The remaining systems software provides a convenient interface between the user and the underlying hardware and between the user and applications programs. Utilities such as file management and screen savers are also provided here. Figure 3.2 (opposite) shows the major functional areas of systems software.

Systems software is platform-specific and so may limit the portability of applications. Additionally, systems software may be classified according to its level of scope. There are three such levels:

- personal — for individual desktop use
- work group — to support a small community of users
- corporate — to support a large organisation.

Often, organisations use all three levels of systems software. Work group and corporate levels normally support multi-user operation. Windows and its variants are the most widely used systems software for individual machines and work groups. LINUX is widely used for server or work group systems and has around 25% of the server market, compared with Microsoft's 55% share (http://content.techweb.com/wire/story/TWB20031008S0013). Despite the availability of LINDOWS (a window interface for desktop LINUX systems), LINUX accounts for only 2% of the desktop market.

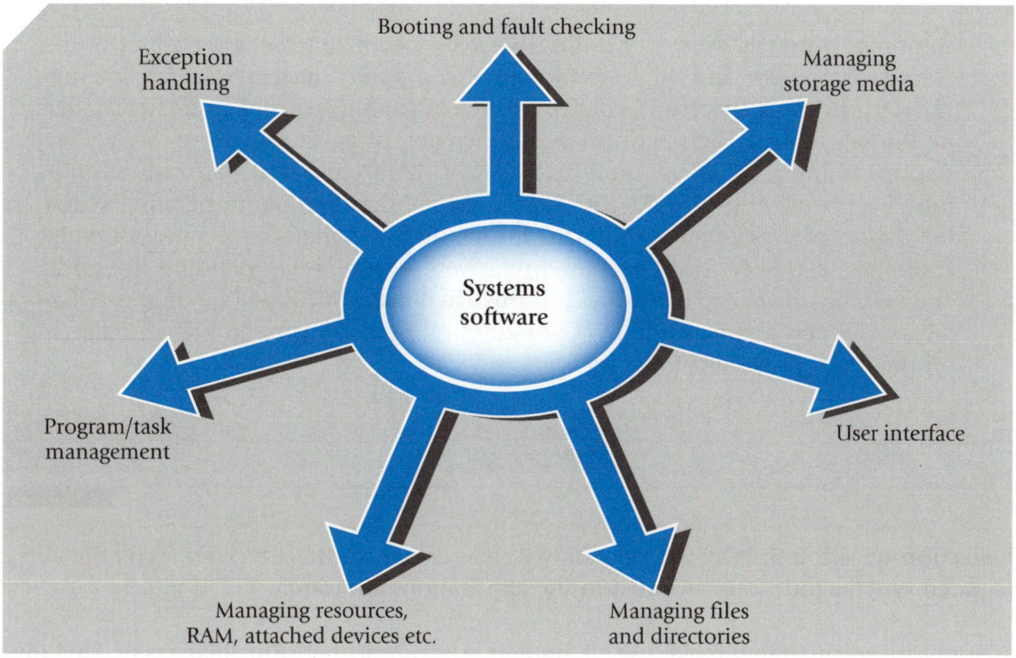

Figure 3.2 Seven functional areas of systems software

Some systems software operates at all three levels, and **UNIX** is a good example of this. Originally developed as a teaching tool, it rapidly became commercially exploited because the source code (the actual high-level language text in which the systems software was written) was made available to anyone who had an interest in developing software for it. There are versions of UNIX for mainframes, workstations and PCs. Since there are well-defined standards for UNIX and no single corporation controls the development of UNIX, it is said to be 'open'. **Open systems** are systems which are compatible and for which anyone may develop software. This contrasts with other systems software which is proprietary and controlled by a single company. Standards for UNIX **graphical user interfaces (GUIs)** were set in the 1980s, allowing it to have the ease of use of other systems software packages.

IS in action

LINUX comes of age

In 1991 Linus Torvalds, a Finnish computer student, released a free version of the UNIX operating system that he called LINUX. In the following years various developers added to the functionality of the software, and its elegant efficiency made it an ideal candidate for use in web servers. Many companies, IBM among them, see LINUX as integral to the development of grid computing. In this view,

(*continued*)

computer power is seen as a utility whereby people access geographically dispersed computers and high-performance computer clusters via the Internet. LINUX provides a cheap and efficient means of enabling such a grid. (Researchers in Illinois built a high-performance supercomputing cluster from Sony Playstations running LINUX (Cass 2003).) All of IBM's hardware platforms are now fully integrated with LINUX, which has become the dominant operating system for web servers (Scannel 2003). This means that IBM mainframes and midrange computers can now run multiple virtual web servers, thus extending the utility and working life of the hardware. It is predicted that LINUX will be on more than 45% of all new servers by 2007 (Galli 2002). Whether this trend will be reflected on the desktop remains to be seen.

Reflection question 5: Why is it necessary to have systems software? Why aren't the required systems functions included in the applications software?

Applications programs make use of systems software to perform their tasks. This division of responsibility allows development effort to be focused on applications and systems software separately. However, applications software depends on systems software in order to function, and this has profound implications for the nature of competition in the software industry.

Communications software

This category includes all forms of computer communication. Over the last twenty-five years, software systems moved through the following discrete phases:

- stand-alone applications — totally independent software not linked to any other computer
- networked applications — software which can use a network if one is present, provided the user knows how to make use of the features
- network-friendly applications — software which can use a network to share information or processing in a user-friendly way
- network-intrinsic applications — applications which have been developed specifically for networks, such as client–server architectures.

The main thrust of competition in the computer industry has moved from manufacture to applications software to systems software, and now it seems likely that communications software is set to become a major battleground. Many software developers ignored this area due to its specialised nature, and certain companies and products managed to consolidate themselves into an expanding area. Early entry into the market allowed these companies to exert an influence on the emerging communications standards and hence secure a competitive advantage over later entries into the marketplace. Just as systems software influences developmental trends in applications software and hardware, the increasing importance of communications means that communications software is exerting a strong influence on the development of systems software. This is considered further in chapter 5.

The nature of competition in the software industry

In the mainframe market sector, which is relatively small, systems and applications software have been very stable when compared with the PC sector. This has permitted one generation of applications and systems software to outlive several generations of supporting hardware.

In contrast, the PC sector is very large and competition is at its most intense. It is important to understand the nature of the relationship between hardware manufacturers and software developers, since this leads to the 'step–lock cycle' which currently dominates the market. A second factor in the development of the PC market sector has been the development of the graphical user interface (GUI).

The step–lock cycle

The argument for the existence of the step–lock cycle runs thus: hardware manufacturers make faster computers, so software developers make more demanding software to take advantage of the increased processing power. Hardware manufacturers then make even faster computers and the software industry responds by developing more complex and demanding software. This increases the total cost of ownership since businesses are forced to upgrade their hardware and software at regular intervals and at considerable expense.

The graphical user interface

Moving to a graphical user interface (GUI) from text-based systems in the 1980s enfranchised a larger segment of the community because interaction with the computer was less difficult and hence users could carry out far more sophisticated tasks. This was part of a movement which has seen the de-skilling of much of computer use. Making computers easier to use has had the effect of increasing the size of the market sector and so increasing the demand for hardware, applications software and systems software as users join the step–lock cycle.

The GUI approach to computing was made possible by the invention in 1967 of the computer mouse by Doug Engelbart (CNN 1997) (see figure 3.3). Pioneered by Xerox PARC and later by Apple, GUIs allowed users to focus on higher level issues rather than low-level systems software. The impact of this mouse device cannot be understated since it changed the nature of human–computer interaction totally. Engelbart has also been very influential in a number of Internet technology areas (Griffin n.d.).

Figure 3.3 Douglas Engelbart with a prototype three-button mouse

Infobyte

The touchy-feely mouse

VirTouch's VTMouse looks, connects and works like an ordinary computer mouse but incorporates technology that allows onscreen action and displays to be presented in a tactile form. The user's fingers sit on two special tactile pads each of which has a number of rounded pins that rise and fall according to what they touch. The sensory experience can be further enhanced by the use of sound. VTMouse enables blind people to play games and use educational and business software in the same way that sighted users do, thus improving their quality of life and job prospects.

Source: information from Adaptive Technology Consulting 2003, 'New computer device will enable blind people to play side-by-side with sighted', www.adaptivetech.net/articles/virtouch_press_release.htm (accessed 27 February 2004).

[**Key concept:** Divide and conquer.]

Apple and Microsoft

The Apple Macintosh was conceived as a total package — hardware and systems software. Technically and ergonomically, the Macintosh was a very user-friendly, well-engineered computer with a slick graphical user interface. Whereas PC users had to understand how the computer worked in order to use it effectively, Macintosh users were free from this constraint and could focus on running applications. The graphical nature of the interface made the Macintosh an ideal vehicle for high-end desktop publishing software and other graphics software and, although Microsoft was firmly focused on the PC market, other software companies met this demand. Apple wanted complete control of its product and so did not allow any other company to manufacture 'Apple clones'. Consequently, while demand for personal computers increased exponentially, Apple's ability to meet that demand increased in a linear fashion, resulting in increased sales but declining market share.

The fact that the IBM PC standard was widely available ensured competition for manufacture as 'IBM clones' hit the market. This in turn increased demand for IBM PC standard software. Apple came to rely on Microsoft to supply applications software, but since the Macintosh market was much smaller than the PC market, the software tended to be developed for the PC first. This eroded Apple's competitive edge in the market, and its market share declined further. The incompatibility of the Apple and PC platforms meant that businesses opted for the PC platform or the Macintosh platform — seldom both. Cost and compatibility issues meant that most companies opted for the IBM standard. Where businesses had a need for superior desktop publishing, drafting or graphics software they opted for the Macintosh simply because the required software had been developed specially for that platform and hence was more mature and reliable (even if that meant running several types of desktop computer), and the superior graphics and ease of use outweighed cost factors. It would be fair to say that Apple's market share has shrunk and then consolidated since the early 1990s to more than 4%. Although the company has experienced financial stress over that time, it should be noted that the desktop arena is not Apple's only market. Servers, printers, monitors, imaging and handheld computing are all part of its portfolio.

- **Reflection question 6:** If Apple had agreed to the manufacture of Macintosh clones, do you think that Microsoft Windows would still be the dominant systems software for the PC platform?

LINUX

The development of **LINUX** is of great interest at this point. The proliferation of the IBM PC standard fuelled the growth of Microsoft Windows. LINUX is a PC version of UNIX which has the potential to weaken Microsoft's market dominance in systems software. The developer of LINUX, Linus Torvalds, has made it available to software developers for no charge. Given a choice between Microsoft's system software for a large fee or LINUX for little or no cost, some people are opting for LINUX. As the user community grows it becomes more worthwhile developing software for the PC/LINUX platform. Users are able to run Microsoft products on a PC using LINUX, although there are minor problems regarding integration. Since LINUX is comparatively small compared with Windows, it has the potential to run more quickly, allowing cheaper server configurations to be used. Its smaller size means that it is easier to secure and control. LINUX is the dominant web server operating system, and it is likely to provide the enabling technology for high-performance, supercomputer clusters on the Internet.

- **Reflection question 7:** In your view should hardware and software standards be determined by market forces, or should they be regulated in some way? Why?

How communications software can break the step-lock cycle

With minor upgrades to applications software every 12 months or so and major upgrades every two or three years, the average business can budget around $500 per machine per year for software. In addition, the useful lifespan of the hardware is around two years without a major upgrade so a further $1000 per year can be added to the operating costs. Although the purchase costs of hardware and the licence costs of software are a minor component of the total operating costs, they are still significant. Most IS managers would like to reduce costs.

A PC has a powerful processor, lots of memory, hard drive, CD-ROM etc. If the software and some of the processing were to be carried out by a computer network, all the PC would need to do would be to communicate with the network, accept input, perform output and handle a limited amount of processing. So simplified systems software is all that is required. Instead of replacing the PC every two years or so, the replacement net computer should have a useful life of at least four years. This view has many influential advocates. The applications software would be resident on a dedicated machine (server) on the network. As mentioned previously, many applications now are client–server and require a network (computer–computer communication) in order to function. In such an environment the user desktop machines are called 'clients' and they access software, data and services from other computers on the network which are called 'servers'. Traditional client–server systems have **fat clients** in which the clients have a large amount of applications software to run. A more modern and cost-effective approach is to have **thin clients** in which the majority of the software is resident on the network. In such an environment, the network becomes the computer.

Simplifying and standardising the client machines means that all updates and software/ hardware upgrades are performed on the network. The management and purchase costs per client machine are much reduced and the task of management is now simplified because the software exists in one place rather than being replicated on every part of the network. It also allows better control of viruses and security. Since the requirements for the client machines are reduced, they have a longer useful lifespan.

Client–server systems make demands on network capacity, and thin clients require even more from both the network and the servers. Would-be adopters should make sure that the network is able to carry the extra traffic and that the server is suitably powerful. The breakeven point for adopting a thin-client solution is around 15 to 20 desktop machines. As we will see in chapter 5, the real cost savings do not arise from the reduced cost of the hardware but from reduced system management costs.

[**Key concept:** Follow the KISS principle (keep it simple, stupid!), i.e. do not introduce unnecessary complications into a system — standardise.]

This approach is being pushed by a number of software developers but is being resisted by the major players. So long as many businesses remain locked in to their desktop hardware and software step-lock cycle, the situation is unlikely to change. To be generally applicable to members of the public, the philosophy is predicated on **pervasive networking** (i.e. communications and networking virtually everywhere, so that the burden of computing is offloaded from desktop machines to a network); but until the communications infrastructure improves, the general public will remain trapped in the step-lock cycle. Most people use only a very small percentage of the total functionality of their software packages and yet they are forced to upgrade to the next version of the software in order to maintain compatibility with the rest of the organisation and business.

Common horizontal applications software

The basic rules for IS success in most areas of business are simple: reduce complexity, reduce diversity and automate routine functions. The most common field for horizontal software is that of office automation. Generally, office automation software performs the following functions:

- word processing
- spreadsheets
- database
- presentation
- electronic mail
- web browsing
- document management
- project management and scheduling.

Word processing, spreadsheets, database and presentation software should be reasonably familiar to you, so the coverage given here will not be detailed. Word processing allows the creation and editing of documents; the use of templates and mail merges saves time and effort. Spreadsheets perform repetitive calculations and allow modelling and 'what if?' analyses of data. Databases maintain records. Presentation software was once taken to refer to products such as Microsoft PowerPoint, which allows the production of lecture slides and animations. Now the definition also embraces the production of documents for online publication and specialist publishing software. These are normally bundled as a software suite, i.e. individual programs that are well integrated, such as Microsoft Office. Alternatively, office automation software is sometimes sold as an **integrated package**, i.e. a single program which carries out several functions. A single program is cheaper but has far less functionality than a software suite.

Electronic mail and browser software

Electronic mail allows written communication and the exchange of documents between people. Time savings result from the reduction in handling physical mail and cost savings result from the reduction in paper. However, the predictions of the paperless office of the twenty-first century seem to have been premature. Again, the multifunctional aspect of modern software can be seen since many of these packages are integrated with web browsers, and others, such as Groupwise and Lotus Domino, incorporate groupware. Groupware is discussed in detail in chapter 4.

Web browsers tend to be an underrated productivity tool. Since many work group and corporate level systems operate using client–server technology, web browsers often provide a user-friendly and convenient means of accessing applications and information via the corporate intranet. Microsoft's Internet Explorer has the major share of the PC market, but other lightweight browsers such as Mozilla are making headway. LINUX/UNIX systems account for only 1% of desktop machines but dedicated browsers are readily available.

Document management

In a contemporary sense, this is really about information management. Information comes into an organisation from many sources, such as fax, letters and email, in addition to the documents which the organisation itself generates. Keeping track of all relevant documents, enquiries, responses and quotations is a major task. Government ministerial offices and legal offices are key users of such software.

Project management and scheduling

Project management software may be horizontal, i.e. applicable to any line of business, or vertical, i.e. specialised to a particular industry such as software engineering. It often integrates with basic office software, allowing time and cost management to be handled with equal ease. Scheduling is often incorporated into groupware; e.g. Groupwise allows online desk diaries to be examined and meetings scheduled at a mutually convenient time.

Evaluating horizontal software

The following guidelines may be useful when evaluating/selecting software:

- Packages should not be stand-alone if at all possible. Look for how well all the software packages can be integrated with each other and other applications that you may be running.
- Use a well-supported and widely used product. This makes technical and user support simpler. Look for something which is relatively easy to manage and upgrade at a reasonable price.

- Can the software be used by everyone? Ideally, standardise operating environments where possible.
- Is it cheaper to have a site licence or individual copies of the software?
- Is this the first release of the software? It may be better to wait until the product is stable.
- Will users require extensive training in the new software in order to become productive? Or is the software easy to learn?
- Although cost is important, functionality and ease of use are far more important criteria for evaluation.

Packaged, customised and custom-built — strategic and tactical implications

In addition to software which is packaged, there is customised and custom-built software. Consultants often advise on software requirements. Some consultants are also **integrators** in that they package hardware and software to produce systems solutions for clients. The most specialised consultancy category in this context is that of the **value-added reseller (VAR)**, companies that take an existing software product and customise it to meet a client's exact requirements.

IS in action

How much is that doggy in the window?

The American Society for the Prevention of Cruelty to Animals (ASPCA) has its headquarters in New York and employs more than 300 staff across the USA. Email is a vital application for internal and external communication. Its Windows-based, mission-critical email server was crashing every second week or so. Each time it happened hours of work were lost, the server had to be rebooted and the Windows operating system had to be rebuilt. There was another knock-on effect on productivity: staff wanted to be able to access the outgoing mail server via the public Internet, but ASPCA's experts said that the Windows operating system was insufficiently secure. Following a major server outage that caused the total loss of email for a whole day, they realised that something had to be done.

The ASPCA went through Siwel Consulting, and the Windows equipment was replaced by two IBM servers running LINUX — and running Domino 6 as the email package. One of the servers was configured as a reverse proxy server to prevent hacking. Users went home as usual and the next day were unaware that they were using a new and more reliable system. The disruption to normal business operations was not noticeable. Eight months after the installation there had not been a single outage.

Besides improved reliability and security, the ASPCA reports that its running costs for the system (licensing, maintenance, Internet service provision etc.) had fallen by 30%.

The ASPCA made its move after establishing a strong business case for doing so. Other organisations might perform detailed problem analysis and conclude that a Windows solution is a more appropriate solution. Note the top-down approach: we begin with business needs and choose an application to support them. The applications dictate the system software, which in turn dictates the hardware that must be used. This much gives us a functional specification. We must then take great care to ensure that the system performance requirements are also taken into consideration when specifying the final configuration.

Source: information from www-306.ibm.com/software/success/cssdb.nsf/CS/TKNC-5V93NZ?OpenDocument&Site=linuxatibm (accessed 27 February 2004)

[**Key concept:** If you don't know what you are doing, find someone else to do it.]

Packaged software

Packaged software is software that can be used 'as is'. It is usually purchased from a reseller without the need for intermediaries such as consultants. The advantages are that the cost is usually low, the product tends to be well supported and relatively error-free, and the software development has already been done. The disadvantages are that the user is unduly dependent on the manufacturer and has to pay for regular upgrades and user support. If users require a feature which is not included in the package, they cannot have it. If the packaged software is vertical (specialised to a particular process or industry sector), then it is very expensive for the user to migrate to a potentially better product due to the costs of licensing fees, training and work flow re-engineering.

[**Key concept:** Don't reinvent the wheel — unless you need to.]

Customised software

Customised software is usually supplied and installed to a client's specification by a value-added reseller. Most software is customisable to a point, but customised software is specially adapted to meet the client's needs as closely as possible. Although this approach eliminates dependency on the software manufacturer to deliver the required functionality, the client is now dependent on the VAR instead. Usually, a software manufacturer will list several recommended VARs so the risk is lessened. Customised software is likely to have more errors than packaged software since the smaller market sector will not sustain rigorous quality control. Clients are not well positioned to take advantage of the increased functionality that software upgrades provide, because to do so would mean recustomising the package. Customised software is much more expensive than packaged software.

Custom software

Companies decide to produce their own software for several reasons:

- There is no suitable package on the market to perform the required task and nothing that can be customised to suit.
- The company is looking to develop a sustainable strategic or competitive advantage and competing firms are using packaged or customised software.
- The company is hoping to recover costs and make a profit by selling the finished product.

The development time for custom software can be significant, often running into several years. Custom software is also very expensive to produce and maintain, and is more likely to have errors and bugs than packaged or customised software has. Perhaps worst of all, if a competitor has access to the package, then key features can be duplicated without the long development time that was originally required. In short, a company could spend much time and money developing a package only to have the advantages that it confers made available to competitors for a fraction of the original cost and time involved.

Table 3.1 gives a comparison of the relative merits of packaged, customisable and custom software.

TABLE 3.1 A comparison of packaged, customisable and custom software

	Packaged software	Customisable software	Custom software
Strategic/tactical advantage	Low	Medium	High
Management and maintenance costs and effort	Low	Medium	High
Specialisation	Low	Medium	High
Cost	Low	Medium	High
Cost and effort of upgrade	Low	Medium	High
Range of functionality	High	Medium	Low
Dependency on third parties	High	Medium	Low

Deciding which path to adopt requires detailed analysis and consideration. Software is an ongoing commitment, not a one-off purchase. Software is an asset and from a financial perspective it should be managed as such in terms of amortisation and replacement.

[**Key concept:** Software isn't just for Christmas.]

IS in action

Hotmail, ICQ and viral marketing

Viral marketing is a phenomenon that relies on existing customers to tell potential customers about a product by word of mouth or, increasingly, by email. When Hotmail was launched, the budget for the project was $US500 000 and marketing was via email. Every message ended with 'Get your free private email at www.hotmail.com'. The catch was that users had to complete a full demographic and psychographic survey. Even so, 12 million users signed up in the first 18 months of operation.

ICQ, an instant Internet-based messaging service, went one better. It did not spend any money at all on promoting its product. Launched in 1996 by Mirabilis (an Internet start-up company in Tel Aviv), the product revolutionised the way in which people conversed online. ICQ's chief technical officer predicted that less than 5000 users would sign up, but within seven months ICQ had more than a million users. Viral marketing saw this number expand to more than 10 million when it was acquired by AOL in 1998. From a simple messaging service, ICQ has grown to support file transfers, voice chat, video chat, SMS paging, to-do lists, birthday reminders and much more. Many small businesses use the SMS features to communicate with their mobile staff. Current subscriptions to the service are in excess of 245 million users with a monthly growth rate of 20%, and users are on PCs, UNIX or LINUX and Macintosh machines. Approximately 70% of registered ICQ downloads are active.

AOL seems unlikely to charge users for ICQ because for one thing there are several competing free products, such as Yahoo's Messenger; for another ICQ acts as a portal on to news, sport and information services. The size of ICQ's subscriber base makes it an attractive strategic partner. In late 2003 Lavalife (the largest technology-based singles service) signed an exclusive deal with ICQ to provide personals content and advertising. There is a commitment to use ICQ's customer database to create 'localised' personals tailored to community cultural standards.

Sources: information from http://company.icq.com/info/press/press_release52.html; and http://searchcrm.techtarget.com/sDefinition/0%2C%2Csid11_gci213514%2C00.html (accessed 27 February 2004).

[**Key concept:** Think globally, act locally.]

The relationship between systems software, applications software and hardware

Since 1985 the nature of the relationship between hardware, systems software and applications software has changed (see figure 3.4). In the early days there was little by way of systems software and the applications software ran everything it needed on the computer.

With increasing complexity, the layer-cake view of hardware, systems software, applications software and user developed. As the systems became capable of a high degree of integration, the relationships between the components became more complex. The systems software provided a convenient interface on to itself (allowing previously text-based system programs to be invoked by a simple point-and-click operation), the applications programs and the underlying computer.

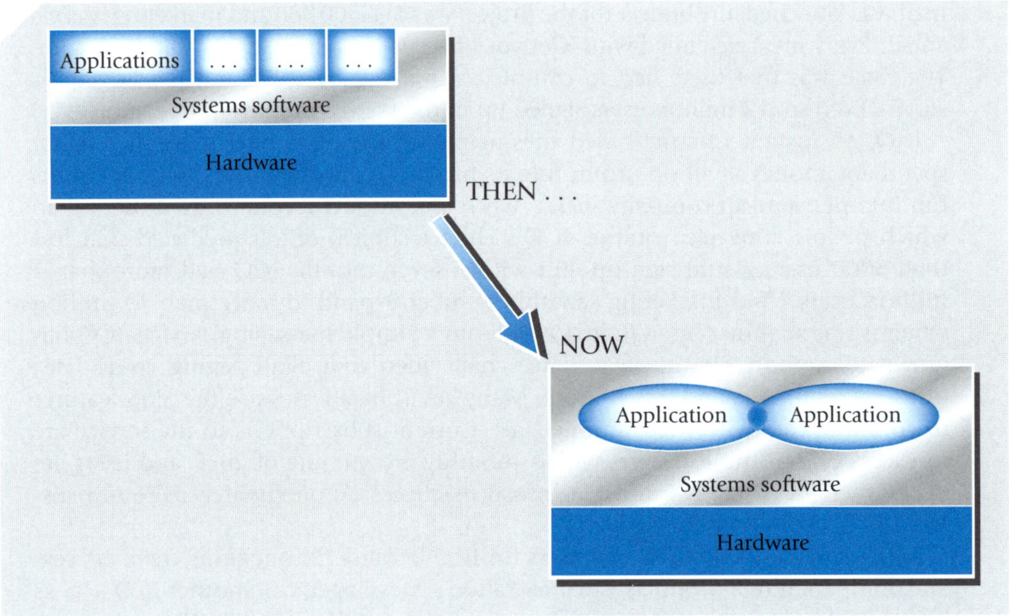

Figure 3.4 The changing nature of the relationship between hardware, systems software and applications software

Intelligent agents

In 1970 one of the biggest problems that managers faced was getting sufficient information quickly enough to run their businesses effectively. At that time there was only around 1% of the information that exists today and computer networks did not permit universal access. In the twenty-first century, finding information is not the problem — finding *essential* information in a vast sea of irrelevance is. The term 'information overload' is widely understood and there is the potential to 'inform ourselves to death'. This overload is one reason the information revolution has failed to deliver the productivity gains which were promised in the 1970s and 1980s.

This is where **intelligent agents (IAs)** come into their own. These are software entities which act on behalf of a user as an intermediary between the user and one or more systems, or between the user and another intelligent agent, in an autonomous manner. The software is programmed according to a set of rules, and some are capable of adapting their behaviour and learning new facts and rules. Because intelligent agents are relatively new, there is no single definition which is accepted in the industry. However, an intelligent agent should have at least five of the characteristics detailed in table 3.2.

TABLE 3.2 Characteristics of intelligent agents

Characteristic	Explanation
Specialisation	IAs are dedicated to particular tasks of a repetitious and often complex nature.
Independence	IAs act independently and, if dealing with other IAs, cooperatively with a minimum amount of inconvenience to their initiators.
Portability	IAs should be portable across hardware, software and networks. Some agents, such as the Microsoft Access database wizard, do not meet this criterion.
Intelligence	IAs make decisions based on supplied or learned rules. Some may exhibit a high degree of 'initiative' and the ability to handle requests which are incomplete or ill defined or which contain errors.
Adaptability	Very few IAs really learn and modify their behaviour, but some are able to note user preferences and conform within certain predefined limits.
Credibility	Users should be able to have confidence in the results which IAs produce.
Friendliness	This applies to most software but it is particularly important in IAs given the productivity gains they bring.

Intelligent agents should not be thought of as true **artificial intelligences (AIs)**. In a classical sense, AIs are attempts to mimic human intelligence generally or at least within a particular domain such as geophysical interpretation. The scope of IAs is much smaller since they are task-focused rather than domain-focused.

Infobyte

Mine, all mine

RETSINA is a multi-agent system (MAS) that supports peer-to-peer interaction between different agent types. The agents communicate with each other and resolve conflicts. A novel application for this technology has been the development of battlefield simulations in which 25 agents cooperate to clear paths through minefields. In real life robots would be used to complete this task. Research continues into cooperation and communication strategies.

Source: www-2.cs.cmu.edu/~softagents/iaai00/iaai00.html (accessed 27 February 2004)

Intelligent agent applications

The following are just a few examples of how IAs can improve personal and corporate productivity.

Reducing the burden of email

Most professional people routinely wade through vast quantities of email, as this is an easy avenue for sharing information. Much of the mail received is 'spam' (junk email) and irrelevant. Intelligent agents can filter email and sort and prioritise messages, allowing users to be more efficient.

Finding and managing information

IAs help users find, categorise, annotate and retrieve information. Once user preferences and requirements are known, an IA can automatically disseminate information on a needs basis. Linking this to another IA which manages collaboration by scheduling meetings and distributing agenda and minutes etc., it is possible to send briefing information to participants according to the level of the pre-existing knowledge.

Finding/negotiating the best price

IAs such as Accenture's Bargain Finder, which finds the best CD price from eight online offerings, are really metalevel search engines in that they use other search engines to do their work. Bargain Finder has been around since 1996, which gives an indication of the level of maturity of IAs. More recently there have been complex interacting IAs which go beyond mere cooperation to a point at which they negotiate with each other to achieve the best overall deal. The package holiday industry is an ideal application for such technology.

User interface

Desks tend to reflect the personality of their owners. Some people are tidy and others work happily with scattered paper; in-trays may be at arm's length or hidden away under piles of files — in short, desks are an expression of individuality and personal productivity. When user interfaces are considered there is a general assumption that one size fits all, and although appearances may be changed cosmetically, few major alterations can be accommodated (Benson & Standing 2000). Microsoft introduced a family of animated agents for web pages that are either liked or despised by users according to their level of expertise. In Windows and Windows NT, users performing non-routine tasks may be interrupted by an agent which says 'It looks like you are trying to do X' and offers help.

Package-specific agents

A novice user of Microsoft Excel might apply borders and shading to each cell separately, or type the same entry for a number of consecutive cells in the same column. An intelligent agent offers suggested contents in order to save typing. It might also suggest that there is a more efficient way to achieve the desired results or even offer to do the formatting for you. Package-specific agents such as wizards help in the creation of documents and the installation of hardware and software.

Software development

Although a high degree of creativity and intelligence is required for the production of software, many routine tasks are involved as well. Just as package-specific agents detect patterns of operation and make suggestions and offer help, so too do software development IAs. The task of embedding one application within another is a good example of something which can be supported via an IA.

■ **Reflection question 8:** If IAs continue to grow in number and capability, will a point be reached at which things will run themselves?

The future of intelligent agents

It is reasonably certain that the burden of information will not diminish over the coming years, nor will the complexity of interacting information systems. Accordingly, IAs will improve in terms of functionality and capability. It is not hard to envisage a future in which IAs confer strategic and tactical advantages. These IAs could be highly individualistic, and implemented in firmware.

Open source vs proprietary software

In the course of this chapter we have touched on the topic of open source code several times. It would be useful to bring our thinking together in a single section. But before we can discuss open source code, we need to consider the nature and relative merits of standards. We touched on the importance of standards in chapters 1 and 2, and now need to make our coverage more explicit. Standards come in three basic flavours:

- *De facto standards:* these are usually established by being a dominant player in the market. As an example, Windows is a de facto standard.
- *De jure standards:* these standards have been ratified or defined by a legal or official standards body. As an example, Internet browsers have to meet standards concerning the interpretation of Hypertext Markup Language (HTML).
- *De rigeur standards:* these are mandatory for reasons that are neither de facto nor de jure, and are often based upon perception rather than reality, e.g. 'this system must support Microsoft's System Message Blocking (SMB)'. SMB is a pre-World Wide Web file service that has perhaps 20% of the total market (compared to Novell's 80% for its Novell Core Protocol) and, although not recognised by any de jure body, is still widely regarded as a standard. An example of a de rigeur standard (now ignored): 'No one needs a computer with more than 640 Kb memory.' Adobe's Acrobat document format interchange standard (pdf) is a better-known example of a de rigeur standard supported by most Internet browsers.

De jure and de facto standards are of most interest to us since these are the most dependable in a business context.

By conforming to de jure standards we can expect to receive certain advantages:

1. De jure standards are future-proof: new standards will have to be backwardly compatible with old ones. This reduces risk.
2. Using standards should give the economies associated with scale: because there is more competition for supply, prices should fall. This also gives a measure of vendor independence.
3. Consolidating to one or two standards reduces the skills base required to run the system, thus reducing training costs and dependency on key staff.
4. Strategic planning is simplified.

A common misunderstanding about standards is that they are about performance. They are not. Standards are the lowest common denominator. They ensure that hardware and software will work together transparently. A major advantage is in transparency of use. High performance is a secondary consideration.

Open source software refers to de jure standards. As an example, LINUX is both open source and fully in the public domain. So anyone can develop code for LINUX. If the code is intended for public distribution, it must conform to the standard. Nobody really cares what organisations do internally. Other software such as Adobe's Acrobat is freely available in the public domain and can be used to transfer documents across different hardware and software systems. However, these are not truly open because the source code is not available to developers.

Figure 3.5 shows a matrix for the classification of software according to whether it is open or closed and proprietary or public domain. The only quadrant for which there is no example is software that is both proprietary and open. Java is a universal programming language. It was developed by Sun and placed in the public domain. Although Java may be used by anyone, the source code for the Java interpreter remains private. Without access to source code we are relegated to being mere users of someone else's software.

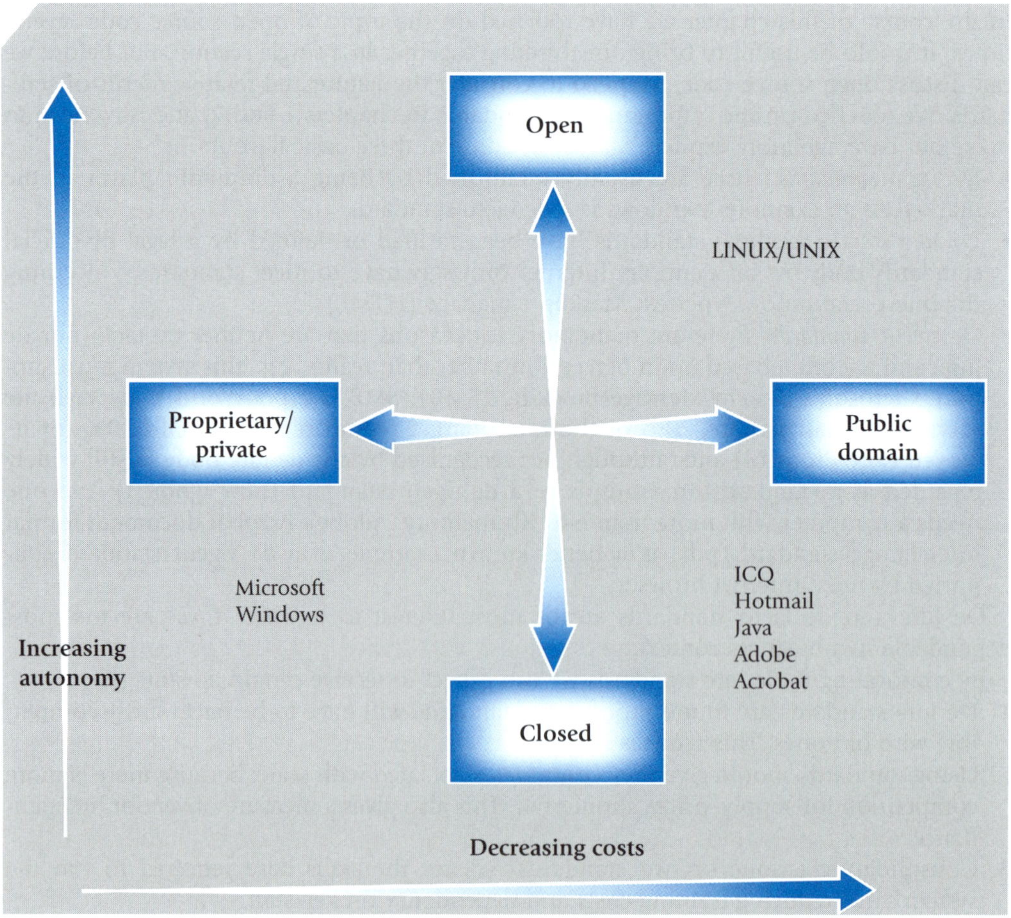

Figure 3.5 A classification matrix for software

The advantages that arise from the use of open source software stem from the fact the software is free. However, licensing costs are not the only factor in choosing whether to go for an open source or proprietary solution. The availability of in-house skills and user support are also significant. Microsoft's domination of the desktop systems and applications software markets simplifies decisions for IS managers but means that there is a huge dependency on Microsoft and no ability to modify the software to match organisational needs. Other criticisms of open source code include a lack of security. However, few people would argue the fact that most hackers and viruses have exploited features in Microsoft software. It was misreported that Microsoft was using LINUX servers in 2003. The simple truth is that Microsoft was being targeted by hackers and resorted to using an Internet-wide caching system provided by Akamai. It was able to minimise the effects of distributed denial of service attacks (DOSs; see chapter 5). An irony of this is that Akamai's systems depend on LINUX for their operation. However, Microsoft is a special case, and most organisations will not face the same volume of hacking or traffic and are usually able to make their Windows-based systems secure via firewalls and good internal security practices. As with most other things, the decision whether to adopt an open source solution or a proprietary one is business-based. Such factors as cost and tactical and strategic benefits must be taken into account. There are no hard and fast rules. Each case must be considered in its own frame of reference.

Summary

This chapter has covered general issues relating to the history and nature of software in order to set a context for tactical and strategic aspects. Most companies rely on software in one form or another to maintain their competitive ability. The key points of this chapter are:

- There are five generations of software, each generation being more abstract than the previous one. The fifth generation, that of natural language processing, has yet to be achieved in a realistic situation.
- The so-called software crisis of the 1970s was overcome by the reuse of programming code, the development of packaged software and the development of user-oriented query languages. Although the effects of the software crisis have been mitigated, they have not been eliminated entirely.
- Software may be categorised as applications software, systems software and communications software. Applications software may be subdivided into horizontal and vertical software.
- Companies which control systems software exert great influence over the development trends of PC hardware and software.
- The pattern of business and competition in the software and processor industries is a step–lock cycle involving the release of faster processors and more sophisticated software which forces customers to upgrade frequently. Computer networks change this pattern by allowing systems with lower specifications to be used as client machines — so-called thin clients — which are cheaper to buy and run and easier to manage because they download most of their applications software from a server as required.
- Most companies opt to buy horizontal software, but might consider customised or custom software for vertical applications. Custom software is a more expensive option and requires investment and commitment if the competitive edge is to be sustained.

- Information overload and trivial tasks have an adverse effect on productivity. Intelligent agents allow many routine and complex tasks to be delegated to an intelligent software entity. These agents can cooperate if required and some may even be capable of negotiation.
- Although open source code appears to be free software and to give more control and independence to adopters, all implications — including user support and ongoing costs — must be considered.

Questions

1. Most manufacturers of word processing software incorporate features which allow their software to handle files produced by their competitors' software. Is this a good strategy? Is there a case for incompatibility as a competitive strategy?
2. Read the fine print of a widely used software licence such as Microsoft Office. Do you think the terms are fair or overly restrictive?
3. Give reasons why LINUX is not capturing a large share of the desktop operating system market. Will this change over the next few years?
4. What are the pros and cons of standardising desktop software for a large organisation?
5. Has Microsoft's domination of desktop operating systems via Windows been a good or bad thing for business? Explain your answer.
6. Is a universal user interface achievable or desirable? Explain.
7. Think of the intelligent agents that you know of. Can you suggest a new type of intelligent agent? What would it do?
8. Suppose you have a software company that has developed a low-cost office software suite (similar to Microsoft's Office software). You have managed to ensure that the product can handle the file formats from all of your major competitors. Your company has a great product, but it does not have a lot of money to spend on marketing. Assuming that you want to keep control of the company and the software, how would you go about promoting the software?
9. Is Java really a universal programming language? (You will need to do a little research to answer this question.)
10. Apart from using ICQ to generate advertising revenue, why else would AOL choose to keep the service free?

Exercises

1. Use the Web to research RFID tags. Now consider the following questions:
   (a) How will this technology transform conventional retailing?
   (b) Do you see any civil liberties or privacy issues associated with the technology?
   (c) Are you able to envisage a new application for this technology?
2. The mouse transformed the way that we interact with computers. How do you imagine you will be interacting with computers ten years from now?
3. Make a list of the pros and cons of controlling web access and email in the workplace. As the IS manager, what line would you take and why?
4. Assume that you have just taken up a position as the IS manager of a sizeable company and have discovered that many employees have illegal copies of commercial software

on their computers. You have also found lots of freeware and shareware products. The company has no policy on these matters.

(a) Make a list of the points that you would make in a presentation to senior management explaining why you need a company policy on pirate software and freeware and shareware products.

(b) List the main elements of your policy (remember to give due consideration to the problems of communicating and enforcing the policy).

CASE STUDY Human resource management

'Let me get this right,' began Sarah. 'Instead of users inputting their own superannuation details into our systems using a web-based system, they have to fill in forms and submit them to a clerical officer for updating? And the same thing applies if they need to file a change of name or address? I know this is a government organisation and that we are under-funded but we must be able to do better than that, surely?'

'That's pretty much it,' answered Chris, 'but it's actually more complicated than that. The system runs on an old PC and prepares a file for submission as a batch job to the mainframe. It was developed in version 2.3 of the software, which is no longer supported by the software company — in fact the software company went broke six years ago. The software needs to run on an old 486 processor because of specific hardware requirements unique to that software. We can't just switch to using something else because there is no off-the-shelf software that we can buy. The mainframe character and file formats have to be preserved and the word length of PCs that succeeded the 486 machines is different. We have been looking for suitable software for ages — I thought you knew.'

'So what happens if that 486 PC dies?' asked Sarah.

'That really depends what it dies of ...' began Chris. 'We keep regular back-ups, and I have a whole range of salvaged spares for the 486 — enough to build three complete computers if need be.'

'Can we develop our own software? We have enough programmers.'

'Well, we could, but we have no design documentation or source code, and the people who developed it left the department ages ago. We could buy new software and then convert all the stored data into the new format — we'd also need to change the mainframe code — unless we ported the system on to a PC platform with a PC-based server. I guess that last option would cost about $50 000, not counting a new server. The other option would be to write our own software. I wouldn't like to put a timeline and cost to that, but it would be expensive. It's not the future that worries me so much as the present. With the current turnover of staff and changes to superannuation, names, addresses etc. I have one person working 45 hours a week just to keep up. Even then it can take up to two weeks for a change to be logged on the mainframe. When we finally run out of spare parts for that PC, we'll have real problems.'

'Not quite,' said Sarah. 'You are the IS manager — you will have problems. You have been with us for more than 11 years and you let this happen. I'll give you a

(*continued*)

week, and by then I expect to know just what you plan to do to solve this and what you can do to prevent a recurrence of similar problems in the future. Otherwise we might have to review your position here.'

'You try it! I'll bring in the union and make a real issue of this. There's only so much that can be done within the confines of the budget I have to work with. We can't afford top-notch people, new hardware and extensive upgrades, and all my attention has been on keeping the mission-critical systems running — payroll, accounting, the HRM database — plus the network. All of those are running well. The network and main systems have more than 98% up time, and most of our help desk calls are resolved in less than 20 minutes. We have no budget for new projects. Although superannuation etc. is important, it's not vital. If it takes a week or two before everything gets updated, then so what? We both know that a new system would pay for itself in two years or so — but we need to have the money up front to develop the new system and it's not forthcoming. I made requests for funding five years ago, four years ago and three years ago. Eventually I got sick of asking. It's not my fault, and it shouldn't be my problem. You have been here for three years — didn't you take the trouble to find out what had been going on when you came here?'

Sarah realised that they were getting nowhere. 'One way or another 30 000 people rely on that system. We have to sort something out. What are the big costs associated with a new system? And why is it so expensive to write our own software?'

'Well, we need a dedicated server and a network upgrade, and the data conversion is a significant cost. We might only really need a snapshot of how things are now. The main database keeps track of payments and other employee records,' Chris responded, 'but even if we could reduce the cost of conversion somehow, we'd still need to find the funds to develop and run the system. It's not only what you see on the screen; we also have to produce code that implements our security and authentication procedures. Given the nature of the application, validation and quality testing would be significant costs. Bear in mind that my staff are really maintenance programmers. They seldom cut new code, and a web-based system would be a new thing for them. Also, because we are slightly understaffed, I would have to pay staff overtime rates or outsource the project. Either of those options would cause a budget blow out — unless of course you have any ideas about how to fund the project?'

'Why can't we just get someone to input the changes directly to the mainframe?' asked Sarah. 'That would overcome the PC bottleneck.'

'That had crossed my mind,' said Chris, 'but there are some difficulties with that — giving a user direct access to the mainframe has security implications — and in any event that only moves the bottleneck from one place to another. Given the age of the main systems, it's easier to work around them. Creating a file with the updates is the only way to go.'

'Leave it with me,' said Sarah. 'I'll explore a few options.'

QUESTIONS

1. Whose side would you take in this argument? Why?
2. Speculate as to what circumstances led to the present state of affairs. How many were preventable?

3. Do you think Chris has behaved sensibly in regarding the superannuation system as low priority?
4. Is there anything else that Chris can do in the short term?
5. Consider Sarah's position. What will happen if she fails to find funding to improve or replace the system?
6. Lack of funding is a major problem in this government department. How would you go about building a case to support an argument for a new system? What funding options would you suggest? (Be creative or radical if need be.)
7. If funding were to be found, would you develop the project in-house or would you bring in an outside company (outsource) to do it? Explain why or why not.
8. Could you establish guidelines to prevent similar problems arising in the future? If so, what would they be?
9. Government departments are not-for-profit organisations. Does this mean that they will always tend to be underfunded, or are there exceptions? (Think of some of the government systems that you know about and what purpose they serve.)

References

Babbage Institute 2001, www.cbi.umn.edu/exhibits/cb.html (accessed May 2001).

Benson, S.P. & Standing, C.R. 2000, 'Irradiating intranet knowledge: The role of the interface', *Journal of Knowledge Management*, vol. 4, no. 3, pp. 244–51.

Britannica 2001, www.britannica.com/seo/j/jacques-de-vaucanson/ (accessed May 2001).

Bromley, A.G. 1987, 'The evolution of Babbage's calculating engines', *Annals of the History of Computing*, vol. 9, pp. 113–36.

Cass, S. 2003, *IEEE Spectrum*, July, vol. 40, no. 7, p. 17.

CNN 1997, www.cnn.com/TECH/9704/09/mouse.inventor/ (accessed May 2001).

Foss, K. 2004, 'Federal court report suggests Microsoft targeting Adobe', *PlanetPDF*, www.planetpdf.com/mainpage.asp?webpageid=3297 (accessed 27 February 2004).

Galli, P. 2002, 'Meta predicts Microsoft move to Linux in 2004', *eWEEK*, 10 December 2002, www.eweek.com/print_article/0,3668,a=34672,00.asp (accessed 22 July 2003).

Glaser, M. 2003, 'Office 2003: Priced to sell?', *TechWeb*, www.techweb.com/tech/software/20030826_software (accessed 27 February 2004).

Griffin, S. n.d., 'Internet pioneers: Doug Engelbart', www.ibiblio.org/pioneers/engelbart.html (accessed 22 July 2003).

Meyers, J. 1999, www.softlord.com/comp/ (accessed May 2001).

Rosoff, M. 2001, 'Effects of the antitrust settlement', *Directions on Microsoft*, www.directionsonmicrosoft.com/sample/DOMIS/update/2002/01jan/0102eotas.htm (accessed 27 February 2004).

Russo, M. 2001, www.history.rochester.edu/steam/hollerith (accessed May 2001).

Scannel, E. 2003, 'IBM, Microsoft launch Linux tug-of-war', *Infoworld*, www.infoworld.com/article/04/01/19/03NNlinux_1.html (accessed 27 February 2004).

Chapter 4

Business information systems

LEARNING OBJECTIVES

After reading this chapter, you should be able to:

- describe the major categories and subcategories of business information systems in current use and the types of business activity they support
- understand the basic functions of databases, their management systems and the advantages that they confer
- understand the types of reports and information that business information systems produce
- understand how the various types of business information systems relate to or operate in a corporate context
- understand the difference between a database and a data warehouse and how both are used
- understand the basic functions of groupware and how it can be used to transform business operations.

4

Introduction

This chapter is intended to give an overview of the different types of information systems in current use. In doing so, it relates the business information systems covered to management levels within organisations since this provides a useful conceptual framework.

The nature of work is such that the higher someone is in an organisation, the less structured and more abstract that person's job is. In contrast, those people lower down the hierarchy have jobs which are highly structured. When automation is contemplated, processes which are well defined and structured are usually selected for computerisation, because the development–effort ratio makes the exercise worthwhile, since well-defined systems are easy to develop. However, functions which are high-level are much more difficult to automate; a senior human resource manager analysing skills deficits and arranging customised training is hard to replace with a computer. In short, the major impact is twofold: (1) the automation of simple processes where timelines and supply chains can be shortened, and (2) providing tools which support higher level functions. In the latter case there are tools which support analysis and modelling in order to facilitate management. The simple data hierarchy 'why? how? what?' is useful as a framing context for business information systems. Table 4.1 shows this simple hierarchy and relates it to business levels and tasks.

TABLE 4.1 The relationship between management levels, data and tasks

Level in organisation	Data hierarchy position	Scope of tasks	Example
Executive level: highly unstructured activities using highly abstract information	Wisdom (why?)	Being able to apply knowledge	Planning to abandon an unprofitable line and introduce a new one
Senior management level: loosely structured tasks using condensed information	Knowledge (how?)	Understanding the meaning of information	Analysing the trends shows that a particular line is no longer profitable
Line management level: summarised data, fairly structured tasks	Information (what?)	Data processed in such a way as to reveal previously obscure trends	Summarised quarterly data expressed in chart form
Operative level: no summarised data, highly structured tasks	Data (what?)	Raw, unprocessed entries	Daily cash entries in a spreadsheet relating to sales lines

Remember the division between knowledge and information that was introduced in chapter 1. Wisdom and knowledge exist only in the minds of people. When people talk about knowing something such as a telephone number, they are really talking about data.

Understanding how to use that piece of data is knowledge. Deciding not to call someone at 3.00 a.m. is an example of wisdom. Although this may seem fanciful, the simple implication is that data and information-based activities are usually well defined and easily automated. When operating in the realms of knowledge and wisdom, most people do not automate the activity per se; it is more cost-effective to provide support tools and environments in which humans can perform their tasks.

This chapter covers a wide range of topics, but the underlying themes are easily understandable. When reading the chapter, keep table 4.1 in mind — think how the business systems relate to the levels of management in the table and what they must do to enable the management tasks to be carried out. In essence, the higher the level of management, the more unstructured and ill defined the tasks become, and information becomes more summarised and less detailed. The lower the level of management, the more structured tasks become, and information becomes more detailed. It is helpful to imagine a three-level hierarchy of information systems — at the lowest level, the main concern is operational matters; at the second level, tactical issues are the main focus; and at the highest level, strategy is the principal issue.

[**Key concept:** Anything that is well structured and defined is a candidate for automation.]

Transaction processing systems

Transaction processing systems (TPS) are the backbone of commerce. Humans have recorded basic business transactions for tens of thousands of years, and the need to do this is believed by many to have given rise to written language. What is a transaction? A transaction is the most fundamental unit of commercial activity. Transactions are indivisible. For example, think about using a bankcard to withdraw money from an account using an ATM. This involves several stages — verifying the card and PIN, establishing the balance, authorising the withdrawal, debiting the account and dispensing the cash. If any subprocess in the transaction fails, then the entire transaction will fail. It is not acceptable to have your account debited but no cash dispensed. Think of transactions in binary terms — they either succeed or they fail; there are no half measures. Beyond the obvious, why do we need to record transaction data?

There are legal requirements, which mean that records must be kept for taxation and audit purposes. The provision of audit trails also allows problems and incomplete transactions to be checked and verified. For example, if an order were received, and the goods were despatched but not received, the failure may be with the shipping company.

Analysing transaction volumes and patterns allows managers to build and manage appropriate business systems, but more importantly this information can be used to devise effective marketing strategies and to integrate them with manufacture and distribution. This also allows inventory loss and pilfering to be quantified. For a chain of retail outlets, it is thus possible to compare the relative efficiencies of individual branches and managers.

Customers, suppliers and business partners might need to have access to transaction details relating to themselves. This allows reconciliation between systems and improves security by lessening the chance of computer fraud. Long supply chains may be shortened if companies use **electronic data interchange (EDI)** while maintaining secure systems.

Employees might need transaction-related information to carry out their daily duties. For example, a ticketing agent needs to check the availability of theatre seats and pricing before proceeding with a transaction on behalf of a customer via a credit card company.

Batch and real-time systems

Batch systems collect and store transaction details for processing at some later time. There is no need for immediacy and high performance and so the computing load can be spread over a greater time period. This also means that a company can have cheaper hardware, and serial storage media such as tapes can be used instead of faster and more expensive random access storage media such as hard drives. Examples of batch systems would include: running a fortnightly payroll system and the way that banks deal with deposited cheques. (The banks make a record of each cheque deposit but the new account balances are not calculated until later when the cheques are processed as a batch.)

■ **Reflection question 1:** Identify two other batch systems known to you.

Real-time systems process transactions as soon as they are received, thus the need for greater speed of response means that hardware and software will be much more expensive. However, there are many applications that have to operate in real time, such as an airline reservation system — Sabre (developed by American Airlines) handles upwards of 5000 transactions per second and has a response time of two seconds. Slower response times waste an unacceptable amount of customer time and render a system uncompetitive. Some leeway is available on retail goods — the customer may go to a competitor, but the business still has the goods to sell and overall profit may not be badly affected. However, for applications where businesses are selling time and space, e.g. a hotel room, another occupant for the room may not be found and profit may suffer badly as a result.

There are many kinds of batch and real-time transaction processing systems, including point of sales systems, **order-entry systems**, reservation systems and general ledger systems (Turban, McLean & Wetherbe 2004).

Point-of-sales systems

You should be familiar with **point-of-sales (POS) systems** from visits to the supermarket, but you may not have thought about what happens in the process. There are a few basic steps:

- The checkout operator scans in the product code.
- The system obtains the price of the goods from a database.
- The above steps are repeated until all the goods have been scanned, and then a receipt is printed.
- Details of the transaction are recorded (but not committed, i.e. made permanent) in the database, including date, amount and method of payment — this includes details of coupons, discount cards, loyalty cards, frequent flyer cards and so on.
- For non-cash transactions, the system verifies that the card is valid and that there is sufficient balance/credit to cover the transaction. At this point the sales record which is held in the register is used by the system to process the request for payment from the credit card company or bank.
- Once payment has been made, the transaction details which have been recorded in the database on a temporary basis can now be made permanent. (Had payment failed, the goods would have been returned to the shelves and the transaction would not have been processed.) The inventory system can now be updated.

A few things are worth noting here: (1) specialised hardware is used to handle input and speed the process — should the bar code be unreadable, the operator can still input the numeric code manually; (2) the number of bad payers is minimised by getting approval 'up front'; (3) at any point in time, the inventory of the store is accurately known, which allows more dynamic stock models to be developed, reducing wastage and increasing profitability; and (4) there is a wealth of information on sales and customers that can be used for marketing purposes.

POS systems are not restricted to supermarkets — they may be used, for example, by insurance agents selling in the customer's home and accessing the system via a laptop and a modem.

Given the high level of expertise required to develop a POS system, many companies simply purchase off-the-shelf or **turnkey systems** (ready-to-roll systems that are customised for a particular line of business).

Order-entry systems

Order-entry systems allow customers to order goods (such as pizzas) and services (such as magazine subscriptions) with much of the functionality of POS systems, but they also handle billing and shipping addresses. These systems usually require customers to be registered. When an order arrives by telephone, fax, email or electronic data interchange, the customer must be verified and records checked. Assuming that the customer is registered and creditworthy, the order will be processed, checked against inventory and shipping instructions issued.

Since input can come from a number of different sources, verification can be handled by an operator or a computer. However, the potential for error is much greater than in a POS system. Operation can be real time or batch depending on the application.

Both POS and order-entry systems can be interfaced with specialised inventory systems that handle distribution and logistics. Consider the problems a company with advanced computerised systems has when dealing with a supplier whose systems are primitive or non-existent. It might take as long as 30 days to place an order and receive the goods. Additionally, since payment cannot be processed quickly, it is not possible to give discount for speedy payment — discounts can be given for bulk purchase but this means tying up valuable capital in stock and limiting the ability to make money.

[**Key concept:** Using information systems is not an option — it is a necessity for survival.]

Reservation systems

Reservation systems were mentioned above in connection with airline and hotel reservation systems. In the past, these systems could be accessed only by organisations or their agents. Since the Internet became a commercial reality, members of the general public are able to make airline, theatre, car hire and hotel reservations with comparative ease. Since customers are dealing directly with the business (i.e. there is no intermediary), the profit margin is greater and discounts can be offered. Many hotels now advertise a special Internet rate.

General ledger systems

There is some controversy as to whether accounting and **general ledger systems** qualify as transaction processing systems. It is suggested here that they do, since updates (transactions) are indivisible and the systems meet all relevant criteria in terms of their need to record transaction data. In most businesses, the general ledger tends to be the confluence for all other transaction processing systems (TPSs) in the business, i.e the general ledger ties everything together. Such systems tend to be sold as integrated modules consisting of general ledger, payroll, accounts payable and accounts receivable. Whether they are 'true' TPSs depends on the degree of integration with debtor/creditor systems.

TPS summary

Ideally, data entry should be as simple and efficient as possible, and bar codes meet both these criteria. However, in reality the data come from a variety of sources and much is captured manually. As emphasised in previous chapters, the aim is to reduce complexity and diversity — standardising forms and input sources can improve manageability and save costs. For example, a large organisation using more than twenty different kinds of forms for similar activities found that by redesigning the forms it was possible to reduce the number of form types to eight.

All TPSs need to be quick, secure and reliable. Increasingly, TPSs are expected to operate 24 hours a day, seven days a week. Extra hardware and power supplies are needed to support this. Problems may arise when accessing the system via the Internet, as periods of heavy demand may reduce performance to unacceptable levels with a corresponding loss of business. TPSs provide the mechanisms and infrastructure for the implementation of transactions. The transaction data are recorded in a database. A good TPS needs good database management and accessibility.

IS in action

Smart cars herald the end of backyard mechanics

In 1938 General Motors' Futurama exhibit invited people to visit the future of 1960 in which radio-controlled cars would drive inches apart at 120 miles per hour on superhighways. Technology hasn't advanced quite that quickly, but the cost of electronics in cars is increasing by 9 to 16% per year. By 2005 electronics might account for 25% of the cost of a midrange car and anything up to 50% for a luxury vehicle. Much of this development effort is focused on improving vehicle performance and safety; after all, failure of a single component can result in injury or death for the driver. Other effort is channelled into diagnostics and vehicle information systems. The various subsystems are equipped with flash memory, which records intermittent faults; when the car goes in for routine servicing, the service station's computers can make an accurate diagnosis of problems. This information is then relayed to the manufacturer to improve the product. Remote diagnostic systems transmit information to service stations and car makers. Service stations can order parts ahead of scheduled servicing, and car makers can minimise the cost of potential vehicle recalls by detecting problems after only a few cars have been shipped, thus avoiding potential liability and litigation. The electronics are complicated, and the

(continued)

documentation is not generally available. This prevents people and non-franchise businesses from servicing vehicles. There have been attempts to legislate to 'protect the rights of American consumers to diagnose, service, and repair motor vehicles purchased in the United States' (http://thomas.loc.gov/cgi-bin/bdquery/z?d107:h.r.02735:), so far without success. Non-urgent matters are recorded for batch processing at the time of service while urgent things are handled in real time. This illustrates three effective strategies of using IS for competition: imbuing products with intelligence, creating umbilical links with business partners, and using technology to create barriers to competition.

Source: information from www.spectrum.ieee.org/WEBONLY/publicfeature/apr02/ecar.html (accessed 1 March 2004)

Databases

'A database is a centralised collection of data.' Thus began a 1982 database course. It is easy to criticise this definition with the benefit of hindsight but it will serve as a starting point. The word 'centralised' is not appropriate because contemporary databases may be spread over a number of different computers and over a wide geographic area, so it is best replaced by the term 'logically related'. Next, the concepts of organisation and management need to be introduced. Any collection of data needs to be easily accessible and capable of being queried efficiently. This leads to the following working definition:

'A database is a logically related collection of organised data.'

Just as there is a distinction between hardware and software, so there is a distinction between data and the means of accessing and managing those data. A database not only has data, it has a **database management system (DBMS)**. Essentially, the DBMS looks after the following functions:

- data storage and retrieval
- transaction/update indivisibility
- user authentication and security
- reducing redundant data (data which occur more than once in the database) to an absolute minimum
- **metadata** management. Metadata are data about data; they describe the data structures and relationships. At an enterprise level, this description is called a schema, and at lower levels the descriptions are called subschemas. The data dictionary falls into this category.

The elimination of redundant data needs further explanation since this is a major advantage of using a DBMS. Without a database, organisations would be forced to duplicate data so that staff could access them; when the data were updated, the change would need to be reflected in each duplicate copy. The consequences of making a decision on the basis of outdated data could be significant, and managing so many copies would be a major headache and very costly. By ensuring that data occur only once in the database, these problems can be overcome. (In practice, some data may need to be repeated for performance purposes but to all intents and purposes the view of the data is consistent throughout the entire organisation.) The practice of removing repeating items from the data is called 'normalisation'. The data hierarchy is shown in figure 4.1. At the lower levels of the hierarchy, things become more detailed and less meaningful — a single byte or even a field conveys no information if it is removed from its context. Even single records removed from their context are of little value.

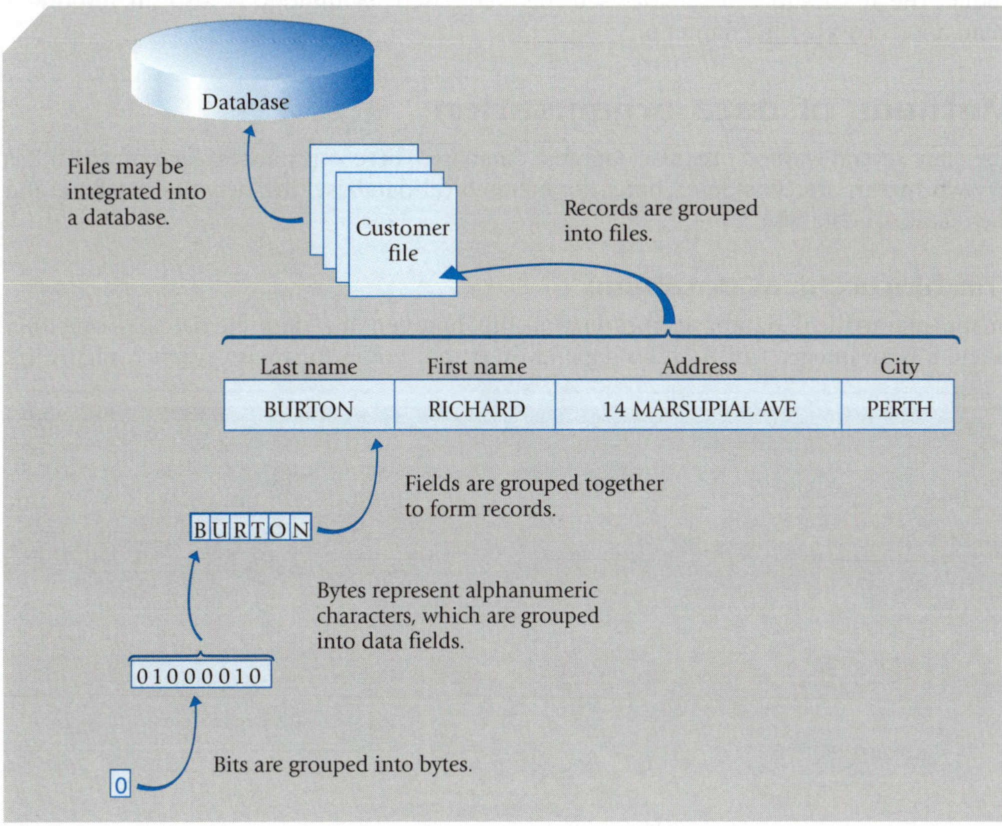

Figure 4.1 The data hierarchy

Separating data from their description (metadata) also simplifies management. If the relationships or structures need to change, then all that needs to be done is to change the description. When discussing software in chapter 3 the concept of third-generation programming languages (3GLs) was introduced. In 3GLs the data were defined inside the programs so maintenance and management were time-consuming, and major alterations were difficult to complete in a reasonable time frame.

Modern databases make use of fourth-generation languages (4GLs). These are much easier to use and allow changes to be made quickly. The most widely used database organisation is based on the relational model. Here, data are organised into tables and relationships are defined within and between tables. Object-oriented databases are a newer approach and may come to predominate over the next 15 years or so. Currently, there is so much investment in relational databases that the situation is unlikely to change in the short term. Most modern databases also make use of client–server technology.

Databases don't just hold current data; they may contain huge amounts of historical data which could be analysed by management. Specialised databases which are used solely to support managerial decision-making and planning for an entire enterprise are termed **data warehouses**. Multidimensional analysis and modelling software is available to allow management to view data in many different ways. Smaller specialised databases which focus on a single application or business unit are called **datamarts** (McKeown 2001). The integration of databases using web-based technology is also an important trend and is covered in chapter 6.

Methods of data organisation

There are several ways to organise data in a database. Three approaches, each of which has its own merits, are considered here: the hierarchical database, the network database and the relational database.

The hierarchical database

In the **hierarchical database**, the relationship between the data elements is one-to-*n*, where *n* is an integer. Child nodes depend on parent nodes for their existence. Figure 4.2

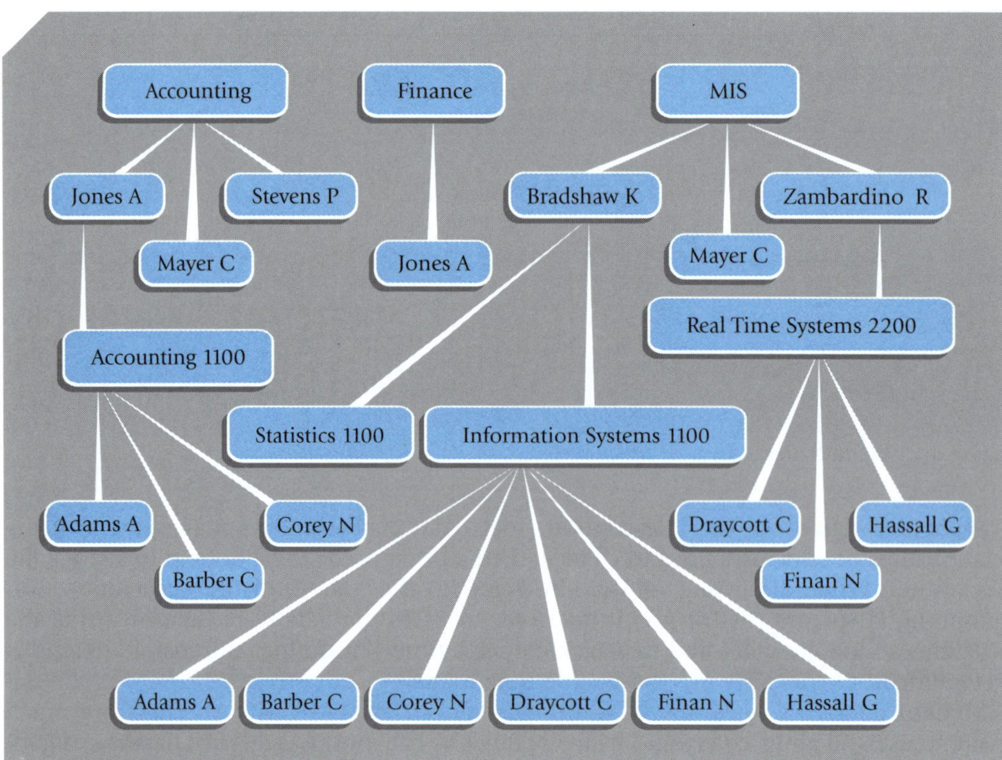

Figure 4.2 The hierarchical database

shows this method. Note that it is not possible to access a child node directly and that deleting a parent node causes access to all its child nodes to be lost. In figure 4.2, Jones works for both Accounting and Finance, and the only way to cope with this is to have two separate entries for Jones which can cause inconsistency problems. This approach is very fast for well-defined queries but potentially slow for more complex queries.

The network database

The **network database** is much more flexible than the hierarchical approach. Figure 4.3 shows this method. Note that it is no longer necessary to duplicate entries for Jones. Here relationships between nodes can be one-to-one, many-to-one or many-to-many. Although it is much more expressive than the hierarchical approach, the complexity of link management makes it unwieldy for complex applications.

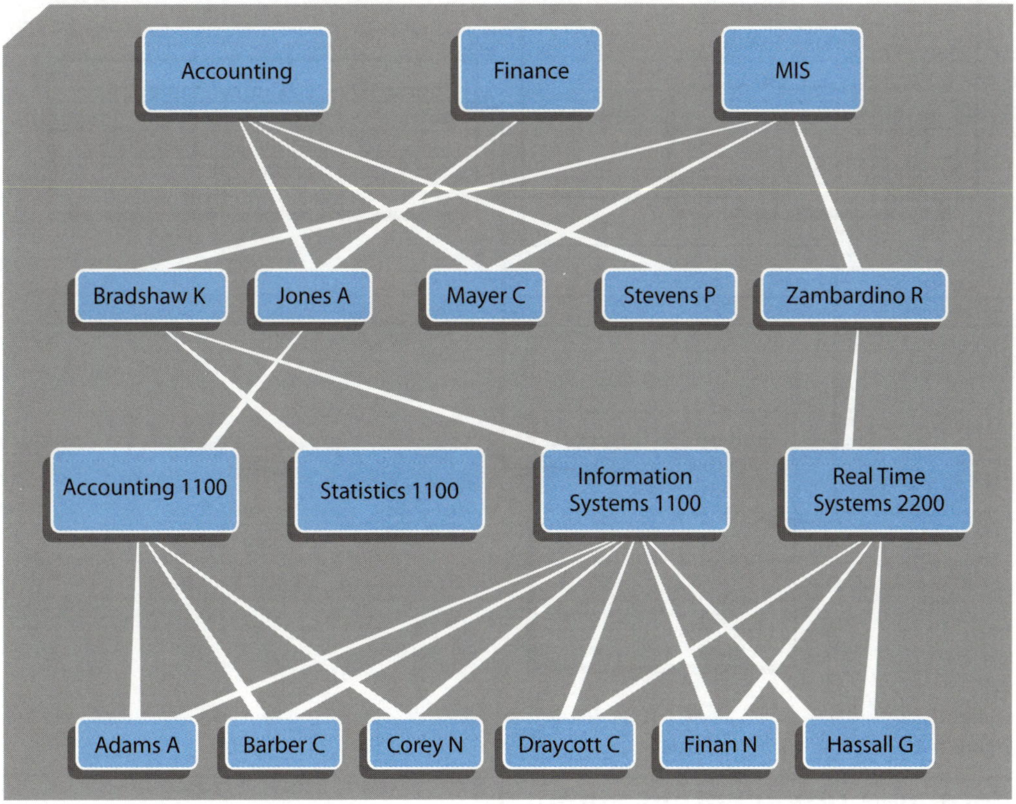

Figure 4.3 The network database

The relational database

The **relational database** is more modern and flexible than the previous methods considered. As shown in figure 4.4, data are organised as a set of relations or tables. Fields in one table can be used to find data in other tables. With the exception of key fields (fields used to find things in the database) no duplication of data is permitted. This results in databases which are easier to manage and update. The relational approach is more expressive since it can handle relationships between tables which are one-to-one, many-to-one, one-to-many and many-to-many (Carter 2000).

Staff ID	Staff	School
09412	Bradshaw	MIS
09614	Jones	Accounting
09041	Mayer	MIS
09361	Stevens	Accounting
09413	Zambardino	MIS

Student ID	Name	Address
00001	Adams	123 ....
00002	Barber	19 ....
00003	Corey	73 ....
00004	Draycott	42 ....
00005	Finan	204 ....
00006	Hassall	3/86 ....

Staff ID	Course ID
09412	C2
09412	C3
09614	C1

Course ID	Course name
C1	Accounting 1100
C2	Information Systems 1100
C3	Statistics 1100
C4	Real Time Systems 2200

Student ID	Course ID
00001	C1
00001	C2
00002	C1
00002	C2
00003	C1
00003	C2
00004	C2
00004	C4

Figure 4.4 The relational database

Database organisation summary

An in-depth consideration of the relative merits of the three schemes is beyond the scope of this text. Simpler queries like those in restricted applications such as transaction processing can be handled slightly better by hierarchical and network databases (Connolly, Beg & Strachan 1999). However, these methods are not as flexible as the relational approach for more complex searches and queries where their performance is much worse than relational models. Improvements in hardware performance have meant that most new large databases have been based on the relational model. Remember that many TPSs are quite old, and there are a substantial number of hierarchical and network databases still in current use.

IS in action

Technology for field operatives takes the hurdle out of herding

The popular image of farming is not that of a high-tech business, but scientific animal husbandry requires sophisticated data analysis and management. Until recently computers were relegated to the offices, and laptops were too delicate to take out into the fields. Dairy and beef farmers who wanted to make full use of information systems had to use handwritten notebooks and then painstakingly transfer everything into the computer. The obvious solution was a handheld computer and dedicated software. New Zealand farmers are now able to use iTouch Business Mobility's M-NOTE software on a Palm handheld computer. Details of herds and individual animals can be displayed and new information input quickly and easily. Individual animals can be identified by their tags, and specialist software from the Land Improvement Council (a New Zealand farmer-owned cooperative) called MINDA can display health diagnoses and lactation and breeding data, allowing farmers to make better informed decisions without having to go back to the office. When the farmer returns home a simple operation synchronises the Palm handheld computer with the main PC so that both systems have the same information. The Palm computer is not 'ruggedised' in any way, but a special plastic pouch is used to allow the system to be used in the rain.

Source: information from www.ericsson.com.au/press/case_studies/20030902_itouch.shtml (accessed 1 March 2004)

- **Reflection question 2:** Can you think of the downside of putting corporate data into highly centralised databases?

Infobyte

Improving medical research

Pharmaceuticals offer huge profit margins, but the cost of research and development is very high. All drugs must perform satisfactorily in terms of their ADMET characteristics (Absorption, Distribution, Metabolism, Excretion and Toxicity); failure in any one of these areas is sufficient to terminate a drug's research and development. Fewer than 40% of drugs get through early trials. The MDL Discovery Predictive Science group has combined a large information base with very sophisticated simulation modules; even so, a huge number of inputs are still needed to model the efficacy of a single compound. As an

(continued)

example, their AIDS database has more than 42 000 entries, which have been tested for antiviral properties with data on dosage response rates, together with full medical and registration information. The simulation modules allow unpromising drugs to be eliminated, and the database allows searches to be made on a number of criteria to find substances that are more effective and have fewer side effects. A key feature in MDL's approach is to house all data in a single database. This allows cross-project analyses to be carried out, and this in turn allows better predictive tools to be developed using larger data sets.

Source: information from www.mdl.com/solutions/case_studies/ADMETreprint.jsp (accessed 1 March 2004).

Management information systems

Management information systems (MIS) sit on the boundary between information and knowledge — they are really support tools providing management with the information needed to do the job. In essence, different kinds of information are able to be accessed and analysed, and summarised reports produced. The reports are used at the highest levels of management to produce long-term strategic plans, and in middle management to improve the quality of service and employee efficiency, or for simple operational matters such as identifying bad debtors. An MIS might access information from one or more TPSs to do its job.

Management information systems can be divided into five basic categories:

- management reporting system (MRS)
- decision support system (DSS)
- expert system (ES)
- executive information system (EIS)
- groupware.

Each of these is considered in turn.

Management reporting system (MRS)

An MRS supports managers who are concerned with operations management and the effective use of the organisation's internal resources. The science of deploying people and materials to achieve objectives is called logistics; at an enterprise level, when a more complete picture is required, we tend to talk in terms of enterprise resource planning (ERP).

For example, consider a company that manufactures ceramic tableware. Materials must be brought into the factory and specialist design services might be required. Kiln maintenance and management require careful production scheduling. Balancing orders and shipping against labour costs is also important. Manufacturing ceramics requires a large amount of energy, so efficient energy management is needed. Deciding which lines are profitable and which need to be replaced will have a large impact on manufacturing. For such a company, an ERP system would enable all these functions to be carried out.

Besides general logistics, accounting and sales information could be presented in summarised/report form to managers. The main types of reports produced are shown in table 4.2.

TABLE 4.2 The main types of reports generated by MRSs, and their uses

Report type	Management level	Report content
Summary	Medium/high levels	Usually statistical, time series information, giving an analysis of the underlying data. Generally speaking, the higher the management level, the more summarised the data. Transactional analysis is quite common.
Exception reports	All levels	Only data/information that falls outside the expected range is presented in the report, e.g. an excessive number of orders placed by a customer who has not paid a bill recently, or an unacceptably high failure rate in manufacture.
Detail reports	Usually lower levels; sometimes higher management levels when summary reports are too coarse-grained to provide information needed to solve a problem.	Tend to be used at the operational level. The period the report covers might be hourly, daily or weekly, depending on the nature of the business. People might want to review the efficiency of sales staff in a department store, or be able to link manufacturing problems to the replacement of tools from a certain supplier.

In addition to the main types of reports, *when* these reports are generated is important. There are three main categories:

- *Scheduled reports.* These are reports generated at fixed intervals (daily, weekly, monthly etc.) and distributed to selected members of staff. The format and content are usually determined in advance. They might feature employee production rates for operations managers, or occupancy rates for hotel rooms, or simple accounting information. They are intended to support managerial decision-making while minimising information overload. In the case of a hotel, a manager might decide to reduce the cost of rooms or offer special deals to established customers in order to increase occupancy.
- *Event-driven reports.* These tend to be generated when an expected event or problem arises. For example, a company might have a multiphase software project to deliver. On the completion of each phase, reports are generated showing the state of progress, budget versus projected etc. Usually, the distribution list is selective.
- *Ad hoc reports.* Sometimes an authorised manager may wish to perform a one-off query. Most modern systems provide managers with the software they need to perform such a task. A manager might want to review advertising expenditure patterns with sales trends to assess the effectiveness of a marketing campaign.

Note that whatever the type of report and its timing, these systems are intended to help managers by automating the routine parts of the job and providing accurate, timely responses. The information is provided by the system — the thinking, knowledge and wisdom (the interpretation and decision-making) are provided by the manager.

Decision support system (DSS)

Up to this point, all the systems considered have used data which are internal to an organisation. A **decision support system (DSS)** *may* use data from external sources. The systems we have considered so far are retrospective, i.e concerned with the past, but a DSS is concerned with both the past and the future. By using existing data, a DSS manager can model possible futures and select the most appropriate strategy. This allows decisions to be made with a greater degree of confidence. A DSS is targeted to a specific functional area.

An example DSS might handle staff rostering and be able to cope with employee illness and leave. It might also allow a manager to see how the business would cope if an employee were to leave or be dismissed. Another DSS might perform detailed analysis of demand, overseas suppliers and commodities, factor in overseas exchange rates and labour costs, and check local manufacturing capacity and costs in order to help a manager establish the viability and profitability of a particular contract/project. Figure 4.5 shows the main components of a DSS. It is important to note that a DSS is for senior management, so it must be very convenient to use. User interface design is a major issue for DSSs.

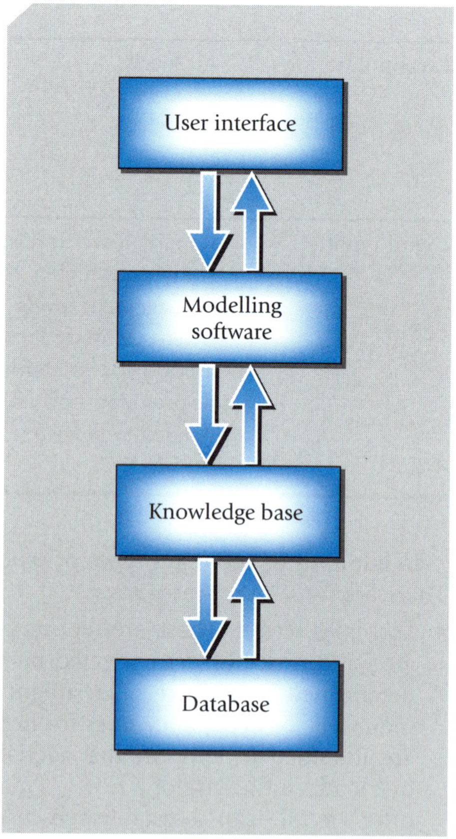

Figure 4.5 Components of a decision support system

The function of each of these components should be clear, with the possible exception of the knowledge base. This contains information about the complicated relationships between data that would be impossible to describe in a database, e.g. balancing manufacturing capacity and cost against demand and profitability.

Although many DSSs are stand-alone, there is an increasing tendency to rely more on humans for expertise and knowledge and use the technology to facilitate and moderate communication. A **group decision support system (GDSS)** has software which improves group decision-making processes — areas of consensus and argument can be identified quickly. GDSSs are frequently used for brainstorming sessions. Usually, staff can contribute to the decision-making process with complete anonymity, and in turn this tends to reduce personality clashes and improve group focus. Special electronic meeting rooms can be used for the purpose, and the use of Internet and related technologies allows for geographic distribution of staff. The role of groupware is vital here and will be examined in detail shortly.

Decision support and data warehouses

A data warehouse differs from a database in several respects. First, it is a management tool only; it is not part of the operational business system. Second, updates to the warehouse are carried out periodically rather than incrementally, as is the case with most live systems. Third, the scope of a data warehouse is greater than that of a database, since data from several different databases may be used. Fourth, instead of information retrieval and simple report generation, **online analytical processing (OLAP)** tools, statistical analysis tools, **data mining** tools and geographical information systems (GIS) are all provided. Finally, the data are organised according to subject area rather than application.

Specialist software is used to remove any duplicate data and to fill in any missing fields before the data are organised into consistent file formats.

Data-warehousing facilitates decision support by allowing more sophisticated analyses than a database alone would provide. However, the degree of sophistication is such that it is possible to search for hidden patterns in the data, going beyond most DSS design parameters, such as a relationship between customer, postcode and expenditure. Other applications include fraud detection, identifying profitable customers, and product repositioning.

Data warehouses are expensive to set up and maintain, often costing several million dollars for large companies, but smaller datamarts may be set up for much lower costs in a short time frame. Datamarts may subsequently be networked into a confederated warehouse environment.

IS in action

Home help

Home Depot is the world's largest home improvement retailer with annual sales in excess of $US55 billion. However, competition in this market is fierce, and Home Depot's ageing information systems and manual business processes were inhibiting its ability to compete. The company had excellent data about sales, buying patterns, services, performance and HRM issues, but this information was held in older legacy systems and was very difficult to access. The objectives were simple: gather and analyse information more quickly and use it to improve the business. Home Depot opted for IBM's Enterprise Data Warehouse running on a set of IBM SMP pSeries servers. In a clustered configuration these servers become a massively parallel system, which gives excellent performance. The main advantage of this physical architecture is that it is modular and scalable, allowing new servers to be added on an incremental basis as and when higher performance becomes necessary. The data warehouse allows the performance of managers to be assessed and can be used to track employee retention rates. However, the main strategic advantage is that Home Depot can develop and deliver individual store merchandising plans and improve its bottom line.

Source: information from www-3.ibm.com/software/success/cssdb.nsf/CS/LEOD-5L72F2?OpenDocument&Site=software (accessed 1 March 2004).

Expert system (ES)

Expert systems mimic the expertise of humans in a specialised field. They may be used to augment the decision-making of humans or may make the decision themselves. Because they are computerised, they are faster than humans and can work reliably (and cost-effectively) 24 hours a day.

Consider the nature of distribution and delivery. Many companies exist to perform this specialised function and rates and tariffs change frequently. An expert system can be programmed with details, delivery routes, schedules and costs for many different companies. An expert system can be used to find the best company to deliver a particular shipment of goods.

In a medical scenario, an expert system can be programmed using information from many human experts. Details of individual case histories might also be available for statistical analysis. A doctor diagnosing a patient's condition would be prompted to input the symptoms and might be asked further questions for clarification. The system might recommend further tests for the patient or be able to identify the condition and provide a list of one or more possible causes with their associated statistical probabilities.

Unlike most computerised systems which require certainty, expert systems can usually handle uncertainty. Expert systems software consists of the three main components shown in table 4.3.

TABLE 4.3 Components of expert systems software and their descriptions

Component	Description
Interface	This is intended to make the system as easy to use as possible, since it may not be used by experts or domain specialists. A good interface will improve productivity of users.
Inference engine	This uses the knowledge base to answer a particular query. It might be simple information retrieval or require the application of deductive logic. Most inference engines incorporate a module that allows a user to see how the facts and rules have been applied.
Knowledge base	This is not knowledge in the true sense but rather where facts and rules concerning the domain of expertise are stored. This 'knowledge' is captured from one or more human experts.

Although some expert systems are developed from scratch, more often companies purchase off-the-shelf packages called 'expert systems shells'. These provide the interface and inference engine, and all the company has to do is build its knowledge base. (This is often referred to as knowledge engineering.)

Many people regard expert systems as specialised types of decision support systems, but they are actually systems in their own right. Although some authors tend to regard expert systems as part of a **knowledge management (KM)** strategy (which is for a community of users in an organisation and is facilitated by groupware), expert systems are usually for individual use in a support role.

Infobyte

Spam with everything

In May 2003 the amount of spam on the Internet exceeded the amount of genuine email (Vaughn-Nichols 2003). Spam has a huge negative effect on productivity, and it reduces Internet and network performance worldwide. Using Bayesian probability filtering and adaptive learning, modern spam filters can remove up to 99.5% of spam. This improves productivity but does nothing to remove the burden from the Internet. A spammer selling an article that generates a profit of $30.00 and spending $3000 to promote it via spam would need to sell only a hundred articles from 30 million emails — a hit rate of only 0.000003333%. Technology is only part of the answer; legislation is urgently needed (Graham 2003).

Executive information system (EIS)

The information needs of high-ranking executives are different from those of lower and middle management. An **executive information system (EIS)** tends to have an enterprise-wide focus and makes extensive use of external data. Superficially, it resembles a DSS but it emphasises data synthesis, display, and trend and cause analysis rather than modelling, which is the focus of most DSSs.

An EIS may make use of hard information (information which is known to be reliable and has a factual basis, e.g. monthly sales figures) and soft information ('speculative' data such as industry forecasts and the views of business gurus). The interface of an EIS needs to make the system very easy to use, since senior executives may not have good typing skills. Because the work at this level is highly unstructured, the underlying software has to be very flexible. Most EISs allow an executive to browse the underlying information without making a query, recognising the fact that humans often discern trends intuitively.

A main ojective of all EISs is to facilitate communication between staff, often as part of a coordinated knowledge management strategy. Increasingly, this is groupware-oriented (see below) and supports remote access by executives who are interstate or overseas. EISs incorporate 'environmental' sensing and actively select news items that executives need to see. A subscription to Reuters and/or other services may yield over 8000 items per day, so the system allows filters to be set so that only news items which relate to set criteria (commodity prices, competing companies etc.) are selected. Because much of the news is still in hard copy form only, some organisations choose to pay staff to select, classify and scan news items into the system.

Many EISs are relatively slow in operation. This is because they tend to rely on relational database technology which does not handle complex queries well. With improvements in hardware and moves towards object-oriented databases, this will change, as it is important to deliver performance where it is most needed.

IS in action

Building confidence

Thanks to its costly building automation system, the Pentagon was able to be in operation on 12 September 2001, one day after a plane crashed into the building in the 9/11 terrorism attacks on the USA. This system was able to close down air vents and manipulate building services so that the fire could be contained to a single sector of the building (Snoonian 2003).

However, it is unlikely that ordinary office buildings will be fitted with anything approaching the sophistication and expense of the Pentagon's systems. In the normal course of events security, air-conditioning, energy control, waste management and fire alarm systems are installed by different specialist companies. If these systems could be integrated then buildings could be made safer and cheaper to run.

BACnet (Building Automation and Control network) is a communications protocol that allows different systems to be controlled from a single console via the Internet or almost any standard network. For Australian businesses which have a high dependency on air-conditioning, energy savings alone might trim as much as 30% from the power bill, but being able to act quickly to contain fire damage or terrorist activity to a single area could be of much greater value.

Groupware

Most **groupware** operates at enterprise, group and personal levels. Figure 4.6 shows the four main functional components of groupware. The boundaries between the components are deliberately fuzzy since there is a high degree of overlap. The four areas do not fill the groupware area entirely, which implies that there is more to groupware than these four components. Staff, intelligent agents, access to DSSs, extranets, order-entry systems and so on might also be considered to be part of a particular groupware system.

The four functional areas shown in figure 4.6 are found at every level of groupware use, whether personal (stand-alone), group or enterprise level. In essence, companies use groupware to create, share, organise and manage information. Many of these functions have been developed separately and are integrated in packages such as Lotus Notes. The communications aspects are handled at a physical level by local area networks and at a logical level by intranets and specialised software. There are many references to groupware with more specialised features (i.e. focused on specific tasks rather than on general tasks as with ordinary groupware). Such groupware forms the basis for computer-supported cooperative workgroups (CSCW) and group support systems. Notwithstanding, most authors would regard groupware as horizontal software.

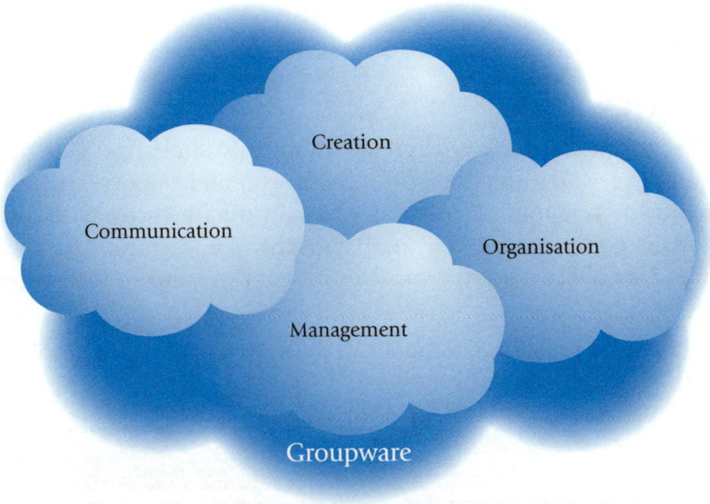

Figure 4.6 The main functional areas of groupware

Communication

Communication may be divided into two main categories: synchronous and asynchronous. In addition, communication may be local or remote.

Synchronous communication means 'at the same time', so the communicating parties are engaged in immediate communication. Local synchronous communication includes electronic meeting room systems. Remote synchronous communication includes videoconferencing and interactive multiauthor screens.

Asynchronous communication implies communication 'at a different time' and email and bulletin boards are good examples. The messages can be read at a later time and replied to when convenient. Obviously, groupware needs to support all communication modes.

Organisation

Since companies wish to have fast, efficient and convenient information retrieval, the documents stored must be classified and cross-referenced in a meaningful manner.

At an enterprise level, many businesses opt for a mixture of databases and web-type technology in which the cross-references become active links to information. Users may need to be alerted to new information, and information may need to be 'aged' or deleted as it ceases to be relevant. Since the documents that need to be cross-referenced might be in a variety of formats — graphics, text file, email, html, scanned text/image files — this is a complex area usually requiring dedicated staff for its care.

At a personal level, there are fewer cross-references and so the task is usually much simpler, e.g. filing and categorising emails by content and author for later retrieval, or linking files together to form a book or web page.

Infobyte

Bicycles with GPS

With crowded roads and expensive cars, Japanese consumers find electric power-assisted bicycles an attractive option. Unfortunately so do Japanese joyriders. A major bicycle manufacturer is now shipping bicycles with a GPS locator as standard equipment. For a small monthly fee (around A$12), a security company is able to track the bicycles in real time and so locate lost and stolen bicycles.

Source: www.industrypages.com/artman/publish/Industry_News_2820.stm (accessed 23 September 2003).

Creation

Staff need to create a variety of files in their everyday activities — spreadsheets, jpegs, databases etc. Many of these are single-author and use files that do not need to be shared. However, some files will need to be shared and some, such as shared files in group decision support systems, will have multiple authors. Editing is included in this area because, when a document is altered, a new version of that document is created. Groupware provides templates for memoranda, web pages, emails etc., and usually supports widely used software packages such as Microsoft's Frontpage. Providing templates ensures rapid development, consistency of style for corporate image, and ease of management.

Management

Single-author, non-shared files do not need to be managed at a high level. However, as soon as information has to be shared, it needs to be managed. At its simplest, this might involve restricting access to certain information for some staff. It might entail automating and authenticating vote-counting for GDSS purposes. Active environments will notify relevant staff when information has been updated. A business might want to restrict email access to some employees, and so on. Essentially the business is concerned with coordinating the activities in the environment. The word 'environment' is deliberate, and is a good way to think of groupware — a pervasive infrastructure that makes personal and business activities more convenient and efficient (Licker 1997). Return on investment is quite high in this area — it is necessary to consider where the main cost savings are to be found and why.

Besides the static rule-driven aspects of management, there are tools which possess a high degree of intelligence which can carry out tasks in an autonomous fashion, such as intelligent agents which are very useful in a groupware setting. Suppose that it is necessary to arrange a meeting or video conference with five members of staff. An intelligent agent can scan their electronic diaries, find a mutually convenient time for everyone, update the diaries accordingly, book the meeting room and video-conference facilities, and supply briefing materials to the participants. It can also, if necessary, inform the catering staff and arrange for refreshments during the meeting. (Intelligent agents are also used in decision support systems and executive information systems to scan the environment for news and so on if it is necessary to brief staff.) Intelligent agents supporting specialised tasks such as project management and problem/progress chasing are increasingly common. Basic scheduling software which accesses employees' electronic desk diaries is provided by Microsoft's Outlook and Schedule Plus as well as products like Powercore's Netscheduler 3. Unfortunately, employee conformance may be a problem. The software works only if all concerned keep their 'diaries' up to date and check the system frequently. These are major implementation and management issues.

Infobyte

Mobile agents

Mobile agents are a variation on the theme of intelligent agents. As the name implies, they are able to 'move' from one computer to another carrying out their work at source. Although mobile agents have been slow to catch on, they do offer certain advantages. Their main advantage is the reduction of network loads. For example, think of downloading a large data set across a network and then performing the analysis. A mobile agent could perform the analysis and send the results via the network.

Problems with groupware

There are several problems with groupware (in addition to the purely technical ones):

- *Information overload.* Since it is so easy to share information, people can be overloaded and are unable to sort out important information from trivial information in a reasonable time frame.
- *Inappropriate sharing of information.* This might include unauthorised access to personnel files or (more commonly) people using the system to socialise and exchange non-work-related information, such as jokes and cartoons. Again, productivity may suffer.
- *Time wasting.* Since it is easy to arrange meetings and conferences, there will be more of them. Many meetings are not productive or essential.
- *Human factors.* Managers often encounter resistance from staff who are opposed to change in the workplace. Careful planning and consultation can do much to ensure a smooth transition.

Despite these problems, informed opinion is that groupware is a cost-effective investment.

Groupware and knowledge management

Definitions of data, information and knowledge were given in chapter 1 and have been reviewed in this chapter. The subjective nature of knowledge is problematic from a management point of view. Whereas the transfer of data and information can be built into computer systems, the transfer of knowledge often relies on social systems for its implementation. Many authors divide knowledge into two basic categories — explicit and tacit. Explicit knowledge is procedural information that can be codified, e.g. how to use a software package, who to contact in the event of X happening. Explicit knowledge is a formal (and usually incomplete) expression of corporate culture.

Tacit knowledge is personal knowledge — experience, and ethical and judicial ability. Tacit knowledge makes use of formal and informal networks and structures, which are hard to codify. When working in teams, people rely on one another's expertise, and learn by observing the techniques and thinking of others and adapting them to their needs. This is a combination of social constructivism and learning by doing. The problem that managers face is that key members of a team may leave at short notice, taking their expertise with them.

The challenge is to make as much knowledge as possible explicit and to create working environments which engender tacit knowledge transfer. For example, think about a company which has an annual performance review of staff before deciding whether to award a pay rise. If financial resources are limited and a person has a high level of expertise in a particular area, then sharing that knowledge with others effectively undermines that person's bargaining position. New paradigms require new reward structures. As indicated before, IS is a people business. Many of the problems are motivational not technical. Adoption of best practices and industry benchmarking is essential if a competitive edge is to be maintained, and this applies to knowledge management, too. Knowledge must be applied to knowledge.

Tacit knowledge relies heavily on social interaction. Some groupware, such as videoconferencing, can support such interaction. Under certain conditions (single-site, small and medium-sized companies), tacit knowledge transfer gets better as the computer systems get worse. This seems counter-intuitive until you realise what is happening. Because the systems do not support knowledge sharing, users are forced to move around the building and talk to other users. In so doing, they are exposed to a wider variety of people and views than they would encounter via the computer system. Face-to-face communication is a very rich form of communication since non-verbal aspects are included in the exchange. This should not be taken as a plea to justify the existence of bad systems. Instead, it is an argument for much better systems that support rich communication.

- **Reflection question 3:** As a manager, how would you go about creating an environment which encourages learning and knowledge sharing?

IS in action

Groupware

As an example of the use of groupware, consider a nationwide department store chain. Ideally, each store needs to operate as independently as possible, but it is sometimes possible to negotiate better deals for larger supply quantities. The time and cost of each purchase should be minimal. Advertising and marketing need to be coordinated at a national level. Expenditure also needs to be matched to budgets and traditional accounting systems tend to report at fixed intervals. This can cause managers to overspend budgets in certain areas.

Examine figure 4.7. The processes are almost self-explanatory but a few things are worth comment. All documentation is electronic, thus avoiding paper trail delays. The groupware server and the main business system exchange financial data each night, allowing purchase requisitions to be checked against budgets (actual and committed). Requisitions meeting set criteria are approved automatically by the groupware server, but those that do not meet the criteria are referred to one or two levels of management at head office for approval. Approved requisitions are then linked to the main business system and orders are issued. The progress of any purchase requisition can be checked via a web browser, and email notifies all relevant personnel of outcomes. Internal ordering systems are simpler and faster. Since payment can be effected on the same day as delivery, suppliers will give discount for prompt payment. Purchasing decisions are based on the most current information available. All in all, this system is more responsive than a traditional system.

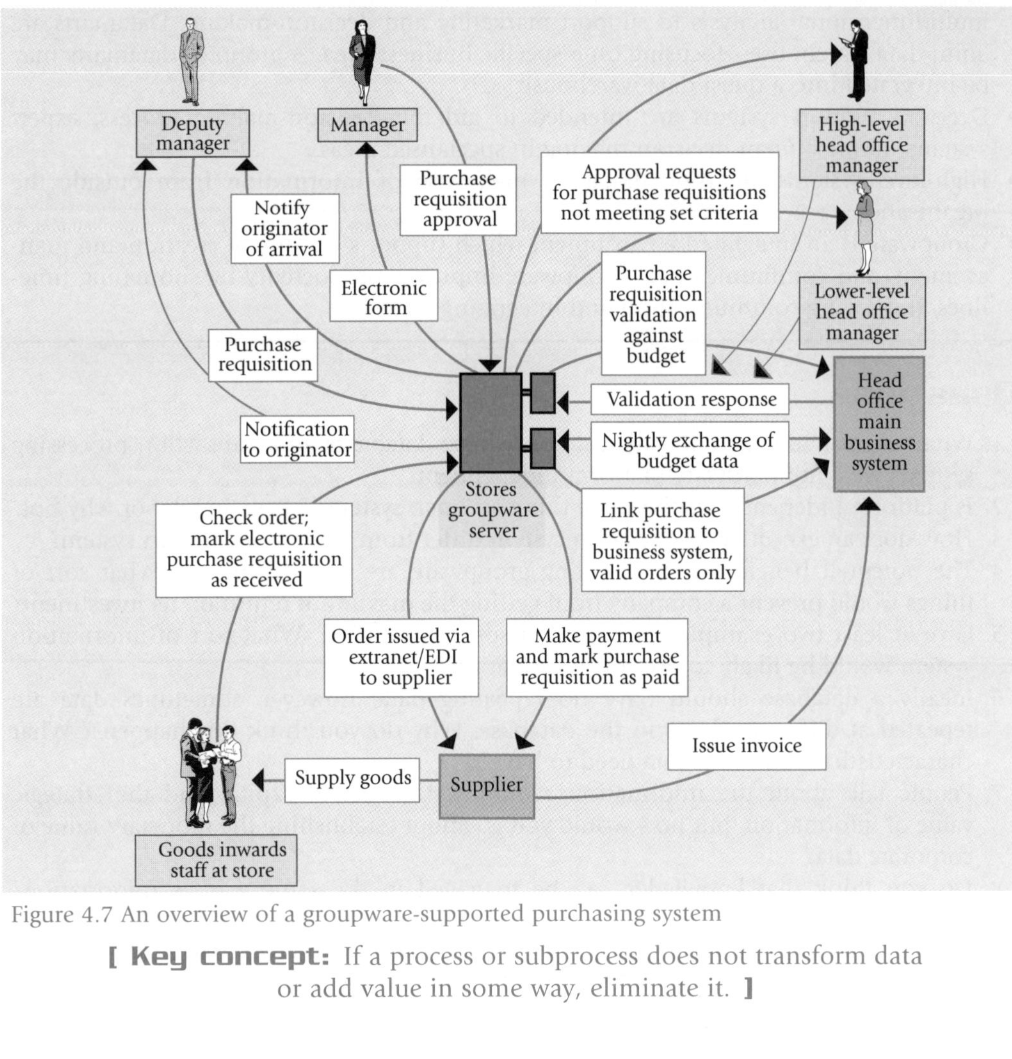

Figure 4.7 An overview of a groupware-supported purchasing system

[Key concept: If a process or subprocess does not transform data or add value in some way, eliminate it. **]**

Summary

The coverage given in this chapter has been both broad and selective; details such as precise database architecture have been omitted in order not to lose view of higher level concerns. The key points of this chapter are:

- Business information systems cooperate in a connected hierarchy. The lower the position in the hierarchy, the more detailed the information is.
- Lower level systems are usually concerned with the automation of basic operational processes, e.g. transaction processing. Higher level systems are concerned with less structured activities, provide a wider variety of easy-to-use tools, and use more summarised (condensed) information.
- Most organisations have logically related collections of data called databases, which are where day-to-day transaction data are recorded. These live systems can be used to generate middle-level management reports. Data warehouses hold archived data from a wide variety of sources and are updated infrequently. Data warehouses are used for multidimensional analysis to support marketing and decision-making. Datamarts are 'mini data warehouses' focusing on a specific business area. A group of datamarts may be integrated into a quasi data warehouse.
- Decision support systems are intended to aid the decision-making process; expert systems mimic human decision-making in specialised areas.
- High-level systems are more likely to make use of information from outside the organisation.
- Groupware is an integrated environment which supports document creation and management, and communication. Groupware improves productivity by shortening timelines, improving communication and integrating systems.

Questions

1. What might happen to an organisation whose databases and transaction processing systems were not hardware platform independent?
2. Is platform independence the same thing as 'open systems'? Explain why or why not.
3. How does an executive information system differ from a decision support system?
4. The potential benefits from adopting groupware are very significant. What sort of things would prevent a company from getting the maximum return on its investment?
5. Give at least two examples of hard and soft information. What sort of information system would be likely to use soft information?
6. Ideally a database should have no repeating data; however, sometimes data are repeated at different places in the database. Why do you think this happens? What characteristics would the data need to have?
7. People talk about the information economy, intellectual capital and the strategic value of information, but how would you go about establishing the monetary value of corporate data?
8. Do you think that knowledge can be managed in the same way as information? Explain why or why not.
9. What characteristics should a transaction processing system (TPS) have?
10. What are the significant differences between a database and a data warehouse?

11. This chapter presented a simple information hierarchy (data, information, knowledge and wisdom). Knowledge management is an important topic in business, what sort of classification scheme would you use to categorise knowledge?
12. Suppose that you had to define the requirements for an information system that would be used in restaurants to record orders and handle billing. What features would you include in the system in order to make it an attractive proposition to the restaurant trade?

Exercises

1. You are the manager of a large hotel in a major city and wish to implement a guest history system. This will allow you to track 'frequent flyers', and bad guests and payers. Records kept might include newspaper preference, snack foods and dietary needs. Specify the information requirements of the system and how that information is to be obtained. Identify functions of the system that would be most useful to management.
2. Your company is about to move to a groupware platform for its 400 non-manual staff. All staff are used to email and web browsers and, although this offers a huge potential return on investment, it could also lead to major problems if the change management process is not well handled. What could you do to minimise the risk of failure? How would you set about the implementation process? (Hint: you will need to think about preparing employees for the change and whether to move everyone to the new system immediately or adopt a more incremental approach.)
3. The misuse of corporate electronic communications causes problems for many companies. Identify the major types of problem and their likely consequences. Next, outline the major elements of an acceptable use policy for staff using electronic communications.

CASE STUDY Ragnarok Video

Competition in the home entertainment market is intense, and for the most part it is dominated by a few large corporations, such as Blockbuster. There are exceptions, such as Ragnarok.

The business was established in 1987 by Michael and Kevin, two science fiction fans who could not get the videos that they wanted from their local video store. Their thinking was that other people with similar interests would pay to rent movies. Initially they ran the business out of a small shop a few kilometres out of the town centre, and soon other science fiction and fantasy fans were driving anything up to 16 kilometres to hire videos. In the early days customers were given six cards, which were used to record video hires. Each video had its own envelope, and when a video was hired, one of the membership cards was put into the envelope, which was then placed in the 'Hired' tray with the due date for return written on it. Customer tracking was a manual process, and reserving videos was an *ad hoc* procedure at best.

For the first three years business was steady, but the early 1990s saw a period of substantial growth. In 1993 Ragnarok Videos moved to its present location on the

(*continued*)

outskirts of the city's business district. The new premises had much more space so Michael and Kevin were able to diversify into cult TV, festival films and foreign language films to serve the diverse local population. Finally in 1995 they moved into mainstream entertainment and began to offer the same range of popular films as might be found in any of the Blockbuster movie stores. Such a varied stock and high volumes of business became impossible to handle manually, and so an off-the-shelf point-of-sale system was installed. Every item has a bar code and a corresponding entry in the electronic stock catalogue. The system was intended to handle sales rather than hires so reservations, enquiries and product tracking are difficult, but it has reduced queueing at the checkout. The system has been in place for seven years now and, although much of the hardware has been replaced, the software has just been ported from one platform to the next, largely unaltered.

Michael and Kevin continued their policy of growth and dreamed of having the largest video collection in Western Australia. In 1997 they took out a lease on the adjoining premises and took on a loan to expand the collection. But profits did not keep pace with growth. In an attempt to generate additional income streams Ragnarok Videos diversified into movie memorabilia, CD and DVD sales, and video game and console hire. These activities have made a difference, but their contribution to profit has been marginal at best. The food and drink vending machines that Kevin had installed in 2000 have made a solid contribution. As it now stands the business is just about in the black and its stock is ageing. The high-profile location is a real advantage to the business, but it is expensive. Rising rents, rates and insurance are ongoing concerns.

A national chain has expressed an interest in acquiring Ragnarok and is offering reasonable terms and continuing employment for Michael and Kevin. However, the founders are not keen to surrender their independence and control.

Ragnarok needs to have a reasonable amount of stock on the shelves for customers to browse through. Although some customers come in with specific requests, most simply make a selection from what is on the shelves. At any point in time no more than 20% of the stock is out on hire. When customers ask if a particular item is available, a staff member makes a quick shelf check. If the item is not found then he/she consults the electronic catalogue to see when it is due for return and offers to reserve it. However, reservations are something of a hit-and-miss affair if a customer is overdue in returning videos. The business operates seven days a week from 10 a.m. to 10 p.m. with 70% of weekly earnings being generated on Friday, Saturday and Sunday. Videos and DVDs are divided into two categories: weekly and new release. New release videos are charged out at $6.00 per night and weekly hires are charged out at $3.00. Customer loyalty is good with most customers visiting the premises at least every two weeks.

A lease on one of the buildings opposite will become available in eight months time. Michael's informal contacts with the local council have told him that a change of use application has been made. It seems that the fruit and vegetable shop is set to become a rival video store. Michael believes that one of the national chains is targetting their business.

If Michael and Kevin ignore the situation they will end up losing their business; Ragnarok does not have the resources to fight a price war with the new video store, which is backed by a national chain. If they accept the offer for their business and sell out, they will lose their control and independence. Somehow they need to trim costs, reposition the business and increase income and profit. Kevin's idea is to try to generate new customers by advertising and try to compete with the new video store when it opens. He argues that they must act now. Michael's approach is to try to generate more income from the customers they already have, but this would involve replacing the older POS system with a newer version that allows product tracking and customer profiling. If anything this will cost more than Kevin's advertising campaign. Currently stockouts (situations when all available copies of a video are out on loan) and the lack of a reliable reservation system are causes of customer dissatisfaction. The problem is that the bank is not prepared to loan any more money until it can see a revised business plan. Kevin has suggested putting the business online since most of their customers have Internet access.

Ragnarok has engaged a consultant to advise on how best to turn the business around.

QUESTIONS

1. Consider Kevin's idea of putting the business online. Is it feasible to do so? What factors should be taken into account?
2. What broad strategies would you suggest to ensure the immediate survival of the business? Do you think that the bank will find these good enough to justify a business loan?
3. Outline the requirements for an information system for Ragnarok (i.e. what must the IS be able to do? What activities should it support?). Remember to think about integrating business processes and supporting them with the IS.
4. Think about the way in which the information system should operate. What sort of queries should it be able to handle? What sort of users will it serve? Any system will require that videos and DVDs are catalogued. How would you catalogue them? (Hint: think about the sort of things that you might want to search for. Categories need not be mutually exclusive.)
5. Consider how you would handle marketing. Do you agree with Kevin's view or Michael's? Given the cash-starved nature of the business currently, any marketing has to be cost-effective. What specific things would you suggest?

References

Carter, J. 2000, *Database Design and Programming*, McGraw-Hill, Maidenhead, pp. 25–30.

Connolly, T., Beg, C.E. & Strachan, A. 1999, *Database Systems: A Practical Approach to Design, Implementation and Management*, Addison-Wesley, pp. 48–53.

Graham, P. 2003, 'A plan for spam', www.paulgraham.com/spam.html (accessed 23 September 2003).

Licker, P. 1997, *Management Information Systems: A Strategic Leadership Approach*, Harcourt Brace, Orlando, pp. 223–45.

McKeown, P.G. 2001, *Information Technology and the Networked Economy*, Harcourt Brace, Orlando, pp. 127–40.

Snoonian, D. 2003, 'Saving the Pentagon', *IEEE Spectrum*, August 2003, p. 23.

Turban, E., McLean, E. & Wetherbe, J. 2004, *Information Technology for Management*, 4th edn, John Wiley & Sons, New York, pp. 330–6.

Vaughn-Nichols, S.J. 2003, 'Saving private e-mail', *IEEE Spectrum*, August 2003, pp. 40–4.

Chapter 5

Communication and networks

LEARNING OBJECTIVES

After reading this chapter, you should be able to:

- understand the differences between digital and analog information, signalling and communication
- understand the differences between asynchronous and synchronous communication
- understand the terms 'simplex', 'half duplex' and 'full duplex'
- understand the difference between circuit and packet switching
- understand what is meant by the term 'protocol' and give suitable examples of local and wide area network protocols
- understand some of the different types of communication media in use today, their limitations and their applications
- understand the principles and implications of wireless and cellular networking
- understand the purpose and use of firewalls
- discuss the differences between local and wide area networks and understand why each evolved
- give working definitions of 'local area network', 'wide area network', 'backbone network', 'metropolitan network', and 'personal area network' and understand their basic technologies
- define the terms 'Internet', 'intranet' and 'extranet', and appreciate how they change the nature of business
- understand the principles behind client–server networking.

5

Introduction

This chapter describes the communications and network technologies on which many information systems rely. Developmental trends and possible futures of communications technology are also covered.

Mainframe computers transformed the way businesses operated in the 1960s and 1970s but the advent of the PC in the 1980s demanded communication in order to fulfil its potential. This combination of information technology and communications technology had a remarkable impact, and with the addition of Internet-based technologies in the 1990s, this impact became truly profound. This was the dawn of a new age and it heralded the imminent demise of corporate management information systems in the accepted sense.

While many organisations have realised this and have undertaken **business process re-engineering (BPR)** in order to gain maximum advantage of the new technologies, there are some who are losing the ability to compete as they cling to the past. When the president of Western Union, William Orton, was offered the exclusive rights to Alexander Graham Bell's telephone for $100 000, he refused, saying, 'What use could this company make of an electrical toy?' (Casson 1910, p. 58). Now, as then, it is vital to think about the future and take advantage of all that technology can offer.

The most obvious manifestations of current technological developments are fusion (fewer devices but with greater capability, e.g. using a mobile telephone to surf the Internet) and fragmentation of society and the market into increasingly specialised (and smaller) areas. This fragmentation arises as a result of increasing media diversity and poses particular problems for advertisers and marketers. From a management point of view, it is possible to construct small and effective teams of people to work on specialised tasks. Such teams can be housed in a single location or distributed nationally or internationally. In all cases, communications technology links members of the team to their client base and to one another.

In order to appreciate the business advantages of networking, it is necessary to review some fundamental aspects of communication.

Digital and analog information

Analog and digital information should be familiar to you from everyday life. Digital information is discrete (discontinuous and almost particulate in nature) and has an allowable range of values. Days of the week are a simple example: as the clock ticks over 2400 hours on a Monday evening, the transition is from Monday to Tuesday; at no point is it Monday *and* Tuesday. It is the same with integer numbers or notes on a piano. There are no intermediate values. The keys of a piano are digital, and there is no value between E and F. The best known example is binary code — 0 and 1 for computer use.

Analog information is continuous and there is an infinite set of values between any two points. A violin allows you to have as many notes as you wish between E and F. The human voice is analog information, consisting as it does of a range of frequencies. Most music is recorded in analog form but is often converted to digital for ease of storage and processing, as is the case with CDs. For example, to show the word 'hello' as analog information would mean using the exact shape of the entire wave. To store it in digital form, only representative values of the information need to be held. The more samples there are, of course, the better the approximation to the original waveform.

Digital and analog signalling

A simple fact may help you to remember the difference between digital and analog signalling — the only time it is possible to have true digital signalling is when a voltage can be applied to a cable. In this case there is a level for 0 and another for 1, i.e. the signal is the information.

In all other forms of communication the signal is a model, representation or analog of the information. Analog signalling involves combining the data with a carrier signal and is referred to as **modulation**.

There is no relationship between the data/information type and the signal type — digital information can be sent in analog form and vice versa.

Digital signalling tends to be used for relatively short distances, principally in local area networks for interdevice communication. Direct digital signalling is also called **baseband** modulation and allows only one channel to be in use on a medium at any point in time. Baseband uses **time division multiplexing (TDM)** to share the use of the medium on a 'turn-taking' basis.

Analog signalling is used for:

- TV and radio
- much of the telephone network
- microwave communications.

Digital signalling is more modern, and is cheaper, faster, simpler and more reliable than analog signalling. Most of these advantages derive from the fact that analog systems tend to use a spread of frequencies for transmission and, consequently, the equipment needs to be more complicated. Digital signalling simply requires that a signal can be interpreted as a '1' or a '0'; the absolute level of the signal is not important. In contrast, analog signalling requires the entire envelope or shape of the signal to be fully recovered and processed. Accordingly, absolute signal values are usually very important in analog signalling.

For radio, TV and telephone communications, an analog carrier wave is modified to convey information. This modification process is called 'modulation' and is a key function of a modem. Since a microcomputer uses digital information and signalling, and the user parts of the telephone network are analog, it is thus necessary to change the computer's digital information to analog for transmission purposes, a process that will need to be reversed at the receiving end. This is why a modem (modulator–demodulator) is needed.

Analog signalling is also called **broadband** transmission. Broadband allows several channels on different frequencies to be in use at the same time (e.g. watching one TV channel and videotaping another channel simultaneously) — this is called **frequency division multiplexing (FDM)**. Digital communication is superior to analog communication in most cases, which is discussed in the next section.

Digital and analog communication

You now understand the difference between analog and digital information and analog and digital signalling. Digital communication may use any possible combination of these with the exception of analog data/analog signalling. In other words, analog information sent using digital signals, digital information sent using analog signals, and digital information sent using digital signals are all examples of digital communication. As mentioned earlier, the only time digital signalling is possible is when a voltage can be applied to a cable directly — accordingly, a digital mobile telephone does not use digital signalling. What makes digital communication superior to analog communication?

People who have used an analog mobile telephone network will be aware of the pops, hisses and crackles that became part of the signal during conversations. Since analog signal reception involves recovering the complete envelope or shape of the wave, the overall communication quality is poor since the wave form is degraded during transmission.

Many analog transmissions use a range of frequencies in the signalling process. The high-frequency parts of a signal are the first to be weakened during transmission. For example, think about hearing someone's sound system from a few streets away — at a long distance all you hear are the low, bass components of the sound; at a medium distance you can hear the midrange frequencies, too; only when you are close to the source of the sound can you hear the entire frequency range.

High transmission speeds require high-frequency waves but these do not travel for long distances. Lower frequencies give greater transmission distances but do not give high transmission rates. Cable transmission distances may be extended by using repeaters and amplifiers, but this adds to the cost and complexity of the systems. Because the signal is distorted due to the weakening of high-frequency components, these devices must be quite sophisticated since they must amplify high frequencies more than low frequencies. This means that most analog communications systems are a compromise, as cost and complexity are balanced against performance.

[**Key concept:** Perfection is not achievable. The 'best' systems make the right compromises.]

Digital communication (using analog signalling) is usually restricted to a single frequency, and thus the amplifiers can be simpler and, hence, cheaper. Since signals can travel further before being amplified, fewer amplifiers are needed, thus reducing the cost further. Also, because less processing is involved, the process is faster, i.e. digital communications are cheaper, faster and more reliable than analog communications.

Returning to the digital mobile telephone, the voice data are digitised and sent via a restricted analog signal using a single frequency. The data are compressed, too, so that they take less time to transmit. When the signal is received, the handset recreates the voice data using the digitised data. Thus the effects of interference and distortion (compared with analog systems) are almost eliminated.

However, there is another advantage — digital communication can make more efficient use of the **bandwidth** or carrying capacity of communications media. Table 5.1 on the following page gives a comparative summary of analog and digital communications.

TABLE 5.1 Comparison of analog and digital communications

Analog communications	Digital communications
Signal may consist of more than one frequency	Signal usually consists of one frequency
Prone to error	Relatively error-free
Relatively costly and complicated	Cheap and simple
Slow	Fast
Not very efficient use of bandwidth	Good use of bandwidth

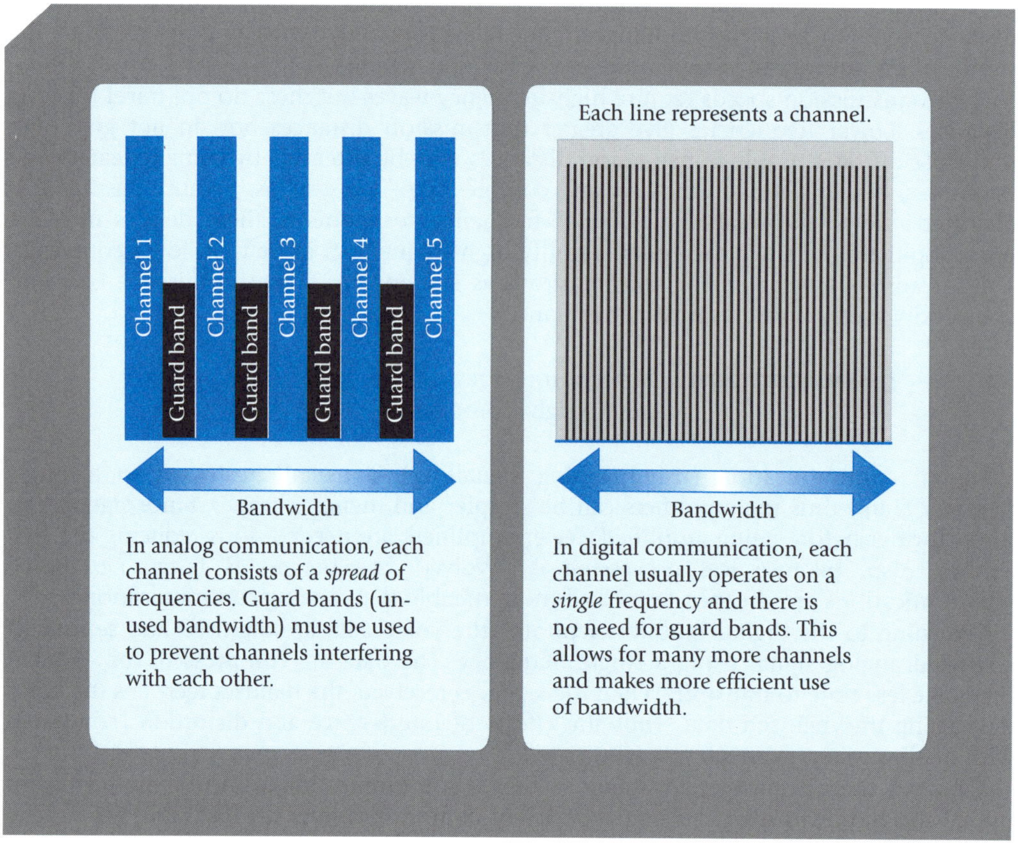

Figure 5.1 A comparison of analog and digital communications in terms of bandwidth usage

Bandwidth is the range of frequencies that a communications medium can carry. The greater the bandwidth, the greater the data-carrying capacity of the medium. Conventional analog transmission which uses a spread of frequencies is very wasteful in terms of bandwidth. Regulatory bodies allocate bandwidth to broadcasters, and it is not a good idea to have two radio or TV channels too close together or they will interfere with each other. Accordingly, there are **guard bands** between stations which enforce channel separation. Digital communications eliminate the need for guard bands, allowing many more communications channels in the same bandwidth. Figure 5.1 gives an idealised pictorial comparison of analog and digital communication bandwidth usage. Moving to a digital broadcast standard with conventional definition television allows for many more TV channels.

Although the superiority of digital over analog has been emphasised in this chapter, analog transmission is far from obsolete. Telstra, the main Australian telecommunications company, is providing Asymmetric Digital Subscriber Line (ADSL) connections to many Australians. ADSL runs at up to 20 times the speed of a normal dial-up Internet connection. The 'Asymmetric' part of the name refers to the fact that different speeds are used for the downlink (from the provider) and the uplink (from the user). Since most users are net consumers rather than producers of information, this is acceptable. Technically ADSL provides digital services, but the transmission remains analog. ADSL and broadband services will be discussed later in this chapter.

However, it should be realised that Telstra is not the only player in this market. Cable TV companies, independent wireless network providers and even power companies are competing in this sector.

Asynchronous and synchronous communication

Asynchronous communication means that there is no real-time relationship between the sending of component parts of a message and their eventual receipt and possible reply. To clarify this, think about sending ten letters to someone over a period of three days. The letters need not arrive in the order in which they were sent and it may be many days before you get a reply (if at all). Letters are asynchronous communication.

Synchronous communication incorporates a real-time element (here and now) and is connection-oriented, e.g. a telephone conversation or a TV broadcast. 'Connection-oriented' should not be taken to imply that there has to be a medium which relates (connects) the communicating parties in real time.

Most local area networks (LANs) are not connection-oriented, although they have connections at a physical level. Consequently, most LANs do not support real-time applications.

However, the use of switches in local area networks is increasing, and fully switched systems do permit synchronous applications.

This is an example of fusion or convergence; the **switch** technology which was previously used in telephone and wide area networks is now being used in local area networks. It also means that voice, video and data communications can all be handled by the same network.

Communication modes

Communication systems can operate in one of three distinct modes. These define the operational characteristics of the system.

- *Simplex*. Data/information flows in only one direction. Television is an ideal example of this mode.
- *Half duplex*. Data/information can flow in both directions but only one direction at a time. Walkie-talkies or CB radios operate in this well-ordered, turn-taking manner. Often there is an acknowledgement that each part of a message has been received successfully.
- *Full duplex*. Data/information can flow in both directions at the same time. The information flows need not be symmetrical in terms of quantity of data transmitted or speed.

Most practical data communications operate in full-duplex mode because half duplex is wasteful of bandwidth. To explain this, think about throwing and catching a ball. When the players are close together, the time is equally divided between throwing, catching and waiting. As the distance increases, so does the waiting time. A typical application operating in half-duplex mode might waste as much as 80% of the available bandwidth in waiting.

■ **Reflection question 1:** There are cases when the communication link is full duplex but the communicating parties use it as though it were half duplex. What reasons might there be for this?

Circuit and packet switching

These are the two major approaches to moving information from one place to another in a network, i.e. how the medium is used. Circuit switching works in much the same way as the telephone. A connection is established for the duration of the communication, data are transmitted, and finally the connection is closed. This approach permits synchronous applications such as video and telephony. Most wide area networks use this approach, but circuit switching can suffer from the same problems as the telephone system, i.e. once a circuit is in use it is usually not available to other users. This means that long messages may cause delays for other users. Circuit switching allows synchronous applications for the communicating parties for the duration of the interaction. Access time (the time spent waiting to use the medium) is not constant and, as a consequence, pure circuit switching may cause problems in non-broadcast situations.

Packet switching involves breaking a message into small components (packets) which are then forwarded through the network to their destination. Each packet may follow a different path to its destination, so each packet must carry addressing information, sequencing instructions and error-control information. Packet switching is used by most local area networks and does not support synchronous applications. Packet switching reduces the delay time by interleaving packets from different sources, although the individual delay time for long messages is likely to increase. The Internet **protocol** TCP/IP (a protocol in this context is just the set of rules that govern the exchange of information; it says what must be done in the event of an error, resetting a connection etc.) is the predominant wide area network protocol and is able to operate on a circuit or packet basis. TCP/IP stands for transmission control protocol/Internet protocol.

Fast circuit switching is a modern hybrid technology (though the concepts were published in the early 1980s) which combines the simplicity and fairness of packet switching with the synchronous transmission abilities of circuit switching. A connection is established for each packet sent, and the access time is so low as to make true synchronous applications possible. It is likely that most networks will migrate to a variant of this scheme. This provides yet another example of technology convergence.

Communications media

Detailed coverage of cabling and media in current use is beyond the scope of this book. However, media can be subdivided into hardwire and softwire.

Hardwire media are media that can be touched. Twisted pair, coaxial cable and optical fibre are all hardwire. The initial installation costs are lower than softwire systems but they are more expensive to maintain and manage. Since the final connection to a networked device is by means of a cable or fibre to a designated network connection point, hardwire systems do not allow a high degree of user/device mobility. Hardwire systems have been around for a long time and standards are well developed, so performance is better than softwire systems.

Softwire ('wireless') media are broadcast systems. They use radiowaves, microwaves or free space optics to handle the communication. They cost more to install than hardwire systems, but are easier (and cheaper) to manage. They allow a high degree of user/device mobility but do not give such good performance as hardwire systems. However, for a temporary installation, one which requires a high degree of flexibility or one where architectural constraints preclude the use of hardwire systems, they are excellent. Satellite systems are very good for broadcasting but not so useful for ordinary communication owing to the long propagation delays that they introduce. Satellites are also affected by sunspot activity and magnetic storms, so for this reason most Internet service providers do not choose to use satellite links as their only source of Internet bandwidth.

Table 5.2 gives a simple comparison of hardwire and softwire media.

TABLE 5.2 Comparison of hardwire and softwire media

Hardwire	Softwire
Set-up costs low	Set-up costs high
Ongoing management costs high	Ongoing management costs low
Not flexible, no mobility	Very flexible, allows great mobility
Good standards and high speeds	Standards now well developed and speeds approaching hardwire capability
May not be an option for an architecturally significant building, i.e. the alterations required to install cabling and powerpoints may not be permitted under local regulations	Can be used anywhere

Infobyte

Terabeam making light work of communication

The final connection from the Internet to a client's premises is often provided by a telephone company. It is usually the slowest and most expensive link in the chain. IT professionals call this the 'last mile connection'. In trying to overcome many of the problems associated with last mile connections, Terabeam has taken a novel approach. Rather than run expensive cable or optic fibre to business premises, Terabeam uses laser beams to achieve high-speed, point-to-point 'connections'. Distribution centres are strategically placed on high buildings, and line-of-sight operation delivers data to optical receivers in the clients' windows. Special tracking systems are required to overcome the effects of buildings swaying in the wind. If a business relocates it is relatively cheap and simple to redirect the service to a new location. Besides providing higher performance and flexibility than conventional systems, it can be set up comparatively quickly. Terabeam assisted in the recovery of communication functions following the 11 September 2001 attack on the World Trade Center in New York, and many companies now use Terabeam as part of their disaster recovery strategy.

Source: www.terabeam.com (accessed 1 March 2004).

Another way to classify media is to divide them into electrical, radio and optical categories.

- *Electrical media*. Electrical media include telephone, twisted pair and coaxial cable. Of these, twisted pair is the most commonly used medium in local area networking. Category 5 cable (CAT5) is baseband twisted pair and operates at 100 Mbps over 50 m. Coaxial cable gives similar performance but over longer distances and tends to be used in network backbones. All electrical media are prone to interference or induced currents due to lightning strikes.
- *Radio*. Apart from radio and TV broadcasts, this category also includes microwave communications such as satellites and mobile telephones. Like electrical media, this category is prone to interference, and for some applications may represent a security hazard since the signals are broadcast.
- *Optical*. This may be a softwire system using infra-red light (not unlike a TV remote control) but more usually means using optical fibres. Optical fibres do not suffer from interference. The limitations here come from absorption of the signal and signal loss at fibre joins. Optical fibres are resistant to interference and lightning strikes, making them ideal for the safe interconnection of buildings in a local area network environment. Because they are not electrical, they cannot be tapped externally, and because they are so thin, they are virtually impossible to tap internally. It is this high degree of precision that makes optical fibres expensive because of the engineering needed to

make connections, but this cost continues to come down as the technology becomes widespread. A single strand of multimode fibre can replace 1800 pairs of telephone lines, which gives some idea of their huge carrying capacity. Fibres are much lighter than copper cables — 1 km of coaxial cable could weigh much more than 1000 kg; the same length of a single optical fibre can be carried easily in one hand. Of course, since much of the installation cost of any cabling is labour, more fibre than immediately needed should be installed to allow for growth.

[**Key concept:** Labour is a significant cost, so it is better to over-engineer the system in the short term than to pay for expensive upgrades in the medium term.]

More on optical fibres

Fibres come in two main types — multimode and monomode. Multimode fibres propagate the signal by total internal reflection and are able to use **light-emitting diodes (LEDs)** as light sources. They are much cheaper than monomode fibres and tend to be used for distances of less than 5 km. They are usually capable of delivering at least 150 Mbps. They tend to be used for metropolitan area networks and shorter haul high-speed links, though they are starting to be deployed in ordinary local area networks.

Monomode fibres have a much smaller aperture (diameter) than multimode fibres — they are so narrow that they approach the physical wavelength of light. At this point, the ray model of light fails and the light can be propagated only as a wave — hence the name *mono*mode. Monomode fibres are very expensive and have to use lasers as light sources. They are used for long-haul communications links (often more than 20 km) and have a much higher carrying capacity than multimode fibres do. In theory, their bandwidth is in excess of 5 Gbps. Speeds in excess of 10 Gbps are possible, but rely on a technique called **dense wave division multiplexing (DWDM)**, which is similar to frequency division multiplexing. Table 5.3 gives a comparison of common communications media.

TABLE 5.3 A comparison of common communications media

	Network	Typical speed	Typical distance	Error rate	Security	Cost
Hardwire medium						
Twisted pair	LAN	100 Mbps	100 m	Low	Average	Low
Coaxial cable	LAN backbone	150 Mbps	500 m	Low	Average	Moderate
Optical fibre	Any	100 Mbps to 160 Gbps	Up to 40 km	Extremely low	Excellent	Very high
Softwire medium						
Radio	LAN	~ 10 Mbps	< 500 m	Moderate	Poor	Low
Infra-red	LAN backbone	16 Mbps	< 100 m	Moderate	Poor	Low
Microwave	WAN	4–32 Mbps	< 30 km	Low to moderate	Poor	Moderate
Satellite	WAN	Up to 8 Mbps	Very long	Low to moderate	Poor	Moderate

Computer networks

'A communications network is a set of independent devices which may exchange information.' This definition is rather more inclusive than many but it has certain merits. First, the word 'independent' implies that no individual device is in control of the communication process — the master–slave relationship of the old mainframe days is all but over. It reflects the empowerment of users via PCs. Second, the word 'devices' is used in preference to 'computers' to convey the idea that networks have types of devices other than computers, e.g. smart printers, servers, interconnection devices. Last, the word 'information' may be construed to mean simple data, processed data, instructions, requests, graphics files, or just about anything. This is indicative of the huge changes that have occurred in business computing in the last decade or so.

Networks are the enabling technology which allows modern systems to function — some people have described them as the 'glue' that holds corporate systems together. The importance of networks is evidenced by the fact that communications costs far outweigh data processing costs for the vast majority of businesses. There are many reasons for networking, and most of these will emerge from our consideration of basic network types and their function.

Wide area and local area networks

Wide area networks (WANs) evolved first and had their origins in telephone network technology. These allowed staff at different mainframe sites to communicate. There were two driving forces behind this — the first was simple commerce (the need to make money) and the second was defence (largely driven by the Cold War between major Western powers and the then USSR). However, in terms of applications, the original emphasis in wide area networking was communication and this has not really changed in the last four decades. WANs tend to be connection-oriented and the separation between communicating parties is usually in the order of tens of kilometres but may span several hundreds of kilometres. Many companies do not build their own WANs but find it cheaper to buy-in communications from a third-party provider or to use the Internet. Increasingly, companies are using a **virtual private network (VPN)** on third-party-provided WAN services and, more recently, on internal local area networks, too. A VPN is a sort of network within a network.

[**Key concept:** It is usually more cost-effective to use someone else's network than it is to build and manage your own. This is especially true for WANs.]

Local area networks (LANs) developed a little later than WANs. Initially, the emphasis was on sharing resources, such as printers and disk drives, and the networks tended to be oriented towards specific functions such as localised data processing or controlling automated industrial processes. The advent of the PC in the 1980s and reduced technology costs allowed the original emphasis of resource sharing to be extended to include communication functions. LANs now provided the information and communications infrastructure for many businesses. They provide basic communications functions such as email and support network-intrinsic software such as groupware. With time, there is no reason to doubt that they will also provide video-conferencing, media streaming and the like. Although there is an increasing demand for synchronous applications in LAN environments, most LANs are not connection-oriented and so do not support synchronous communication. An analysis of current trends suggests that this will change. Most LANs are contained within a single site (and many within a single building) and the separation between communicating parties is usually in the order of a few thousand metres.

A **backbone network (BN)** is a special kind of LAN that interconnects everything on a single site, including other smaller LANs (LAN segments), into a single, cohesive whole. The backbone may operate at a much higher speed than other parts of the network and may use different networking technology from the rest of the site.

Personal area networks

Personal area networks (PANs) have evolved in recent years to support the increasing number of peripheral devices that PCs need to communicate with. Operating at a variety of speeds and over short distances (see later in this chapter), the emphasis is on the convenience of local mobility. Typical products for home use would include Bluetooth and WiFi networking.

Cellular and wireless communications

Few people would have anticipated the take-up rate for the various forms of wireless communication now available. Essentially there are three main uses: telephony, data transfer and communication between PCs and peripheral devices (personal area networking). We will examine cellular and wireless approaches.

Cellular communication systems

The principle of cellular communication is simple. The service area is divided into 'cells', each of which has a low-powered transmitting station at its centre. As a user moves from one cell to another, the stations negotiate a graceful handover so that the communication does not drop out. The use of low-powered stations means that transmission frequencies can be reused in non-adjacent cells to increase the service coverage. In order to achieve a handover, the cells must overlap as shown in figure 5.2 (where the overlap is shown for *some* cells by means of circles, but conventionally cells are represented as hexagons). To prevent interference, adjacent cells must use different frequencies.

Cells come in several varieties. *Macrocells* are for low population density areas, and the transmitters are more powerful than ordinary cells. *Microcells* are created by splitting a normal cell as the demand increases, and the transmitters are much lower power than an ordinary cell. Microcells can be further subdivided to create picocells. *Umbrella cells* are sometimes used to improve the effectiveness of a microcell cluster. Someone driving a car through such a cluster would require a large number of handovers. So when the speed of a user unit is sufficiently high, it is handled by the umbrella cell rather than the microcells. *Selective cells* are used whenever a 360-degree transmitter is impractical, or not needed, such as tunnel mouths or adjacent to high-power electricity installations.

Cellular systems underpin mobile telephone technology. Contemporary mobile phones do much more than handle voice communication; they are also able to handle data communication. Older systems used Cellular Digital Packet Data (CDPD) to allow users to surf the Web, but the speeds were very low. CDPD is regarded as obsolescent technology. Code Division Multiple Access (CDMA) looks set to replace CDPD. Current versions operate at speeds of 2 to 4 Mbps.

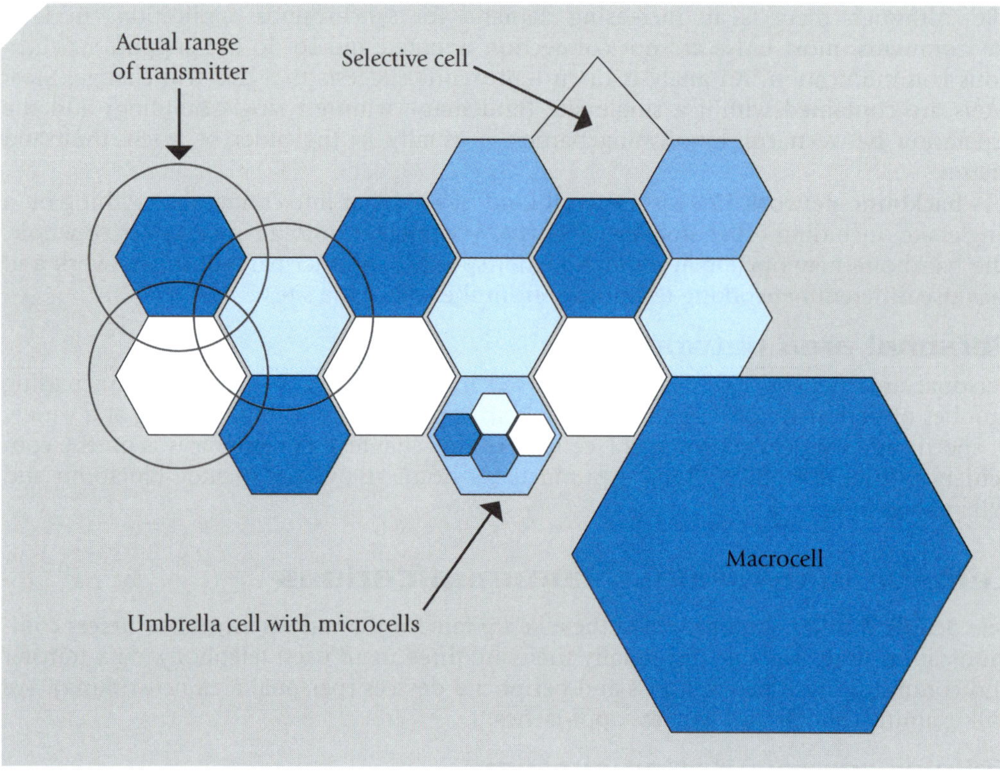

Figure 5.2 A simple cellular network showing different cell types

Mobile commerce is expected to make extensive use of mobile phone technology, but the lack of global standards is posing obstacles in the medium to short term. Mobile phone tariffs tend to make mobile data communication an expensive option, and the small displays and keypads on phones do not make for good-quality web surfing.

Bluetooth

Bluetooth was developed to support communication between PCs and peripheral devices, but the technology soon found its way into mobile phones and handheld computers. Bluetooth (named after Harald Blåtland, the 10th-century Danish king, known as Bluetooth, who united Denmark and Norway) can operate in either packet or circuit modes at speeds less than 2 Mbps for voice and data (typical circuit operation would be 64 Kbps). It uses a cellular approach, and a Bluetooth picocell allows up to eight devices to be networked within a 10-metre radius. A picocell has one master and several slave devices. Up to 10 Piconets can be overlapped to form a scatternet — frequency limitations prevent more than 80 devices being used in a scatternet. Although the range of a picocell is normally restricted to 10 metres, it is possible to increase this range to 100 metres by boosting the power of the transmitter.

The founding companies (Ericsson, Nokia, Toshiba, Intel and IBM) have been at pains to ensure that the technology remains relatively inexpensive, but it seems likely that higher-speed wireless networking such as IEEE802.11a,b or g will eventually supersede Bluetooth on the grounds of superior performance. Hewlett Packard is shipping PDAs that support both standards in the interim.

Wireless networking

Given that Ethernet is the dominant standard for local area networking, it is logical to expect a mobile version. In fact there are three main varieties. IEEE802.11 is the 'umbrella' standard for these networks. The 'a' version supports transmission speeds up to 54 Mbps at distances less than or equal to 20 metres; the 'b' version (popularly known as WiFi) gives 11 Mbps at less than or equal to 100 metres; and the 'g' version provides 54 Mbps at distances less than or equal to 50 metres.

A newer kind of wireless network called ultra-wideband supports 100 to 500 Mbps over distances of less than or equal to 10 metres, and this will support high-definition multimedia in the home.

Pervasive networking

The take-up rate for mobile and wireless networking is sufficiently high to support pervasive networking. All the term 'pervasive networking' means is that networking technology is finding its way into many different kinds of technology. Televisions, DVD players, video-cameras, cars, refrigerators and so on are having networking capability installed. Even devices that already have networking capability are having to support several communication protocols. PDAs are being shipped with Bluetooth, IEEE802.11b as well as the usual infra-red communication ports. Figure 5.3 gives a comparison of the different technologies in terms of range and speed. There is much debate about which will come to dominate, but it seems likely that most devices will support several networking standards if only because of the substantial market penetration already achieved. Ultimately slower standards are likely to be superseded.

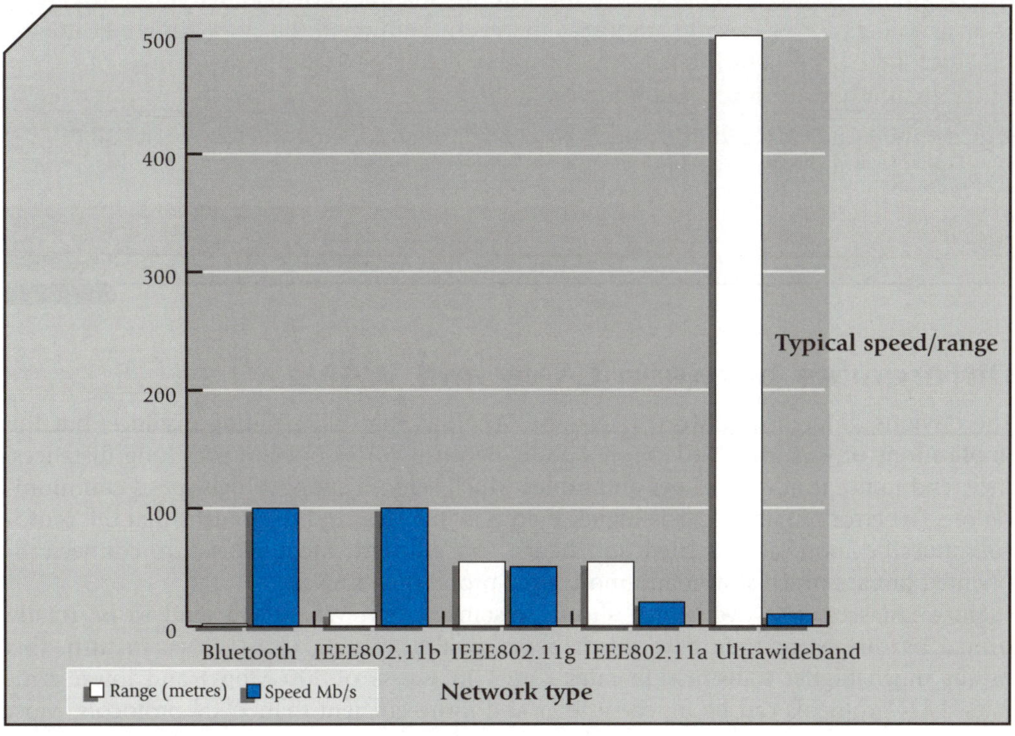

Figure 5.3 Comparison of wireless networking

What are the practical implications and applications of pervasive networking? Freedom from cables in the home is one major advantage; apart from power cables, monitors, TVs, printers, scanners, speakers and so on will need no direct connection to each other or a PC. A whole new range of geographic-specific applications will become available, and homes will become more user-friendly. A PDA will function as a universal remote control, not only for entertainment devices but also for communicating remotely with home lighting, security and climate control systems.

Increasingly networks make use of wireless technologies, and some hubs are able to support synchronous communication and operate as 'wireless switches'.

[**Key concept:** The smaller you are, the more you will pay for bandwidth.]

Infobyte

Wide, wider, widest

Most wireless technologies use a relatively small portion of the available bandwidth to deliver high performance. Ultra-wideband (UWB) uses at least 500 Mhz of the available spectrum to deliver blistering performance over short distances. This enables DVD players to communicate with standard and high-definition TV sets simultaneously — so-called 'killer' applications for most communication systems. Other applications include moving large image files from digital cameras to computers and even keeping all the clocks in the house accurate. Such performance and flexibility is likely to lead to the demise of Bluetooth and slower technologies.

Source: Aiello, G.R. and Rogersons, G.D. 2003, 'Ultra-wideband wireless systems', *IEEE Microwave*, June, pp. 36-47

Differences between LANs and WANs

The obvious difference between LANs and WANs is that of operating distance, but the implications of this are a little more subtle. Because WANs operate over long distances, they tend to use third-party lines and cables which seldom support high-speed communication. The error rate in WANs is higher than it is in LANs, and this means that the protocols must be more complicated and hence less efficient. Most WANs are connection-oriented but are much slower and more error-prone than LANs.

Since LANs operate over much shorter distances than WANs and tend to be totally owned by one party, they have much better quality cabling than WANs. In turn, this means much higher transmission rates (often in excess of 100 Mbps) and lower error rates. LAN protocols can be much simpler and more efficient than WAN protocols. Most LANs are not connection-oriented and so cannot handle synchronous applications.

Contention versus controlled access

The most widely used LAN technology is called 'Ethernet'. This accounts for approximately 75% of the world's LANs, and it operates on a 'contention' access basis. Any connected device can transmit whenever there are no other transmissions in progress. If any other stations start to transmit, then the transmissions will collide and data will be lost. The affected devices will try to resend after a random wait. The more heavily loaded the network is, the worse the problem becomes. This seems very wasteful, but most LANs are not heavily loaded. Access times are generally low and the network is cheaper to install than its competing technologies. Since Ethernet accounts for most of the world's LANs, most of the technical development effort is also focused here.

A previously widely used networking protocol, token ring, uses controlled access — possession of a token guarantees exclusive rights to transmission. This is much better under heavy loading but the performance under light loading is much worse than Ethernet because of the complexity of access management. This strategy is seldom used now for new networks, since most of the technical developments are taking place in the Ethernet sector.

Metropolitan area networks

Metropolitan area networks (MANs) are a relatively recent phenomenon. The advent of reliable, high-speed communications media such as optical fibres has allowed simple, efficient LAN protocols to be used over much greater distances. The emphasis in MANs is one of interconnection — they allow dissimilar networks on different sites to interconnect and cooperate. MANs often provide gateway (access) services to remote networks and applications.

Table 5.4 provides a comparison of the different network types.

TABLE 5.4 A comparison of different network types

	Personal area network (PAN)	Local area network (LAN)	Backbone network (BN)	Metropolitan area network (MAN)	Wide area network (WAN)
Emphasis	Peripheral interconnection	Resource sharing	Interconnection	Interconnection	Communication
Speed	Low to high	High	Very high	Very high	Relatively slow
Protocol	Simple and efficient	Simple and efficient	Simple and efficient	Simple and efficient	Complex and slow
Distances	Very short	Short	Campus scale	Metropolitan scale	Long

Other reasons for networking

Resource sharing and communication have been the prime movers in the development of networks. Another reason for networking is the need for systems which have 'fail soft' potential. (**Fail soft** is the ability of a system to detect component failures and temporarily modify its processing to prevent irretrievable loss of data.) If part of a networked system goes down, because processing and data are distributed it is possible for the business to continue its operations by using other parts of the network, e.g. if a local server goes down a business might be able to use a remote server. Performance will be reduced for the period of the outage but the business can continue to trade. Some organisations operate on a 7 × 24 basis (i.e. seven days a week, 24 hours a day) and make extensive use of redundant networked hardware. In the event of faults, the system will continue to function at a normal level and identify the faults for later repair. The ability not to lose business far outweighs the extra hardware and management costs. To put this into context, the management costs for a local area network for one year will far exceed the purchase costs of all the hardware and software.

Basic local area networking technology

LANs consist of devices which allow PCs to access the network, communications media, devices which interconnect cables, and software which facilitates network management. These are considered in turn.

PC network interface card

Each computer and networked device such as a server or printer needs to have a **network interface card (NIC)**. In a PC, the NIC is installed in one of the spare expansion slots on the computer's motherboard (refer to chapter 2). The NIC allows the computer to 'talk' to the network.

Cabling

At a physical level, the network makes use of a communications medium. Although softwire (wireless) media are available, most installations will use cables of some kind. LAN cables come in three basic varieties:

- *Twisted pair.* This is the most widely used medium in local area networking. The older standard (Category 3, usually called CAT3) is used for telephone links and can handle communication speeds up to 10 Mbps. However, most LANs now run at a higher speed and the newer standard (CAT5) can support speeds of 100 Mbps and is the preferred option when building new networks.
- *Coaxial cable.* This is similar in appearance to the cable that is used for TV. It supports slightly higher speeds and longer distances than CAT5 cable but is more expensive. It was often used for network backbones (the core cabling of a LAN). Advances in twisted-pair cabling and optical fibres are tending to make coaxial obsolete for most LAN applications.

- *Optical fibre.* This is the most expensive and the most reliable medium. Because it uses light instead of electricity, it is immune from interference. It gives very high speed transmission (frequently in the order of gigabits per second) and is very secure since it is almost impossible to tap. It is also used for long cable runs between buildings to avoid the effects of lightning.

Infobyte

Smash repairs

Most car accidents result in only minor damage to panel and paint. However, preparing an estimate and getting approval from insurance companies adds a considerable amount of delay to what should be a simple process. A West Australian business uses specialist software to help it prepare estimates and prepare a parts picking list. Digital images of the damage, together with an electronic copy of the estimate, are forwarded to the insurance companies for on-the-spot approval. When the customer books the car in for repair, details from the estimate are used to feed into the workshop loading and scheduling system to ensure optimum loading and guaranteed completion times.

Interconnection devices

Interconnection devices tend to operate in two ways: (1) broadcast, in which a message is transmitted throughout the entire network (a **hub** operates in this way), and (2) directed, in which messages are 'targeted' to their destination. Directed devices may operate at a hardware level, such as switches, or at a higher level in software, as is the case with **routers**. Of course, for messages to be sent, received or forwarded, every device in a network has to have an individual address.

Routers process network traffic and forward messages along preprogrammed paths (hence 'router' since they route messages) and in larger networks find an alternative path in the event of circuit failure. Routers have a high degree of software intelligence, and since they operate at a higher level than switches and hubs, they are able to provide privacy and security. Routers are also able to handle several different LAN protocols. However, since a full consideration of routers and hybrid devices is beyond the scope of this text, the discussion will be restricted to the most commonly used devices in LANs, i.e. hubs and switches.

Hubs and switches

LANs use interconnection devices to provide connection points between computers and other network devices. These simplify the process of network design since the developer can focus on the central infrastructure of the network. The main tasks are to design efficient cable runs and to ensure that the network has scope for growth. Most developers install more and better cable than is required initially, and make sure that interconnection devices have spare ports to accommodate growth. If this seems extravagant, remember that the yearly operating costs of a LAN far exceed the installation costs. Remember, too, that most of the cable installation costs are for labour, and return visits for upgrades are relatively expensive. The basic infrastructure for a LAN should have an effective lifespan of five to seven years. Hubs may be hardwire or softwire such as WiFi hubs.

Ethernet-type networks (the most commonly used local area networking strategy) tend to use hubs or switches. Hubs are really broadcast devices, i.e. everything that is input on one port is automatically output on every other available port. This is wasteful since every computer will receive a message whether it needs to or not. However, for a small, lightly loaded network, this may be permissible. Hubs cannot support modern synchronous applications.

Switches are selective (i.e. directed), and make connections only between computers/ devices that need them. A 32-port hub can handle only one communication at a time but a 32-port switch can handle up to 16 communications between pairs of computers/ devices at the same time. Switches allow synchronous applications and give much better performance than hubs. Accordingly, many newer LANs are based around switch technology. Figure 5.4 (opposite) shows the difference between a hub and a switch. To clarify the distinction, think about an internal telephone system. If this were wired using a hub, then every extension would ring whenever a call came in or was made, and all workers would have to answer their telephone in case the call was for them. Also, people could not make a call if another call was in progress. Using a switch allows calls to be made on an individual basis and several calls to be made simultaneously. In short, switches make much better use of bandwidth.

Network operating system

A network operating system (NOS) is also required. This assists in basic network operations management and allows user accounts etc. to be set up easily. Novell Netware, LINUX and Windows-derived products are well-known examples. Although these provide 'nuts and bolts' features of network operations, they should not be confused with higher level software whose function is network management. The distinction is analogous to that between word processing and desktop publishing software.

[**Key concept:** In LANs, performance is vital, so if the budget will stand it, opt for high-speed synchronous communication.]

Satellites

In 1945, the science fiction writer Arthur C. Clarke, in an article in *Wireless World*, proposed the idea of using geostationary orbits for communications satellites (he did not, as popular opinion has it, actually invent the communications satellite). In Clarke's view, three satellites would be sufficient to provide world coverage, with each satellite acting as a line-of-sight relay for communications. The link has to be line-of-sight because satellites use microwaves. Astonishingly, Clarke never patented his idea because he thought it would never be achievable in his lifetime, as he commented in an interview: 'It is with somewhat mixed feelings that I can claim to have originated one of the most commercially viable ideas of the twentieth century, and to have sold it for just $40' (PBS 2000).

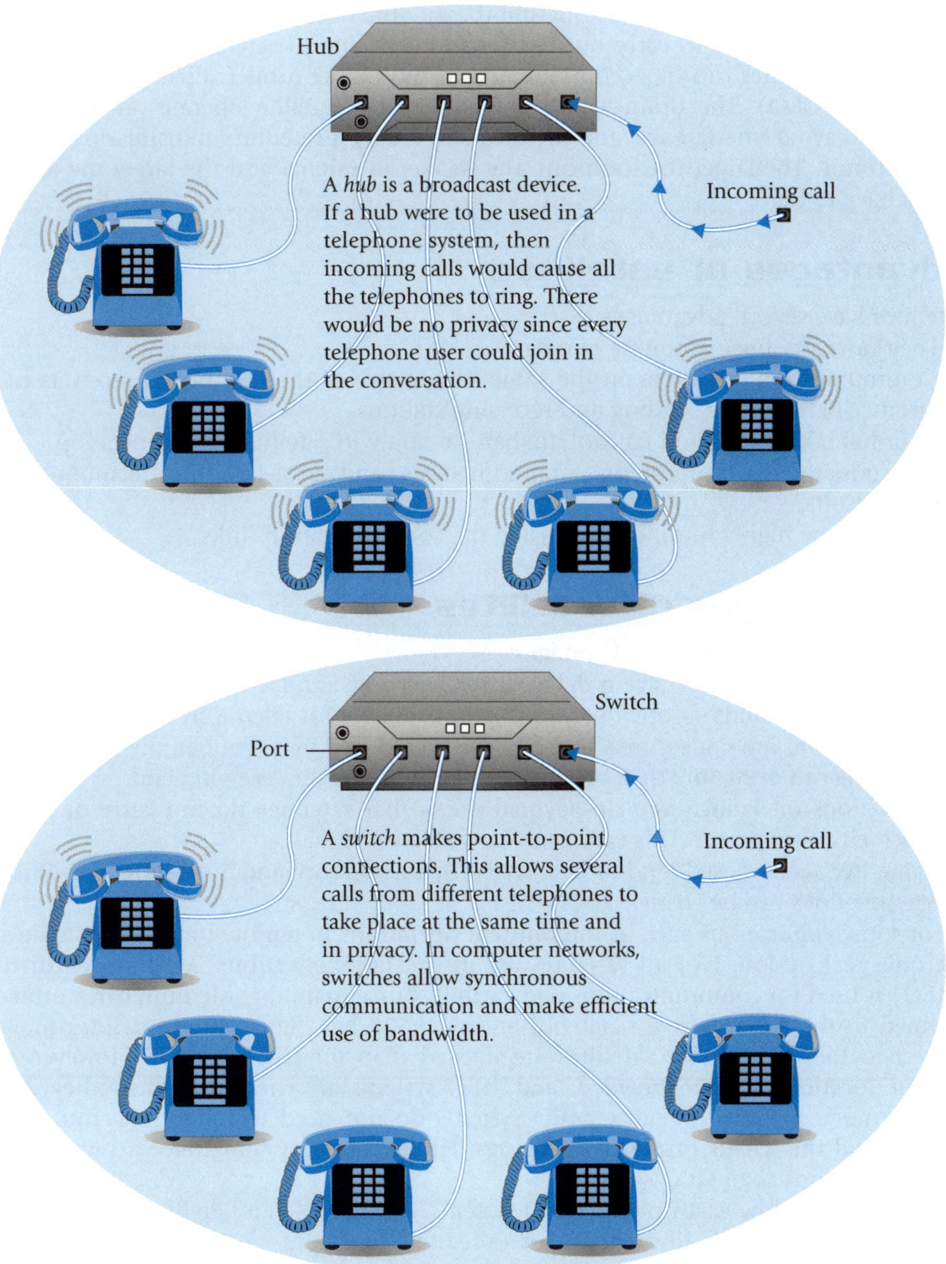

Figure 5.4 The difference between a hub and a switch

The 'Clarke' orbit is at a distance of 35 680 km above the equator, and here a satellite tends to maintain the same position relative to the Earth. (Some variations in orbit occur since the Earth is not perfectly spherical; accordingly, satellites burn fuel to maintain their position. Eventually the fuel runs out and the satellite's orbit decays, hence the interest in using the space shuttle to carry out repairs and servicing to satellites in orbit.) Approximately 150 satellites can be accommodated in the Clarke orbit (called **geosynchronous earth orbit, GEO**). The uplinks and downlinks of a satellite operate on different frequencies to avoid interference, and the area covered by a satellite's transmissions is called the 'footprint'. The larger the footprint, the weaker the signal and the larger the receiving dishes have to be.

Advantages of satellites

Satellites have several advantages:

- They can carry huge amounts of data.
- Communication costs remain the same irrespective of the number of receivers or the distance between the sending and receiving stations.
- National boundaries and control are hard to apply to satellite communication.
- Transmission errors occur on a random basis, and error-handling techniques yield good results.
- Users can be highly mobile while using the communication links.

Disadvantages of satellites

Satellites also have several disadvantages:

- A one-way circuit may have a delay of 0.25 seconds, and a two-way link may have a delay of 0.5 seconds — obviously, this is not suitable for telephony.
- Transmissions are not secure since they can be received by anyone in the footprint area. Encoding can overcome this, but it adds to the cost at the receiving end.
- Restrictions on launch vehicle payload mean that satellites do not carry or generate much electrical power. This can result in weakened signals.
- Some frequencies used tend to be affected by interference and atmospheric conditions.
- Satellite links can be costly.

For some applications such as intermittent operations in remote locations, satellites are the only real option. Not all satellites are in geostationary orbits. **Medium earth orbit (MEO)** is used for communications and earth resource mapping. Medium earth orbits are inclined to the equator at a height of around 9600 km. Since these satellites move in respect to the Earth, more satellites are needed than for GEO systems. However, GEO satellite locations are overcrowded, and MEO systems are cheaper because they do not cost so much to put into orbit. MEO systems do not need to be as powerful as GEO systems and this yields further cost savings. Finally, MEO systems have a much smaller signal delay time than GEO systems.

There are also **low earth orbit (LEO)** systems, positioned at a height of 640–1600 km. Launch costs are much lower than for other satellite types, and because the distances involved are much less, both satellites and users can handle less powerful signals. Many more satellites are needed to provide coverage, since the satellites frequently change their position relative to Earth. LEO satellites were the underlying technology of the Iridium project (a system that originally proposed 77 satellites and for that reason was named 'Iridium' after the element with the atomic number 77). The underlying idea was simple

— take the concepts of a mobile phone and put the base stations into orbit. This would give a worldwide mobile network for voice and data communication. (The quoted coverage of current mobile phone networks tends to be based on percentage of population with access rather than geographic area in which the service is available.)

The Iridium concept was bold and total project costs were to be in excess of $US5 billion for hardware alone, but it was decided that the potential profits justified proceeding. However, the project was not a commercial success and Iridium became bankrupt in 2000. Other LEO systems (e.g. Globalstar) are still in use.

Infobyte

Securing the ubiquitous PDA

With the advent of wireless networking the humble PDA looks set to become the device of choice for controlling household systems and multimedia devices. It also seems likely that the PDA will take on mobile phone functions via cheap wireless headsets. Since PDAs store a lot of personal data they pose a significant security threat. How can you be certain that nobody else can use your PDA? Passwords alone might not be enough to guarantee protection. Some PDAs already require thumbprint identification, and stronger security measures are on the way. Locating technology will allow a stolen PDA to be traced and disabled. Once again, technology convergence is a major driver of development.

The Internet

The Internet is a network of networks, each network having its own acceptable use policies. Nobody owns the Internet, and it exists in many different countries. The term 'Internet' is not to be confused with the World Wide Web (the Web, or WWW); the Internet (or Net) is the hardware and the Web is the hypertext environment that sits on top of the Net and makes it easy to use. (Hypertext was developed at CERN, the European Laboratory for Particle Physics, in the 1980s by Tim Berners-Lee, a physicist who wanted a more interactive database.)

The Internet has its origins with the US military. The need for reliable communications and networks that could still operate if they sustained heavy damage led to the development of the routing methods and addressing schemes which became TCP/IP (the world's most widely used network protocol). This resilience has been a double-edged sword as far as governments are concerned, because it is almost impossible to control the Internet and still maintain adequate performance. The Internet spans national boundaries and so the question arises as to which jurisdiction should apply. As hackers are wont to say: 'The Internet finds a way.'

[**Key concept:** The smaller you are, the more you will pay for Internet use.]

Reflection question 2: Is it possible to censor the Internet?

The combination of Internet and web technologies has allowed users to access Internet resources in a relatively friendly way. Graphical browsers such as Netscape mean a simple point-and-click style of operation. The downside of the Internet is that performance is variable since it depends on network loads. Additionally, security is a concern for many organisations. There is a huge amount of investment being put into re-engineering the Internet to deliver the performance people require. In the early days of public Internet access, little was needed other than simple text transfer. Currently, users expect interactive chat, graphic file transfers, Internet telephony and video-conferencing technologies. Much of the revenue needed to fund the technology comes from Internet advertising.

Security is another major issue. There is no intrinsic security on the Internet, so all that can be done is to take precautions at the sending and receiving ends. This might entail physical measures such as proxy servers (devices which hide internal network details from outsiders) and logical security measures such as passwords, authentication and encryption. Notwithstanding, provided proper care is taken, the Internet is more secure than the average automatic teller machine.

Earlier, a reference was made to the phenomenon of technology convergence. All networks simply move information from one place to another, so why does the technology have to be different? You may have used Internet telephony, a piece of software that allows your $3000 computer to emulate a $20 telephone handset. Currently the quality is not good, because the Internet's routing protocol introduces delays into the communication. However, the cost more than compensates for this; a local call to your Internet service provider costs a few cents and you can talk for as long as you wish. Compare that with charges of more than $1 per minute to countries such as Malaysia. It is much cheaper to send faxes via the Internet using secure technology, and many companies in the USA do this as a matter of routine. At the 1997 International Switching Symposium, World Telecommunications Congress, more than 2500 professionals were surveyed as to whether they thought that the telephone systems and the Internet would be separate technologies by 2010. The overwhelming response was 'no'. Also, when the infrastructure of the Internet is sufficiently good, video and music may be reticulated into the home. Here, again, the convergence of data communications and media technologies may be seen.

IS in action

Broadband bicycles

The Laotian village of Phon Kham endures a tropical monsoon climate that combines blistering temperatures and heavy rains. The village is located in a valley and has no telephones, electricity or running water. Its inhabitants are refugees from the Plain of Jars (named after the Bronze Age urns found there), which suffered saturation bombing during the Vietnam War averaging one plane load per minute. Lee Thorn used to load bombs on to US aeroplanes during the war and became a peace activist when his service ended. The villagers told Lee that they needed to communicate with the outside world, partly to ensure that they got the best price for their rice and handicrafts but also to keep in touch with family and friends. Lee was sympathetic and made contact with Lee Felenstein (designer of the world's first laptop). Between them they began to specify the system.

The computer had be very cheap since the average Laotian annual income is less than $A325. It also had to be easy to maintain, have low power consumption and be capable of withstanding the extremes of the Laotian climate. The most startling feature was that it should have no moving parts; traditional hard drives would be replaced by flash memory. A high-gain antenna would send signals using a WiFi connection to a solar-powered relay station on a local mountain. From there the signal would need to travel 11 km to Phon Hong where telephone and Internet access were available. The final computer was the equivalent of a 133 MHz 486 system (such a system would have been considered state of the art in about 1990 by Australian standards) and was capable of withstanding total immersion in water without damage. Bicycle power was chosen on cost and climate grounds. A simple car battery powers the entire system, and one minute of pedalling produces five minutes of air time. The lack of any commercial software in the Lao language meant that existing software had to be 'localised'. Anoussak Souphavan (an IBM employee) produced a Lao version of LINUX, which he called 'Laonux'.

The project overcame many technical problems and worked because it was driven by the end-users. Many projects intended to bridge the digital divide fail because they are driven from the top down by outsiders.

Although the use of the system was delayed by bureaucratic wrangling, the developers have had enquiries from 40 countries where power and communications infrastructures are not well developed.

Sources: information from www.cia.gov/cia/publications/factbook/geos/la.html#Geo (accessed 1 March 2004); www.jhai.org (accessed 1 March 2004).

Internet access

Within most sizeable businesses, the networking is high speed and high quality, but when it comes to home and small business users, high performance is often difficult and expensive to maintain. In Australia the main telecommunications provider has a virtual monopoly and hence has no vested interest in providing new services since there is no effective competition. Most Australian users have simple dial-up access and, owing to line quality and modem pooling (i.e. how Internet service providers (ISPs) share out the bandwidth) few if any are realising the 56 Kbps speeds that their PC modems can reach.

Broadband services require a special kind of modem and provide a higher-speed access (although usually much less than 0.5 Mbps). These are based around Digital Subscriber Loop (DSL) services, which have the advantage of not tying up phone lines for network access. In most DSL variants, including Asymmetric Digital Subscriber Loop (ADSL), data transmission uses different frequencies from those allocated to voice transmission (the 'Asymmetric' part of name comes from the fact that most people and businesses consume more information that they produce and hence do not need the up and down links to operate at the same capacity). ISDN is an older technology also offered, but both ISDN and ADSL are relatively expensive options when download limits and speeds are considered. In areas where cable TV systems are well developed it might be possible to get high-speed downloads via the TV cable; however, the uplink to the ISP must be made by telephone. One- and two-way satellite options are available, but these are also quite expensive. For many Australian businesses dial-up access and ISDN are the most cost-effective options since they are restricted to the telephone system for historical reasons.

It should be realised that the actual infrastructure of the Internet is relatively good; 'last mile' connections are where delays usually occur, most notably where the telephone infrastructure is obsolescent. Here, wireless DSL might provide an effective solution. As a final comment, note that good communications speeds are not synonymous with good Internet performance from a user point of view. Internet performance requires efficient domain name service (running at the local Internet service provider) and good subscriber-to-dial-up-connection ratios.

Reflection question 3: Given advances in Internet technology, do traditional telephone companies have a long-term future?

Intranets

The problems with the Internet from a corporate perspective are:

- lack of performance
- too much information to search through
- potential lack of security and an inability to restrict access
- an inability to impose control on content and presentation aspects.

If a company has its own privately owned and controlled internet, then these problems are not an issue. This is the guiding principle behind the development of intranets, which have user-friendly graphical browsers and make corporate information resources available to staff in a convenient manner. The return on investment (ROI) for intranets may be as high as 2000%. (According to Ian Campbell (2000) at International Data Corporation, which conducted an investment study of Netscape intranets, Cadence Design Systems Inc. in California achieved an ROI of 1766%, and Silicon Graphics Inc. achieved an ROI of 1427%.) Think about maintaining a web-based telephone directory for an organisation with 3000 staff and a high staff turnover — the listing would be up to date and available at all times, and would save on time and paper, compared with a hard copy. The range of services that may be accessed might include groupware, organisational charts, staff directories and corporate databases. Restricting access to specific groups is a simple matter of network management.

Extranets

Whereas intranets are for internal use and the Internet is for general use, extranets are somewhere between those two. Extranets are networks that form umbilical links between a company and its suppliers and/or customers. Extranets frequently (but not exclusively) make use of Internet technologies such as browsers. The connections between sites can be private or public — in the latter case, security and data encryption are very important.

While intranets shorten timelines and improve the delivery of information inside an organisation (and hence improve knowledge management), extranets do the same for suppliers and customers. Shortening timelines improves cash flow and enhances the competitive edge. (Just-in-time delivery systems were discussed earlier in this text and will be revisited when e-business is discussed.) There is an important psychological aspect about extranets — they make customers, clients and suppliers part of the enterprise. As mentioned in chapter 1, Harley-Davidson Motorcycles uses 'materials as needed' (MAN, not to be confused with metropolitan area network) in its factories, and its extranet allows parts and product information to be disseminated to its North American distributors and dealers. The dealerships are then able to give better service to their customers and reduce their investment in parts on hand. The benefits move up and down the supply chain.

Client–server issues

In client–server environments, client machines make requests for a service (e.g. printing, Internet access) and a dedicated device on the network responds to the requests. Most modern databases operate in this way.

[**Key concept:** In any system, try to allocate computer processing so as to minimise the load on critical central resources.]

Client–server architectures have been a major force in the development of both application software and local area networks over the last two decades. The distribution of processing between client and server is a major factor in design. Sometimes, the client merely provides an interface on to the server-based system, whereas in other approaches the client may carry out a substantial amount of processing (recall the mention of thin and fat clients in chapter 3). There are two things to note:

- Client–server architectures give a very clear division of responsibility between client and server. Placing critical data and applications on to dedicated servers means that they are easier to control and manage (duplicating corporate data and applications on every desktop would be a managerial and security nightmare). There is a third component in the client–server system — the network. Each component in the system may be developed and managed separately, thus allowing a clearer management focus.
- Client–server systems are network-intrinsic and their very nature places huge demands on the networks which support them. Client–server systems generate a lot of network traffic, i.e. they have been responsible for a rise in LAN numbers and are a driver in improving network performance.

Usually, servers are accessed via a LAN, but there is no reason they should not be remote. Client–server architectures may be simple two-tier systems or they may use other devices as intermediaries between the client and server (so-called N-tier client–server systems).

Often, when general-purpose (horizontal) software is being used at an installation, it is downloaded on to the client from the server each time it is required. This places a huge demand on the network, so why is it done in this way? First, software licences may allow a certain number of people to use the package at any one time, and since not every employee needs to use the package at the same time there is a potential cost-saving. Second, downloading the software each time overwrites any viruses that find their way into the system. Since files with an '.exe' suffix are prime targets for viruses, this may be an effective strategy. Of course, this is merely one facet of an entire set of security procedures that a company might adopt.

Network security

Although most 'hacking' originates from inside organisations, networks provide the main vector for computer viruses and denial of service attacks (DOS). Most people are familiar with computer viruses, but denial of service attacks might require some explanation. A DOS uses network and/or system commands in such a way as to interfere with systems performance or to cause a system to crash; the misuse of 'ping' would be a good example. In order for networks to function every connected device must have a unique address. From time to time we might need to 'ping' a device to see whether it is present on the network and to check the transmission times. The 'ping' command allows us to do so. The format of the command is 'ping' followed by the Internet protocol (IP) address of the device (e.g. ping 131.251.138.15). The pinged device *must* then reply to the 'ping' command. Hackers can obtain a valid IP address and use it as the source address of their 'ping' command; however, they send out many thousands of such commands to different addresses listing the target machine as the source address. When devices replay to the 'ping' they overwhelm the target machine.

Firewalls

Firewalls give limited protection against viruses and DOS attacks, but they do restrict unauthorised access. Firewalls can be dedicated hardware devices or might be implemented in software on a single PC. There are two main types of firewall: packet level and application.

Packet-level firewalls

A packet-level firewall inspects source and destination IP addresses of incoming and outgoing data packets. Only packets with acceptable addresses are allowed through. Obviously this does not prevent hackers obtaining the IP addresses of trusted business partners and using those to sneak their packets through the firewall. Because every packet entering or leaving the business must pass through the firewall, there is no time to inspect the contents since this would cause processing delays. Consequently another kind of firewall is needed.

Application-level firewalls

Whereas most organisations have only one packet-level firewall, they will have an application-level firewall for each mission-critical application. These firewalls carry out 'stateful inspection'; that is, they examine the contents of the data packets to make sure that their content is appropriate for the application they are guarding. Only 'good' packets are allowed through. The combined use of packet- and application-level firewalls reduces hacking but does not eliminate it, so specialist intruder detection systems (IDS) will still be needed. The effect of hacking on e-business will be covered in chapter 10.

IS in action

I spy with my little program

Many people browse the Internet at home or at work, blissfully unaware that their computer could be relaying every keystroke to a third party. This was the case with Peter, a graduate student in IS/IT. As he was accessing his bank account online, he noticed that his computer's performance was poor. The connection speed seemed fine, and he had no 'heavy' applications running. He decided to check his Internet settings and discovered that his DNS (domain name service) was being redirected to a computer that did not belong to his Internet service provider, so every time he needed to find a web site, his computer had to send a message to that computer and wait for a reply. Fearing that a hacker was trying to steal his bank account details, he broke the connection, reset his Internet options to what they should have been and closed down his computer. When he restarted the machine he found that his changes had been overwritten and that his DNS was again diverted to California. After six or seven hours trying to find out what was going on, he decided to back up all his data and reinstall the entire systems software. This at least fixed the problem but left the cause unanswered.

To prevent a recurrence Peter installed spyware detection and elimination software and a software firewall to protect his computer. This allowed him to monitor all incoming and outgoing traffic, and so he was able to see would-be hackers. After reconnecting to the Internet he was able to use his firewall software to track the hacker to a particular machine in California. He informed the authorities. Unfortunately the company behind the spyware could not be prosecuted because their activities of 'market research' had been ruled to be legal in the USA. Peter was furious. It did not seem fair that a foreign company could hack into his computer, see every key stroke that he made, reduce his Internet performance and put him to a lot of time, trouble and expense. His researches led to him to discover that as many as 55% of his friends' PCs had spyware hidden on them, most of those computers being in government and business — and these people were technically literate and very capable. The percentage of naive users running spyware is unknown but is presumed to be high. The most important thing he learned? Security begins at home.

[**Key concept:** Networked systems tend be a compromise between high security and high performance.]

Future developments

Currently, more than half the world's population has never even seen a telephone, let alone used a computer to access the Internet. These people are being asked to leapfrog several generations of technology and culture, and it must be acknowledged that this is a huge shock to the psyche. However, most people's view of the information systems world is very PC-oriented, and this influences the way they think. The basis of competition in the industry has been outlined in chapters 2 and 3, but there are two research directions that might change the PC emphasis. The first of these is wearable computing, with its emphasis on portability, and the second is wireless communication. Using a keyboard is a very slow and inefficient method of interacting with a computer. Voice recognition and speech processing systems offer a way to speed things up.

Steve Mann of Toronto University has a different vision. He has been involved in personal cybernetics and wearable computing since the 1970s. His inventions include WearComp (wearable computing with networking capability) and Eyetap, a technology that provides visual information fed to the human eye. Eyetap can be concealed in spectacles or in contact lenses. The eye operates as both camera and display, enabling people to link into information resources and to communicate with each other. A third invention of Mann's, which comprises a brainwave monitor as another input/output to the WearComp, gives rise to a 'telepathic' experience. As mentioned in chapter 1, Professor Kevin Warwick of Reading University has implanted microprocessors into his own body to communicate with computers (Warwick 2003) and more recently with similar devices implanted in his wife. In all of this, it is mobile communications that is the prime driver.

In this sort of environment, the humble PC will disappear and much of the software that people take for granted will go with it. After all, why would you bother to send a memo when you can send a swift videogram? Everything you want to access by way of music, information and video will be available. Given that writing evolved as a way of making information more permanent and widely available, what impact will all this have on literacy? What will be the effect on business? The wireless technologies that enable mobile commerce will see the PDA or mobile phone become the nexus point at which conventional retail and e-commerce meet.

Infobyte

Cable TV revisited

Whereas most people see ultra-wideband (UWB) communications as replacing older cable systems, Pulse-Link Inc. see UWB as a means of increasing the capacity of older cable TV networks. The underlying concept is simple: inject low-power UWB signals into digital and analog cable TV systems. These signals will coexist with existing TV signals and (since the amplifiers have to cope with a broad range of spectrum) are able to travel over the entire network. The attraction is that retrofitting high-speed Internet and high-definition TV technology to older cable networks will be a relatively cheap option. Tests have shown that downstream speeds of 1.2 Gbps with upstream speeds of 120 Mbps are feasible, opening up a new range of applications.

Source: www.pulse-link.com (accessed 1 March 2004).

IS in action

Broadband helping to make government smaller

As a result of a policy of cost-cutting, government in British Columbia has downsized extensively over the past few years. While outsourcing has accounted for much of this, the use of communications technology has enabled many mail and 'over the counter' services to be put online. However, from a customer point of view there are two difficulties. The first is simply that of access. Many British Columbians do not have Internet access. The second has to do with the quality of access. In order to achieve a satisfactory level of service, customers need to have broadband access to government systems.

In 2003 it was announced that the British Columbian government would be outsourcing its largest ever contract to bridge the 'digital divide'. The scope of the project is the provision of broadband access for every British Columbian community. The project is being handled by the AGTI consulting group. (The name is an acronym of 'A Group of Terrific Individuals'.) Although British Columbia is the third-largest province in Canada, its population is spread throughout cities and huge expanses of countryside.

Generally speaking, when one thinks of large third-party networks the telephone companies spring to mind. However, it should be realised that their networks evolved to support the needs of voice traffic and so tend to have restricted bandwidth (carrying capacity) in comparison to more modern data and media networks. Even when broadband access is available, the speeds provided are far from fast and the distances over which the service is available are restricted. Figures for the USA show that the telephone companies are meeting less than a third of the demand for broadband and are using obsolescent DSL technology to do so. The bulk of the remaining market share is being met by independent wireless DSL providers, cable TV companies and even power companies. It is estimated that broadband should reach 40% of American homes by 2006. Estimates for Canada are more difficult to obtain but should closely parallel the US figures.

In the population centres of British Columbia, the cable TV networks are well established and hence well positioned to provide high-speed Internet access. For the telephone companies this represents a fundamental change in business, and it requires a substantial investment to provide high-speed services to the majority of existing customers. So no single technical solution is possible. Citizens with broadband access will continue to receive a better level of service than rural people with dial-up access, and it seems likely that this state of affairs will continue for some years to come.

Discussion

Early in this chapter, hardwire and softwire systems were discussed. There is much talk in the business community about which will come to predominate. Mobile phones are commonplace now and Internet technologies are finding their way into many handheld devices. The technology for portable DVD players using special headsets that give the perspective of large-screen TV is already available. Information-carrying capacity (bandwidth) is not a problem, but cost is the current deterrent. Most IS professionals hold the view that hardwire technology will persist for long-haul communications and most LAN applications for the next 10–15 years, whereas softwire (mobile) communications will predominate at the personal level.

The direct impact of Internet technologies on business is substantial, and there are few businesses whose style of operation will not be changed to a great extent. The implications of this are rather more subtle. In the past, businesses used proprietary technologies to manage internal affairs. Very few businesses actually used those technologies to communicate with the world at large. Now the situation is different — businesses are still maintaining those older legacy systems but, increasingly, access to them and other corporate resources is tending to be web-based, i.e. the systems and/or access to them is more distributed than in previous times. In short, the fundamental nature of corporate information systems has undergone an irrevocable paradigm shift. The technology used inside the organisation is virtually the same as that used between the organisation and its clients/customers and the market at large. The difficulty MIS managers face is where to put the boundaries between internal and external systems. It is quite clear that people will not be able to think about corporate information systems in quite the same way again.

Summary

Networking has transformed the way many companies do business. It has enabled small business to operate globally and made it possible for companies to form strategic alliances and partnerships in their supply chain and customer relationship management. Communications have changed the cost balance of technology and so offer ways to save money (thin clients would be an obvious example). Mobile communications are in the ascendancy, and it seems likely that many people will access network services in this way. Larger networks such as those that form the Internet are most likely to remain with hardwire communications, simply because they can carry much more data at much higher speeds. If networking allows us to do these things, it does so at a price because allowing outsiders to access our systems via a network can pose significant security risks from computer viruses and other hacking. Firewalls can improve network and system security, but they add to the cost and complexity of network management.

The key points of this chapter are:

1. Networks are the 'glue' that holds our systems together, and economics favour networked rather than centralised systems. Although mainframe computing will be the only option for some organisations, that market is contracting and consolidating. Physically distributing the components of a system also helps to improve its resilience to failure.

2. The number of networked applications continues to increase, but networks themselves are converging. Historically we had data, telephone and media networks. Increasingly we find networks that are able to handle any kind of traffic.
3. Business and domestic users are demanding high-speed synchronous applications, such as video-conferencing. Many existing networks will have to be replaced or upgraded to meet this demand.
4. As with other hardware and software, adherence to internationally recognised standards is important — strategically, tactically and financially. The fewer standards we can use in an organisation, the easier management will be.
5. Hardwire systems will continue to be important in larger networks, but over the next three to five years, personal network access is most likely to be softwire or wireless.
6. Information systems security is always important but it is even more so in a networked environment. Firewalls can go some way towards protecting important applications and data resources, but there is a trade-off. Secure systems tend to be slow, fast systems tend to be insecure. It is important to establish a level of security that is commensurate with risk.

Questions

1. Give two examples of synchronous and asynchronous applications.
2. Over the next ten years, which do you think will predominate and why: hardwire or softwire systems?
3. In a LAN setting, which is more important: network performance or adhering to internationally recognised standards?
4. Use the Internet to research affordable video-conferencing and Internet telephony. How good are those technologies? How successful are those products likely to be over the next five years or so, and why?
5. Why is satellite communication best used for media and data communication purposes rather than telephony and video-conferencing?
6. Will optic fibre render satellite communications obsolete? Explain why or why not.
7. What advantages do optic fibres have compared with other forms of hardwire media?
8. Technology convergence is a major feature of networking. Use the Internet to research fast circuit switching. Which does it resemble more: packet switching or conventional circuit switching?
9. Digital TV offers (potentially) many more channels than analog systems. Is this a good or bad thing for (a) the consumer and (b) business?
10. Assume that national networking infrastructure is sufficiently advanced to allow a referendum to be held on contentious issues currently before government. Voting on these issues will be handled (securely) via the Internet. Will this lead to a fairer, more democratic society? Could the size and role of government be reduced?
11. Why are many telephone companies falling behind in the race to provide customers with high-speed Internet access and communications?
12. Is it possible to make a networked system too secure? Explain why or why not.

Exercises

1. Suppose that you have been retained to advise a business on how to choose an Internet service provider. What basic criteria would you suggest?

2. The advances in digital TV are allowing for a greater degree of interactivity with consumers. Access to media services are faster than ever before and include Internet access and online ordering of goods. Form a discussion group and consider the following questions:
   (a) Why would companies prefer this mode of operation rather than Internet-based e-commerce?
   (b) Would such a scenario mean the end of e-commerce? How could e-commerce companies react to prevent this?
   (c) Is it likely that media networks will replace the Internet in a domestic situation?
3. Form a small group and discuss the following. The original design concept of the telephone was to relay concerts into the home — almost the equivalent of radio broadcasts. Assume that the quality of telephone cabling is good enough to provide multiple audio entertainment channels and voice communication and the Internet uses the AM/FM radio bands. How would the operation of business and entertainment differ from current practice? Would the two systems remain separate?

CASE STUDY Magic Box

Magic Box is a Perth-based multimedia company. The founders, Mike, Sue, Amy and Brian, graduated with majors in multimedia and e-commerce and, frustrated with the local jobs market, decided to start their own company. In addition to themselves, in their first two years of operation they employed three other people for secretarial and technical support. Since then the business has grown to employ twenty-two people, seventeen of whom are actively engaged in multimedia development. The nature of their business is simple: they create web pages and interactive web sites for West Australian businesses, and they are currently thinking of expanding into interstate and overseas markets. Their business is healthy.

Currently every developer has a high-end PC for development work. The founders also have high-end laptops, which they use when travelling or presenting to existing and potential clients. There are two other laptops available to other staff according to need. Portable data projectors are used for presentations and company meetings.

Magic Box makes extensive use of Internet resources and, owing to its location, is forced to use three ISDN lines. Broadband is not available. Networking is handled via a switch and CAT5 cabling, which was installed two years ago. The networking solution is switched Ethernet. There are two servers; one for development work and the other for email and web access. The desktop machines are two years old and due for replacement. Both servers have been replaced recently and have plenty of spare capacity. The laptops are less than a year old, since they can be issued to company directors under favourable tax provisions.

Being located in the outer suburbs has kept rent and rates low, but a recent analysis has shown that it would be more cost-effective to move closer to their main client market and try to get closer to the city centre. An entire floor of an office building in an inner-city location has become available. Currently there is no cabling or Internet access and the lease is short term, but Mike does not see these matters as problems. 'If things are OK we can negotiate an extension. If things are really good we will need somewhere larger. If things are bad then we move back to the sticks.'

Sue engaged a network consultant to design a network for the new premises. He recommends using a new high-speed communications company called Bright, which is a subsidiary of the local power company. Bright has been operating for a few years and has a reasonable client base, but the company is in start-up phase and currently operates in only a few suburbs. The rationale here is that Bright can provide 100 Mbps speeds, which is far faster than the telephone company can supply. The cost of the service is marginally higher. The contract with the existing Internet service provider will remain in place. Nobody has a problem agreeing with this. The consultant's report then offers four basic options:

Option 1: Retain the existing servers and replace the client machines with ordinary, high-end PCs. This option requires that the building be fully cabled and a new switch be installed.

Option 2: Replace the servers with higher-specification machines, and replace the client machines with thin clients. This option also requires that the building be fully cabled and a new switch be installed.

Option 3: Retain the existing servers and replace the client machines with ordinary, high-end PCs. Instead of using a hardwire solution, it is proposed to use IEEE802.11g to create a WiFi network.

Option 4: Replace the servers with higher-specification machines, and replace the client machines with thin clients. Again it is proposed to use IEEE802.11g to create a WiFi network.

Here, everyone has an opinion. Mike is in favour of option 1 since it closely mirrors the current situation and he knows that it works reasonably well. Brian understands the cost benefits that thin clients can bring but is worried about the performance aspects. Can thin clients really deliver the performance needed? He is also worried about what happens if the network goes down, because then nothing will work, whereas at least fat clients can be operated in stand-alone mode.

Sue and Amy find the wireless options very attractive. To be able to move around the building and yet be able to communicate with the network is an advantage that they appreciate. Sue has heard that wireless networks are easier and therefore cheaper to manage. Adding new machines and relocating equipment is also simpler.

There is no consensus of opinion, and nobody wishes to push it to a vote or make a decision. After all, there is a stigma attached to making the wrong decision. In terms of cost there is not enough difference to choose between the four options. Thin clients are definitely cheaper to install and manage, but there are concerns about performance and reliability. Wireless options are a little more expensive to set up but are cheaper to manage.

Mike looks around the table at his colleagues. 'What we have here is paralysis by analysis ... How do we move on from here?'

(*continued*)

QUESTIONS

1. What are the likely consequences of making a bad choice?
2. How should Magic Box proceed from this point? You will need to think politically and operationally.
3. What other information would you need to make a decision?
4. Which option would you recommend and why?
5. Would your recommendation be different if the lease were longer term?
6. Do you think that the consultant is right to recommend using Bright as a communication provider? What are the risks?

References

Casson, Herbert N. 1910, *The History of the Telephone*, McClurg & Co., Chicago.

Cherry, S.M. 2003, 'The wireless last mile', *IEEE Spectrum*, September 2003, pp. 18–22.

Fitzgerald, J. & Dennis, A. 2002, *Data Communications and Networking*, 7th edn, John Wiley & Sons, Hoboken, NJ.

Premier's Technology Council 2003, 3rd Report, 23 September 2003, www.gov.bc.ca/bcgov/content/docs/the_ptc_report_q3.pdf (accessed 21 November 2003).

Warwick, K. 2003. 'The potential for implant technology', *Proc. European Journal on Engineering in Information Systems Applications* (EJEISA), vol. 5, no. 1, pp. 1–7.

Chapter 6

Systems integration: information systems at work

LEARNING OBJECTIVES

After reading this chapter, you should be able to:

- understand the relative merits of centralised and distributed IS organisation
- understand what is meant by operating as an unallocated cost centre, an allocated cost centre and a profit centre, and the advantages and disadvantage of each approach
- explain the various job types that are available in the IS industry, what they entail and what abilities they require
- understand what outsourcing is and what may be outsourced, and the considerations that must be taken into account before outsourcing
- understand the need for systems integration and the various strategies for achieving this
- understand what is meant by enterprise resource planning systems, the advantages that they confer and their applications
- understand what is meant by application service provider (ASP) and how small–medium enterprises may take advantage of ASP services for systems integration.

6

Introduction

This chapter focuses on two broad aspects: (1) the organisational aspects of IS, including the staffing function, and (2) systems integration. Hardware, software, communications and different kinds of business information systems have been considered in previous chapters. Now we need to look at how all these interact in a commercial context. Organisations are seldom, if ever, in the position of having a 'clean slate' when devising systems solutions. In the case of a small business, it is sometimes more cost-effective to start from scratch. But in most medium and large enterprises, there are systems that have been developed without reference to each other which are crucial to the operation of the business. A classic example is a company which has several different PC networks and which runs a mainframe for much of its transaction processing. The development effort for the mainframe systems is measured in hundreds of people-years, and since those systems still meet the requirements, they will not be replaced in the near future. Such systems are termed 'legacy systems'. The challenge is making the different systems in a business become a well-integrated, cohesive system that is convenient to use. Success often depends on appropriate organisational structures.

Information systems management — centralised or distributed?

In general, management consists of five basic functions: planning, organising, directing, controlling and staffing. For the purposes of this chapter, only organising and staffing are covered.

There are three terms that are frequently confused: IS infrastructure, IS architecture and IS organisation. *IS infrastructure* is all the hardware, software, systems and people of the IS division. Infrastructure is about providing an IS environment within which corporate systems can operate. Infrastructure-based approaches are usually geared to maintaining the status quo and often lack detailed focus. *IS architecture* is a framework or plan which shapes the hardware aspects (including future trends) of corporate systems. *IS organisation* defines reporting responsibilities of staff, organisational structure, mode of financial operation and managerial responsibilities of staff.

Centralised information systems organisation

Many of the arguments that suggest that databases are better than a collection of independent file systems can be used to justify the centralised model. Centralising resources eliminates duplication and achieves economies of scale. Less expenditure on hardware, software and personnel is needed. These advantages are not limited to IS; human resource management, purchasing, legal and other areas can all be centralised. Certainly, in a centralised environment it is easier to maintain control over processes, people and systems. However, the downside of this approach is twofold. First, unless business processes are highly streamlined, the IS division can take too long to respond to the needs of its clients; most organisations respond to this problem by making sure that the public face of IS (the help desk) has a very visible presence and a fast response time. Second, there is the risk of costs rising since IS personnel are too far removed from the business processes. Much depends, of course, on the size of the organisation, and in smaller businesses the IS division *has* to be centralised because it is so small. Usually, in the centralised approach, a single person, the **chief information officer (CIO)** has responsibility for the entire IS function. This arrangement is shown in figure 6.1.

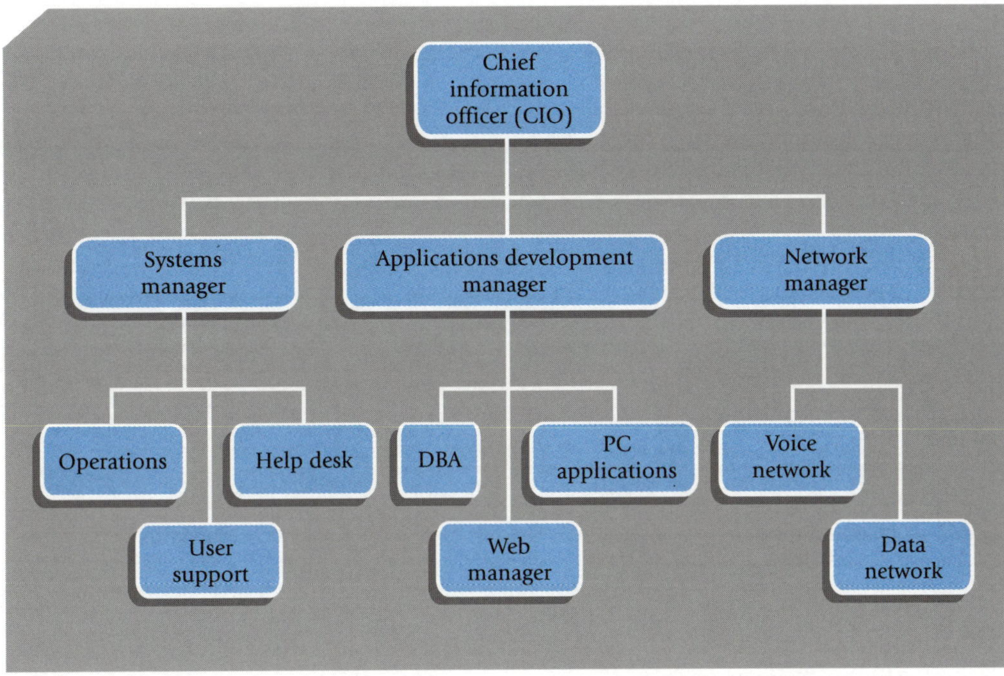

Figure 6.1 Centralised IS organisation

Distributed information systems organisation

This view is perhaps best regarded as a set of centralised IS divisions within an umbrella management structure as shown in figure 6.2. Here, the mini-IS divisions are contained within separate business units. Now there are **divisional information officers (DIOs)** who report to their divisional managers, but they may also report to the corporate CIO (if the CIO role remains, then that person is usually equal in status to a divisional manager).

Devolving responsibility down to divisional level allows divisions to select the most appropriate solution to their systems problems based on local knowledge and experience. Since the locus of control is much closer to the client, responses should be quicker. Divisions have their own hardware, software and staff.

Most DIOs are concerned with vertical systems (not company-wide systems but systems specialised to the needs of the division). Accordingly, the corporate CIO still maintains responsibility for the development and management of systems which span business units. The disadvantage of this is that there may be substantial duplication of resources. Equally, there may be a greater capacity to meet the systems needs of the divisions, and this in turn may confer a business advantage that outweighs the cost of duplicated resources. Additionally, the reporting structure tends to produce a matrix-like model.

In organisations that have distributed their IS division, there is a tendency to duplicate hardware, software and personnel. For example, one organisation had fifteen separate web servers when only five (plus a back-up) were needed. The excessive hardware and management costs were reduced following rationalisation. Additionally, the organisation employed several web developers of whom four were underworked. Another problem with the distributed approach is the potential loss of tacit knowledge transfer between IS staff as staff in the core IS division are reduced.

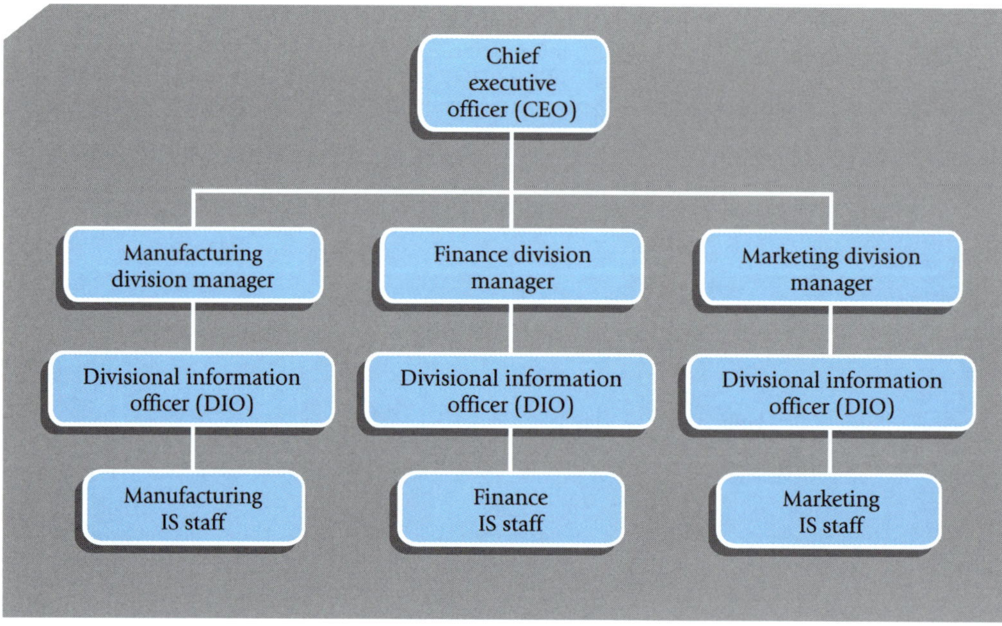

Figure 6.2 The distributed IS function

Hybrid information systems organisation

Many businesses opt for a mixed structure in which systems development is devolved to the divisions, but all live systems are managed centrally. This reduces unnecessary duplication of resources but still permits a high degree of autonomy within divisions. As with the distributed approach, managers have to ensure that IS staff maintain skills and that each division is aware of systems under development by the other divisions.

Funding the information systems function

There are three basic approaches to funding the IS function. The IS division may operate as an unallocated cost centre, an allocated cost centre or a profit centre. Each of these approaches is examined below.

Unallocated cost centre

In the **unallocated cost centre** model, the IS manager receives a one-line budget to cover expenditure for the whole year. This sum is usually taken off the top of everyone else's budget prior to allocation. In short, IS is considered to be an organisational cost. If the IS division is providing services to several large divisions, there is bound to be conflict between those various departments regarding what IS services and innovations are required. So budget allocation can be politically difficult if there are many competing requests. The IS manager has to be tactful and professional in order to make this work well. Requests from users/clients need to be supported by cost–benefit analysis. This means talking to internal clients at length about needs and plans. From the perspective of other division managers, there is a loss of control and status that follows the flow of funds from their budget to the IS budget. If accounting controls are not rigorous, IS costs can escalate.

Allocated cost centre

Operating as an **allocated cost centre** within the company means that costs are allocated for services to internal clients. Although no money will leave the company, there is still the added complexity of internal accounting and budget transfers. However, this has some advantages. First, it may eliminate any cross-subsidy from one division to another. Second, it makes for a more responsive relationship between the IS division and the internal clients. Third, the accounting information is very useful for planning purposes since it reveals patterns of use and growth that enable the IS division to meet the future needs of the organisation. This prevents the demand for information systems services exceeding the capacity to meet them. Usually load thresholds are set — besides the disaster threshold (the point at which the business fails), there is the pain threshold (the point at which the business begins to suffer). Most responsible IS managers raise an alert when the load comes within 20% (or some other arbitrary value) of the pain threshold. This gives the IS division some time to respond to the problem and develop avoidance strategies.

[**Key concept:** Anticipate clients' needs. Ideally, the only time a client should know that there is a problem is after it has been fixed.]

Profit centre

In the **profit centre** model of operation there is no distinction between internal and external clients, and the IS division competes for both kinds of client. This allows users to choose who will carry out the IS function on their behalf, and there is a chance that the work will go outside the company. The IS division is in direct competition with external companies and so is motivated to be as efficient as possible, but there is still a risk of the operation being outsourced. Perhaps most significant of all, costs to other divisions are likely to rise. Divisions which operate as profit centres tend not to carry out developmental and experimental work since this has to be done on a cost recovery + profit basis.

Some information systems job descriptions

All IS staff need to have good problem-solving and communication skills, and need to be flexible and adaptable and able to work on several things at the same time. Creativity and attention to detail are important. Depending on their level within an organisation or project, IS staff may also require organisational and managerial skills. Curiously, some employers seem to put hard technical skills a little lower on their shopping list. A graduate looking to find a first position in the IS industry should have the following skills:

- a working knowledge of basic business disciplines and processes
- basic computer literacy
- the ability to identify information requirements
- the ability to outline design requirements and/or specify system requirements
- the ability to program in third- or fourth-generation software product
- experience in using a software development tool.

Business knowledge is at the top of the list because information systems exist to support business. If you understand what the business does, it is much easier to build a system to help the business to do it. If not, you are at a disadvantage. However, if you are lacking in some of the other skills in the list, do not despair — in the authors' experience more than a third of IS professionals did not have an IS background before they entered the profession. There are examples of biology, philosophy, liberal arts, history and literature graduates who have made the transition into IS and done very well. The demand for IS professionals exceeds the supply that universities are able to produce. Most employers accept that they will have to train graduates before they become profitable.

Reflection question 1: Is a background in mathematics and logic an asset in the information systems industry?

As with much else in the IS industry, job titles, descriptions and terminology vary greatly from organisation to organisation. In the following sections the most common terms are used.

Chief information officer

The position of CIO is synonymous with director of IS, director of MIS, manager of IS services and so on. Essentially, this person is responsible for all information activities and resources and reports to the most senior levels of management. It is important that the position has sufficient status within the organisation since much effort is devoted to organisational politics. Besides leadership, planning and organisational skills, the CIO requires good people skills, since the job requires negotiation with staff and motivating them to achieve goals. CIOs also spend a substantial amount of time educating management about IS and MIS from a strategic perspective. Basic financial skills are also needed, since part of the brief is to secure all the resources required for the IS division.

In companies which are too small to support a full-time CIO, the role is often given to the head of accounting or finance, because cash flows and information flows often coincide.

In some larger organisations, the CIO role may be augmented by separate DIOs (divisional information officers) for each business function, as shown in the distributed IS organisation in figure 6.2.

In the past, cynical IS people would say that CIO stood for 'career is over'. The thinking behind this was the CIO was as far up the hierarchy as an IS professional could rise without a business/management qualification. This has been seen in other disciplines and it explains the popularity of MBA courses. More recently, information has come to be regarded as a strategic resource and CIOs are now being promoted to the highest levels in the organisation. Other authors also tend to this view (Kerrigan 2002).

Systems manager/operations manager

The **systems manager/operations manager** is responsible for the entire day-to-day running of the IS division from an operational perspective, overseeing technical staff who maintain and upgrade hardware and software. All operational policies and procedures fall within this area. Service-level agreements, maintenance and back-up schedules are all carried out here. Monitoring the systems and gathering information for planning and security purposes is also a major responsibility. Budgeting and acquisition may form part of the portfolio. Depending on the organisational structure, the help desk and user-support functions are frequently located within the systems manager's responsibility.

■ **Reflection question 2:** Help desk functions should be centralised for planning and control purposes. But they also should be distributed so that users receive prompt assistance from a familiar and friendly person. What are the relative merits of each approach?

Database administrator

Very few companies have separate data and database administrators, preferring the single viewpoint that a combination of these positions gives. Thus the **database administrator (DBA)** operates from an enterprise-wide perspective, establishing data requirements for projects and applications. Additionally, the DBA refers to company policies and establishes all necessary data access and security policies and translates business rule into data integrity constraints (e.g. 'a client may not have more than $30 000 credit' is a business rule that is enforced via the database). Database design, data organisation and maintaining the data dictionary are all within the DBA role. More specifically, the DBA performs database back-ups and disaster recoveries and ensures that the database delivers the required level of performance to users.

Network administrator/manager

The **network administrator/manager** is responsible for all corporate network LANs and WANs; increasingly, this includes voice networks. The role usually entails planning and staffing for network function. Network administrators are also responsible for the day-to-day running of the networks and operational management. As noted in chapter 5, corporate communications are vital and, accordingly, network administrators are better paid than most other technical managers. This role requires a strong technical emphasis and most network administrators have technical qualifications only.

■ **Reflection question 3:** If there is a single corporate LAN which handles voice and data communications, which does it most resemble, a data network or a telephone network? Why?

Solutions architect

When organisations use systems that have enterprise-wide significance, reconciling the needs of different stakeholder groups and applications is an essential role. A **solutions architect** usually has a technical background with good business knowledge and excellent communication skills. Much of this job is about eliciting information and knowledge requirements throughout the organisation, consolidating and rationalising those needs and then providing infrastructure-based solutions. Solutions architects are especially useful in enterprise resource planning (ERP) settings. The job title is relatively new and is something of a superset of software engineering and business analysis.

Project architect/applications development manager

In larger organisations, there is the potential for several departments to develop similar software packages leading to duplication and waste of resources. The **project architect/ applications development manager** monitors and helps coordinate all software development activity. As seen in earlier chapters, it is important to reduce diversity and complexity, and this usually entails strict adherence to hardware and software standards. The project architect is involved in the definition and enforcement of these standards. In centralised IS organisation, this role is frequently subsumed under the CIO role. However, in distributed IS organisation, the project architect position is particularly important. Leadership, organisational ability, communication skills and people skills are very important in this role. Typically, project architects have experience as analysts and programmers but this is not always the case.

Many systems have the potential to cost vast sums if they malfunction. It is cost-effective in such situations to use rigorous design and specification methods and strict quality control and testing. It is important to design systems with testing in mind. Testing may be carried out by the project team (benevolent testing) or by people from outside the team (adversarial testing). In larger organisations the project architect is responsible for developing and implementing quality procedures. In smaller organisations, testing is often the duty of systems analysts and programmers.

Project manager

A **project manager** is usually assigned to a particular project for its duration. The goal is to deliver systems that meet user requirements and corporate standards on schedule and within budget. Since much of the work involves supervising technical work, the project manager often has a technical background. Much of the rest of the work involves human resource management, and so managerial skills are also valued. Sometimes, the project manager may provide business expertise in a particular area (domain specialist), in which case the reporting structure expands and the project manager may report to, or liaise with, a technical manager. Although most project managers are appointed for the duration of the project only, some are regarded as permanent management positions.

Web manager/administrator

Web-based technologies are used to facilitate systems integration, provide uniform interfaces for corporate information and so on. It is often the case that a company's intranet resources are overseen by a **web manager/administrator**. This person has responsibility for the development, delivery and integration of all web resources, and works with the DBA and network administrator to ensure that systems are safe and secure. The web manager usually has a background in web development.

Systems analyst/business analyst

The **systems analyst/business analyst** role is frequently the graduate entry position into the IS industry. The systems analyst is involved with every aspect of the system development life cycle with the exception of programming. The definition of requirements and design/specification of the system are where most of the effort is expended. The whole system life cycle revolves around the analyst who acts as a liaison point between technical staff and business clients, translating business requirements into system requirements. Business skills are usually crucial to this role.

The analyst requires excellent communication and presentation skills, organisational ability, and an understanding of the programming process.

Although the analyst is distanced from the technology, increasingly companies look for analysts who have experience in using computer-aided software engineering (CASE) software. There is a tendency to call any analyst with CASE experience a software engineer, but software engineers are much closer to the actual process and often perform detailed design work and develop and test codes. Software engineers generally do not have business expertise. It is the authors' experience that analysts are involved in the system requirements definition whereas software engineers are not. Most companies will train their analysts in the use of CASE tools, but do not necessarily train software engineers in business.

Programmer

As the job title implies, a **programmer** produces software. However, the definition of software is now far broader than it used to be and most businesses include web development (with the exception of specialist graphic design), customisation of packaged software, fourth-generation products and high-level code as part of the programmer's portfolio. The role is often combined as programmer/analyst.

Programmers do not need to have a business education, although it may restrict their progress at a later date.

Most employers expect an applicant for a programming position to have two to four years of tertiary education and the ability to program in at least one language or product. Industry-based qualifications and certificated courses are very well regarded by employers.

Within the programmer role there is the position of specialist or **virtuoso programmer**. This person specialises in certain problematic areas of coding. For example, a virtuoso programmer might rewrite parts of systems software in order to improve performance of an application, or write code which integrates one application with another. Virtuoso programmers produce very efficient code and their background is steeped in technology.

Chief technology officer

Many organisations do not have a **chief technology officer (CTO)**, so the role is taken on by the CIO. Larger organisations often find it useful to have a person in this position. The CTO is responsible for keeping abreast of technology and the market, briefing other staff on his or her findings and outlining plans whereby the business could take advantage of the new technology within its existing IS framework in a cost-effective manner.

Some businesses prefer to distribute the role over a number of industry specialists, such as network administrator and database administrator. These people meet at intervals to brief one another on their own area and combine their views. The existing IS plan can then be reviewed in the light of their findings. In many ways, this has advantages over a single CTO since individual excesses tend to be moderated by the group. It also makes people more aware of what their colleagues actually do, and hence helps divisional activities to be more concerted.

Training officer

The training needs of IS professionals are sufficiently different from those in other business areas to warrant special treatment. In fairness, only large organisations actually have a special person in this role. Most training needs are determined by line managers and staff themselves.

Organising training in the use of a new system for end-users usually comes down to the project manager. The importance of such training should not be underestimated. Users can make or break a system. If they are trained to use it effectively, they will accept the system and be more productive. If they are not trained or are badly trained, then they will make mistakes and criticise the system. You should view training as relationship marketing and encourage others to do the same.

[**Key concept:** Appearances aren't everything, but if you don't look professional you won't get the job.]

■ **Reflection question 4:** From a personnel management perspective, are older staff unsuited to modern systems development? Justify your answer.

Outsourcing

Most companies choose to maintain their own IS infrastructure, enabling them to exercise control over the whole IS domain. But there are other options. **Outsourcing** means paying a third party outside the organisation to perform specific functions such as data processing, application development, communications, or electronic data processing audit. In so doing, organisations try to reduce the size of the IS infrastructure and the number of staff, and hence cut costs. The trick is to achieve these things without compromising the organisation's short-, medium- and long-term ability to compete.

However, outsourcing can be high-risk. Having divested itself of its IS equipment and staff, the organisation no longer has the infrastructure to perform the outsourced functions itself if a problem arises with the service provider.

Advantages of outsourcing

There are considerable advantages to be gained from outsourcing, provided that the conditions are right to do so.

- It has the potential to reduce costs. The word 'potential' is used advisedly, because even when an application is outsourced it is important to maintain strategic management in-house. Another factor that is often overlooked is the cost of overseeing the outsourced contract — making sure that the provider delivers the levels of service in the contract and that all submitted accounts are correct. If employees are to be made redundant, the costs of payouts have to be considered here.

- It allows consolidation of the IS division.
- It reduces fluctuations in staffing levels.
- It reduces dependency on key personnel.
- It allows management to focus on business rather than on technical issues.
- It gives improved reliability and system availability (the service provider can justify a higher level of investment in hardware since the provider enjoys the benefits of economies of scale).

[**Key concept:** If it's not your problem, don't take ownership of it (unless you really have to).]

Disadvantages of outsourcing

Although there are undoubted benefits to be gained from outsourcing, note that the activity is not without risk. There are downsides to outsourcing:

- It removes knowledge of business processes from the organisation with an associated loss of control.
- It leads to a loss of corporate culture and experience if staff are retrenched.
- It can make it difficult to use information strategically.
- It ties the company to the service provider, often denying any competition.
- It may increase costs.
- It prevents the consideration of enterprise-wide IS and may restrict strategic planning.

What to consider when outsourcing

ABC — accept nothing, believe nothing, check everything — is particularly useful advice in the outsourcing context. There are many things to consider, and the following is a selection of the most important.

- What is the track record of the provider? Is the provider well established and dependable?
- Is the application which is being outsourced of high strategic value? If the answer is yes, then outsourcing may not be a good idea since you will lose control over your competitive edge.
- What is the nature of the relationship between the organisation and provider — customer? client? partner? Power differentials are important here.
- How flexible is the contract? What happens if things go wrong? Is there a get-out clause and provision for damages?
- How is the service to be monitored?
- What is the pricing structure? Is it possible to renegotiate charges at intervals?
- What is your investment position? If you have just invested heavily in hardware and software, the outsource provider is unlikely to save you enough to recover your costs. On the other hand, if you are approaching the end of an investment cycle, then the equipment and software is verging on the obsolete. It may be a good time to outsource.
- Does the application vary substantially in load and throughput? It may be a good thing to outsource.
- Is this an area where it is difficult to attract and retain staff? Again, this is a suitable candidate for outsourcing.

- What are the privacy, security and intellectual copyright positions? Can the provider guarantee that your data will remain confidential? If you have developed software for a particular application, does the provider have the right to use and develop it? If that software gives you an advantage in the market, can you prevent the provider using it for other clients?
- Are you diversifying into a new area and wish to reduce your capital commitment? Outsourcing may provide a cost-effective option.

IS in action

Why outsource outsourcing?

Many organisations view outsourcing as a means to cut costs. Often they apply the same thinking to the outsourcing project itself and try to do without the help of a consulting firm to guide the process. There is an unfortunate tendency for companies to confuse cost with value. A good consulting firm is not cheap, but their charges will be justified if their involvement prevents major problems and costly mistakes; even completing a project more quickly can save money and give a company a tactical competitive advantage. As with any move into a new area, there is a learning curve involved — unfortunately there is more to it than learning a few new techniques. Successful outsourcing project management requires: extensive market intelligence, detailed knowledge of emerging technologies, human resource management skills, the ability to manage change, financial management skills and sufficient experience to be able to negotiate legally binding service-level agreements and pricing structure. Once the true costs have been ascertained a consulting firm will look like an economic option. Kathleen Goolsby (2003) noted that the use of consultants had a direct relationship to the success of outsourcing projects: 80% of clients who used consultants reported a smooth transition to the new system compared with only 20% who did not use a consultant. More than 60% of companies that did not engage a consultant subsequently experienced relationship problems with their outsource provider. It is difficult to estimate the losses involved, but it is likely that they would be significant.

[**Key concept:** If you do not know what you are doing, it is not a good idea to do a lot of it.]

■ **Reflection question 5:** You are negotiating an outsourcing contract. Your costs per transaction are $1.20. The outsource provider has offered a price of $0.80 per transaction and has guaranteed to hold the price for the next seven years. Assuming that everything else in the contract is acceptable, would you accept the offer? Explain your answer.

Outsourcing summary

Outsourcing was a major trend in the 1980s and 1990s and is still popular. It needs to be considered in a climate of corporate downsizing and the corporatisation of government. Although many case studies have been published which present outsourcing in a positive light, there are some disaster stories. However, very few companies wish to publicise failure. Of those companies that consider outsourcing, approximately 60% choose not to proceed. Also, many companies that have outsourced in the past are now rebuilding their infrastructure. A loss of control can affect a company's ability to compete. Outsource providers tend to be large, well-established companies such as IBM, with a long history and a secure asset base.

Not all downsizing is necessarily high-risk, nor need it involve a bona fide provider. In areas which are well defined, a business might look to establish a strategic complementary alliance with a third party. For example, consider an organisation which has retained its mainframe systems but has provided a PC-based network to improve the performance of its applications. The distributed system has removed much of the load from the mainframe, which is now underutilised and is no longer a cost-effective option. An agreement with another company which is in a similar position could lead to both companies sharing a mainframe installation. Cost savings are substantial, and there is virtually zero impact on control, staffing and planning. Disaster recovery and contingency arrangements can also be handled in this way. Two companies might agree to provide mainframe data processing for each other in the event of a systems failure. Companies frequently outsource long-haul communications and Internet service provision.

A strategy which yields cost savings similar to those of outsourcing is competitive tendering. If the IS division runs as a profit centre, then it tenders for work in the same way as external companies, but this can lead to overcharging for some services in order to subsidise a tender to secure the contract for new work. The amount of developmental work carried out also tends to reduce (see the discussion above on profit centre IS).

Islands of information and proprietary systems

Many large organisations still have complicated heterogeneous hardware platforms and applications. A typical portfolio might include:

- old, high-volume, mainframe-based transaction processing systems using **proprietary systems** software and non-relational proprietary databases; the centralised application usually has a large network of non-intelligent terminals (IBM's IMS is a good example)
- moderately old divisional or departmental MIS-operational applications running on proprietary midrange computers using relational but proprietary databases
- online applications which make use of divisional or departmental client–server LANs
- relatively new divisional or departmental operational applications running on open (non-proprietary) client–server platforms; often these are UNIX servers hosting open relational database products such as Oracle.

This scenario leads to the development of 'islands' of information, i.e. corporate information that is not universally accessible throughout the organisation. Although individual processes may be automated, the business as a whole is not, so islands of automation also develop. Applications cannot share data easily and users cannot access all relevant corporate data from their desktops. This limits the ability of the organisation to compete effectively. Because the architecture is fragmented, IS staff cannot change the IS infrastructure to reflect changes in business requirements in a reasonable time period. Moving to a position where changes can be made in a reasonable time frame and systems can be integrated normally involves the use of open systems.

Open systems

Chapter 5 discussed the importance of standards in networking to simplify communication between computers. Discussions in earlier chapters also highlighted the importance of standardising hardware platforms. Systems are said to be **open systems** if:

- they can be connected to other standard components easily
- they can exchange data easily
- they are hardware-platform independent
- they use internationally recognised standards rather than proprietary ones.

Open systems reduce cost and risk since future systems are guaranteed to be compatible with present ones. Accordingly, changes to systems will be evolutionary rather than revolutionary. Oracle, a relational database company, specialised in converting corporate data into standard formats and ensured that its database software was available for every industry-standard platform. This allowed business to break free from proprietary traps and achieve openness at the data and application levels.

However, although a company may be committed to an open systems path, there may be problems handling legacy systems. **Legacy systems** often impair a company's ability to make changes to application functionality without changing the existing IS infrastructure. Changing the IS infrastructure is usually not possible without changing the way in which business applications operate. There are three basic ways of handling legacy systems in the corporate IS plan: forward engineering, reverse engineering and wrapper engineering.

- **Forward engineering** is the usual way in which systems are developed, but the presence of legacy systems can hinder the introduction of new systems. However, if it has been decided that a new system is justified, then processes can be re-engineered and the legacy system replaced by the new system. In many cases, simply discarding the legacy system is not a cost-effective option.
- When a company depends on the legacy system and there is insufficient system documentation or a lack of knowledge about the underlying business processes, then **reverse engineering** may be the only option. Here, the behaviour of the system is used to derive a new set of system requirements which, in turn, are used to design an optimised system. Again the legacy system is discarded, which may prove costly.
- Usually, financial constraints and the risk of introducing a massive amount of change in one go prevent companies adopting forward or reverse engineering solutions for legacy systems. A more conservative approach is to leave the old systems as they are but 'wrap' them in newer, more friendly systems, thus providing a more convenient interface to users and other systems. This is termed **wrapper engineering**. This makes it easier to integrate the legacy system into the corporate system. Usually there will be a migration plan for the legacy system's final replacement. Many enterprise resource planning (ERP) systems operate in this manner, making older systems more flexible and useful.

Infobyte

Extending mainframes into web services

If you have made an international flight recently, the chances are that you have made use of web services to make your reservation and check in. You can use your PC or mobile phone to make your arrangements, and most people will use a credit card at the airport when checking in. The airport card reader accesses credit card clearing-house systems to verify your personal information and allows you to check in, make a booking or changes via a touch screen. Should the first attempt at verification fail, the system will access other clearing houses. Making a reservation makes use of at least three databases: the airline reservation database, the frequent flyer points database and the credit card clearing-house database. Optionally the web service could check a database for arrivals and departures to make sure that your flight is on time. The web service acts as a user-friendly kiosk interface with previously private systems (Castro-Leon 2004).

Systems integration

It is not only legacy systems that cause problems for systems managers. Often, modern systems have been selected for their particular ability to handle a specialised application. Differences in data formats and networking standards may prevent these systems from being integrated into the corporate IS resource. This has an effect on productivity and effectiveness. There are three aspects of systems integration:

- *External integration* entails interconnectivity and interworking between business partners' systems. This was touched on in earlier chapters when discussing using IS to form umbilical cords between companies. Web browsers, computer networks and electronic data interchange play a large part in this process.
- *Internal integration* refers to the integration of the company's web-based systems with the company's core application systems. It also implies that the core applications themselves are closely integrated. There is an underlying assumption that the applications are built with standard **application program interfaces (APIs)**. This allows new functions to be added quickly and with minimum risk on a modular basis. Some authors refer to this as **componentisation**.
- *Infrastructure integration* refers to the integration of IS infrastructure and applications. It also includes the integration of infrastructure components. It is important that the applications are independent of, and insulated from, the underlying infrastructure since this allows either to be changed without the need for expensive and disruptive changes to the other.

When it comes to managing systems integration, there are two main schools of thought. The first is to have an overall migration plan in which the current systems are moving towards a more uniform solution which uses fewer standards. The second ignores the technical problems of hardware and software integration and seeks to achieve integration at the application level by using high-level software which enables all information resources to be accessed in the same way regardless of hardware platform or data format. This is termed **enterprise application integration (EAI)**. Organisations which have a slowly evolving IS portfolio tend to opt for the former whereas organisations with a diverse and rapidly changing portfolio tend to opt for the latter.

IS in action

Elegant sufficiency vs wholesale ERP

Profit margins are so tight that an Australian supermarket trading six days per week might not start making any profit in a particular week until Saturday afternoon. Competition in the UK supermarket sector is also intense. Sainsbury's held the number 1 position until late 1995, when Tesco became the dominant player. At a time when the rest of the UK grocery industry was moving to a supply chain management (SCM) system called Efficient Customer Response, Sainsbury's ignored the warning signs and announced its belief in the superiority of its systems. It was merely a question of time before the chairman would be asked to step down and be replaced by a more progressive executive team. The history of the deployment of IS and IT in the grocery industry has tended to be one of tactics rather than strategy. A company might have difficulty in managing its staff and buy a human resource management system. The same company might realise that its delivery trucks are underutilised and buy a logistics system. At some later time integrating these systems would prove hard. Other companies undertaking massive ERP implementations found that the cost of software licences was a very small fraction of the total implementation costs and that the payback times were in the order of several years. Sainsbury's now has a policy of only implementing projects that can be completed in less than thirteen weeks and which provide 100% investment return in six months. The company's view is that IS people need to resist the urge to re-engineer on a large scale and should make only those alterations that are strictly needed to achieve core objectives. So far the strategy is paying dividends (Wheatley 2002).

Enterprise-wide client–server architecture

It is not simply a matter of connecting existing applications. The different networking standards and data formats actively prevent this. A more reasonable approach is to allow users to access a wide variety of applications directly from their desktop machines using a Windows-based graphical user interface. This includes the mainframe legacy systems. This relies on open client–server architectures on an enterprise-wide scale. In short, the legacy systems may be left as they are, but extra functionality in one of the non-server tiers in the client–server architecture needs to be added. Accordingly, a new application might take data from several legacy systems, remove redundancy, pool the data, and re-present it for information or analysis in a new, more meaningful format. Such an approach improves the performance of older applications by removing unnecessary work from legacy mainframes and presents opportunities for downsizing.

Faced with a choice between rewriting or redeveloping existing applications (forward and reverse engineering) or replacing/augmenting the systems using a company-wide enterprise resource planning package such as SAP, many organisations have opted for the latter.

Implementing a modern ERP system which includes applications and technical infrastructure is an expensive option, but the advantages that it confers may justify the investment. Specifically, ERP provides:

- applications software that yields functionality in line with industry best practice
- complete horizontal and vertical integration throughout the enterprise
- applications which are tailored for their environments, which includes languages, currencies and legal frameworks
- simplified applications development due to componentisation.

Besides overcoming the islands of information and automation identified above, ERP systems are intended to support **business engineering (BE)**. BE is more than just the automation and improvement of existing processes — here, the emphasis is on organisational flexibility. This means that a business is better positioned to respond to a changing environment quickly. With BE, processes are considered in a rich information environment and their relationships with other processes are important. Businesses are still trying to reduce product cycle times, speed cash flow and improve customer service, but ERP (when properly deployed) should engender individual and team creativity. In terms of chapter 1, this is the transition from the industrial age into the information and knowledge age.

IS in action

Six principles for successful CRM implementation

1. Define a vision for CRM — this should conform with the company's strategic plan. The system itself is largely defined by business rules, but ultimately it will be customers who make it a success so involve them at an early stage.
2. Find champions and advocates — all important projects need to be driven at the highest levels of management, and technology is a major driver of CRM. However, it is middle management who must carry the message to staff, and that message must be clear.
3. Seek employee endorsement for the vision — personalise the benefits and avoid presenting information in an abstract way. Instead of talking about a 'typical customer', talk about George, the production manager of company X.
4. Set realistic milestones — the key to most successful projects is people management. If goals are too large, complex and far away, staff tend to lose motivation. A good project plan will ensure that staff experience success at regular intervals.

(*continued*)

5 Manage staff with a degree of sensitivity — change causes problems. If staff are properly informed — for example, being told: 'Things will be difficult for the next two months while the new systems are bedded in' — their expectations and coping strategies will be realistic. Compare this with being told: 'Everything will be wonderful from day 1.'
6 Ensure that improvement is ongoing — once the system is in place, every aspect of it — technology, training and so on — must be re-examined from customer, company and employee perspectives with a view to maximising effectiveness and system satisfaction.

IS in action

Toronto Life runs on webbed feat

When most people think about customer relationship management (CRM), they tend to think in terms of manufacturing and logistics, but the principles apply equally well to services, information and media. For some time Toronto Life Magazine (TLM) had been running an email magazine called *Preview*. At best this part of the business was revenue neutral, but TLM wanted to turn *Preview* into a profit centre. The newsletter was already well liked by customers, but TLM needed to make it more valuable to customers and advertisers. One of the nice features about web-based systems is that they have the potential to be 100% trackable, enabling a wealth of useful marketing information to be gained.

After some deliberation, Intervision-CRM was chosen to host the system, which supports two important strategies. The first is to shift advertisers away from banners and buttons to a sponsorship/partnership mode of operation. This changes the underlying business model, but the increased sophistication of the system makes it worthwhile to advertisers and marketers. The second takes into account the diverse nature of Toronto's 5.5 million inhabitants and allows 'regionalisation' of content down to individual suburbs, such as the large Greek community in Danforth. The system has already yielded a 13% increase in click-through rates for feature content, and there is the potential for better returns.

Source: information from Intervision-CRM, www.intervision-crm.com/pdf/Toronto_Life_PR.pdf (accessed 15 March 2004).

Extended ERP (EERP) systems

SAP is the best known vendor of ERP solutions. Typically, the modules provided on the mySAP.com e-business platform include:

- mySAP Workplace
- mySAP Supply Chain Management
- mySAP Customer Relationship Management
- mySAP E-Procurement
- mySAP Product Lifecycle Management
- mySAP Business Intelligence
- mySAP Financials
- mySAP Human Resources
- mySAP Marketplace
- mySAP Industry Solutions.

All these are predominantly internally focused except for E-Procurement, Supply Chain Management, Customer Relationship Management and some aspects of Business Intelligence. Supply Chain Management requires the interconnection of all partners — business-to-business (B2B) links from suppliers are referred to as 'upstream links', and business-to-customer (B2C) links are referred to as 'downstream links'. Extended Supply Chain Management involves both upstream and downstream links. An ERP system is said to be an **extended ERP (EERP)** system if it incorporates electronic commerce functionality.

Upstream links are used for **supply chain management (SCM)** (the practice of linking one's suppliers into core business processes). Large organisations have been practising SCM for some years because they can justify the huge investment required for internal ERP systems. About 65% of SAP's customers are large companies with revenues in excess of $US200 million. ERP deployment typically costs several million dollars and extends over several years. The question arises as to what can be done to ensure that small–medium enterprises can realise the potential benefits of ERP.

We need to comment on the development of SCM systems in recent years. As networking and e-commerce technologies (such as EDI) have improved in their capabilities, so the SCM systems that they support have increased in their levels of sophistication. From handling the needs of a single factory, SCM systems are now complicated systems of interconnected online hubs, as shown in figure 6.3 on page 168.

[**Key concept:** There is a trade-off between integration and flexibility — the better integrated a system is, the more difficult it is to make changes to it.]

ERP and SMEs

Small–medium enterprises (SMEs) cannot afford the huge investment required to build enterprise resource planning systems, and the cost of using electronic data interchange networks is prohibitive for smaller organisations. Usually, SME customers are not connected to the supply chain electronically, and if they are they may have proprietary networks and systems that actively prevent interconnection. The inclusion of web-based electronic commerce components in ERP packages (shopping carts, catalogues and so on)

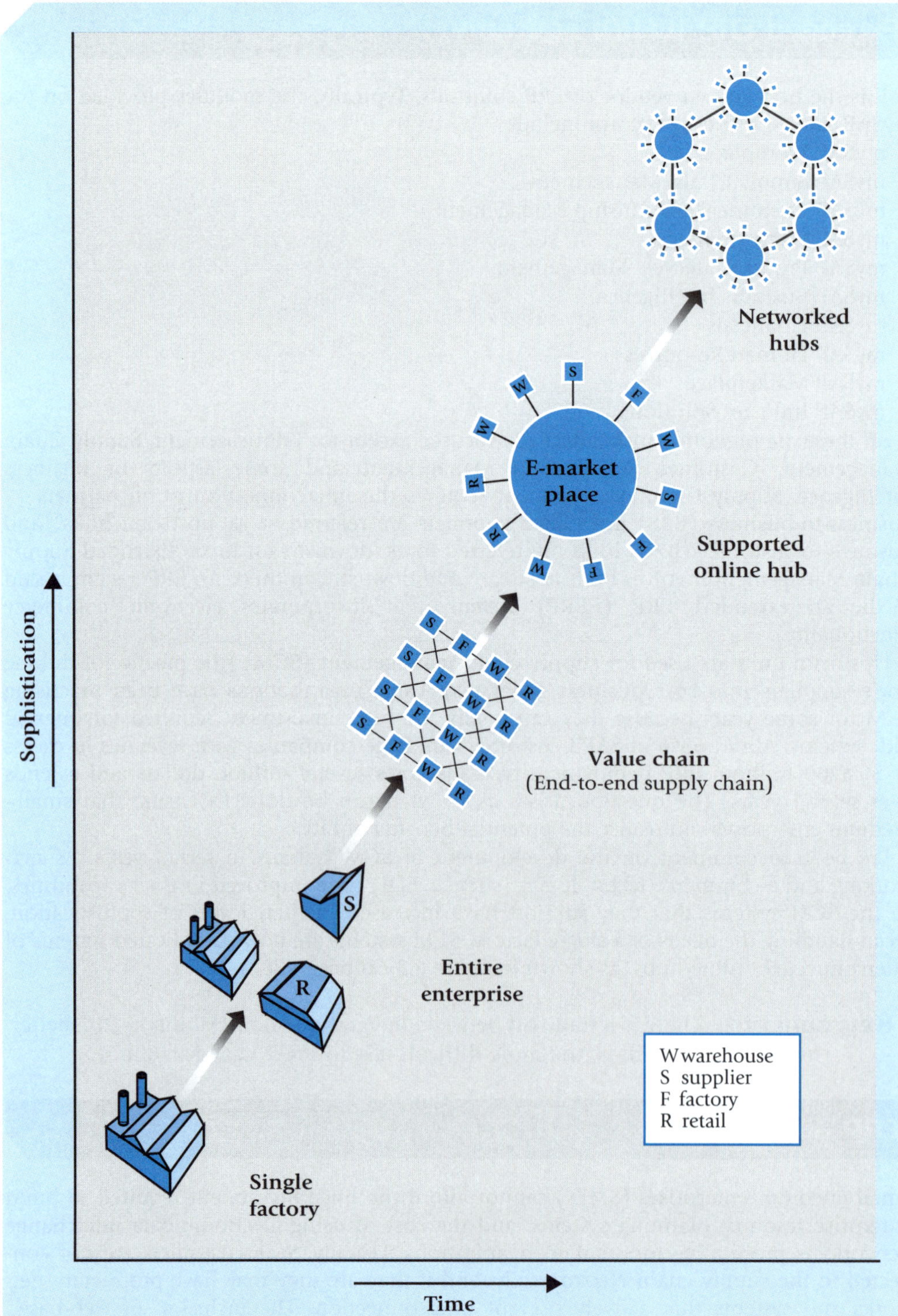

Figure 6.3 The evolution of supply chain management systems

reduces barrier costs and improves accessibility for B2B and B2C links. However, when ordering a computer online, for example, the web ordering system needs to interface with the distribution systems, manufacturing systems and component supplier systems, so that delivery can be guaranteed within a certain period. Given the need for just-in-time delivery, this integration is vital to the business process. Most ERP systems usually lack the intelligence to search through masses of transaction data and make suggestions. Nor, as a rule, are they able to sense the environment and use external data in decision-making processes. For supply chain planning, business partners need to be aware of each other's patterns of demand and the implications for their own manufacturing/supply systems. Good ERP systems should provide these features.

The use of web-based technology in ERP systems provides a level of convenience when accessing the system that fits well with SMEs. The cost of ERP systems is a deterrent, and thus a form of outsourcing has emerged which enables SMEs to have access to ERP technology and permits a cheap 'implementation'. An **application service provider (ASP)** is a person or a company which installs (and possibly customises) prepackaged software applications (such as ERP) on its own computer systems and then allows its customers to access those applications. Payment schemes are usually similar to rental agreements, since pay-for-use approaches might reduce cash flow to the ASP. The initial costs associated with implementation and ongoing costs associated with management are now the responsibility of the ASP. Of course, the ASP will rent the application to as many clients as possible in order to increase income. Figure 6.4 shows a typical ASP scenario, in which all that the SME needs is Internet or virtual private network (VPN) access using Java-compliant web browsers running on thin clients. (Recall from earlier chapters that thin clients simplify management and reduce costs under most conditions.)

As mentioned before, a major business trend is to deal direct where possible. There is potential for the independent software vendor to fill the role of the ASP itself.

It is difficult to generalise about the ASP market, but it would seem that ASPs come in three main flavours. Each poses risks for businesses.

The first is the specialist ASP. Here profit margins are high because the expertise required is of a high order. Specialist ASPs are unlikely to suffer bankruptcy, but they are often subject to takeover bids. In this event the distinctive nature of the service ensures that it has a strong identity in the new structure. The strategic advantage of the service is high.

The second group has a broader focus, usually on an industry sector. The broader focus means that there is more competition and so profit margins are smaller than those of specialist ASPs. These ASPs are more likely to be involved in friendly mergers than in direct takeovers, but since they are providing services that are already provided in a competitive market, they can lose their identity in the new business. This in turn can pose problems for their clients as the services provided might deteriorate or be reorganised.

The last flavour of ASP is that of the generic provider. Here the ASP provides nothing special, and competition is intense and profit margins are low. Takeovers and mergers are common, and bankruptcy in the face of fierce competition is nothing unusual. The effect on a business is disruptive but not catastrophic. Here the strategic advantage of the service is low.

The simple rules in choosing an ASP are pretty much the same as they are for any other outsource provider. We are looking for an organisation which is big enough to maintain its identity in the face of competition and which can deliver the required services at an affordable price. Usually the larger the organisation, the greater the pool of skills it has to draw on. What is not immediately apparent from figure 6.3 is the effect that SCM has had

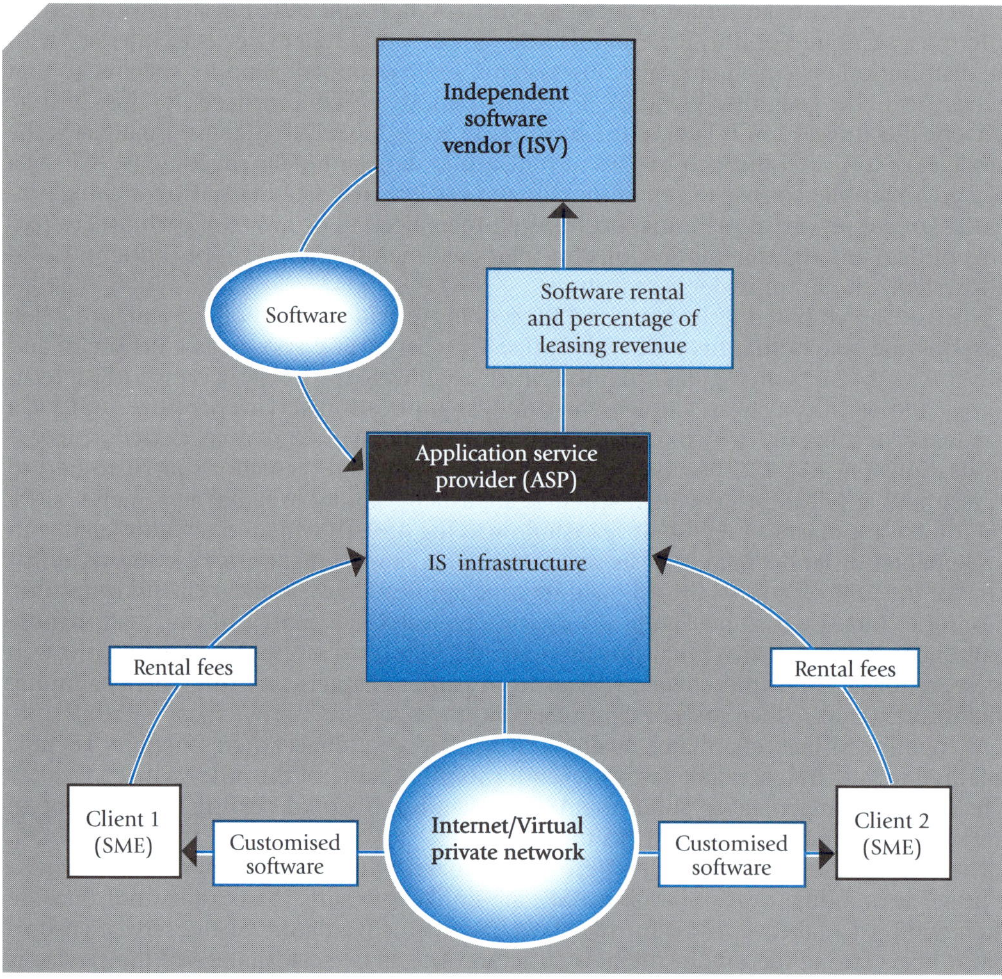

Figure 6.4 A typical ASP scenario

on geography. Locality is much less of an issue since SCM can be Internet-enabled. This in turn enables smaller companies to take part in the processes, thus increasing competition and reducing prices. Figure 6.5 shows the predicted increase in the ASP market from 2004 to 2007.

Just how much money can an SME save by using ERP via an ASP? Forty per cent is a typical figure. Products such as PeopleSoft carry an annual licence fee of around $US150 000, which doesn't include the cost of support, service, and hardware and software infrastructure. It is true that the rental costs will accrue rapidly, but if the SME is not in a position to deploy its own ERP system owing to cost constraints, this is the only way in which it can obtain the competitive advantages that ERP gives. Careful cost–benefit analysis is vital in reaching a decision.

- **Reflection question 6:** Why would it make good business sense for an ERP software company to let companies have its software for free?

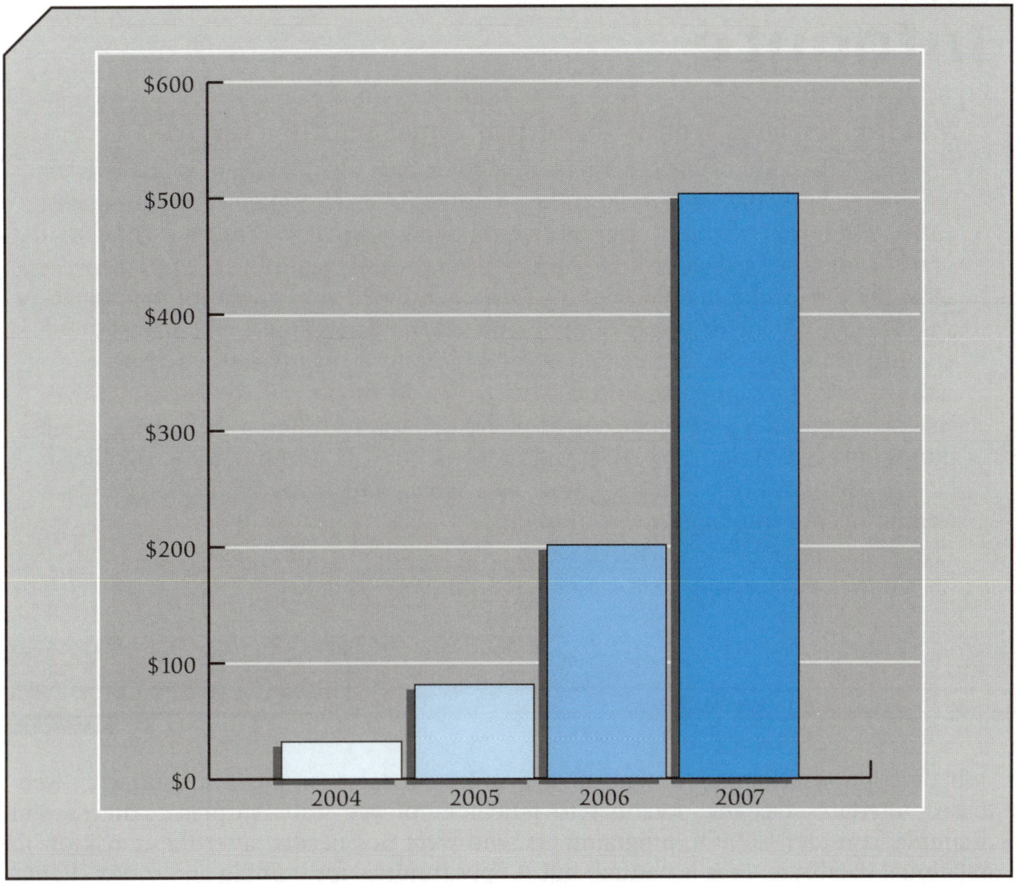

Figure 6.5 Predicted growth in global ASP market, 2004–07
Source: data based on trends observed by ASP News 2002 in CRM Daily, www.crmdaily.com/perl/story/17437.html (accessed 10 December 2003).

Problems with introducing ERP or other changes

Introducing any new system has associated risks. People generally are resistant to change, and too much change in one go can destroy a business. We said in chapter 1 that IS is a people business and that it is important to make sure that integrated solutions are achievable from a personnel point of view. The following guidelines are useful in this context:

- Involve staff in the planning process and project management — they are stakeholders in the enterprise, so they should be stakeholders in the new system.
- Provide incentives for change, productivity-based payments or a more manageable workload.
- Introduce change gradually. When introducing groupware, it may be best to start with a small group of technically able people who will benefit most quickly from the new system. From that point, good training programs will allow the system to 'snowball'. However, this is not an option for all systems.

Infobyte

Making sense of trends: is software just another service?

Growth in the sales of customer relationship management software is predicted to remain relatively flat, at least until the end of 2007 when a global market value of $A98.4 billion is predicted. By contrast the growth in CRM services exceeds that of CRM software and will reach $A55.9 billion by the beginning of 2007, services accounting for more than 56% of the total. So how do we account for the discrepancy in trends? The disparity in the predicted trends is due to two main factors. The first is the growth in outsourcing. The second is an increasing use of application service providers. Additionally there are ongoing expenses associated with systems integration and management. Although experts differ in their views, some things remain certain: CRM, ASP and outsourcing will continue to be significant factors. The trend of viewing software as a service rather than a product marks a significant shift in management thinking.

Source: www.forrester.com/ER/Press/Release/0,1769,739,FF.html; www.fujitsu-siemens.es/solutions/aspect/index.html (accessed 15 March 2004).

- Job descriptions change. Moving to a distributed database environment with web-based interfaces has the potential to render employee skills surplus to needs. For example, consider COBOL programmers who were not needed after the transition to relational databases. Fear is natural, but if opportunities for training and career change are offered, most people can make the transition fairly comfortably.
- Gather information on the performance of the new systems from the users, and involve them in the shakedown trials.
- Take the opportunity to introduce total quality management (TQM), quality circles or other forms of participative management.

When attempting to integrate business systems via ERP or other means, it is important to realise that there may be some mutually antagonistic departments or divisions. It is vital to find the best all-round compromise. As with any system we need to focus on four views:

- the business view (why is the system needed?)
- the functional view (what will the system do?)
- the technology view (how will the system be constructed?)
- the implementation view (how will the system be deployed, managed and updated?).

Most systems have a degree of complexity but enterprise-wide systems need to cope with conflicting needs, complexity, diversity and uncertainty within the confines of a single architecture. In order to make progress, operate on a divide-and-conquer principle (this is common to many design and management exercises). Reducing the overall problem to a set of manageable chunks allows progress to be made in several areas concurrently. In practice, these 'chunks' are referred to as 'views' or 'domains' — they are really stakeholder perceptions of the underlying system. In this context a stakeholder could have a business or technology perspective or a combination of the two. A solutions architect normally carries out these functions, matching the required functionality to available ERP components and subsystems.

[**Key concept:** There is a limit to how much change an organisation can take at any one time — maximise the effectiveness but minimise the impact.]

IS in action

Reinventing Kodak

George Eastman's role in making Kodak one of the world's most successful companies is well documented. His slogan 'You push the button, we do the rest' defined the company's business model. Based on traditional film and printing processes, Kodak suffered as its customers switched to digital photography. In 2003 the company announced that its future lay with digital technology, despite the fact that its own digital businesses had failed to turn a profit. Reaction in the marketplace was mixed, but Kodak's share price dropped and its credit rating was assessed as BBB minus (not quite junk level). Kodak's own analysts predicted that digital technologies would account for 50% of the company's profit and 60% of its sales. Although profit margins on conventional film processing are higher, Kodak sees it as a diminishing market. Advances in digital camera technology mean that picture density is almost as good as conventional film: a 4 megapixel camera can produce good-quality poster-sized prints. Customers are also able to be more selective about the shots they use and can use software packages such as Photoshop to clean up flawed images.

In common with many businesses embarking on digital projects, Kodak has made effective use of the World Wide Web and formed strategic alliances. Australian customers can download special print software from Kodak and then email their selected prints to their local Coles supermarket for printing. Although the service has a three- to four-day turnaround time, customers have the convenience of collecting their prints when they do their shopping. Alternatively, Kodak Australia can direct users to the nearest photolab that supports the service. Any digital image can be processed, but Kodak's software warns users if their selected images are of inferior quality. Prints can be delivered to any Australian address for family or business reasons. Note how Kodak is breaking down geographic barriers and 'piggy-backing' on existing technology and trends. It is too early to say whether digital photography will save Kodak — the problem is that other companies are able to compete in similar ways. Somehow 'You click the mouse and we do the rest' doesn't have the same ring to it.

Sources: www.forbes.com/infoimaging/2003/10/21/1021kodakbattlepinnacor.html; www.kodak.com.au

Summary

People are as much a part of the system as hardware, software and communications, and in many ways they are the most important part. Understanding the various jobs and roles in the IS industry is essential if you are to appreciate how the entire enterprise operates. Integrating the various islands of information and automation into a cohesive enterprise-wide system pays dividends since it extends the range of control over all business processes including business-to-business and business-to-customer links. The key points in this chapter are:

- Jobs in the IS industry are many and varied and subject to continual evolution. Most require good communication skills and business knowledge.
- Systems integration is important in reducing costs and maximising the return on investment in older systems. It also improves the ability of an organisation to compete.
- Outsourcing is often a key part of the IS plan.
- Integration may be vertical (specialised to a business function) or horizontal (general enterprise functions).
- Systems integration should be accompanied by business engineering to ensure the effectiveness of the processes. The integration may be achieved by redeveloping systems (forward and reverse engineering) or incorporating them into a modular ERP system.
- Most ERP systems are expensive but give good tactical and strategic advantages, such as freedom from proprietary systems, application and data independence, easier infrastructure planning and change. Usually, ERP systems are viable only for large organisations.
- The development of application service providers (ASPs) has allowed SMEs to have access to ERP and other software.
- When introducing systems integration, ERP or any system, it is vital that the process of change is handled well. This involves stakeholder analysis and an inclusive management style. People make or break systems.

Questions

1. Given that a distributed organisation of the IS function is more responsive to the needs of end-users and clients, why do most businesses choose to centralise the IS function? (You should give at least three reasons.)
2. What are the risks for a large business that does not impose strict standards for the hardware and software configuration of its desktop machines?
3. Think about large-scale re-engineering (such as ERP) versus continual improvement for large business systems. What are the relative merits of each approach? How much depends on the nature of the business?
4. In order to shorten timelines for important large-scale projects, businesses often outsource the software development. What problems could stem from this stratagem? What are the potential rewards? Why might a company choose not to develop its own staff?
5. Several Australian companies will not employ systems analysts unless they have a business background or business qualifications. Do you think this is a reasonable policy? Give supporting reasons for your answer.

6. Explain the difference between forward engineering, reverse engineering and wrapper engineering. Take care to outline the circumstances under which each would be used.
7. Although operating as an allocated cost centre is the preferred option for many IS divisions, difficulty arises in allocating costs to departments. Identify some costs that are difficult to allocate, and suggest a workable solution.
8. With any large-scale project such as ERP implementation, staff turnover is a major problem. Suggest strategies to (a) avoid the problem and (b) minimise the effects of staff turnover on your large-scale project.
9. An ERP implementation for a large corporation might cost more than $200 million and extend over five years before the full business benefits are realised. Smaller companies often use an ASP to save time and money. Is this a viable option for large companies? Give supporting reasons for your answer.
10. How does business engineering differ from business process re-engineering?
11. Explain the difference between vertical and horizontal integration. Which do you think is easier to achieve, and why? Which is more profitable, and why? Which is more useful, and why?
12. Many businesses see ERP systems as being necessary but not of strategic advantage. The view they take is that there is a disadvantage in not having ERP. Do you think this is a return to more traditional modes of business competition, or is the technology still a prime influence on business strategy?

Exercises

1. You will be in charge of a project that will change the way a large group of people work in your business. No jobs will be lost as a result of your project, and it is expected that the project will improve the company's profits by 4 to 7% per annum. At the moment the project is in the planning stage, but it is expected that work on it will begin in the next six months and that it will be completed within nine months. The staff association representative has managed to find out about the project and is expressing concern at the lack of consultation. What strategies would you employ to ensure that your project is successful?
2. You are putting together a project team to carry out a feasibility study for an Australian whitegoods manufacturer. The company in question has a turnover of nearly $800 million and is considering the adoption of an ERP system. Discuss this scenario with other students, and try to define your 'dream team' for the feasibility study, taking care to identify the personal and technical skills each team member would need.
3. Review an information systems course syllabus from a university handbook or online source. In your view, does it adequately prepare students for the world of work? What (if anything) is lacking? What else might be done to improve skills acquisition in students?
4. Modern management methods attempt to empower rather than control staff. Implicit in such an approach is that staff mem bers know exactly what is required of them and what they are allowed to do. Some companies actually produce a bill of rights for employees. Identify seven rights and their associated responsibilities for employees. Remember that the goal is to make the business more effective. If you are working in a small group, discuss the proposed rights and identify the seven most useful proposals.

CASE STUDY OZChem

OZChem is a Melbourne-based company that specialises in the design, development and supply of laboratory equipment for hospitals, universities and the private sector. It needs to be able to supply most items in a very short time frame whereas more expensive items such as mass spectrometers might take as long as ten days to source and supply. For its complex toxicology systems, OZChem deals with a few approved installers. For almost everything else the company is self-reliant. Like most businesses of its type, OZChem is obliged to maintain relatively high levels of inventory and is heavily dependent on its suppliers to meet delivery schedules. A recent history of late deliveries and frustrated customers has led to OZChem instigating an inquiry into the cause of the problems. The consultant's report criticised OZChem's ordering and delivery systems, its management culture and its old-fashioned policies and procedures.

Since then much of the senior management of the company has been replaced with younger, more progressive types. The new IS manager, Caroline Black, has a good background in IS and an MBA, but this is the first time that she has had sole responsibility for the IS function. The manager in charge of logistics, Peter Ritchie, has risen from the ranks and does not have a university degree. One of the recommendations the consultant's report made was to examine the feasibility of introducing ERP systems. Caroline produced a strong case for using an ASP to develop and run OZChem's supply chain management systems using industry standard software. The executive management team supported this initiative, and Australasian Systems Solutions was selected to develop and host OZChem's systems.

In the interim Caroline has been re-engineering OZChem's internal legacy systems. The company intranet was launched four months ago, and most internal systems now have web interfaces on to them, including wrapper-engineered legacy systems. With the support of the management group, Caroline has replaced the old stock control system, which was specially developed, and replaced it with a proprietary system that is compatible with web protocols and services. When she proposed buying an 'off-the-shelf' logistics system, Peter hit the roof.

'You think you can just wander down here fresh out of university and tell us how to do our work? I have been running this division for 15 years with no problems that are our fault. I know we have had a few difficulties of late, but we depend on our suppliers — if they let us down, we let our customers down. We could increase stock levels, but that would decrease profit. We don't have that many unhappy customers anyway. This system will have no knowledge of our customers and limited intelligence when it comes to planning deliveries. I know how our customers operate, what they want and how they want it. I will fight this all the way. If you do manage to get the system in place, I promise you that it will not yield the benefits that you expect. It's just change for the sake of change.'

Caroline does not handle confrontation well. She simply turned on her heels and walked back to her office.

In her in-tray was a letter from Australasian Systems Solutions saying that the company had been taken over by Total Logistics, a large American company that had a relationship with a different software company than that used by Australasian Systems Solutions. The letter explained that there would be some delay in the development of the system, but that all OZChem's supply chain needs would be met in a reasonable time frame. The letter also included an option to cancel the agreement. The next piece of correspondence was a memo that detailed the huge increase in the number of help desk calls as staff struggled with the new intranet and different interfaces with once-familiar systems. Besides the user problems there were technical problems associated with system integration.

At 12 o'clock Alan, the deputy IS manager, asked Caroline if she wanted to go to lunch. He asked how her day had been and listened intently as she told him what was going on. He nodded sympathetically and then paused. 'I am not sure how to tell you this,' he began, 'but I have been asked if I'd be prepared to take your job. I said that I would need to time to think and I would need to see exactly what was on offer.'

Caroline stood up and knocked the remains of Alan's lunch into his lap. 'You're in on it too!' she spat. 'As soon as men like you see a woman in a position of importance, you just have to undermine her.' Alan slowly stood up and leaned over the table.

'Your gender has never been an issue for anyone at OZChem,' he snapped. 'You have undermined yourself. You created the problems that put you into this situation — you put them right! Just don't come to me for help.'

QUESTIONS

1. What would you do in Alan's position?
2. What mistakes do you think Caroline made in handling staff, system changes and the supply chain management project?
3. How serious an impact is the takeover of Australasian Systems Solutions by Total Logistics?
4. If you were on the management team of OZChem, what would your next move be in relation to Caroline's employment?
5. If a decision were made to retain Caroline, what conditions would you impose on her subsequent conduct?
6. Is Caroline's position irredeemable, or can she extricate herself from this situation? Explain your answer.
7. If you were in Alan's position and had accepted the IS manager's position, what steps would you take to sort out the mess?

References

Castro-Leon,E. 2004, 'The web within the web', *IEEE Spectrum*, February, pp. 37–40.

Goolsby, K. 2003, 'Cost vs. value of using an outsourcing consultant', www.outsourcing-best-practices.com/cost.html (accessed 15 March 2004).

Kerrigan, P. 2002, 'The changing role of the CIO', http://au.fujitsu.com/FAL/CDA/0,1531,350~1436,00.html (accessed 15 March 2004).

Wheatley, M. 2002, 'Shorter, faster, cheaper, better', *PM Network*, vol. 16, no. 5, pp. 42–7.

Chapter 7

Introduction to systems development

LEARNING OBJECTIVES

After reading this chapter, you should be able to:

- explain the purpose of the systems development lifecycle
- describe the skills needed by systems analysts
- describe each stage of the systems development process
- explain the purpose of CASE tools
- compare the variety of data- and information-gathering techniques
- provide an overview of data and process modelling
- explain the role of methodologies in systems development
- provide an overview of a number of alternative systems development approaches.

7

Introduction

This chapter provides an introduction to the topic of building information systems otherwise known as **systems development**. The **systems development lifecycle** serves as a framework for developing information systems. The classical phases of analysis, design, implementation and maintenance provide a logical and structured approach for building systems. Data are valuable resources in organisations and require effective management. Data and process modelling provide the **systems analyst** with methods to manage and document the data and the processes that modify the data. Software such as CASE tools (computer-aided software engineering) is commonly used for improving the development process, and techniques such as rapid application development (RAD) and joint application design (JAD) can be used for speeding up project timelines. Different problems require alternative systems development methodologies. Some situations may need softer, people-centred approaches rather than structured engineering methods, especially where there are differences of opinion as to what is best for the organisation.

We are concerned here with explaining general development approaches and techniques that are applicable to most types of systems development situations. The World Wide Web affects many systems development projects today, and specific details of web applications development are covered in a separate chapter.

The systems development environment

Earlier in the book we explained that an information system in a business environment is made up of a number of components. These usually include people, hardware, software, policies and procedures, data and information. The components of the information system do not operate in isolation but are closely interwoven with the fabric of the organisation. Information systems are often complex systems that operate in complex environments. Systems development methods are techniques, often diagrammatic, that aim to simplify this complexity both for developers and users. A systems analyst needs to understand these methods and develop a toolkit of methods and techniques to manage existing systems and to help in the creation of new ones. Two key techniques for IS professionals are the modelling of 'data' and the modelling of 'processes' in organisations.

[**Key concept:** 'A picture is worth a thousand words.' Systems development uses diagrams and tables, wherever possible, to model the system.]

The development processes used in building an information system involve following a series of steps. Although information systems could be developed in an informal way, there is usually a more formal process, or methodology, that is used in organisations.

The systems development lifecycle

Every systems analyst has heard of the systems development lifecycle (SDLC). It is important to become familiar with the basic concept. The SDLC is a structured framework for developing information systems. It breaks down the development process into various phases and provides a project management context to work within. The main phases are analysis, design, implementation and maintenance (see figure 7.1), and these are briefly outlined below.

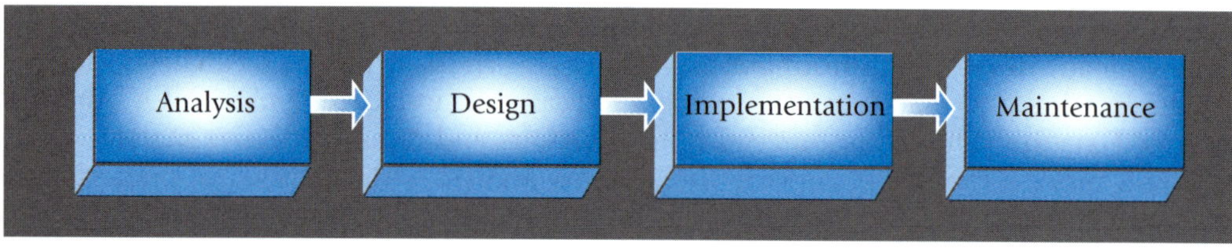

Figure 7.1 The systems development process

[**Key concept:** Divide and conquer — break up the problem or task into smaller components and solve each subproblem.]

- *Analysis*. The analysis phase concentrates on gathering information about the current and proposed systems. It is important that the feasibility of making changes is continually assessed. The requirements of the new systems are gathered and form the basis of the logical design which details what data and information will be processed but not the technologies that will be used. This phase uses modelling techniques to describe the processes and the data within the organisation.

■ **Reflection question 1:** What are some of the potential consequences of a poor analysis phase?

- *Design*. Once the requirements of the new system have been obtained, the new system has to be designed in detail. This involves specifying all components of the system including the design of the database, network infrastructure, the policies and procedures, and the software.
- *Implementation*. After the design details have been worked out, the system must be constructed and put into place. The software has to be written, or set up if it is an off-the-shelf package. A large amount of testing and training takes place before the system is finally handed over to the users.

[**Key concept:** Analyse, design and then implement is the basic problem-solving approach underlying much of systems development.]

- *Maintenance*. You will notice businesses changing how they interact with their customers on a regular basis. Most information systems undergo changes as time progresses. These may be the result of changing requirements or errors being detected in the system. As a consequence of the need for change, resources must be set aside each year for maintaining a system.

The four commonly used phases can be broken down into further stages (figure 7.2). Systems development textbooks have different names for some of the stages or some stages may be combined or even further broken down, but the seven stages in figure 7.2 form a logical breakdown of the systems development lifecycle. The lifecycle can be amended for alternative systems development approaches such as prototyping (discussed later).

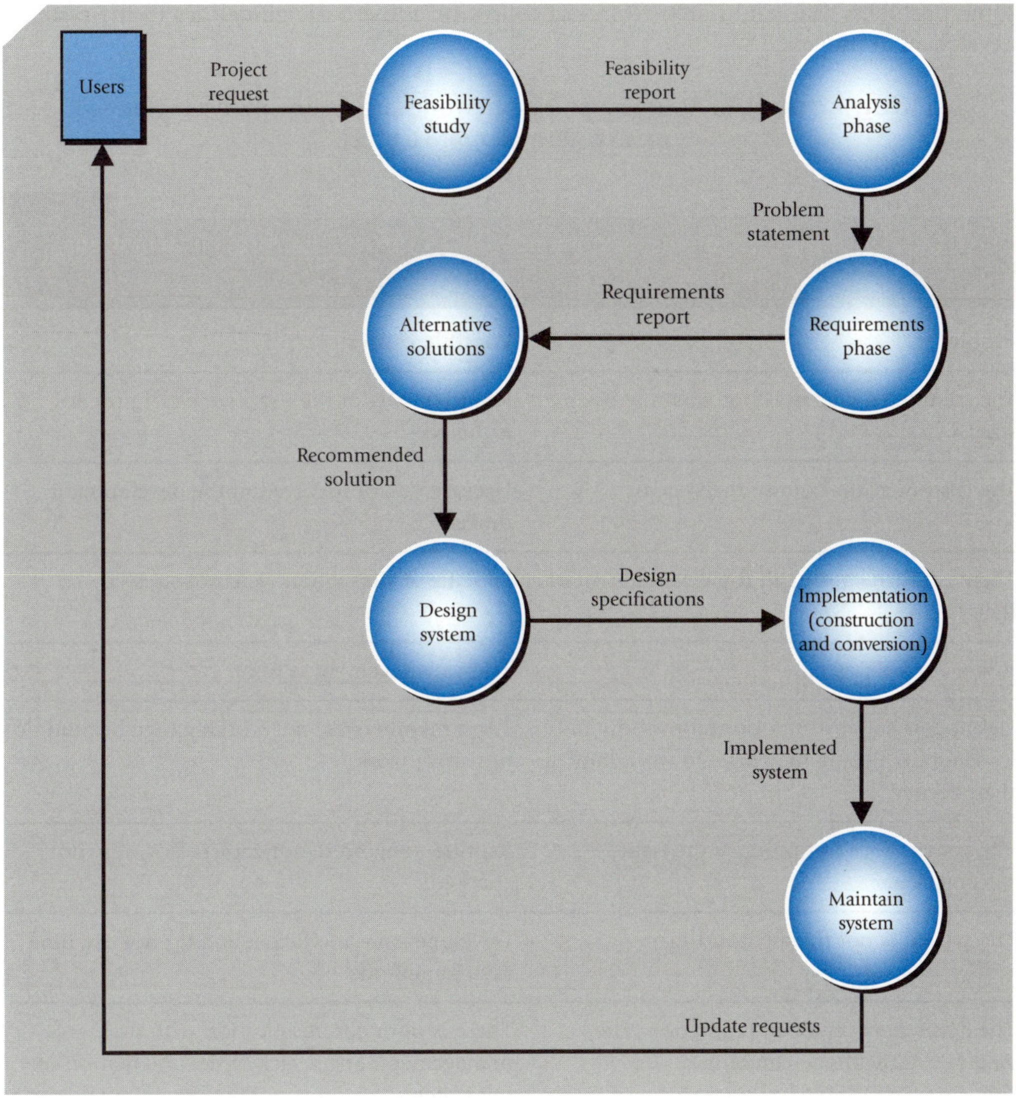

Figure 7.2 Systems development lifecycle

The broad phases of analysis, design, implementation and maintenance are used in many situations. Building a house, for example, requires a systematic approach. The requirements of the owners need to be considered in relation to major specifications such as the size of the house and the number of rooms. All the requirements need to be specified in a design drawn by the architect. The implementation phase involves the actual building of the house and, of course, as every home owner knows, continual maintenance is needed. Perhaps later down the track the home owner will require some major structural modification such as an extra bedroom or a kitchen extension.

The structured lifecycle approach evolved as a reaction to the problems of developing information systems in an ad hoc or unsystematic way. There are several inherent dangers in developing an information system without some type of framework. Table 7.1 lists some problems that could arise from not following some basic guidelines in the systems development process.

[**Key concept:** Structure and frameworks are nearly always preferred to an informal approach.]

TABLE 7.1 Some problems associated with an informal approach to systems development

Problems	Possible causes
The completed system is not what the users want.	Requirements of the users were not properly gathered.
The customers do not use the system.	Users were not involved in the development process.
There is much conflict in the development of the system.	Benefits of the system were not stressed.
Resources are wasted.	Team management is poor.
Developers suffer from poor motivation and low morale. People may have to work harder than needed.	Team members are not working together and do not share work.
The system does not produce the right information.	Requirements were not gathered or were not checked.
The system is not finished on time.	Developers are inefficient and do not use time-saving methods.
The developers get a bad reputation. The system is difficult to maintain.	There is poor communication with user management, and a lack of documentation on the system.

■ **Reflection question 2:** Can an approach to developing information systems be too structured?

The skills required by systems analysts

To effectively develop information systems, the systems analyst requires a wide range of skills. Many of these are general skills which are important in most aspects of business and will need developing throughout the analyst's career. As you read through the next section, ask yourself where your strengths lie and which skills you should work on.

Making a frank appraisal of your skills set is sometimes a painful exercise but a necessary one if you want to improve your chances of landing that challenging job or gaining that important promotion.

Communication and interpersonal skills

Have you ever heard anyone stand up and give a marvellous yet seemingly effortless presentation which informed and entertained the audience at the same time? Chances are that the person making the presentation had worked hard on his or her presentation skills for years and had also put a lot of preparation into the presentation itself. The same applies to that wonderfully constructed memo, letter or report.

Systems analysts require effective writing skills as they have to write many reports, memos, emails and letters throughout the systems development process. Well-structured and well-presented reports are important tools for communicating with users and senior managers. Oral presentations are also important in helping to guide the team in the development of the system, to report to managers on progress, and in requests for resources. At times, analysts will need to be enthusiastic in 'selling' the system to users and managers. The ability to relate to people, form working relationships and effectively negotiate are useful skills which the analyst should develop.

Infobyte

The need for business skills

As IS comes under increased pressure to deliver business value, there is a growing demand for IT staff with a blend of business skills, communication skills and sound technical skills. An additional factor creating the need for business skills is the blurring of the boundaries between IT, marketing and business development. Knowledge of the business means that developers can focus on the creation of systems that add value to the organisation and know how to use information systems for competitive advantage.

Analytical and problem-solving skills

Many problems arise when dealing with computerised information systems. The analyst must be skilled in analysing and solving problems. Rather than looking upon them as a continual series of problems, many analysts see them as challenges and opportunities for improving the system.

The solution of problems may require creative thinking; this is an especially useful skill in the systems design phase where **multimedia interfaces** can provide a competitive edge.

Technical skills

Systems development requires an understanding of the technical issues related to technology in order to make sound recommendations concerning the systems design details. Programming, for example, is usually a very involved and intricate task that demands a 'technical' aptitude and eye for detail. Project management skills include managing resources and people as well as time, and require technical methods, techniques and software. Project management is a fundamental skill which the analyst must be conscious of and make every effort to develop.

[**Key concept:** Systems development requires a blend of business, communication and technical skills.]

The tasks involved in each stage of systems development

Earlier in the chapter you were introduced to the four key stages of systems development: analysis, design, implementation and maintenance. The following describes in more detail the tasks that need to be carried out as part of the systems development lifecycle. Not all information systems projects require that every stage and task be completed fully. Remember, the systems development lifecycle serves as a framework for development and does not need to be used in exactly the same way on all projects.

Information systems planning

IS planning is an important issue for many IS managers and is covered in more detail in a later chapter. However, it is worthwhile looking at IS planning in relation to the systems development lifecycle. Due to the rapid changes in information technology, organisations are seeking to harness technology to help drive the business. IS plans are seen as a way of strategically positioning the organisation in terms of its use and development of information technology. An IS plan includes broad directions for the technology platform, the network infrastructure, the software architecture, and the key data and processes of the business, as well as identifying the IS/IT expertise and skills required by the organisation. Future project requests can be assessed from the perspective of whether they fall in line with the IS plan. This can reduce the danger of becoming side-tracked by projects that are not aligned with the organisational strategy and goals.

Infobyte

Drivers of m-commerce

It is often asserted that people will adopt mobile commerce (m-commerce) to purchase entertainment-related services like buying movie tickets. One survey conducted in Finland (Anckar 2002) found quite the opposite. Although all service types serve as motivators for adoption to a certain extent, it is the routine services that constitute the primary driver to taking on m-commerce.

Routine services are those that are used on a regular or even daily basis, such as mobile email. This suggests that m-commerce adoption is mainly driven by the need to improve efficiency and to add convenience and flexibility to our daily routines rather than excitement or entertainment. M-commerce can be used in similar ways in the workplace to improve efficiency and flexibility. It is important for systems developers to be aware of technology developments and trends in society since they can address these issues and trends in the information systems plan.

Feasibility phase

A project is initiated as a result of a user request, a management initiative, or the analyst's suggestion. The **feasibility phase** has a simple aim: to determine whether the suggestion or proposal is a worthwhile one. It may involve gathering information on, and understanding, the current system if there is one. Problems are identified and the benefits of solving them are assessed. If no current system exists, then research may be carried out on similar systems in other organisations. The feasibility phase is a preliminary investigation which tries to identify the scope of the project and determine the project's validity. On occasions, potential broad solutions are suggested and estimates of costs and benefits are made. Of course, at this stage, all the costs and benefits are difficult to identify and quantify. A more detailed cost–benefit analysis is often left to subsequent stages when more detailed information is known. The outcome of the feasibility stage is a feasibility report on the project, which is typically presented to management. A decision must then be made on whether to move on to the next stage of the lifecycle, to cancel the project, or to shelve the project for the time being until conditions become more favourable.

[**Key concept:** Anything you do in systems development requires justification.]

IS in action

Collaboration rules!

Employees of organisations are more mobile than ever before, making them difficult to reach. A study has found that between 25% and 35% of employees at large organisations in the US are mobile, spending at least 20% of their time away from their primary workspace. The use of email, voice mail, mobile phones, personal digital assistants and video-conferencing is helping co-workers and customers communicate, but even these technologies present problems because in many cases they are not integrated.

(*continued*)

The solution for the University of California, Berkeley is to deploy the Oracle Collaboration Suite in order to create a unified messaging solution based on a single inbox that contains various message types such as email, voicemail and faxes. The project was started by the desire for an enterprise calendar system. The existing system being used was Meeting Maker. The system worked at the departmental level but did not scale up to enterprise level, crashing often and forcing people to re-enter data.

Oracle Calendar, which is part of the Oracle Collaboration Suite, was chosen for a number of reasons:

1. It could cope with the 15 000 staff and 32 000 students.
2. The Oracle Calendar works across operating systems. This is important since there are many operating systems in use on campus, and integrating with existing systems was not a problem.
3. Oracle was perceived to offer stable software products, and so the risk of problems or errors with the system was thought to be low.
4. The Oracle Collaboration Suite offers other modules of interest. The suite has strong wireless underpinnings, which is important to the university.

The University of California's requirements highlight a number of systems development issues, such as the scalability of solutions, a unified solution, integration with existing platforms, reliable software vendor selection, and catering for the needs of users for mobile applications access.

Source: adapted from http://otn.oracle/oramag/oracle/03-may/o33collab.html (accessed May 2003).

Analysis phase

A systems development project usually involves an examination of the current operations and systems. For example, in assessing the development of a new order processing system, the existing system should be analysed to gain an understanding of the strengths and weaknesses of that system. The problems associated with any information system fall into broad categories (see table 7.2). The costs associated with the problems can then be estimated. This information can be used to justify the expense of the new development. If the proposed system is completely new, then this phase can be used to research systems in other organisations.

When analysing the current system, analysts conduct a detailed investigation that uses various information-gathering techniques such as interviews, observation and questionnaires (see the later section on information gathering). The study phase typically requires considerable end-user involvement. Data-flow diagrams are commonly drawn to document the existing system and form part of the documentation for the stage together with a study phase report which identifies the key problems and associated costs.

TABLE 7.2 Common problems found in information systems

Symptom of problem	General problem
Managers find it difficult to make decisions	Lack of information
Customers complain about invoices	Inaccurate data
Reports are not used	Inappropriate level of information
Complaints about delivery times are received from customers	Too slow in producing information
Users do not know how to query the database effectively	Expensive information

[**Key concept:** IS problems usually fall into the categories of speed, accuracy, relevance, availability and expense.]

Requirements phase

After studying the current system, analysts must try to define the requirements for the proposed system. Again, this phase requires much end-user involvement and uses a range of information-gathering techniques. This phase of the systems development lifecycle is a logical one. The emphasis is on defining what is required in terms of the information requirements rather than how the system should be physically implemented.

The requirements of the proposed system can be documented using process models (data-flow diagrams) and data models (entity relationship diagrams). A computer-aided software engineering tool can be used to develop and store the documentation of the system. A presentation can be made to user management at the end of the stage to communicate the essential requirements of the proposed system.

Infobyte

Have you really considered all the users?

A significant percentage of users, particularly of web sites, have some form of disability. Indeed, many vision-impaired people rely heavily on the Internet for information. Because these people use screen readers, careful attention should be given to each web page to ensure that table content is summarised, graphics and videos have text summaries and that the page is effectively formatted when read by screen readers.

The role of CASE

Computer-aided software engineering (CASE) is used in the development process to manage the vast amount of data and information that is gathered. It provides diagrammatic modelling tools and, in many cases, validation of the logical and physical designs (see figure 7.3). The **data** (or **project**) **dictionary** is the repository of data input through templates in the CASE tool (see figure 7.4). Eventually, every aspect of the system is modelled and recorded in the software and this should be kept up to date once the system is implemented. **Upper CASE tools** focus on the analysis and design phases of the systems development lifecycle and **lower CASE tools** concentrate on the implementation and maintenance phases. The advantages of using CASE tools are:

- they improve the quality of system documentation (i.e. better presentation, fewer errors and omissions)
- they improve the quality of the completed system
- they improve communication between analysts
- they improve maintainability of system
- they can potentially speed up the development process.

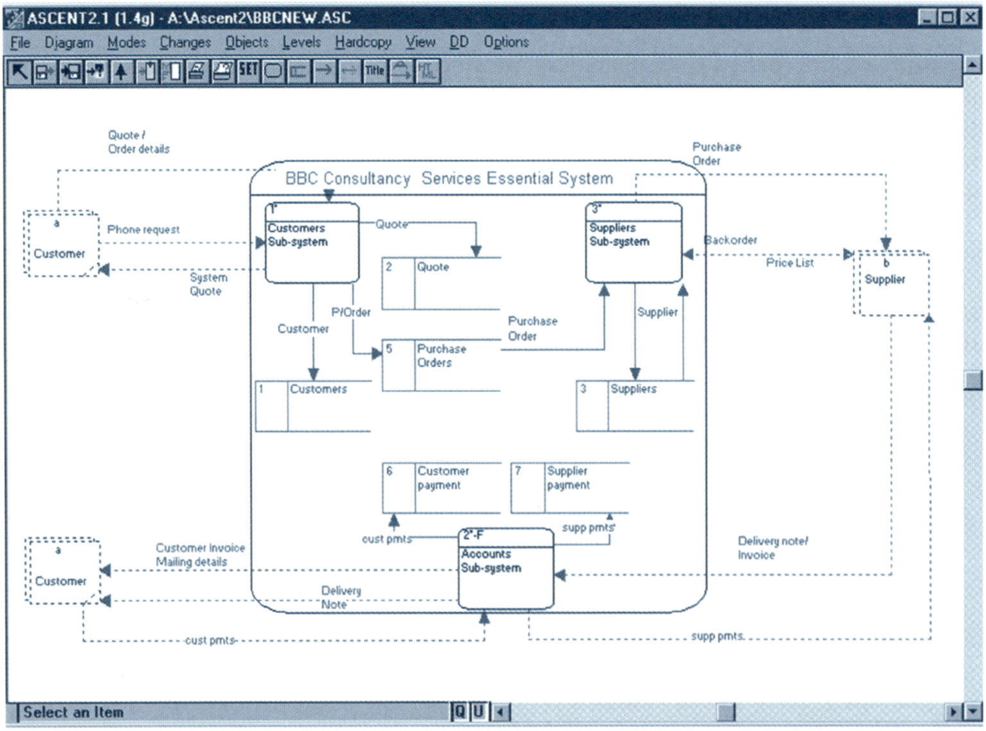

Figure 7.3 Data-flow diagram drawn in a CASE tool
(*Source:* Knowledge Base 2001)

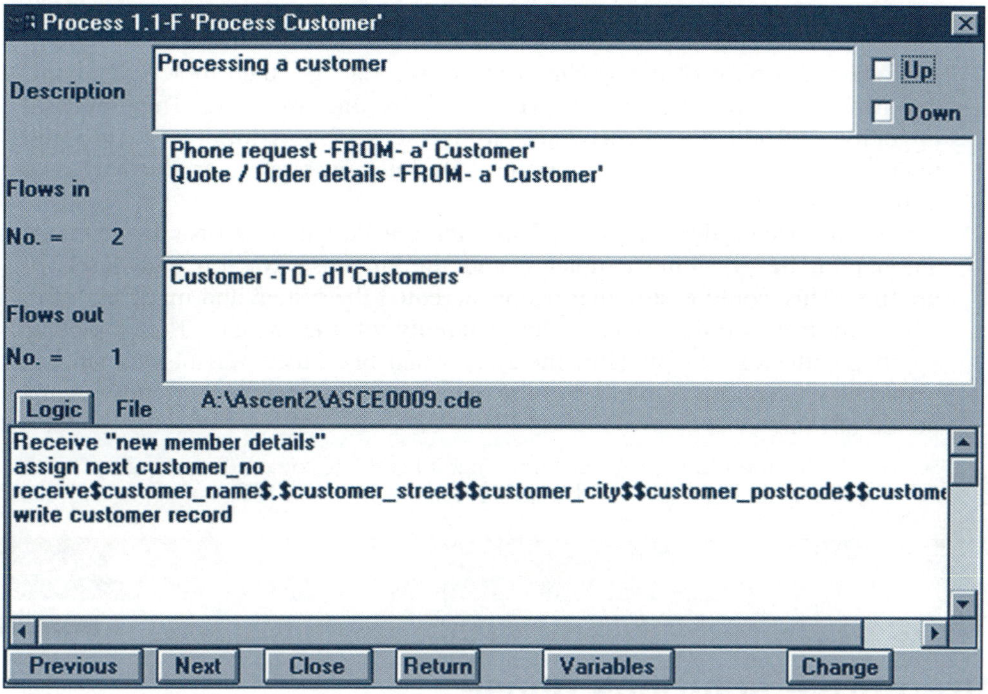

Figure 7.4 Data dictionary entry in a CASE tool (*Source:* Knowledge Base 2001)

IS in action

Court management information system

The European Court of Human Rights in Strasbourg had a real information-processing problem whereby it felt it was drowning in applications. The court needed a way of managing and processing the increasing number of applications, which had grown to 35 000 per year.

The court developed a court management information system (CMIS) to manage the operations of the court and process the applications. The system delivers benefits to the organisation because it creates an integrated database of digital documents. Applications have to be registered and tracked to create an online database. Most of the applications are rejected — as many as 85%. The system integrates with the court's document management system, event management, automation of tasks on case files, search screens, model letters, timetable generation and reporting module. The system has more than 400 users, which will increase to 600. More than 2000 forms and model letters were developed to save time re-creating standard letters. Any external document can be input to the system electronically or scanned whereas internal documents automatically go into the system.

(*continued*)

The planning stage for the system took six months, which involved user group sessions and a pilot of the system. The project manager then took a 'big-bang' approach since the system was converted in one weekend. This involved migrating 500 000 documents into CMIS. The system is intuitive to use and requires only two hours of training. Overall, processing productivity was improved by 60%.

From a systems development perspective the design increased the levels of automation by providing templates, and the emphasis was on high levels of usability. This would ensure that people accepted the system and made use of it, which in turn would increase the reliability of the system. The 'big-bang' approach after various pilots of the system had been tried was needed since it would have been impossible to run the old and new systems concurrently for any period of time.

Source: adapted from http://mimage.hummingbird.com/alt_content/binary/pdf/collateral/ss/dm_echr.pdf (accessed May 2003).

Alternative solutions phase

The **alternative solutions phase** involves identifying possible implementation solutions for the requirements. Ideally, several options are proposed rather than one, and the analyst presents these to management to decide on one. Alternative options might include a fully automated system, a partially automated system, or using alternative technology. The option of keeping the system as it is should be included as a way of comparing the proposals. The technical details of each alternative system are specified and the costs estimated. Much depends on the resources and the type of system being developed as to the level of detail for each specification. Time constraints do not usually allow the developers to specify all candidate solutions in absolute detail.

[**Key concept:** Always assess the implications of making no changes to the current system.]

Design phase

Systems design is a physical stage of the systems development lifecycle because it concentrates on how the proposed system will be designed. All aspects of the proposed systems have to be designed (see table 7.3).

Database design is a common and critical part of the systems design phase of the SDLC. The characteristics of a well-designed database are many, but here we focus on the key characteristics:

- Minimise redundancy of data. This requires that data are specified only once within the database. Although it is not always practical to do this, the objective is to minimise the amount of redundancy or duplication of data that is likely to create update problems in the future.

- The database should be flexible to the needs of users. In other words, a user should be able to create reports and obtain relevant information on the basis of their own requirements. If the database is designed with flexibility in mind, this should be achievable.
- The data within the database should be reliable and accurate. If the database is properly designed, it is more likely that the correct data will be input and errors will be trapped. Also if data are not duplicated, an update requires the updating of just one data set rather than two or more.
- The database should be designed to respond quickly to requests. Careful design and fine-tuning of the database will provide fast retrieval of data.

Of course, a database that is well designed should be easy to use and understand.

TABLE 7.3 Activities of the systems design phase

Activities of systems design	Description of tasks
Software and hardware acquisition	Sourcing and buying hardware and software. Evaluating vendor recommendations.
Database and file design	Setting up the database. Fine-tuning the performance of the database.
Network design	Designing the data communications infrastructure.
Input design	Designing forms and input screens.
Output design	Designing reports and output screens.
Interface design	Designing the user interface (usually graphical user interface).
Software or program design	Designing the software for modularity and reusability.
Design of methods, procedures and controls	Timing of events and specifying the conditions they operate under.

Hardware and software acquisition

Hardware and software may have to be acquired for the proposed system. If there is to be a substantial investment in technology, then this task needs considerable effort. If company officials are sure about the hardware and software required, then they can approach various vendors and ask for quotes for the products. Warranty agreements, price of products, quality of equipment and reputation are all factors to be considered in choosing a supplier. Other factors such as whether the supplier is a local company that will collect equipment under warranty for repair can be important as there are usually delays involved when distances are greater.

If the decision-makers have not decided on particular hardware and software, they will require vendors to make recommendations with justifications in this area. The requirements of the organisation should be outlined for the vendors who should respond with their suggestions. The vendors' proposals can be ranked using a scoring system which allocates points on a scale of 1 to 10, for example, for each feature of the recommendations.

IS in action

Systems integration at the ABS

The Australian Bureau of Statistics (ABS) has over the years assembled a diverse range of applications, platforms, architectures and toolsets. The 250 applications require 200 people to manage them. In addition to the range of applications there is also a diverse range of hardware and operating systems.

The ABS IT team decided it was becoming too difficult to manage such a diverse range of applications. However, it had a large investment in the systems and could not afford to abandon them. The ABS also wanted to find ways of making its data more accessible to the community at large.

The solution to these problems lay in the concept of component interfaces and web services. These technologies allow a modular software development approach whereby the software can be clipped together in a building block fashion.

To test development environments, a prototype system was created to assess the interoperability, ease of use and effectiveness of each environment. A range of development environments were evaluated, but in the end Microsoft's Web Services and .NET was chosen.

.Net had certain advantages:

- it worked well with multiple vendors and in a range of environments
- it was based on industry standards
- it supports a choice of programming languages, which leverages the existing skill set in the organisation.

From a systems development perspective, the ABS's case is interesting since it had identified an increasingly common problem: independent systems that need to cooperate. A prototype environment was developed to test the potential solutions, which led to a decision on the most suitable tool. A key factor was leveraging existing skill sets, which would reduce delays due to the learning and training associated with adopting new programming languages. The decision would help developers to be productive from an early stage.

Source: adapted from www.microsoft.com/australia/business/casestudy/studies/the_australian_bureau_of_statistics.asp (accessed May 2003).

Implementation

Implementation is the phase in the systems development lifecycle when the system is built and tested (construction phase) and then handed over (conversion phase). Of all the phases, this usually takes the most amount of time. In fact, a lot has to happen during implementation.

There are a number of major tasks to be completed during implementation, including:

- altering rooms and buildings
- coding programs
- testing programs
- installing hardware
- systems software set-up
- installing applications software
- installing the network
- database set-up
- keying data into database
- further testing
- putting security measures in place
- testing security measures
- training staff
- updating documentation
- handover of the system
- reviewing the system.

■ **Reflection question 3:** Which of the tasks above are not necessary when a software package is bought rather than developed?

The most important aspect of systems implementation is project management, which is the scheduling of events and the organising of people to achieve set goals. Many projects run over time or over budget because of poor project management. Projects may run over time for several reasons:

- Estimations of task duration may have been over-optimistic. This often happens as a result of trying to win contracts or being too eager to please project sponsors.
- Poor project management skills of the project leaders can lead to a failure to see all the tasks involved and the capabilities of the team.
- The project team may be poorly motivated. They may be lacking incentives to complete the project on time.
- Clients may be poorly motivated. Staff can drag their heels and put up obstacles if they are resisting change.
- The skills of the project team may be inadequate for the tasks. They may not be the right people for the job or they may not have had sufficient training.
- People may be unwilling to be accountable and take responsibility for corrective action.

Testing

Computer-aided mistakes can have severe consequences. Mistakes that result from software or hardware problems can lead to loss of life or loss or damage to property, or financial loss. Computers are used in many critical situations such as:

- controlling air traffic
- flying aeroplanes
- for hospital treatment
- manufacturing processes.

The effects of undetected errors in such systems are potentially disastrous. Recent cases have involved giving cancer patients too great a dose of radiation over a prolonged period (software error) and an aircraft falling from 9000 to 6000 metres in a few seconds (software error).

We can all see the seriousness of such cases. Mistakes in the business world can also be very costly; for example, a bank recently processed the debits and credits twice for one day (software error), and there have been reported mistakes occurring in mortgage calculations.

Determining who is responsible and hence liable for computer-aided mistakes can be a legal minefield. A number of factors have to be taken into account, such as:

- whether the error resulted from a mistake in the program (developers)
- incorrect data stored in a file or database (the users or possibly the developers)
- whether the person using the computer was incompetent or was badly trained (users)
- inadequate requirements provided (user or developers)
- inadequate requirements gathered (developers).

In other words, the problems in relation to a computer system not working properly can result from a wide range of factors. **Testing** aims to minimise the number of errors appearing in a system and to ensure the system performs adequately. These might seem straightforward objectives but, in fact, testing is far from straightforward.

Testing is an ongoing task. After every phase of the systems development lifecycle, developers test the accuracy of the system by:

- going over the work
- going through the documentation with users
- referring back to earlier stages of the SDLC and overall project goals and aims to see if everything is consistent.

The main focus of testing is during construction and delivery of the system. The testing is carried out by the systems developers and the users of the system.

The systems developers test the software as it is being written and then the system as it is being put together. There is some time during implementation when the developers work with the users to test the system. There is usually some time after the system is handed over when the users test the system alone and report back to the developers (see figure 7.5).

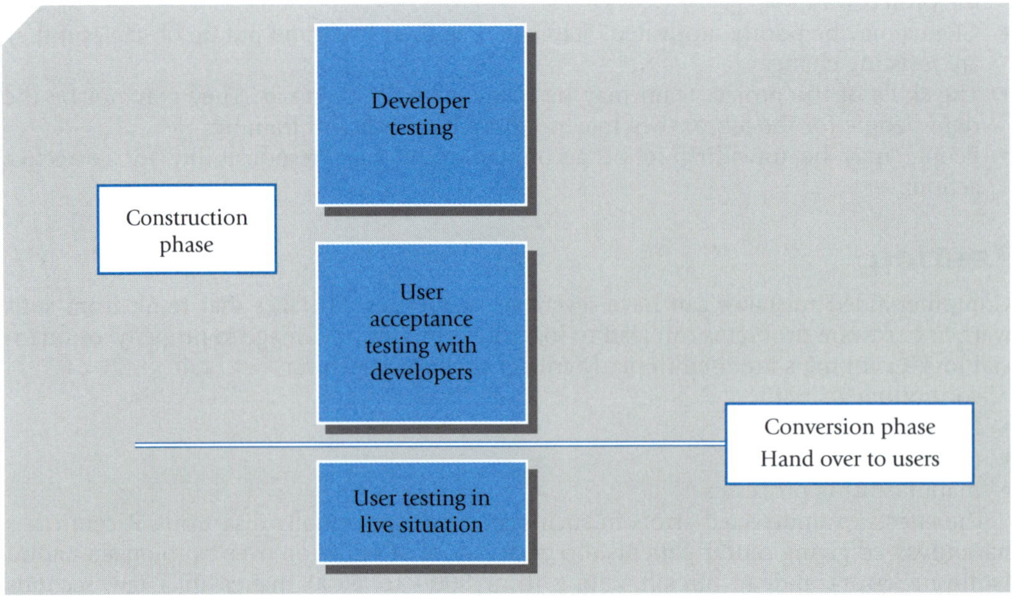

Figure 7.5 Testing during implementation

Systems conversion

Systems conversion is a stage in the project when processing changes over from one system to another. There are several ways that conversion can be carried out.

- *Direct conversion* — on a set date, dispense with old system and start with new system.
- *Parallel conversion* — run both systems for a time.
- *Pilot conversion* — the system is tested in one location before others are converted.
- *Phased conversion* — subsystems are implemented one at a time.
- *Evolutionary conversion* — this takes the perspective that a system evolves in small increments rather than radical changes from old to new.

Maintenance

Maintenance projects can be divided into two categories. The first category concerns correcting errors in the system. The errors may have been detected during the systems development process but left to a later date for correction. The second category concerns detecting errors when the system has been running for some time. The problems are logged and attended to in batches if they are deemed not to be critical. If they are critical to the system, they must be attended to as soon as possible.

Changes will need to be made to the system at various times due to changing requirements. These changes may come about because of new regulations, changed preferences, or new techniques which can improve the performance of the system. A change to a system can be a significant project in its own right and may require following the systems development lifecycle, albeit a shortened one.

[**Key concept:** The cost of maintaining a system often amounts to more than the initial cost of developing the system.]

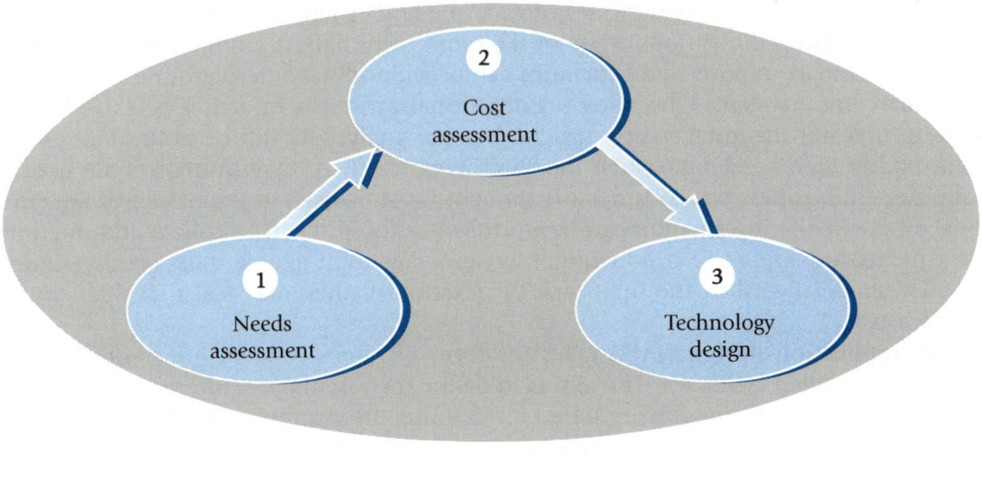

Figure 7.6 Key stages in the development of small systems

The lifecycle for small systems

Clearly, in a small business or where a small system is concerned, not all tasks will be performed to the same level of detail. However, the systems development lifecycle is still a good framework to work within. The emphasis with small systems will be on the needs assessment and associated cost assessment leading to the technology design (see figure 7.6).

Information gathering

Fact-finding or information gathering is undertaken at various stages throughout the systems development lifecycle. It is particularly important in defining the problem(s) and the requirements. Researching design options and the technology also require information-gathering techniques. There are nine common fact-finding techniques:

1. Analysing company documentation.
2. Analysing forms, files and database records.
3. Visiting other organisations.
4. Researching topics in magazines and journals.
5. Observation of the systems in action.
6. Questionnaires.
7. Interviews.
8. Informal conversations with users.
9. Joint application design (JAD).

■ **Reflection question 4:** Is there any particular order in which information gathering should be carried out?

The systems analyst must be skilled in gathering information. Table 7.4 (opposite) gives some of the strengths and weaknesses of each method. There is much that can be determined by accessing the various types of data and information within the organisation. Analysing company reports and brochures can provide valuable background information about the current system. Observing organisational processes in action is a useful technique to find out the glitches in a system, but the analyst should be aware that people often modify their behaviour when they are being watched. Questionnaires are used in many areas of business but considerable thought must be used in the design of the questions, otherwise the information can be worthless or too difficult to collate and interpret. The same hazard applies to conducting interviews. The right people must be interviewed, and they should be asked the right type of question or they may feel that their time is being wasted.

Joint application design (JAD) takes the form of intensive workshops with key personnel and a skilled facilitator. The aim is to define the essential requirements of the new system. JAD can reduce the time required for defining the requirements and be very effective if the workshops are properly organised and structured.

[**Key concept:** The systems analyst must be skilled in gathering information.]

TABLE 7.4 The strengths and weaknesses of information-gathering techniques

Method	Phase(s) used	Strength of the method	Weakness of the method
Analysing company documentation	Feasibility Analysis	Gives good background information.	May be out of date. May not reflect reality.
Analysing forms, files and database records	Feasibility Analysis	Good for detailed information.	May be out of date.
Visiting other organisations	Requirements	Learn from others' mistakes.	May not be possible to gain access to other organisations.
Researching	Design	Valuable sources of information from experts.	May not be easy to find relevant information.
Observation	Analysis Requirements	Can find out first-hand how things work.	May give a distorted view of events and work.
Questionnaires	Feasibility Analysis Requirements	Can involve a large number of people in a cost-effective manner.	Not easy to construct, or few may reply, or difficult to get detail.
Interviews	Feasibility Analysis Requirements	Can get detailed answers.	Time-consuming and sometimes difficult to arrange.
Informal conversations	Analysis	Good for finding out problems.	Can give a distorted view.
Joint application design	Requirements	Shortens the time to define requirements.	May not be possible to get key people for enough time.

Systems modelling

At this point it is worth introducing an overview of systems modelling methods. At the start of the chapter we said that data modelling and process modelling were part of the systems analyst's toolkit. In fact, the two most commonly used types of modelling in systems development are data modelling (entity relationship diagrams) and process modelling (data-flow diagrams). The two methods are complementary but were never originally designed as cohesive modelling techniques. However, there are a number of systems development methodologies which use both modelling approaches. An entity relationship diagram represents a static view of the data in a system and the data-flow diagram is used to model the dynamic aspects of the system or how the data is changed (processes). Most CASE tools facilitate the development of both techniques and the details and cross-references can take place in the data dictionary.

Data modelling

Data modelling is a method of organising and documenting a system's data. The models produced are considered to be logical models as they are implementation-independent. They form the early stages of the database design. Although the data are always changing in a business, the types of data collected are fairly stable. Data are usually more stable than processes and hence some methods put the emphasis on data modelling. One methodology that does this is James Martin's Information Engineering (Martin 1989).

[**Key concept:** Data change less than processes.]

Entity relationship diagrams

The **entity relationship diagram (ERD)** is a data-modelling technique that shows the relationships between the data within a business. It is not a technique to show how data is implemented, created, modified or deleted. Figure 7.7 shows an ERD for a company's order processing system. This ERD forms the basis of the database design and, as can be seen from the diagram, implies that data will be stored on customers, products, orders, and so on.

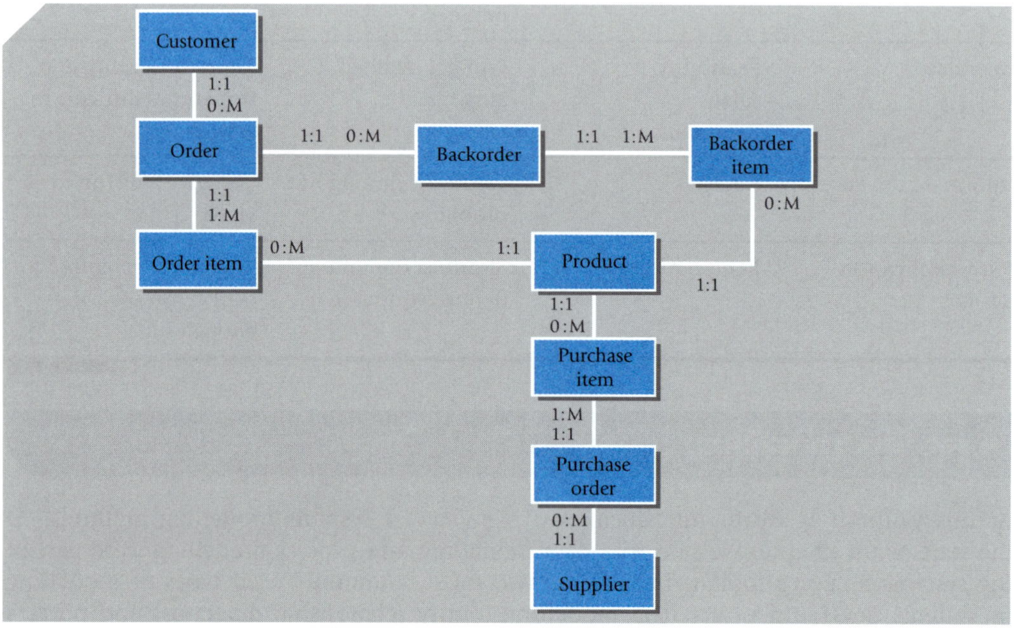

Figure 7.7 Entity relationship diagram

A data entity is anything, real or abstract, about which we want to store data. A rectangle is used to denote a data entity. Each entity has a list of attributes to describe it with one or several of them acting as the key or unique identifier. The following is a list of example entities:

Machine	Book	Contract
Applicant	Borrower	Contractor
Order	Client	State
Campus	Patient	Customer
Project	Purchase order	Quote

A data relationship is shown by a line between the entities. The relationship between entities can be made more explicit by defining the degree of relationship. The degree of relationship between entities is denoted by:

[0:M]zero or many

[1:M]one or many

[1:1]only one.

The entity relationship diagram in figure 7.8 shows products being ordered from suppliers and can be read in the following ways:

- A purchase order is filled by one and only one supplier. This is a [1:1] relationship.
- A supplier fills zero or more orders. This is a [0:M] relationship.
- A product is contained on zero or more purchase orders. This is a [0:M] relationship.
- A purchase order contains at least one product. This is a [1:M] relationship.

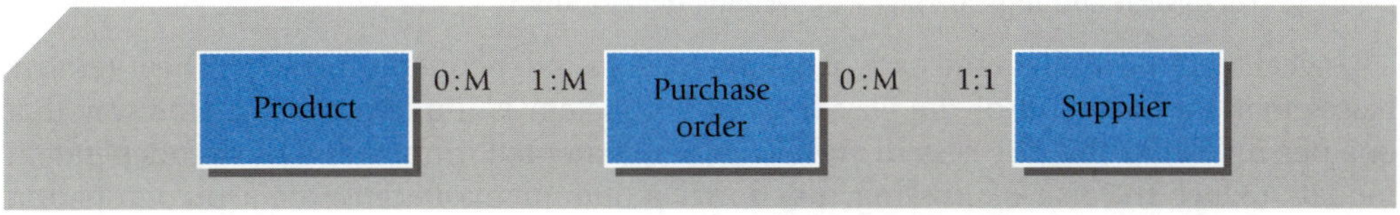

Figure 7.8 Part of an entity relationship diagram to show the ordering of products from suppliers

Of course, all entities are described in the data dictionary within the CASE tool (see figure 7.9 at right).

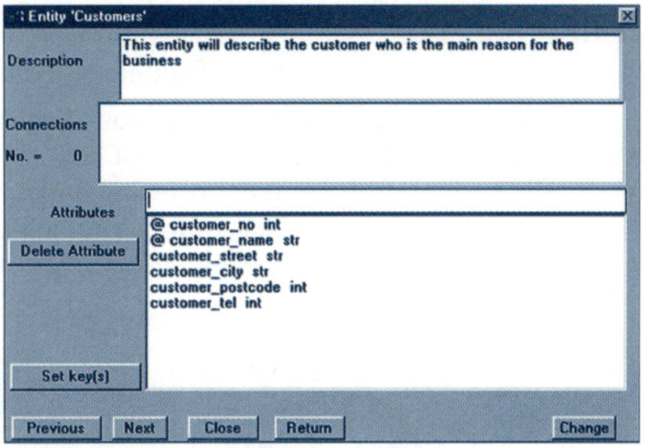

Figure 7.9 Data dictionary entry for an entity

Process modelling

All the actions that take place in a company, such as an order being received and dealt with, are processes. **Process models** using data-flow diagrams model system processes and are commonly used by systems analysts. They can be used to model both the existing system and the proposed system.

Reports as a form of communication have been partially replaced by diagrams in systems development for a number of reasons: diagrams are less ambiguous; diagrams show relationships better; and diagrams summarise material.

Data-flow diagrams can either show the physical details of implementation or be logical diagrams without the physical details. As figure 7.10 shows, they can be used:

- in the problem definition phase during analysis (physical data-flow diagrams)
- to view the current system logically (logical data-flow diagrams)
- in the requirements definition phase (logical data-flow diagrams)
- to describe alternative solutions (semi-physical data-flow diagrams)
- in the design stage (physical data-flow diagrams).

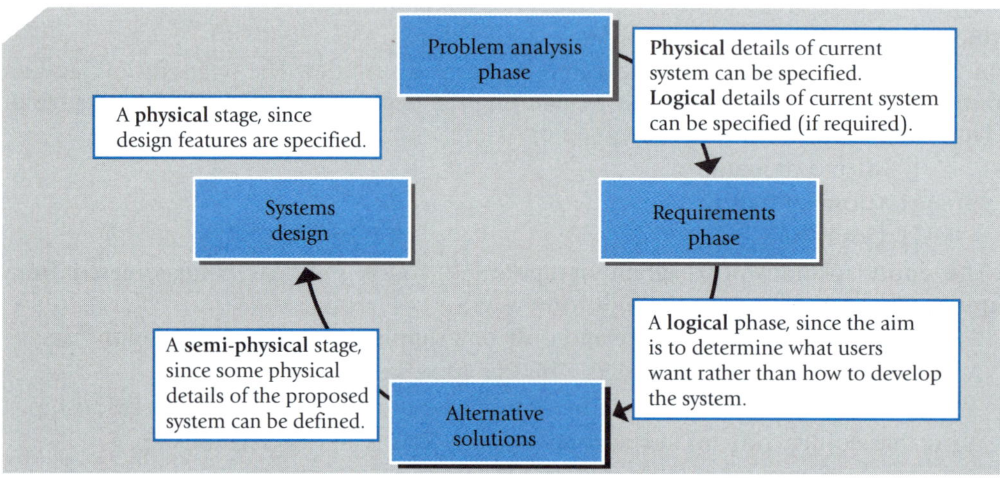

Figure 7.10 Physical and logical stages of systems development

Logical data-flow diagrams are implementation-independent models. They remove biases that are the result of the way the existing system is implemented, or the way that one person thinks that the system should be implemented. Implementation-independent models reduce the risk of missing functional requirements because of a preoccupation with technical details. They allow the analyst to communicate with the user in a non-technical way when gathering requirements.

[**Key concept:** Avoid specifying physical features of the system before you know the information requirements.]

There are four symbols used in data-flow diagrams (see figure 7.11(a) to (d)):

- the *data flow* symbol shows the flow of data (a)
- the *process* symbol shows the processing of data (b)
- the *entity* symbol shows data coming into and going from the system (c)
- the *data store* is a symbol to show the storage of data (d).

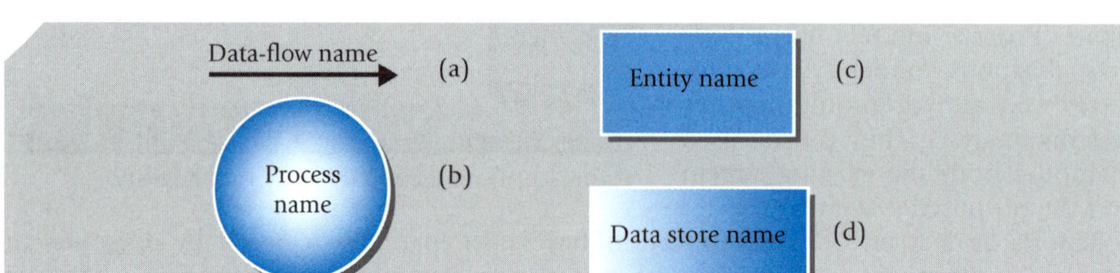

Figure 7.11 Symbols used in data-flow diagrams

A data-flow diagram for an order processing system is shown in figure 7.12.

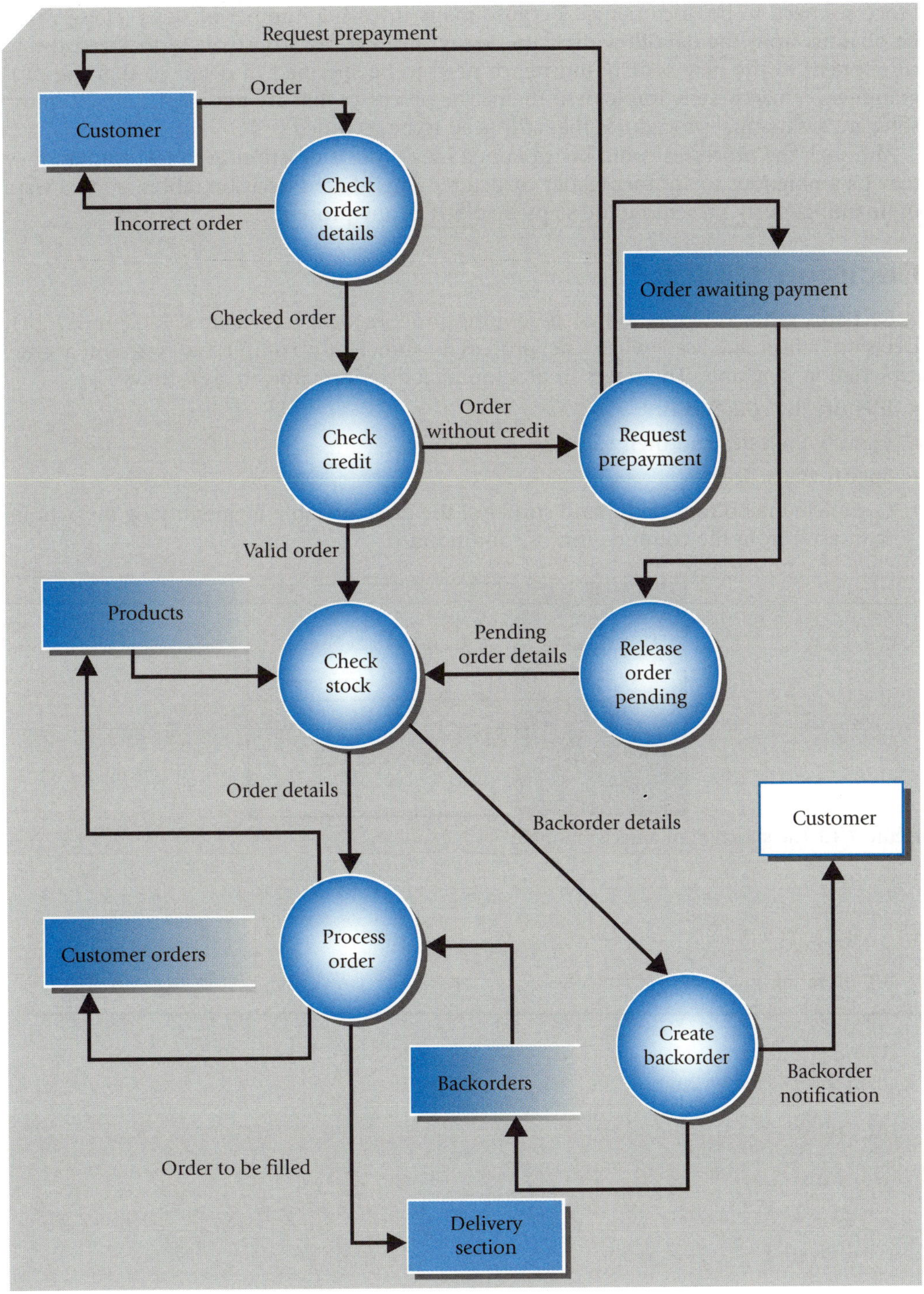

Figure 7.12 Order processing diagram

Data dictionary entries

Processes need to be documented because many involve a number of steps. These won't be obvious from the data-flow diagram. Many of these processes will form the software component of the new system and hence need to be specified in detail so that the programmers can accurately implement them. The processes that are not implemented in the software are manual procedures that still need to be recorded.

Although the processes could be explained by a process description in text format, they may be ambiguous to another reader. Structured English and decision tables are two ways of unambiguously presenting the steps involved in any process.

Decision tables

A **decision table** is a method of describing process logic (see figures 7.13 and 7.14). Decision tables are used when the process is sufficiently complex to warrant a clear explanation in a table. The stages in developing a decision table are as follows:

- Identify the conditions.
- Identify the rules and their values.
- Specify the actions.
- Complete the bottom right-hand corner of the decision table by identifying the actions that result from the combination of conditions.

Conditions	Condition values
Actions	Action values

Figure 7.13 The structure of a decision table

CONDITIONS	RULES											
Credit rating	A	B	C	A	B	C	A	B	C	A	B	C
Over 26?	Y	Y	Y	N	N	N	Y	Y	Y	N	N	N
Employed more than three years	N	N	N	N	N	N	Y	Y	Y	Y	Y	Y
ACTIONS												
No credit						X						
Credit level A		X	X	X	X			X	X		X	X
Credit level B	X						X			X		

Figure 7.14 An example decision table

Structured English

Process logic can also be defined using **structured English**. The decision tables are used for defining business policies and structured English can be used for defining business procedures. The two are complementary techniques (see figure 7.15). Structured English uses a restricted set of terms, file and attribute names to describe the high-level logic. There is no set vocabulary for structured English but its style must be brief and to the point. It relies on the use of repetition, condition and sequence statements.

```
For each credit application
  Case 1 (credit rating A) then
    If age < 26 and employed < 3 years then
      assign credit level A
    else
      assign credit level B
    end If
  Case 2 (credit rating B) then
    assign credit level A
  Case 3 (credit rating C) then
    If age < 26 and employed < 3 years then
      assign no credit
    else
      assign credit level A
    end If
  End Case
```

Figure 7.15 An example of structured English

Systems development methodologies

So far in this chapter you have gained an understanding of the systems development life-cycle and common systems modelling techniques. The principles of the SDLC form a framework for developing information systems. Because the SDLC is a general approach it needs an extra slice of formality to be really useful in organisations. This formality commonly takes the form of a standardised set of rules and procedures for developers of information systems to follow. When the extra formality is added the approach is called a **methodology**. The aim in this section of the chapter is to present an understanding of information systems methodologies and to provide insights into a number of well-known IS development approaches.

An **information systems methodology** can vary from a series of steps used in solving a problem to a general approach to problem solving, or it can even be a philosophical approach. Depending on the nature of the problem and the contextual environment, any one or a combination may be appropriate to use in the systems development process.

We define an IS methodology as a collection of philosophies, phases, procedures, rules, techniques, tools, documentation, management and training for developers of information systems.

Generally, the components of an IS methodology describe:

- how a project is to be broken down into stages
- the tasks to be carried out at each stage
- the outputs to be produced
- the actions or events to be carried out
- the constraints to be applied
- the support tools to be used.

A methodology is often used as a project management tool to create a better end-product, a better development process and a standardised process. There are two main types of IS methodologies: structured methodologies and behavioural methodologies. The lifecycle discussed in this chapter is characteristic of traditional structured methodologies. Examples of these include information engineering and structured systems analysis and design methods (SSADM). Structured methodologies, although not really scientific, tend to draw on the credibility of the scientific method.

[**Key concept:** Choose a methodology appropriate to the situation.]

Behavioural methodologies

Behavioural methodologies take an organisational perspective. The real complexity in an organisational setting comes about as a result of the interaction of the components of the system. The system encompasses such things as the people, technology, protocols, procedures, organisational culture and politics, and the wider business environment. The **soft systems methodology (SSM)** is perhaps the best known behavioural methodology used in information systems (Checkland & Scholes 1990).

Examples of IS methodologies

Information engineering

Information engineering (Martin 1989, 1990) is a methodology that takes a data-driven approach. This means that data models and data modelling are at the heart not just of any one system but the organisation as a whole. The enterprise-wide approach to systems development is also the reason it puts such an emphasis on systems planning. Process modelling is given some attention but is not given the same priority as data modelling. The methodology is supported by a CASE tool called information engineering workbench (IEW).

Object-oriented methodology

Although **object-oriented development** has much in common with the structured approaches described in this chapter, it differs in that it focuses on the notion of objects that encapsulate both data and methods (processes). This means that objects can be developed and then reused in other parts of the system without worrying greatly about their internal structure. For example, suppose there is an object which is a picture. It could be developed to include the method to display it on the screen so that if the object is reused in another part of the system it carries with it the code to display it. The object acts as a self-contained feature of the system.

Traditional structured techniques were developed when data was mainly text-based. Increasingly, systems have to store multimedia information and hence object-oriented methods are seen as a more appropriate way of handling these diverse forms of data. Object-oriented development has also made an impact on web applications through the use of Java applets. Java is an object-oriented programming language which can be used for developing web applications or stand-alone applications.

A **class** serves as a template from which to create objects. The class defines the properties (data values) that can be stored for an object and the methods or functions that can be performed on the data. For example, a STUDENT Class could be created that provided a template which included a student's personal details, such as First_Name, Last_Name, Date_of_Birth, Sex and so on. The methods could be Add_Student(), Delete_Student() (see figure 17.16(a)). This class could then be used to create objects that store students' actual personal details (see figure 7.16(b)). Classes can be arranged in hierarchies to improve reuse through a technique known as inheritance.

Student
PROPERTIES Student_ID: First_name: Last_name: Date_of_birth: Sex:
METHODS Add_student() Delete_student()

(a) Class for student

Student: 095614
PROPERTIES Student_ID: 095614 First_name: James Last_name: Jones Date_of_birth: 23021980 Sex: Male
METHODS Add_student() Delete_student()

(b) Object for student

Figure 7.16 A class and object

There are a number of advantages of object-oriented approaches from a systems development perspective:

- Reuse of objects is encouraged. This cuts down on the development time required for new systems as objects are reused when new subsystems are developed.
- Systems are more reliable. As an object is a self-contained entity with its own data and processes, they should be reliable and robust, and are less likely to have undesirable effects on other parts of the system. Also the reuse of objects that have been tried and tested improves the reliability of systems.
- Consistent development paradigm. Object-oriented approaches cover analysis, design and implementation by object-oriented programming languages.

- Flexibility is improved and complexity is reduced as the basic objects can be used like building blocks that can be drawn into the development of new subsystems.
- Objects are based on features of the business that are unlikely to change rapidly as opposed to the specific information needs of users at any given time.

From a systems development perspective, objects need to be defined along with their relationships to other objects for the system being developed. This is termed **object modelling**. The properties (data) and methods (procedures) for each object would then need to be detailed. Although a range of object-oriented methods has been developed, the Unified Modeling Language (UML) is widely known. UML includes a range of modelling techniques for identifying and presenting the objects in s system and the relationships between them.

Prototyping

Prototypes have been used by engineers for many years. They generally develop a small-scale working (or simulated) model of a product. In systems development, a prototype is used to supplement the systems development lifecycle in order to define requirements and/or try out designs. Structured methodologies were seen to concentrate on documentation and were perceived as inflexible. If the users were uncertain about their requirements, the methodology became a barrier to the progress of the project. Developers became frustrated by this scenario and many questioned the need for full documentation on all projects. Prototyping was seen as a partial solution to some of these problems. It relies on tools that enable the interface to be specified quickly. Examples of prototyping tools are Microsoft Access and Visual Basic. It can be used as part of rapid application development (RAD), the main aim of which is to quickly put together a system shell by using structured methods, joint application design (JAD) techniques and prototyping methods.

Four types of prototyping have been identified: feasibility prototyping, requirements prototyping, design prototyping and implementation prototyping (Whitten, Bentley & Dittman 2000).

Feasibility prototyping

This is used to test the feasibility of a specific technology approach that might be used for an information system. For example, a college wants to improve its enrolment procedures, since too much time is spent on keying in the data, and it is believed that students could possibly input the data directly into the computer system. Hence, a prototype is designed to test a range of student reactions to inputting the details of enrolment. In other words, it allows some input and simulates some basic searches. On the basis of the students' reactions, the college can decide whether or not to go ahead.

Requirements prototyping

This type of prototyping is used to define the users' requirements. It is used as a tool to encourage interaction between users and developers. The prototype is composed of screens which have menus, icons and forms to illustrate the types of data to be captured or output. Users can then use the screens as a prompt to give further information. The actual design of the screens is not really important.

Design prototyping

The user interface of the system can be developed and shown to users. The users assess the ease of use, the layout, the order of input fields, help messages and so on, and provide feedback to the developers who can then modify the prototype. After several iterations the interface should be in line with what the users find acceptable to work with. However, the prototype may not become the finished system; another tool may be seen as more appropriate for implementing the software.

Implementation prototyping

When the design prototype is extended to become the actual system it is called an implementation prototype. In this case it would not include certain editing and security features which would be added later.

Prototyping is not a return to development without a methodology and documentation. The development process needs to be managed and, ideally, used alongside another methodology. It should be used with set objectives in mind, such as for a small project, or as part of the design of the interface of a large system. It is not a panacea for all systems development problems.

Rapid application development

Rapid application development is a systems development approach which aims to speed up the development process. It combines prototyping, CASE and joint application design (JAD) in an iterative cycle until the users and developers are satisfied with the system designs. JAD involves collecting requirements in a group-based situation. The developers and users work closely together with an emphasis on getting the system developed. It was put forward by James Martin as a reaction to the problems with methodologies that followed a more traditional systems development lifecycle where the development process was thorough but often seen as time-consuming.

- **Reflection question 5:** Why do you think developing systems quickly is of concern to systems developers?

Infobyte

Agile software development

Agile software development can be defined as a method of software development that aims for customer satisfaction through the early and continuous delivery of useful software components. The approach tries to reduce the failure rate associated with many software projects.

Agile software development is really a bundle of ideas based on the following principles:

- Start with only the essential requirements.
- Develop, complete and accept code in small increments.

(*continued*)

- Use small development teams.
- Have members of the team work together on writing and checking code.
- Involve non-IT executives in project teams.

Extreme programming (XP) is a development method derived from the agile development approach with the same aims of improving software development times and reducing the risk of project failure.

Soft systems methodology

Soft systems methodology (SSM) grew out of dissatisfaction with structured techniques for their underestimation of the issues associated with defining the problem(s) with the current systems and in defining a way forward. Peter Checkland developed the methodology not just as an information systems methodology but as a general problem-solving approach (Checkland & Scholes 1990). SSM has seven stages but has, at its core, the development of 'rich pictures' and the ethos of empowering users to decide on the acceptability and desirability of any changes to be made. The rich picture is a freeform sketch drawn by the user. It incorporates such things as concerns, challenges, issues, politics and competition. The SSM sessions are facilitated in such a way as to promote open discussion based on the idea that real progress cannot be made until the issues and concerns are acknowledged.

Summary

The systems development lifecycle and the techniques and methods embedded within it provide systems developers with a framework to work within. However, there are a number of different types of approaches to building information systems, and all have their applications. The key points in this chapter are:

- The systems development lifecycle (SDLC) provides a structured framework for building information systems.
- Identification of problems and requirements is carried out during analysis before detailed design issues are considered.
- CASE tools (computer-aided software engineering) can be used to manage and document the development of systems.
- The design phase involves database design, network design, software design, design of reports and forms, interface design and design of organisational procedures.
- Cost, warranty, leasing arrangements, and the proximity of the supplier are some of the factors which may need to be considered when acquiring hardware and software.
- The system requires a significant amount of testing before it is eventually handed over to the users.

- The systems analyst needs to be skilled in the various information-gathering techniques and ideally should have sound business skills.
- Entity relationship diagrams (ERDs), data-flow diagrams (DFDs), decision tables and structured English are techniques to model and describe the data and processes in an organisation.
- The term 'information systems methodology' is used to describe the approach to developing an information system.
- Object-oriented methodologies form an alternative development approach which involves specialised analysis, design and implementation techniques.
- Prototyping, rapid application development (RAD) and joint application design (JAD) are methodologies that emphasise user involvement and speed of development.

Questions

1. Why do you think that improving the time taken to develop information systems has been a major concern in the industry for many years?
2. Imagine that you have been asked to get involved in the development of an information system as part of a team. You are surprised to find no methodology is being used. Explain to the rest of the team some consequences of not using some form of methodology or guidelines.
3. Can any phase of the systems development lifecycle be omitted?
4. Why are communication skills so important for a systems analyst?
5. Explain the value of drawing a rich picture as part of the soft systems methodology.
6. Do you think prototyping would speed up the development process? Explain your answer.
7. How does process modelling differ from data modelling?
8. Where is process modelling used in the process of developing information systems?
9. Where is data modelling used in the process of developing information systems?
10. What is the value of developing a decision table?
11. What advantages are usually put forward in relation to CASE tools? Can you see any disadvantages of using a CASE tool in the systems development process?
12. Explain the advantages of using object-oriented methodologies in developing systems.

Exercises

1. Using an organisation with which you are familiar, identify an information system problem of some kind or some situation that could be improved with the introduction of a new system. To help you spot areas for improvement, use table 7.2, especially the general problems column. Also think about complaints you or others have made about some aspect of the organisation and try to work out how an information system could improve things.
   (a) Explain the general and specific aspects of the problem or the need for a new system. Try to list the costs associated with the problem and the benefits to the organisation if the situation can be improved.
   (b) If possible, talk to employees of the organisation to gain first-hand insights into the problem and to test if your initial assumptions were on the right lines.

(c) Suggest how the problem can be solved.
   - If you were conducting a thorough systems analysis, list the information-gathering techniques that you would use to find out more about the problem or situation.
   - How and where would data-flow diagrams be useful in the analysis of the situation?
   - Suggest an outline design for the solution of the problem. Specify what the solution would require in terms of (1) hardware, (2) software (new software or modification of existing software), (3) change of organisational procedures and (4) training of users.

2. Work through the chapter and list all the possible delays that could occur during systems development. Alongside each point suggest a way the delay could be prevented or minimised.
3. Review the skills required by a systems analyst. Assess your capabilities and limitations in relation to these skills. Try to give yourself a score (out of a maximum of 10) for each skill. Justify your decision, and provide an example that demonstrates your use of the skill in the past. Present the skills analysis in a table.

CASE STUDY Developing systems at XL Ltd

XL Ltd is a printing and packaging company. It deals mainly with large companies and has around 2000 customers in total. There are, on average, 200 orders per day. The company is a family-owned organisation and many of the employees have worked for the organisation for many years. It is not a technologically innovative company but the staff know they must update their approach or suffer the consequences. The managing director is worried that sweeping changes may be hard for some employees to accept and so is concerned about how the entire process is handled.

XL Ltd had separate software systems for the processing of orders, accounts and stock. This arrangement was seven years old and was not integrated very well as the three systems were developed at different times and did not have a consistent interface, although data could be transferred between the systems. The interfaces to all three systems were not very easy to use for many of the employees. The managing director believed this to be the cause of many errors in the system as terms and key words were different in each system.

Besides order processing, accounts and inventory systems, XL Ltd wanted to investigate the use of the following systems:

- *Transport delivery system.* XL would like a system that produces a listing that includes the routes for the delivery of the goods. This will be used by the drivers so that a more economical delivery process is maintained. Currently, a member of staff works on the delivery routes for the drivers.
- *Marketing systems.* The company wants to use the data and information in the systems more fully to market more effectively to its customers. There is data on all orders for the past seven years.
- *Ordering via the Web for customers.* The managing director is conscious of the danger of being perceived as an old-fashioned company. She is still not convinced of the merits of ordering via the Web but would be very interested in hearing a proposal to do so.

The managing director and the new IT manager called a meeting with the senior members of the organisation to discuss the information systems at XL. The IT manager was given overall responsibility for the development of the new systems.

The IT manager explained that XL did not have the in-house expertise to develop the new systems and should go about selecting a good software development company to do much of the software selection and development while XL employees could do most of the analysis. The managing director explained that XL did not have a great deal of money so any outside involvement should be kept to a minimum. As a result, the IT manager selected two IT staff (Bill was asked to act as systems analyst and Jane as junior analyst).

Bill asked Jane to start gathering information on the problems and requirements of the new systems. Jane had little experience in doing so but decided to talk informally with a number of people in the organisation. The reports they gave were somewhat conflicting as some staff liked the existing systems and hinted that they would be very displeased if any major changes were made. Other staff appeared at their wits end with the information systems and suggested radical changes. Jane knew that the managing director wanted improvements and so chose not to spend time gathering more information from employees as this would only confuse matters further. She presented her findings mainly on the basis of her own dealings with the information systems in the organisation and passed them off as representative findings and requirements from the users.

Bill spent time modelling the data and processes related to the existing systems in a CASE tool that XL had recently acquired. Once he had received Jane's documentation about the users' requirements, he started creating models for the new systems. Once this had been done, a presentation was made to the managing director and senior staff who, although not fully understanding the implications of the models presented, were in agreement that the system should now be developed.

In consultation with the IT manager, who had been spending much of his time trying to oversee the corrections to the existing systems, a decision was made on the purchase of software. Jane was given responsibility for any customisation of the software.

To avoid employees clinging to the old systems it was decided to start with the new systems on 2 January after the New Year holiday break. Many problems were reported, and many of the employees threatened to walk out if they were not rectified quickly. The managing director was most upset and asked the IT manager to report on the situation immediately.

QUESTIONS

1. Outline the main causes of the problems that led to the disastrous situation at XL Ltd.
2. Did the team responsible for the changes follow the systems development lifecycle phases? What aspects of the systems development lifecycle were missed out?

(continued)

3. What approach would you have adopted if you had been responsible for the changes?
4. XL did not conduct a proper feasibility study. What were the consequences of not conducting a feasibility study, and what should it have included?
5. How would you have dealt with the concerns of the managing director about the staff coping with the changes?
6. Was the team responsible for the changes adequately skilled for their roles?
7. What can be done at this stage to salvage the situation at XL?

References

Anckar, B. 2002, 'Adoption drivers and intents in the mobile electronic marketplace: Survey findings', *Journal of Systems and Information Technology*, vol. 6, no. 2, pp. 1–18.

Bavington, A. 1995, 'Experiences in the use of the structured systems analysis and design methodology (SSADM) in a service organisation', Master's thesis, Edith Cowan University, Perth, Western Australia.

Checkland, P. & Scholes, J. 1990, *Soft Systems Methodology in Action*, John Wiley & Sons, Chichester.

Knowledge Base 2001, http://knowledgebase.server101.com (accessed January 2001).

Martin, J. 1989, *Information Engineering*, vol. 1, Prentice Hall, Englewood Cliffs, N.J.

—— 1990, *Information Engineering*, vols 2 and 3, Prentice Hall, Englewood Cliffs, N.J.

Whitten, J.L., Bentley, L.D. & Dittman, K. 2000, *Systems Analysis and Design Methods*, McGraw-Hill, New York.

Chapter 8

Strategic information systems management

LEARNING OBJECTIVES

After reading this chapter, you should be able to:

- explain the significance of strategic information systems planning in organisations
- describe various forms of competitive analysis that can be used in IS planning
- explain how IS/IT can be used as a strategic driver
- describe the components of an information architecture and its importance in IS strategic planning
- explain the advantages and disadvantages of outsourcing the information systems function
- explain the relationship between developing dynamic and innovative organisational culture and effective information systems.

8

Introduction

Anyone who owns a personal computer will know how quickly technology changes. Those who use technology at work or at home may sometimes think how they can make their work or life easier, be more efficient or just have more fun with hardware upgrades or new software. Large business organisations are no different — with the exception of fun perhaps. In the rapidly changing business environment, managers must constantly assess the contribution that technology and new or improved information systems can make to their organisation.

Who is responsible for keeping an organisation at the forefront of IS and IT developments so that it is competitive in its business sector? Although good ideas can come from anyone in an organisation, the bulk of the responsibility for developing leading-edge information systems rests with the senior IS management team. They must give considerable thought to these issues. Leading-edge IS strategies rarely happen by accident. Information systems managers have the responsibility for developing IS strategy and managing the day-to-day IS operations of the organisation. This chapter focuses on the process of developing IS strategy and chapter 9 examines the operational aspects of IS management.

There are a number of ways to go about developing IS strategic plans. It is not the aim of this chapter to cover them all, but rather to explore some examples of IS strategic thinking to provide insights into the ways that IS can be maximised for organisational advantage. The concept of competitive advantage is examined, together with how information systems can be used to gain a competitive advantage. Other strategic approaches include developing an IS/IT architecture, using IS/IT to support the business goals of the organisation, and using IS/IT to improve efficiency and effectiveness through value chain analysis.

The importance of strategy

A **strategy** is a plan for achieving medium and long-term goals. When this is specified for an organisation in a document that covers such things as the vision and mission of the business, the organisation's goals and how it will achieve them, then it is called a **strategic plan** (Bartol et al. 1998).

Strategic planning has been much maligned in recent years. Some critics pointed to all the strategic plans that were resting on the shelves of senior executives that were never referred to after they were initially completed. However, this is not a fault of strategic planning itself but rather a failing of management to follow through and implement the plans. Critics may argue that in a rapidly changing business environment there is little point in developing large-scale detailed plans which quickly become out of date. Those in favour of strategic planning argue that a loose-fitting, general framework or plan is better, one that can accommodate changes in technology and in the business environment. As you work through the chapter, consider this argument and make up your own mind about the usefulness of the approaches.

- **Reflection question 1:** Can you think of other reasons why strategic plans might never become reality?

A strategic plan is important for two main reasons. First, it provides the organisation with a focus and clear mission which can be communicated to employees, suppliers and customers. People work better and more productively when they understand what the aim of the business is. They can make decisions more easily and effectively if they have a clear understanding of the organisation's goals. A clear strategy can be useful externally as suppliers and customers know what the organisation stands for.

[**Key concept:** Strategic planning enables a company to focus on what is important.]

Second, in the process of developing a strategic plan, the organisation should be able to identify where its strengths lie and how it can create or maintain a competitive advantage over other organisations.

IS strategic planning is concerned with helping the organisation achieve its strategy. For example, if a business had a strategy to tap into global markets, then IS management would look at how the IS could support this. One option would be to look at how the Internet could be used to reach new markets. This would need to be specified in the IS strategic plan. You might be thinking that the IS strategic plan is constantly changing, and to some extent you are right, since the IS strategic plan is a dynamic entity and needs to be continually updated in line with the organisation's strategy. However, because a strategy contains high-level goals, it stays relevant for longer than many would think.

Customer relationship management (CRM) is a business strategy to manage customer relationships on a long-term basis in order to add value. CRM becomes a strategic focus for the organisation when it embraces management, strategy and organisational culture. Thus, it cannot be effective if viewed solely as a technology solution.

Infobyte

Customer relationship management (CRM) systems highlight a lack of strategic planning

Properly understood, CRM is 'a philosophy that puts the customer at the design point, it's getting intimate with the customer,' [says Liz Shahnam, CRM analyst with the META Group]. Mike Littell, president of the CRM Division of EDS [in the United States] agrees: 'We view CRM more as a strategy than a process. It's designed to understand and anticipate the needs of the current and potential customer base a company has.'

Jim Dickie, managing partner of Insight Technology Group, says that while the basic idea behind CRM is simple, implementations are often ruined because 'CEOs are suffering from techno lust, in love with shortcuts, and are operating with a sense of urgency. As soon as anyone in any industry does this right, everyone else wants to jump on the bandwagon and have an instant solution.' When CEOs see the technology their competitors are using to bash their brains out, they simply order the same stuff for their company. 'There's so much pressure on CEOs to do it now that they usually manage to avoid doing it right,' Dickie says. Buying technology before you have your CRM business goals clearly in mind leads to disaster (Sims 2000).

IS/IT as a strategic driver of the business

In the early years of computerised information systems, the focus was on automating the day-to-day transactions of the business and thereby producing significant cost savings. These transaction-based systems contained great volumes of data in files which could be interrogated and summarised to produce management information. Decision support systems were more interactive systems which managers could use to improve their decision making. However, the view of the role of IS was one of supporting the rest of the organisation. In more recent times, there are cases where IS has taken on the role of **strategic driver** in organisations. In other words, the information systems are not just supporting other functions in the business but are the main reason for a company improving its position in relation to its competitors. In this sense, the information systems become a strategic driver for the business.

For information systems to be considered strategic, they should be helping the organisation achieve its goals and objectives and not just playing a role in the operational aspects of the business.

[**Key concept:** New technologies create opportunities for improvement and competitive advantage.]

Information systems management in organisations

IS management in larger organisations operates on several levels. A key person is the **chief information officer (CIO)**, who has overall responsibility for the information systems and for developing the IS strategy for the business. The CIO does not typically get involved with operational (day-to-day) activities of the IS function, but works with functional managers to ensure the IS are delivering the desired services.

The executive board of a business is responsible for developing the strategy of the organisation and will be led by the **chief executive officer (CEO)**. The CIO advises the board on IS issues and strategy and implements the board's directives.

The CIO may be called the IS manager in smaller organisations but has similar responsibilities. However, the position may call for more involvement in operational activities and any crisis that might arise.

Other management responsibilities within the IS function include the project manager, who takes charge of particular projects, and senior systems analysts, who are responsible for managing other analysts and programmers.

The role of strategic planning

You may have heard the saying 'If you fail to plan you plan to fail'. This is true of running a business. It is important for any business organisation that wants to operate effectively over the medium and long term to have a vision and strategic plan. A strategic plan should provide a focus for an organisation. Without a strategic plan, a company will concentrate on the day-to-day activities and lose sight of the big picture. The 'big picture' in this case is developing the goals and strategies to stay ahead of competitors. Strategic plans can be developed at several levels of the business and should ideally be integrated. The plan should be communicated to all stakeholders. An effective strategic plan which is properly communicated has the potential to radically improve the fortunes of a business. Any new CEO or CIO will work hard on developing a strategic plan for the company. It is the best chance of getting things working in the required way.

■ **Reflection question 2:** Can you think of personal examples from any area of your life when you used a form of strategic planning?

A strategy is a large-scale plan used to achieve long-term goals. However, a corporate strategy is made up of a number of components (see figure 8.1 on p. 218), which are discussed in later sections of this chapter. An organisation should have a **vision statement** which defines in a few sentences the company's main purpose. For example, Western Mining Corporation (WMC) is a large mining company with the following vision:

> WMC Resources is a minerals company determined to be BEST. We are committed to optimum Bottom-line performance, Environmental responsibility, the Safety and wellbeing of our people, and to Teamwork and leadership.

Interestingly, WMC's vision statement is not concerned solely with financial profitability. Of course, a business organisation has to be profitable at some point in its existence to be a viable entity. Nevertheless, other factors are increasingly being given consideration, including the environment and social issues, which are both reflected in WMC's vision. The safety of employees is also part of its social vision.

A vision statement can be expanded further, as in WMC's case, to communicate broad organisational aims in a **mission statement**. These aims should provide a steering mechanism for the functional units where more detailed objectives and goals can be specified along with strategies to achieve them. WMC's mission statement is:

> Our aim is to maximise shareholder value by finding, acquiring, developing and operating or participating in mineral resources projects around the world.

Looking at WMC's vision and mission, you can see key aspects of the business outlined. Although it is a short mission statement, it suggests many issues which can be a focal point for employees in the company. In some respects it provides a systems perspective, i.e. it recognises that everything is connected to everything else.

[**Key concept:** An holistic or systems perspective recognises that everything is connected to everything else and is important in achieving organisational success.]

A vision statement and mission statement are only two components of a strategic plan. Organisations typically develop strategies at three different levels: corporate, business and functional (see figure 8.2 on p. 219). The **corporate-level strategy** is developed by the senior people in the business. It can cover new business directions, the closing of some operations and the allocation of resources between branches of the company's operations.

Business-level strategy applies to organisations that have (semi)autonomous businesses operating independently. These businesses need to develop their own strategies as they are usually in the best position to do so. However, the business strategy should support the broad aims of the corporate strategy. In smaller organisations, the business unit level is not applicable.

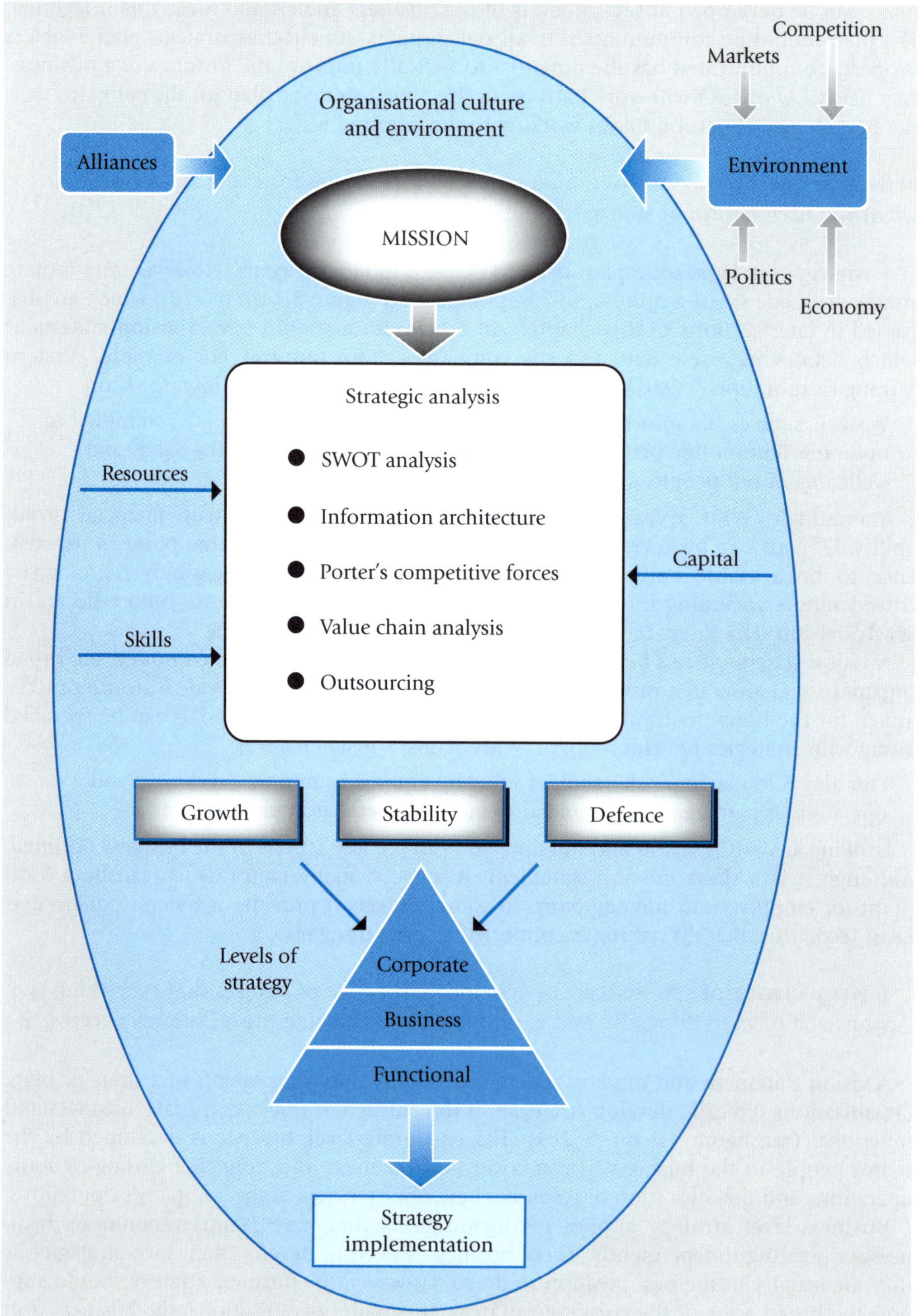

Figure 8.1 The components of corporate strategy

Functional-level strategy is concerned with plans at the functional business level such as marketing, information systems and finance. Effective strategies at the functional level can provide a competitive edge to the organisation as a whole. For example, the development of electronic commerce via a well-designed web site has the potential to improve market share for an organisation.

Coordination across the different levels is essential for strategic planning to be effective. For the corporate strategy to have any effect, it must be backed up by plans at the business and functional level that are aligned.

[**Key concept:** IS strategy formulation follows a top-down approach.]

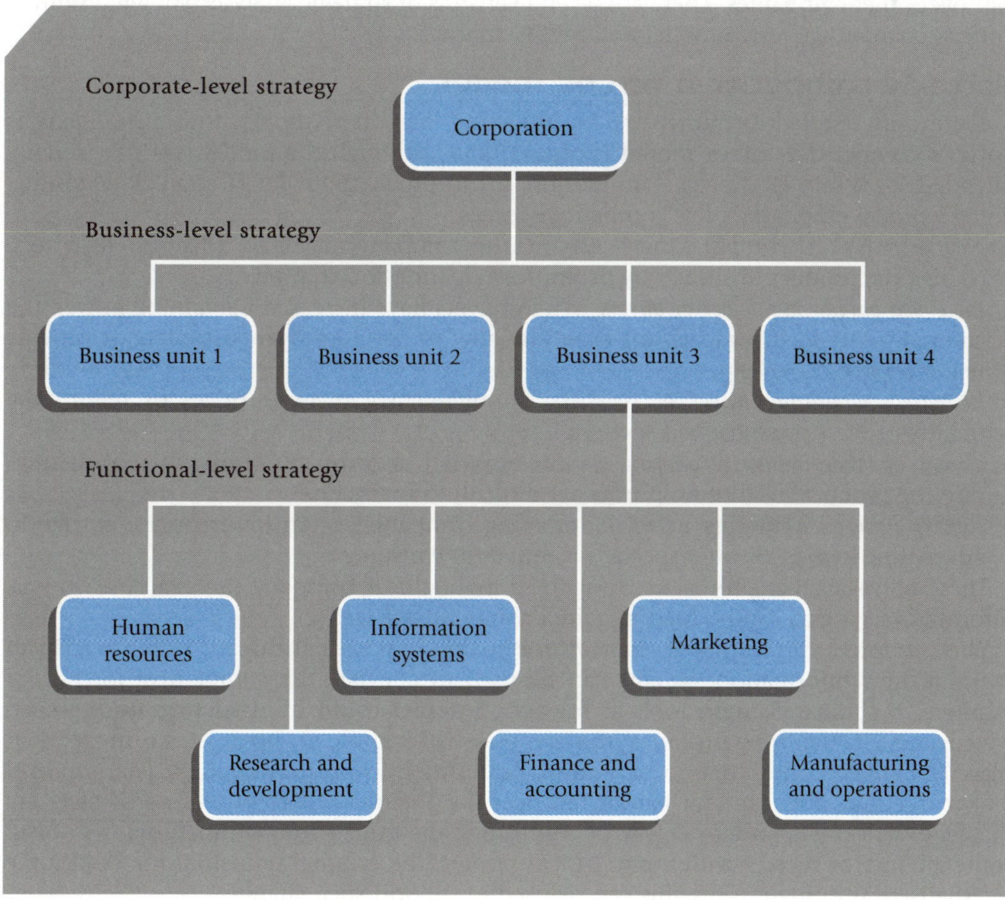

Figure 8.2 Levels of organisational strategy

The aims of IS strategic planning are to improve the performance of the business, to gain a competitive advantage, to add value to business processes, and to improve productivity or reduce costs. It should not be driven by the desire to adopt technology as an end in itself. In other words, there should be sound business reasons for adopting the technology. However, this does not prevent the technology, in some circumstances at least, becoming a business driver.

Strategic analysis approaches

Information systems can contribute to the strategic direction of an organisation in many ways. In the following sections, several strategic planning approaches are examined, each with their own strengths and weaknesses.

Competitive analysis

Competitive strategic analysis takes into account the competition in the business environment and the potential of using IS and technology to gain a competitive advantage over other companies. There are several versions of strategic analysis. We will examine Porter's competitive forces model and SWOT analysis.

Porter's competitive forces model

A commonly referred to framework for analysing the competition within an industry is **Porter's competitive forces model** (Porter 1985). Although the model was not initially intended for use in IT strategy formulation, it can prove useful for IT strategic planning. Porter's model emphasises five competitive forces:

- *New entrants.* To combat a new entrant, the company may have to lower its prices, change the product in some way or improve distribution channels.
- *Increased bargaining power of buyers.* When buyers have increased bargaining power, the company should investigate, for example, how to develop loyal customers or provide better service.
- *Increased bargaining power of suppliers.* Suppliers may increase prices or reduce the quality of their products and services.
- *Threat of other industries offering substitutes.* When a company finds other companies offering product substitutes, profits are difficult to maintain.
- *Rivalry between competing sellers.* Competing companies often lower prices, engage in advertising battles, or offer special incentives to consumers.

These all mean that profits are difficult to maintain. A company can examine how its information systems can be used to gain a competitive edge.

The five forces can form a framework for analysing potential threats. IS managers can examine how information systems can be used to alleviate the competitive forces. For example, a company might look at how the Internet could be used to promote cost-effectiveness in acquiring products from suppliers, or it could set up an electronic marketplace (e-market) or join one to have more flexibility in choosing suppliers. (An e-market is a market-like environment conducted over the Internet where buyers and sellers are matched with one another.) A way of controlling the threat from competitors is to form some alliance or merger with them. In this respect, the external industrial forces become internalised. Information systems can be used to support such changes.

Some might argue that Porter's model is a reactionary approach to strategic planning since changes may not be proposed until the threat becomes severe. It is also mainly concerned with competition — if there is little direct competition, there may be no impetus for change and improvement.

SWOT analysis

SWOT analysis is another form of competitive analysis (Thompson & Strickland 1995). The competitive situation for a company is assessed by examining its strengths (S), weaknesses (W), environmental opportunities (O) and threats (T). The competitive analysis will yield different results for each business examined. However, there are some broad categories of strengths and weaknesses that may be a useful aid in the analysis (see table 8.1).

TABLE 8.1 SWOT analysis examples

Internal to organisation		External to organisation	
Strengths	**Weaknesses**	**Opportunities**	**Threats**
Sound management	Poor administrative procedures	Growth market	Skills shortage
Greatest market share	Low profit margin	New government legislation	Recession in economy
Latest technology infrastructure	High staff turnover	Advantages of new technology capitalised on	New product developments create obsolescence of current materials
Highly skilled staff	Poor market image	Expand into new markets	Increasing competition
Low-cost product development	High-cost product development	Niche product	New legislation

The 'S' in SWOT analysis relates to the internal strengths of the business, such as streamlined administrative systems or technologically adept staff. The internal weaknesses of the organisation can be detailed in much the same way. The wider environment can be scanned for economic, technological and social trends that can be exploited. New government legislation may create an opportunity for some organisations, e.g. government departments may require suppliers to conform to new software standards. This creates opportunities for software consultants and IT-training organisations which could help companies become accredited. The external threats need to be considered because future prosperity depends on how the organisation deals with these.

Consider the travel industry, for example, and in particular the role of the travel agency. A strength of many travel agencies is the personal customer service they provide. This, in turn, often results in a high level of customer loyalty. Many travel agents have expert knowledge on certain holiday destinations and have a wealth of experience in the industry. One of the weaknesses of travel agencies is that they typically offer only what is available through their customer reservation systems, which is quite a restricted set of options. Many travel agencies also operate on small profit margins. Of course, there are opportunities in relation to using the Internet. Threats come from all sides — from airlines offering direct ticket sales to consumers and from online travel agencies and travel brokers marketing directly to the consumer.

Infobyte

Small business and the Web

Many small companies realise that e-business is influencing the way business is conducted and that it is likely to transform their business sector. Many have recognised the opportunities provided by the Internet, even developing their own web pages, but they are not obtaining significant returns from their investments. Studies have revealed that more attention should be paid in their planning to the strategic impact of e-business. This highlights the need for support systems for small business that provide them with information, access to knowledge and expertise on e-business.

[**Key concept:** Strategy development requires people to be aware of what is happening in the external business environment as well as what is happening internally.]

Gathering information about the business environment from various sources is known as environmental scanning. Environmental scanning is not a form of competitive analysis in its own right but rather a technique for helping in competitive analysis. It can be used, for example, to identify opportunities and threats in the business environment as part of a SWOT analysis. The Web can be a useful environmental scanning tool.

IS in action

Environmental scanning using the Web

Companies must have effective methods for obtaining information about the changing business environment. They need to build changes into their strategic plans to take advantage of opportunities and minimise the impact of emerging threats.

Companies pay substantial amounts of money to market research institutions for market information. However, organisations also gather their own information and data. Some information is gathered through informal networks of contacts. Increasingly, the Internet and the World Wide Web are being used to gather information on competitors, trends and changing consumer buying patterns.

The Web is a cost-effective tool for gathering competitive intelligence. People may be using the Web for environmental scanning without being aware that they are doing so. Many employees gather information on trends and competitors while using the Internet for some other purpose, and share this with colleagues, either face to face or by email. This is informal environmental scanning. Some companies employ people to spend some of their time doing environmental scanning. As the amount of data and information available on the Web continues to increase, it is likely that it will be increasingly used for environmental scanning.

As an example, an MIS department in a university could use the Web for environmental scanning. The type of information a department can gather includes:

- the number of similar courses being offered in the same state and country
- course fees charged by other universities
- target market of other universities
- course content and teaching methods
- trends in other countries for certain courses
- staffing profiles.

[**Key concept:** Use the tools around you to maximum advantage, in this case, the Web for environmental scanning. Most people use only a small percentage of any tool's potential.]

Reflection question 3: What types of information may be difficult to find on the Web?

Information architecture

The management information systems (MIS) function of the organisation should develop its own strategic plan which supports the corporate plan. This will cover its own mission and strategic directions, and identify opportunities and threats. The MIS strategic plan's main thrust is to develop and explain the information architecture that will provide the best return for the organisation. The **information architecture** defines the data, processes, information, organisational network and the stakeholders; information technology trends and opportunities are explained; the technology to support the business aims of the organisation is defined.

Clearly, the information architecture should be aligned with organisational business goals. The terms 'information architecture' and 'information technology architecture' are sometimes used interchangeably. However, the IT architecture is actually a subset of the overall information architecture for an organisation.

The IT architecture defines the computer hardware and network infrastructure, and includes the network, systems and applications software. Your own university or college will no doubt have put considerable thought into its IT architecture so that it can provide the best service possible to students. IT staff would have taken into account the need for general and specialist software, such as PCs running Windows software and desktop applications and more specialist scientific applications. The university's IT management would have thought through the effectiveness of the network and the compatibility issues of machines with different systems software. They will also be aware of the issues related to students connecting to the university systems from home. The aim in this type of environment is to provide a high level of service to each student but at the same time make the systems work together in a cost-effective manner. If the organisation has a general IT architecture which is regularly updated, serious issues related to performance, support and compatibility will be avoided.

The data systems within an organisation should be considered as part of the information architecture. A company that takes an enterprise-wide view of its data and information is more likely to effectively manage it so that data redundancy, duplication and errors are minimised. Compatible database systems, data warehouses and web databases all need to be considered.

The adoption and use of applications software within a company require planning. Unregulated adoption of software packages has implications for incompatibility of files, training and support for the software, and the expense associated with separate licensing agreements.

The organisation of the IS function needs to be considered. For example, the IS function must decide whether to be concentrated as a group, or release some staff to work closely with users in other departments and build up specialist knowledge.

[**Key concept:** Developing a coherent information architecture is always near the top of IS/IT manager's wish list.]

IS in action

Jailhouse IS architecture

Rapid population growth and a commensurate growth in crime has led to overcrowding of the prisons in Arizona's Maricopa County. In addition to building new jails, a review of the criminal justice system highlighted the need for the various justice agencies to integrate their information systems. The existing systems were plagued by redundant data, errors created through manual data entry, poor interface design and lack of data sharing.

The county's five major criminal justice agencies each had an IT department as well as unique hardware, systems, databases and operating systems. The county established the Criminal Justice Information System Agency, which encompassed representatives from each agency to create a convergent IS architecture to improve data-sharing.

To reduce the influence of the various political interests of the separate agencies, an independent consultant was engaged. The consultant produced a report that included integration requirements, architecture options and a list of recommendations. The list became the basis for the new architecture on which the five agencies agreed.

Source: information from CIO, Todd Datz, 'Jailhouse talk', March 2003, www.cio.com/archive/030103/case.html (accessed June 2003)

Alignment of information systems with business goals

The development of information systems is usually considered a business decision, not just an IT decision. There are IT decisions to be made, of course, but any IT development should be driven by the business needs of the organisation. Generally, information systems should follow a top-down approach so that the resulting systems are aligned with the strategic objectives of the organisation.

Western Mining's mission statement, discussed earlier in the chapter, suggests the need to strategically align the information systems function with the organisational goals. IS can be used to help manage mineral resource projects. The global focus of the company means that its systems are tightly integrated to facilitate global communication. Systems to provide information for decision-making purposes to save costs would be aligned with the goal of maximising shareholder value. This may include business intelligence software to provide an extra level of analysis and data mining. The vision statement stresses the environment and safety issues. IS can be used to support these areas, too. Monitoring the environmental impact of mining and modelling the likely impact of future mines can be done with geographical information systems. Safety data can be gathered, analysed and presented using a spreadsheet package.

It is worth considering potential outcomes from developments which are driven by information technology without due consideration of the strategic directions of the business. These types of projects can result in systems that:

- take too much time and money to develop because they do not have the full backing of senior people
- do not provide a significant return to the organisation because they are peripheral to the core business needs
- displace other, perhaps more worthwhile, projects from being developed as they consume organisational resources
- are not maintained effectively and eventually become a problem for the business. The information systems may be poorly perceived by the customers and/or employees.

There is a place in organisations for experimentation. Systems may be trialled and the returns monitored. However, they must be recognised as experiments with appropriate budget allocations which the organisation can afford to write off if the experiment does not produce worthwhile results. Projects that use leading-edge technology or use technology in an innovative way and are aligned with corporate strategy have the potential to provide a competitive advantage for the business.

Business process re-engineering

The concept of **business process re-engineering** emerged in 1990 (Hammer 1990) and was further developed in a work produced by Hammer and Champy in 1993. They define business process re-engineering (BPR) as the fundamental rethinking and redesign of business processes to achieve dramatic improvements in critical, contemporary measures of performance. Their approach implies a radical approach to business change. Manganelli and Raspa (1995) suggest that a clean-slate approach to re-engineering is not always necessary as the business may have great strengths which require developing and improving. Therefore, incrementally improving or replacing key processes may be the preferred strategy. BPR is helped by information technology and takes an added-value customer focus to the redesign and integration of organisational processes.

For example, an organisational process in a university is the student enrolment process. Many universities re-engineered this and related processes so they could be conducted over the Web. Before re-engineering, students completed paper forms and queued up at enrolment time to submit their enrolments for that semester. The forms were checked by the administrative clerk and passed over for input into the computer system. If a student changed his or her mind, a change of enrolment form had to be completed. This involved a great deal of time from the perspective of both student and administration. Re-engineered enrolment systems on the Web have the advantage of flexibility since students can enrol from home or work at any time of day or night. The university does not need as many staff to receive and check forms and input the data, as data are now input directly by students. The re-engineering of this function has saved universities considerable money and provided a more flexible and convenient system for users.

Using value chain analysis for strategic analysis

Value chain analysis is, perhaps, a lower level form of strategic analysis than, for example, SWOT analysis. In value chain analysis, the organisation is seen as a large input–output system. The inputs are resources brought into the organisation, processed in some way to add value, and then marketed and sold as outputs. The chain is usually supplemented by after-sales service. Value can be added at various points throughout the chain, such as acquiring products or resources more efficiently. The costs associated with each step and task in the value chain are determined. The costs are then compared with competitors' costs, and changes can be made to gain or sustain a competitive advantage.

Figure 8.3 is a value chain showing where web applications can contribute at each stage. The value chain consists of primary and support activities. The primary activities are the key tasks and processes that return the most value. The secondary activities support the primary activities and do not provide the same level of returns. These include administration, research and development, human resource management and information systems development. Web applications can contribute to both primary and secondary activities. The approach results in incremental improvements to the organisation.

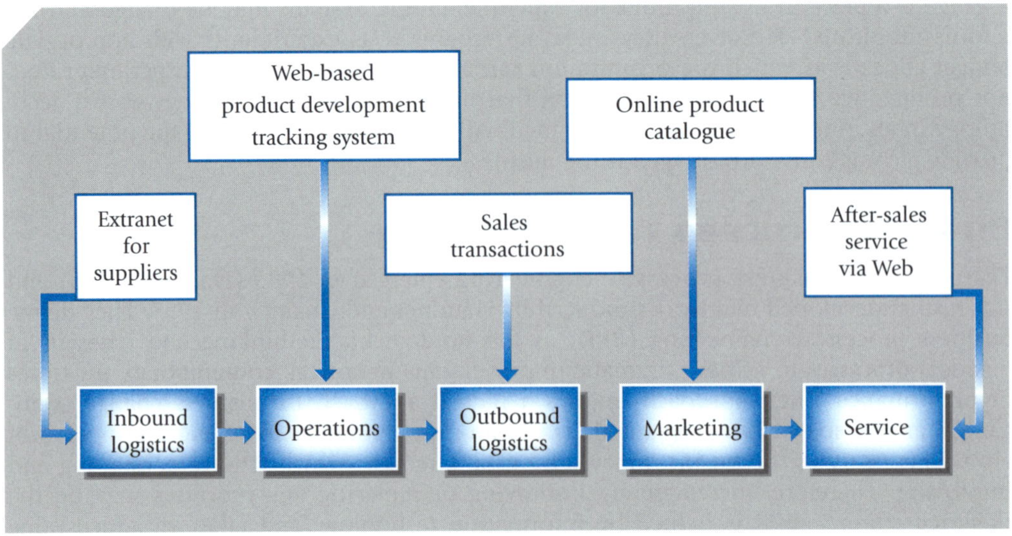

Figure 8.3 Uses of the Internet to add value to the primary activities in the value chain

IS in action

Making improvements to the value chain through ERP

US wine and spirit business Brown-Forman Corporation employs 6500 people and sells into 130 countries. Its brands include Jack Daniel's and Southern Comfort. Although about three-quarters of the company's sales are from wine and spirits, Brown-Forman also manufactures and markets high-quality consumer goods such as china and luggage.

To ensure ongoing profit growth in an increasingly competitive international environment, the company needed to reduce costs and improve service. The solution was to ensure that production, inventory and distribution capabilities met the demands of the market by developing new supply chain processes. The proposal put forward was strategic in nature, with the following goals:

- to improve performance relative to competitors
- to reduce lost sales because of a lack of stock
- to lower inventory levels to reduce production and carrying costs
- to strengthen partnerships with distributors and suppliers.

These goals were achieved in part using enterprise resource planning software (mySAP Supply Chain software). From a value chain perspective the major areas of focus were inbound and outbound logistics and inventory. The results of the project meant that over a 12-month period global inventory levels were reduced by 23%; product availability was maintained at more than 99.9%; transportation costs were decreased by reducing the number of carriers from 140 to 35, and the need to airfreight urgent shipments was generally prevented. A major benefit of the software was that it avoided the need to increase staff numbers by 80% in the area of planning support.

Source: adapted from: SAP AG, SAP case study, 'mySAP supply chain management at Brown-Forman', 2003, www.sap.com/solutions/scm/ (accessed June 2003); Brown-Forman Corporation Annual Report, www.brown-forman.com (accessed February 2004)

Outsourcing as an IS strategy

For strategic reasons, some organisations have decided to outsource some or all of their IS/IT function. **Outsourcing** in this context means off-loading the responsibility to an external organisation. One of the main reasons cited for doing this is cost savings, although there are others.

Various forms of IT outsourcing exist. For example, the external organisation might be used to manage the project but the people actually developing the system are internal to the organisation. This arrangement would be made when complex project management skills are required or when there is a history of projects not being completed on time or budget. On the other hand, a company might write the requirements definition and manage the process but have the external service provider actually develop the systems.

What are the benefits of IS/IT outsourcing for a company? Several benefits are shown in table 8.2. But the strategic importance of IS/IT in an industry sector and to an individual company is the key issue. Much depends on the resources and skills available in-house and how the existing systems are integrated with critical business processes. The benefits assume that a suitable and effective external agent is available and that the company is satisfied with the service provided.

TABLE 8.2 The benefits of outsourcing

Benefit	Reason
Savings in IS/IT	Reduces staffing levels. Reduces IS/IT training. Reduces cost of IS/IT recruitment. Saves on hardware and software (some data may be processed at external service provider's site).
Better planning	Easier to determine budget and, therefore, to plan.
Better decision-making	Management is free to focus on other areas of business.
Access better skills	External agency is the expert.
Access better hardware and software	IT/IS is the core business of the external agency.
Knowledge transfer	Internal staff may learn from external agency.

The literature on outsourcing suggests that the benefits outlined in table 8.2 do not always eventuate. For example, over time the external service provider may increase prices significantly, thus posing the question whether it is cost-effective to outsource. A company might feel that the level of service declines but it is locked in to the service provider contractually.

It may be difficult to gain a strategic advantage from information systems when the main responsibility for IS is handed over to an external agency. Although service providers may work hard to keep the contract, it is unlikely they would be as strategically focused as the company employing them.

■ **Reflection question 4:** What are some other problems associated with IS/IT outsourcing?

Infobyte

Offshore partnering

Outsourcing across continents is increasing rapidly. This is termed 'offshore partnering', and it is driven in many cases by the desire to reduce costs. High-quality labour in such countries as India is the answer for many companies in the USA, UK and Australia. A growing number of senior executives with offshore experience are willing to look at this type of option. However, outsourcing internationally is not without its problems, especially in relation to working across time zones and in different cultures.

[**Key concept:** There are always two sides to any IS/IT issue.]

Strategies for creating a dynamic environment

Most strategic analysis approaches are based on outlining a strategic direction with complementary goals and objectives. Many organisations use one or a combination of strategic analysis methods, such as SWOT analysis, Porter's competitive forces model or value chain analysis. However, another approach to developing a competitive organisation is to focus less on developing long-term goals and objectives and more on creating a dynamic and creative environment which organically spawns ideas and develops effective courses of action. The former approach is one where senior management set the strategic agenda in a top-down fashion, whereas in the latter approach there is much wider scope for ideas and creativity. Although the two approaches may appear to be opposed, they are not, in fact, mutually exclusive. Making the development of the organisational environment a key focus does not preclude strategic analysis in other forms being carried out. Goals, objectives and action plans are still needed but there is likely to be a much wider ownership and responsibility for setting strategy.

So what is driving the push for dynamic environments and new organisational forms? In a rapidly changing business world, companies need to be able to innovate to maintain a competitive advantage. Organisations must also be agile and able to change quickly to take advantage of opportunities and innovations. These attributes require new company structures. For example, rigid hierarchical management structures are notorious for slowing the decision-making process and, indeed, for killing innovation. Newer management approaches and organisational structures are moving towards the characteristics shown in table 8.3.

TABLE 8.3 Features which characterise new business environments

Organisational feature	Traditional company	Dynamic company
Structure	Hierarchy and bureaucracy	Dispersed personnel and outsourcing
Defining features	Optimising existing processes Slow and methodical Conflict covered up	Innovation — create new processes Speed as a competitive edge Openness
Boundary role	Clear boundaries between functions Knowledge 'silos' Computers play support role	Few boundaries, knowledge sharing Networks and alliances Computer systems and networks essential
Business approach	Product and structure define company	Service and innovation define company
Decision making	Precision and certainty Avoid risk Centralised decision making and ideas	Live with uncertainty Take risks Decentralised decision making — ideas come from anywhere

When an organisation embarks on recreating its organisational culture, it needs to develop appropriate information systems. The technological infrastructure in 'learning organisations' (i.e. companies with an ability to learn quickly) where knowledge workers predominate is typically quite sophisticated. It consists of widespread use of email, groupware for document management and control, a multifunctional intranet for knowledge management, heavy use of the Internet and the Web, powerful database query interfaces, and perhaps business intelligence software.

Other aspects of creating a dynamic organisational environment are examined in later chapters. Here, we examine one particular approach which is related to creating a learning environment and managing knowledge effectively as an organisational strategy. The two concepts have a great deal of overlap and so are discussed together. The aim with both is to develop the intellectual capital within the organisation and in so doing achieve greater success against competition.

Knowledge management and the learning organisation

Knowledge management has been proposed for a number of years as a method by which organisations can improve productivity and sustain a competitive advantage in increasingly knowledge-based economies. Despite the interest in knowledge management, there is still some ambiguity in relation to the term, particularly in commercial circles where it is sometimes used interchangeably with information management. However, knowledge management can be viewed as the process of creating, storing, managing, accessing and sharing tacit knowledge (in a person's head) and explicit knowledge (documented in books, intranets and so on). It relates to the corporate memory of an organisation and its intellectual capital.

A simple classification of knowledge is shown below:

- Know-why — explanatory knowledge, scientific knowledge of principles (laws of nature)
- Know-how — skills, the ability to organise resources to achieve desired outcomes
- Know-who — social knowledge, refers to specific social relations, e.g. who controls the resources needed in a particular situation
- Know-when/know-where — economically useful knowledge about markets
- Know-what — catalogue knowledge.

Many diverse companies are effectively developing knowledge management programs. These are applied to cost reduction, process improvement, improving productivity, improving time to market and increasing innovation. The types of applications include frequently asked questions (FAQs), best practices, problem-solving software, decision support systems, resource management systems, and asset management systems.

The term 'learning organisation' was used by Peter Senge (1990) to describe companies whose ability to learn quickly will provide them with a competitive edge. Although a learning organisation might generate new knowledge, it might not necessarily manage it effectively. This is where the learning organisation and knowledge management go hand in hand. Companies need to learn quickly in a rapidly changing environment, and efficiently manage and share the knowledge gained.

[**Key concept:** The success of information systems is inextricably tied up with how the organisation functions as a unit. Informations systems are not islands.]

Infobyte

Knowledge management technologies

A study by the Cranfield University School of Management investigated the potential of technology in supporting knowledge exploitation. Although email has been seen as the main tool for sharing knowledge, it is expected that the Internet and intranets will be the key tools of the future. They are richer technologies in that they can easily integrate text, audio and video data and hence provide contextualised information. The trend is the move from data and information to richer content with a focus on knowledge. This is in part due to the complexity and ambiguity associated with knowledge management (Cranfield 2000).

IS in action

Knowledge management systems at Motorola

Many of the world's leading organisations are taking knowledge management seriously. Management at the mobile, automotive and broadband communications company Motorola realised that, with 140 000 employees in more than 400 cities around the world, it faced a host of knowledge management challenges. As Philip Stockwell, Motorola's Internet technologies group manager, said, 'We have to be able to communicate and share critical information across functional and departmental lines; and we need the ability to raise awareness of projects, communities, and product development practices.'

Trying to integrate the skills and knowledge of so many people for any given project was difficult. The company worked with OpenText Corporation to build a global intranet called COMPASS. COMPASS serves as a central information store, a collaborative workplace for work groups and a medium for enterprise-level communication for more than 30 000 users. It is one of the world's largest knowledge management solutions.

Each business unit that uses COMPASS is responsible for its own knowledge management, library structure and content. Most units have a 'Knowledge Champion' who serves as the administrator, posting information into the group's COMPASS area and assigning user privileges. The system also includes version control features.

Some criticise knowledge management initiatives for not delivering value to the organisation. Motorola is convinced that the system has resulted in improved productivity and a reduction of product time-to-market while maintaining product quality.

Source: adapted from 'Come together', *The Manufacturer*, December 2003, www.themanufacturer.com/content_detail.html?header=article&contents_id=1805&t=manufacturer_us (accessed 13 February 2004).

Summary

Strategic planning seems to be more of an art than a science. There are many ways to go about using IS within organisations and no one strategic planning approach can guarantee business success. However, the methods presented do provide a starting point and framework for examining the potential of information technology and information systems in organisations. The key points in this chapter are:

- A strategy is a medium-to-long-term plan outlining the goals of the organisation.
- The information systems plan in an organisation should be aligned with the organisation's strategic plan.

- IS managers can use one or a number of strategic planning methods, including various forms of competitive analysis such as Porter's competitive forces model and SWOT analysis.
- There are occasions when the information technology can act as a strategic driver in its own right.
- The information architecture is a plan for the organisation's information and technology infrastructure.
- Creating an effective knowledge-based organisational environment is a strategic direction facilitated by information systems.

Questions

1. How should an IT strategic plan relate to an organisation's strategic plan?
2. How can IS be used to competitive advantage in organisations?
3. How can the strengths, weaknesses, opportunities and threats (SWOT) analysis be used for IS planning?
4. What is meant by an 'information architecture'?
5. What role can value chain analysis play in strategic planning?
6. What are the likely consequences for organisations that do not perform any IS strategic planning?
7. Identify one strength and one weakness or limitation for each IS strategic planning method.
8. What are the perceived benefits of outsourcing the IT facilities of an organisation?
9. Why are changes to an organisation's culture often required when implementing new information systems?
10. How does knowledge management differ from information management?

Exercises

1. Choose an organisation with which you are familiar — it could be your own university. Outline what you consider to be the information architecture of the organisation. In groups of four, brainstorm the likely changes to this information architecture over the next few years.
2. In small groups discuss how you acquire, record and share knowledge as part of your university or college course. Try to make the distinction between information and knowledge. Share your experiences as a group with the rest of the class. What role (if any) does technology play in your knowledge management experiences?
3. What would be the advantages and disadvantages of outsourcing the IT facilities of an organisation with which you are familiar?
4. Interview a senior IS professional about their organisation's IS strategic plan. How was it developed? What methods and techniques were used? If there is no plan, ask about the consequences of not having a plan.
5. Perform a SWOT analysis on an organisation with which you are familiar. How can IS/IT be used to build on the strengths or take advantage of opportunities? How can IS/IT be used to alleviate or address any of the weaknesses?

CASE STUDY AP Consulting

AP Consulting Group is a leading management, information and technology consultancy, operating worldwide from thirty-five offices. It was started in North America more than thirty years ago. The company took over a consulting group in the UK eighteen months ago and a consulting group with offices in Singapore, Hong Kong and Japan six months ago.

AP draws on the knowledge and expertise of 2000 employees, whose skills span a wider range of capability than any other major consulting firm. Its consultancy services — strategy, performance improvement, IT, technology, human resources, recruitment, program and project management — are helping its clients to transform their businesses in order to achieve significant increases in value, profitability and effectiveness.

Recently AP re-examined its business processes and found that its offices and service groups did not communicate as well as they could. Expertise was not being used to the fullest to create a competitive advantage.

The success of the consultancy is based on being able to provide total business solutions on a global basis. Historically, parts of the AP Group had been insular because they were geographically distant. Now with the acquisition of the UK group and the group in Asia matters have become worse. The offices in each region have a different culture on a regional and organisational (group) level. The group based in Japan, Singapore and Hong Kong has a particular type of organisational culture, and the UK offices are often quite bureaucratic, which has tended to work against the creation of ideas and innovation. There is a perception that the UK offices don't want to be dictated to from North America and prefer to work autonomously.

The aim now is to come together globally and share not just best practice but also common and standard practice throughout the firm. For example, AP has built up methodologies over many years, but they need to be shared. There is a real need to communicate and share knowledge among service practices, industries and regions. Basically, they want to manage knowledge more effectively.

The information technology infrastructure is fragmented. Each region has its own systems and ways of providing information technology support. There is a need to integrate these systems and set some standards for the organisation as a whole.

Overall, the IT problems and the information and knowledge management problems reflect the problems associated with integrating the newly merged companies as one entity. The company's board realises that strategic thinking is required in relation to IT.

QUESTIONS

1. Explain how various strategic IT planning approaches could help AP in its current situation.
2. What are likely to be some of the benefits of integrating IT, data and knowledge better throughout the organisation?
3. Should AP concentrate on getting the basic IT infrastructure integrated first before it looks at managing knowledge more effectively?

References

Bartol, K., Martin, D., Tein, M. & Matthews, G. 1998, *Management: A Pacific Rim Focus*, 2nd edn, McGraw-Hill, Sydney.

Cranfield 2000, 'Releasing the value of knowledge — a Cranfield School of Management and Microsoft survey of UK industry', www.microsoft.com/uk/knowledgereport (accessed March 2001).

Hammer, M. 1990, 'Re-engineering work: Don't automate, obliterate', *Harvard Business Review*, July–August, pp. 104–12.

Hammer, M. & Champy, J. 1993, *Re-engineering the Corporation: A Manifesto for Business Revolution*, Nicholas Brearley Publishing, London.

Manganelli, R.L. & Raspa, S.P. 1995, 'Why re-engineering has failed', *Management Review*, pp. 39–44.

Porter, M.E. 1985, *Competitive Advantage: Creating and Sustaining Superior Performance*, Free Press, New York.

Senge, P. 1990, *The Fifth Discipline: The Art and Practice of the Learning Organization*, Doubleday/ Currency, New York.

Sims, D. 2000, 'What is CRM?', CRMGuru.com, 21 March 2000, www.crmguru.com/content/ features/sims01.html (accessed March 2001).

Standing, C. & Vasudavan, V. 2000, 'The travel industry and Internet commerce: Lessons from Australia', *Journal of Tourism and Recreation Research*, vol. 25, no. 3, pp. 45–54.

Thompson, A.A. & Strickland, A.J. 1995, *Strategic Management: Concepts and Cases*, 8th edn, Richard D. Irwin, Inc., Homewood, IL.

Chapter 9

Managing the information systems function

LEARNING OBJECTIVES

After reading this chapter, you should be able to:

- explain the difference between tactical and operational IS management
- explain how IS managers manage people and relationships
- understand the importance of creative thinking skills for IS staff
- describe the key areas that IS/IT managers need to monitor to maintain the performance and effectiveness of the information systems
- understand the main issues related to information security and data privacy in organisations
- explain methods and approaches for effective management of IS projects and development teams.

9

Introduction

Information systems managers have the responsibility of managing the tactical and operational activities related to the running of the IS service. Tactical issues relate to short-term plans, procedures and policies, whereas the operational activities relate to the day-to-day tasks that must be carried out to maintain the IS service effectively for the organisation. How they carry out these tactical and operational activities is shaped to some extent by the organisation's existing short-, medium- and long-range strategies. A well-managed information systems function in an organisation should have a strong alignment between the IS strategy and IS tactical and operational activities. These activities involve managing people and relationships, delivering an effective IS service to a range of users and managing IS projects. This chapter examines each of these three interrelated activities in turn, starting with the management of people and relationships.

Managing people and relationships in the IS function

An important part of an information systems managerial role is the effective management of people and relationships. These include information systems professionals, users of the systems, senior management, customers, suppliers and external alliances. Managing the relationships between these different groups requires some guiding principles, which are discussed below.

- *Responsibility of management.* The IS manager must take the responsibility for making things happen; in other words, being proactive. This is especially true in flatter organisational structures since the manager cannot rely on being given orders from above. On the tactical and operational levels decisions have to be made to resolve problems, avoid problems and take advantage of opportunities. The strategic plans discussed in chapter 8 will guide much of this decision-making, but the manager must be prepared to take responsibility and make decisions.
- *Development of boundary roles.* IS managers cannot afford to have an inward focus. Although day-to-day operations need managing within the IS function, managers should become involved in boundary relationships. These are, for example, the interfaces between the IS function and other departments of the organisation and the interface between the IS function and suppliers or customers. Boundary relationships were once the responsibility of either executive managers or more junior people in the organisation responsible for selling and purchasing. These boundary relationships should be considered strategic focal points and as such require managing on an operational level.
- *Development and use of communication systems.* IS management must effectively develop and use communication systems to foster relationships between IS staff, users, customers and suppliers. This needs to take into account what will be communicated, how often it will be communicated and the modes of communication. For example, an IS manager might hold short weekly briefings or meetings to keep IS staff aware of project developments and organisational issues. Email might be directed at relevant individuals or groups or communicate urgent information. If a dialogue exists between the IS function and its clients there are less likely to be misunderstandings in relation to expectations, which should lead to a better working relationship.

- *Create and maintain an effective working environment*. An open and transparent management style is characteristic of the network style of management and is more likely to engender trust between groups (Limerick, Cunnington & Crowther 1998). Trust is seen as a key value in the network organisation. Managers cannot monitor their employees — or, for that matter, their business partners — all the time; nor should they try to. They have to communicate core directions and values, support employees along the way and trust that they are responsible enough to do their jobs well. If employees are empowered rather than monitored they will be more innovative and probably work harder and longer. In this model the manager becomes a facilitator in the network rather than a custodian of resources.

Information systems may be used to support the status quo or power brokers in an organisation. Although this is sometimes desirable, IS become part of the problem when they become rigid and prevent organisational progress. For the IS manager, knowledge of changing organisational structures and the reasons behind them is important so that even on a day-to-day basis decisions are informed by where the organisation is heading and the potential role that IS and IT can play. Indeed, even on a personal level the managerial style of the IS function will need to be sensitive to the changing world of work and the aspirations of the IS staff and users.

Reflection question 1: Do you think there could be resistance from some managers to change their management styles?

[**Key concept:** IS can be used to transform organisations.]

Infobyte

Looking for a mentor?

Ever wondered what it takes to get on in the information systems profession? Well, certainly IS skills are important as well as the more generic communication and problem-solving skills. However, many consider that a mentor is important, too. A mentor can provide medium- to long-term career advice and advice on how to solve difficult business problems. The mentor might typically be someone who displays qualities that you admire in the way that they work and make decisions. It might take time to find a suitable mentor as that person might not be in the same organisation as you. Some suggest that the mentor should not be your manager as it should be someone higher up in the organisation with more senior experience. You have to be comfortable with your mentor and be able to speak openly with them.

Reflection question 2: If IS managers are struggling to keep up with the rate of change in each area of information systems, how can they manage effectively?

Managing IS professionals

An important aspect of information systems operations is acquiring and training effective staff. High-quality staff will have considerable input into the ongoing information systems developments. They will influence the medium- and long-term returns from the operations. Companies that take a longer-term perspective of their endeavours will create a staffing plan that identifies responsibilities for current staff and a plan for acquiring additional staff.

Each IS professional should have regular performance reviews with the IS management and plan their training requirements. Motivated IS professionals require challenges in their day-to-day responsibilities and are very concerned about developing skills that are in demand. The IS manager needs to allow staff the opportunity to work on exciting projects rather than being involved entirely with maintaining older systems.

Managing internal and external relationships

The IS management team must manage the relationships with other departments and functions in their organisation. This would involve working with senior management throughout the organisation to obtain high-level requirements and feedback on the service provided by the information systems function. A service mentality is very important since, if the image of the IS function is poor, it is unlikely to obtain high levels of funding, and it might even find that more IS services are outsourced. Users of the information systems must be trained adequately and effectively supported through responsive help desks. Surveys should be conducted on a regular basis to obtain feedback on the level of service being provided.

The IS function in a large organisation is likely to interface with a wide range of external organisations and individuals. These can include customers, suppliers, banks and partner organisations. The IS managers must develop good relationships with these groups in order to meet their requirements and to be perceived as being responsive and proactive.

The role of power, politics and culture in information systems

No discussion of IS management would be complete without explaining the role of politics and power (Jasperson et al. 2002). Since the late 1980s researchers in the IS field have been increasingly interested in the importance of the social and political factors in information systems development (Hirschheim & Newman 1991). In this context 'political' refers to the clash of conflicting agendas that can surface in the struggles for recognition, resources, career progression, power and influence. Political struggles can be seen in the situations that involve user resistance. According to Grover, Lederer and Sabherwal (1988, p. 145), 'user resistance to management information systems is common'. There are several different reasons why systems succeed or fail, but recognising the role of politics is crucial to understanding user resistance. In some circumstances, user resistance might be due in part to a perceived threat regarding a reduction in someone's autonomy, an increase in their workload or an invasion of their territory.

Politics has been given some attention, especially in its relation to power, by organisational behaviourists (Thompson & McHugh 1995). Managers often tend to rationalise their activities in terms of technical skills and choose to ignore the influence of politics.

Pfeffer defines the internal politics of organisations as 'Those activities within organisations to acquire, develop and use power and other resources to obtain one's preferred outcomes in a situation where there is dissension or uncertainty about choices' (Pfeffer 1981, p. 10). Thus, people seeking influence often have to work within sectional interests or networks (coalitions).

Reflection question 3: Why do you think people often assume that organisational politics is a bad thing?

[**Key concept:** Information systems are social systems, not just technical systems!]

IS in action

The politics of information systems

The CIO of Wyoming's state government found that working in the public sector involved more political issues than his previous experiences in the private sector. However, the politics of information systems depends a lot on the culture of the organisation, and politics can still be rife in private companies.

The following are examples of political and cultural issues on an organisational level that William Campbell found during his reign as CIO of the Wyoming state government. He was hired to develop and implement a formal IT program for the executive branch of government. This involved developing a single enterprise architecture, a mechanism for financial governance and a structure for overcoming problems with suppliers. The project was expected to save $US70 million over two years.

The problems that arose included:

- *High organisational turbulence.* As soon as the CIO was hired there was a change of governor. The new governor was not supportive of the project.
- *Slow provision of funding.* The funding and budgeting mechanisms had to be done at least a year in advance, and there was no flexibility in the system. This meant that the earliest the project could get started was 18 months away!
- *Protection of turf.* Each meeting showed just how much each department wanted to protect its power base. This meant that decisions that improved the quality of the system as a whole were difficult to obtain.
- *Prevalence of politics.* The project contained financial controls and corrected past abuses of the system. The state auditor responsible for financial controls saw this as an incursion on his responsibility and tried to derail it. Eventually the governor fired the CIO at the request of the auditor.

Source: adapted from William Campbell, 'How to survive in the public sector', www.cio.com (accessed July 2003).

The IS manager must be able to manage and promote projects and relationships within and outside the organisation. The political component is the development and management of the relationships. Internal and external promotion of activities requires support in terms of people and resources. The IS manager requires a good understanding of the organisation and its internal politics, and must be skilled in developing coalitions. Political skills can help a person sell their ideas, acquire resources and get things done.

Successful individuals in organisations spend a great deal of time developing relationships. This process is termed networking. Networking enables the individual to relate to subcultures in the organisation and to become aware of the internal political processes.

Culture has been recognised as being an important consideration in information systems development and management. Organisational culture and national culture are two main levels at which cultural issues can be seen. Organisational culture can be defined as the shared values and norms that exist in an organisation which involve common beliefs and feelings, regularities of behaviour and a historical process for transmitting values and norms (Vecchio et al. 1997).

Organisational culture can have a positive influence on organisational effectiveness when it supports organisational goals, is widely shared and is internalised by organisational members (Bartol et al. 1998). It can be influenced through time by such things as policies, procedures and management strategies, in addition to the recruitment of people from different backgrounds and age groups. Organisational culture is generally seen as a unitary entity, although it could be argued that it is possible for radically different cultures to exist in the same organisation (McKenna 1999).

IS managers are increasingly working with clients and suppliers from different countries that do not share the same business culture. Multinational companies might assume that cultural differences are not great enough to present problems in their own organisation, but this is unlikely to be true. Hofstede (1991) classified culture in relation to a number of attributes. 'Power distance' is the extent to which the members of a society accept that power in institutions and organisations is distributed unequally. 'Uncertainty avoidance' is the degree to which the people in a group or society feel uncomfortable with uncertainty and ambiguity. This can lead to beliefs that support the promise of certainty and is characterised by conformity. The 'masculinity/femininity' metaphor is used to convey the tendency in a society to value achievement, heroism, assertiveness and material success (masculine), as opposed to a preference for relationships, modesty, caring for the weak and the quality of life (feminine). The last characteristic of culture is 'individualism/collectivism'. Western culture is often described as individualistic or independent whereas Eastern culture is seen as being collectivist or interdependent. Individualistic (independent) cultures focus on the self and what makes the individual different from others. In collectivist cultures a person's feelings and thinking are more influenced by social relationships with others and the individual's role in the group. In independent cultures individual goals dominate and ties between individuals are weak. In interdependent cultures strong groups with lasting ties dominate (Hofstede 1991).

The trend of organisations outsourcing software development to a company in another country is increasing. Many IS departments now have experience of dealing with cultural differences. Their awareness of the cultural differences and their ability to manage culturally diverse teams are likely to influence the success of the project outcomes (Walsham 2002). It is argued that culture has been looked at too simplistically since within one country there are often culturally diverse groups that need to be considered (Myers & Tan 2002).

[**Key concept:** When working in teams, always take cultural differences into account.]

■ **Reflection question 4:** Can you think of an example of the possible influence of cultural differences on the development of information systems?

Innovation and creativity

There is no simple answer to the question of how to be creative or how to be innovative. Some people are better than others at being more creative and some organisations appear more innovative than others do. However, there are approaches, techniques and skills that can be used to develop a more creative and innovative environment.

For organisations to be successful in today's business world, they must accept that what they did yesterday may not be appropriate for tomorrow. In other words, organisations must not only accept change but also be prepared to encourage change.

To become more innovative, organisations need to value people with ideas and encourage brainstorming sessions. When expertise is not available internally, it should be brought in via new people or consultants. Organisations should become learning environments and should learn from the successes and failures of other organisations. Innovation and entrepreneurship should be rewarded. Risk-taking should be encouraged and limited failures tolerated. Of course, organisations should invest in training, and help staff experience new situations and new working environments. All the points mentioned apply to the IS arena also. Staff who can creatively use IS/IT to solve organisational problems are in big demand.

Infobyte

Managers struggling to communicate

The senior managers who manage IS projects in organisations are struggling to communicate with their team members. The rate of change in information systems and technology has meant that there are many specialised areas. For example, agile computing and development, web services and web development, changes in hardware and changes in software development paradigms have all created a set of complex concepts and terminology that need to be mastered. Senior managers have responsibilities in addition to managing projects, which has meant that they find it difficult to update and develop new skills in the range of new development paradigms. This has led to a communication problem with team members whom they supervise as they don't have the same technical knowledge and therefore don't speak the same language!

■ **Reflection question 5:** Have you any other ideas for fostering creativity in employees?

Managing information systems operations

The overall performance and effectiveness of information systems need to be managed. This involves making sure that the operational activities (daily activities) are aligned to the IS strategic plan. The IS strategic architecture serves as a framework for guiding the daily decisions that have to be made.

Operational management includes monitoring and evaluating the performance of the computer systems and quality of IS service provided. This usually involves monitoring all aspects of performance, including:

- data quality — data produced by the systems must be accurate and have a high degree of reliability
- response times — time to retrieve data from database systems must be acceptable to the users
- network and server reliability — network access should be maintained at high levels of reliability; if access to the network servers falls below a certain level (for accessing email, for example), then users will start to complain
- hardware reliability — computer systems, printers, scanners etc. must be reliable
- licensing agreements — these need to be adhered to
- Web access performance — previously, the focus was on accessing internal systems but now most organisations are accessing data and information from outside the organisation
- security issues — system security needs to be continually monitored and any breaches rectified.

Policies and procedures related to the above should be developed and communicated throughout the company.

A related issue is the enforcement of standards across the organisation for the acquisition of hardware and software. Some of the benefits of such standards are:

- support costs are reduced
- system complexity is kept to manageable levels
- training costs are reduced
- discounts are available for bulk purchasing
- expertise is built up more easily.

■ **Reflection question 6:** Which issues or areas are likely to cause most problems for IT managers?

[**Key concept:** Performance and effectiveness of IS can always be improved.]

Typically, new technology is adopted at different times by organisations (see figure 9.1). The timing of adoption can be classified into five stages. The innovators are a small minority who adopt the technology very early on. They are followed by a more significant minority who are still early in the adoption cycle. A larger percentage of companies are not leaders but still adopt before many other organisations. The other 50% of adopters can be divided into late adopters and laggards. There is plenty to be gained by being an early adopter of technology, but many companies do not want to be innovators since they may want the technology to be tested in the marketplace before they use it, thus reducing the risk of problems associated with it.

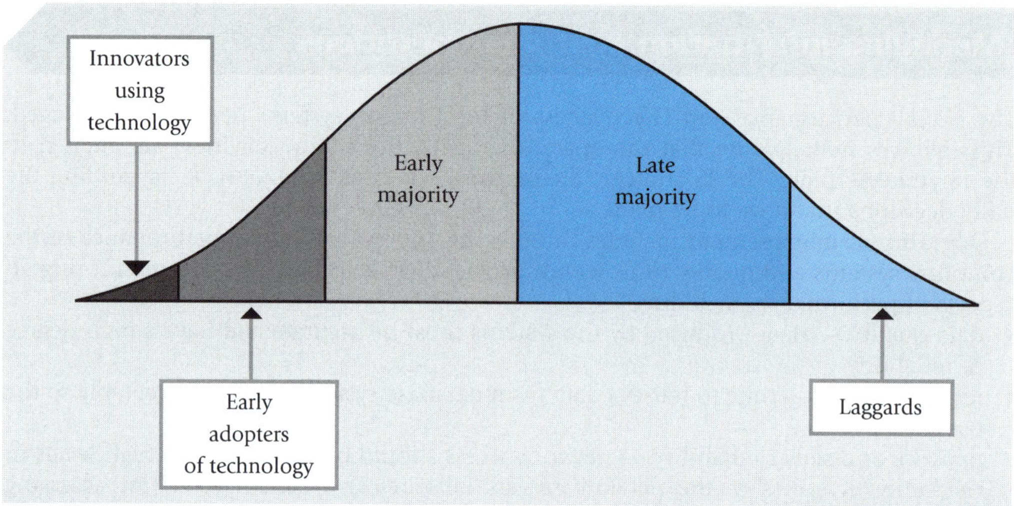

Figure 9.1 Stages of technology adoption

Information systems continuity planning and security management

Information systems continuity planning is concerned with protecting the organisation against disruption to the running of the information systems, the failure of systems or subsystems, and disasters such as fire and floods affecting the information systems. In fact IS continuity planning is one part of business continuity planning, and the two should not be confused. 'Business continuity planning', as the term suggests, examines the entire business and would typically include areas that are less dependent on information systems.

IS continuity planning encompasses security measures. Developing an IS continuity plan should be high on the agenda of any information systems department. It should outline the general policies in relation to continuity planning and security, the levels of security that should be adopted, the key risks related to the systems, disaster recovery procedures and the people responsible for maintaining continuity and security.

Security includes the physical environment as well as the software environment. Once in operation the security measures and procedures need to be monitored and evaluated for effectiveness.

Risk analysis

Developing adequate security measures is all about the assessment of risk. Even with the costliest of safeguards put in place there can be no guarantees that the system will be 100% secure. Therefore the levels of security required are determined by factors such as the value of the data being protected and the types of potential threats to the system.

There is a cost to putting security measures in place. Some of these are purely financial costs and others may be considered as an inconvenience. IS professionals should assess the value of the data and information they are about to protect, what the likely cost of system disruption would be, and the possible loss of business that would arise from a disruption. For instance, there is little point in putting high-cost security measures in place to protect low-value data and information. However, only the organisation can put a value on the loss of business or the data being protected. There is always a trade-off in terms of aiming for an ideal level of security and the costs associated with it.

The systems designers must assess where the main threats to the system are. Do they come from within or outside the organisation? Are the main threats likely to be deliberate acts of malicious damage or accidental events? Most of the problems in any security environment arise from not attending to basic security measures adequately.

Infobyte

IT staff and ethical issues

The IT manager should be aware of the ethical issues surrounding access to information. The Ethics Committee of the British Computer Society recently highlighted how IT can be used to both open up and restrict access to information. As a result, IS/IT professionals are in a special position of sometimes deciding on the level of freedom or restriction in relation to information access. Usually, legislation provides the guidelines, but in other cases it is a matter of personal conscience. In relation to confidentiality, decisions are sometimes less clear, since data may not be clearly labelled as confidential.

Companies should create a policy clarifying what employees are allowed and not allowed to do on the Internet. The general feeling is that employers should clarify their policy on their employees' surfing during work time.

Physical security

Physical security aspects of IS include protecting the hardware, monitoring access to buildings and taking back-ups. Servers and other hardware should be in a secure location with a locked door accessed only by authorised personnel. However, this issue is probably not so significant within a networked environment, because the software and data on the Web server or accessed via the Web server can be modified or deleted by a variety of methods.

Access to buildings should be monitored because unauthorised people are a potential threat to computer system security — they may access confidential data both on the system or from printouts. Many companies have a sign-in procedure where the 'visitor' provides a reason for being there and is given a badge to wear while on the premises. Anyone not recognised and not wearing a badge is challenged. In high-security situations, guards are employed to challenge people at the entrances to buildings. This level of security and associated expense is warranted where valuable data are stored or where a high level of confidentiality is required.

The Web server, application server and database server, if these are being used, should be protected against power surges. After a system crash, there should be adequate procedures for the rebooting of the system and restoring the service to the users.

Back-ups of any transactions should be taken and a copy stored off-site in case of fire or other accidents. How often should you take back-ups of your data files? It depends on how much the files have changed since the last back-up. For a small business, it is generally worthwhile taking back-ups on a daily basis. Don't overwrite the previous day's back-up but work on a three-day cycle so that by the fourth day the back-up is overwriting the data from three days previously. That way there should always be some data to fall back on. Taking back-ups daily might seem like a lot of bother — but not when you think about the time and trouble involved in recreating a day's lost work.

Software security

Software security for information systems could be the subject of a book in its own right. The following covers the main issues from a security management perspective.

Network security

A firewall (see chapter 5) can protect a network or system by separating the organisation's intranet from other systems within the organisation or outside the organisation. Note that not all threats come from outside the organisation.

Developing an effective firewall system is not easy. There can be a tendency to become too severe in what is allowed in and out of the organisation and also in monitoring too much of the communication. If a security policy has been developed for the organisation, then this will help in defining the level of firewall security needed.

The management of virus attacks

When corporate networks have a connection to the Internet or allow files to be transferred from disks, they run the risk of **virus infection**. The Internet is a threat to security through use of email attachments and downloaded files. Each user needs to have an up-to-date virus scanner that can detect and delete the most recent strains of a virus.

The number of people accessing data over the Internet has become a major security issue for companies. As far as downloading files is concerned, there are a number of factors which users should be aware of. They should avoid or minimise the downloading of files, whether software or documents, from sites which have no reputation to lose. Downloading files from major software vendors is some assurance that the files will not contain code that has malicious intent — files are more likely to have been checked and their quality assured before they are released to the public because the company has its reputation on the line. A personal site does not have the same type of reputation at stake when providing free downloads. Free software should also be viewed with some suspicion for much the same reasons, particularly if it is from an unrecognised software vendor.

There are potential problems with accessing web sites which use Java applets, even though Java has been made secure by not allowing applets to write to the user's hard disk without permission. However, many users give permission to store configuration information for the applet on the disk because they are unaware of the consequences or they trust the site they are downloading from. These downloads can result in a number of problems.

A policy on Internet access should be developed and disseminated within the organisation. It should clearly explain the potential problems associated with Internet use. This, in addition to an effective firewall system, should safeguard the organisation.

Authentication

Authentication deals with proving the identity of a person. Passwords, hardware tokens or smart cards, or biometric properties, such as fingerprints or retinal patterns, are all forms of authentication. Passwords are the most commonly used — although also probably the most abused — form of security measure. Users predictably choose names and favourite words as their passwords and sometimes write them down, and before long a system that could be effective becomes quite ineffective. The system should force users to develop passwords that are:

- longer than five characters
- a combination of characters and digits
- changed regularly.

Biometrics can be used as an alternative or supplement to passwords in authentication systems. 'Biometrics' refers to the technologies for measuring and analysing body characteristics, such as fingerprints, retinal patterns and voice patterns, so they can be checked automatically. Factors to be considered in the choice of a particular characteristic include public acceptability, ease of use and accuracy levels.

Fingerprints are the most widely used biometric today. Iris identification is even more accurate than fingerprints; however, a small percentage of people cannot use those systems because of an inability to stabilise their iris. Biometrics can be foiled by a sudden change in a person's body; for example, a cut finger might mean a person cannot log in.

Threats to computer systems come from different categories of people and not all have malicious intent:

- *Employees*. Poorly trained staff can be a threat to the security of systems and can create several problems for maintenance staff. Disconnecting equipment or trying to use systems for which they are not trained can be potentially damaging to the overall effective running of the system. Disgruntled employees may deliberately attempt to delete or alter files and are difficult to stop since they have authority to use the system.
- *Other users*. Suppliers or customers may have access to systems through the Web.
- *Hackers*. The antics of hackers have been reported for some years now. A distinction is sometimes made between 'hackers' (those who do not damage the system in any way but gain unauthorised access) and 'crackers' (those who gain unauthorised access with the intent of deliberately creating problems such as deleting files).
- *Criminals*. Some people gain access to systems for personal profit, such as accessing credit card details without authorisation.

[**Key concept:** Most security problems arise from not implementing the fundamentals of security effectively.]

■ **Reflection question 7:** Would your passwords stand up to scrutiny?

Companies are spending more on trying to keep their systems secure. As a consequence of IS continuity planning, the information security policy of an organisation is taking on increased significance. Organisations have typically been reactive rather than taking the initiative in relation to security — only when there has been a breach of security or the auditors have planned to visit does the information security policy become a hot issue again.

IS in action

Biometrics in action

Biometrics is beginning to catch on in the business world. Israel's largest bank, Bank Hapoalim, has begun using biometric signature identification to combat some of its security problems, in particular to reduce losses from fraud.

The bank needed a system that would ensure the security of transactions and be easy to implement and operate. The solution was to add a sample of each customer's signature to the bank's central database. The technology learns the variations of each signature, including pressure, acceleration, speed and rhythm. This creates a unique personal profile, which is updated over time in response to natural changes that occur in the signature. The signatures are encrypted and compressed to be stored in the database. Customers then sign on an electronic pad in any branch of the bank. (The bank holds 2.5 million accounts and operates in Europe and North, Central and South America as well as in Israel.)

Besides improving security, the system cuts down on time spent checking, reduces paperwork and provides faster customer service in bank branches. There is even potential to use a personal digital assistant to make online transactions from home.

Source: information from www.signature-perfect.com/docs/wn_case_study_bank_hapoalim.pdf (accessed 30 July 2003).

High rates of staff turnover in the IS/IT industry have meant threats are likely to come from a broader range of people. In the days when mainframes were commonly used, people used to stay in one position longer and knew that they would be one of the first suspects if anything happened. When an increasing proportion of an organisation's IS operations are outsourced and when there are a number of temporary workers in IS support, establishing trust can be made more difficult. Security policies have to consider staff turnover in all sensitive positions (Connolly 2000).

IS in action

Councils demonstrate lack of continuity planning

Local government councils are increasingly reliant on information systems, and this has created a new set of risks for them. The increase in e-government initiatives, along with a growing potential for the misuse and abuse of information in relation to data privacy and ethical use of information, has added to the concerns. Local governments have now become targets for hacking and virus attacks. On top of this, natural disasters can strike at any time.

Local councils in Queensland, Australia, have been criticised for not implementing business continuity plans. Queensland's Auditor-General is worried by the lack of continuity planning and access controls by many local councils.

Queensland's local government is not the only one to come in for criticism as the State of Victoria and the Northern Territory have been recently found wanting in this area. The Queensland Auditor-General's report for Local Government stated, 'Poor and ineffective system access controls form the majority of the information systems [concerns] raised by the audit.'

Some of the main areas of concern identified were:

- users being given inappropriate levels of access
- inadequate controls over passwords
- inadequate monitoring of access to systems
- inadequate monitoring of system usage.

In addition, there have been ineffective hardware security measures, poor backup procedures and even poor data validation controls. The report strongly recommended the councils put in place effective plans to provide better information systems continuity.

Source: Australian IT, 'Councils scolded over IT plans', http://australianit.news.com.au/articles/0,7204,6194967%5e15441%5e%5enbv%5e15306-15319,00.html (accessed 8 August 2003).

Data privacy

Related to information security is the issue of **data privacy**. The increasing amount of personal data stored in computer databases has created a major issue in modern society in terms of protecting the privacy of the individual. Many organisations including government departments, universities, schools and banks keep personal details of students, customers and so on. If there is a serious breach of confidentiality and these details fall into the wrong hands, it could result, for example, in fraud, unsolicited phone calls from businesses, or harassment.

The onus is on the companies that store such personal information to protect the data and act ethically in relation to their use. Many countries have legislation to protect the rights of the individual in this area, and companies which do not adequately protect personal data are fined. Legislation also gives people the right to ask for copies of their personal records to determine if they are correct, since inaccurate data can have serious consequences, such as being refused credit because of an incorrectly recorded bad debt. Together, data privacy Acts and freedom of information Acts provide some comfort in an increasingly digital world where data can be rapidly copied, merged and transferred over networks and the Internet.

■ **Reflection question 8:** Have you experienced an invasion of your privacy as a result of personal data being used for a purpose other than the one it was intended for?

Managing projects and development teams

IS managers spend a great deal of time managing projects and development teams. A US study in 1995 found that a large percentage, as high as 40%, of IS projects were cancelled before completion, with many others overrunning on time and budget. It is worthwhile identifying the critical aspects of project management and the underlying reasons that some projects fail.

Senior executive support

Significant initiatives require senior management support. If the operation has a strategic impact on the organisation, then everyone should know about it and get behind it. Despite new trends in organisational structures, staff still take a lead from senior management.

Projects can easily run into problems if they do not have management backing. Team members may find that people are not so cooperative in providing information or are slow to respond to requests. They may even find that the project is continually being questioned, even though it has been given the go-ahead. Having highly visible senior management backing for an application oils the political machinery within a company and makes the developers' tasks so much easier. Senior people can lend support to the development of information systems by being involved in various ways: (1) in the creation of strategy, (2) by being part of the first tier of the ongoing management structure of the project, and (3) by taking a high profile throughout the project and communicating with team members and the rest of the staff at regular intervals about the progress and significance of the initiative.

Assessing the organisation's requirements

The organisation's requirements must be accurately assessed. Information systems projects should have a clearly defined strategy. Some information systems initiatives do not provide the return on investment that the organisation had hoped for because what was expected was never clearly stated. Thus the developers deliver a system which fulfils the requirements as specified but is not good enough to produce significant returns to the company.

Defining the scope of the project

Developing information systems within a company can take many forms. Hence, development team members need to be clear on the scope of the initiative they are taking on. To do this will typically involve some form of feasibility assessment which includes a definition of the scope of the project. Doing this can avoid arguments later on over the success of the delivered system. To clarify the scope of the project early in the proceedings is a worthwhile investment in time and energy, and radically improves the chances of a successful application being delivered.

Assessing the most worthwhile projects

Many projects are undertaken without paying due regard to return on investment. Focusing on the applications that maximise the returns means that the benefits are quickly brought back to the company and the perceived success of the system acts as an impetus to develop other applications.

Being wary of changing requirements

The scope of the project can change along the way. When this happens without a conscious decision being made, it is known as 'scope creep'. It arises because enthusiastic managers begin to see the beneficial implications of the applications being developed and so suggest further applications or requirements be considered. The team leaders must assess how critical these suggestions are to the overall success of the system. If they are outside the scope of the current development and are not critical, then they should be logged but not tackled immediately. If they are critical and are within the scope of the system, then they should be built into the requirements and planning adjustments made accordingly. The major difficulty with scope creep is that the resources for the project are stretched so far that the success of the project overall comes into question.

Blending team member skills

Team members must have the right blend of skills to tackle the project. Often this must be considered well in advance since some skills and knowledge take a long time to acquire. Besides technical skills, team members need to continually develop their communication skills. Project management skills need to be developed through training and on-the-job guidance and experience.

Setting realistic targets

Many managers set unrealistic project deliverables and targets in the hope that they will be given the go-ahead with the project. In other words, the project is often doomed from the start because the deadlines and returns are not possible to achieve. Managers and team members must be wary of falling into this trap — they should not commit to unrealistic targets or present inaccurate progress reports.

Infobyte

IS failure and requirements specification

Despite new techniques, new software systems and improved hardware, the business world is still plagued by IS failures. This means that some projects are delayed, some exceed their budget and some are cancelled completely. The IS department creates a specification based upon user requirements. However, some argue that specifications are sometimes too complex, which leads to project blowouts! Others argue that project specifications can be too lean and hence miss vital requirements. Also, developers must be wary of letting users dictate too much detail, including technical solutions. The art is to achieve a balance in terms of the level of detail in the requirements specification.

Monitoring project progress

Monitoring the development refers to gathering information about the status of the project and comparing it with the initial plans and targets. Monitoring can be undertaken on three levels: tasks completed (including time), expenditure and quality.

Tasks not completed on time, budgets blowing out, communication problems and high levels of stress are all signs of poor project management. A project can be monitored by checking the tasks that have been completed compared with the tasks that should have been completed according to the project plan. This is helped by identifying 'deliverables' throughout using strategy reports or reports detailing requirements, designs and prototypes. Each module or phase of the project can be summarised in a report. For project management purposes, meetings are held to determine what has been accomplished and what should be accomplished in relation to the overall goals of the initiative, to identify new problems, and to revise the project plan for the remainder of the project.

If monitoring highlights project problems, team leaders must take corrective action. However, if there is no hope of achieving any of the deliverables, the project may have to be cancelled.

Corrective action

Problem projects may require different types of corrective action. A new project plan, which is realistic and achievable, must be created to reschedule events. There may be scope for running two tasks in parallel when more is known about the project and the team members.

The priorities of individual team members can be reviewed. It may be that some members have not been assigning priorities correctly and so not working on the most critical tasks. This is a chance to review workloads and assess time and project management skills.

People may at times lack the necessary motivation to work in a sustained fashion at a high level of quality. This problem may be fixed on a short-term basis with additional rewards. If there is conflict between team members, this might be resolved by the sensitive reshuffling of personalities across teams. However, in the longer term, motivation problems can be resolved only by new attitudes within the organisation. In some cases, this may involve retrenchments and acquiring more motivated staff. Motivated staff still require careful management and usually need a constant stream of achievable targets and challenges to remain motivated. Staff may require on-the-job training, especially junior staff. If staff lack specialist skills, a short intensive training course may be appropriate to rectify, or at least improve, skill levels.

Additional staffing for a project may at first glance seem the easiest way to get the project back on track, but there are several potential problems associated with this option. Good help is hard to find, especially at short notice. People who are new to a project that has been under way for some time have a steep learning curve to overcome. They will not be aware of the key issues and problems and may therefore need considerable help and information before they can be fully productive. Providing help may take people away from their tasks and therefore slow the project down overall.

Using charts in project management

Explaining project schedules and monitoring project progress can be enhanced with the aid of various charts, tables and diagrams. Two of the most commonly used techniques in project management are Gantt and PERT charts, which can both be developed and maintained using software such as Microsoft Project.

A **Gantt chart** is a form of bar chart that show the activities of a project and the amount of time each task will take (see figure 9.2). The time required for each task is estimated. Once this is done, the tasks are listed on the left-hand side of the chart in their intended order of completion. The period for the project is defined along the top of the chart from left to right. A bar is drawn on the chart for each task with the left of the bar identifying the start date for the task and the right of the bar indicating the completion date for the task. If there is no bar for a task, this means there is no activity associated with the task during that period.

The charts can be presented at several levels. A top-level chart can show the main stages of the project with other levels breaking down the main stages into more detail. The main benefit of Gantt charts is as an aid in monitoring project progress. Given a certain date, it is easy to see what activities should be in progress. Of course, these charts are continually revised and updated, and hence project management software has become indispensable to project managers.

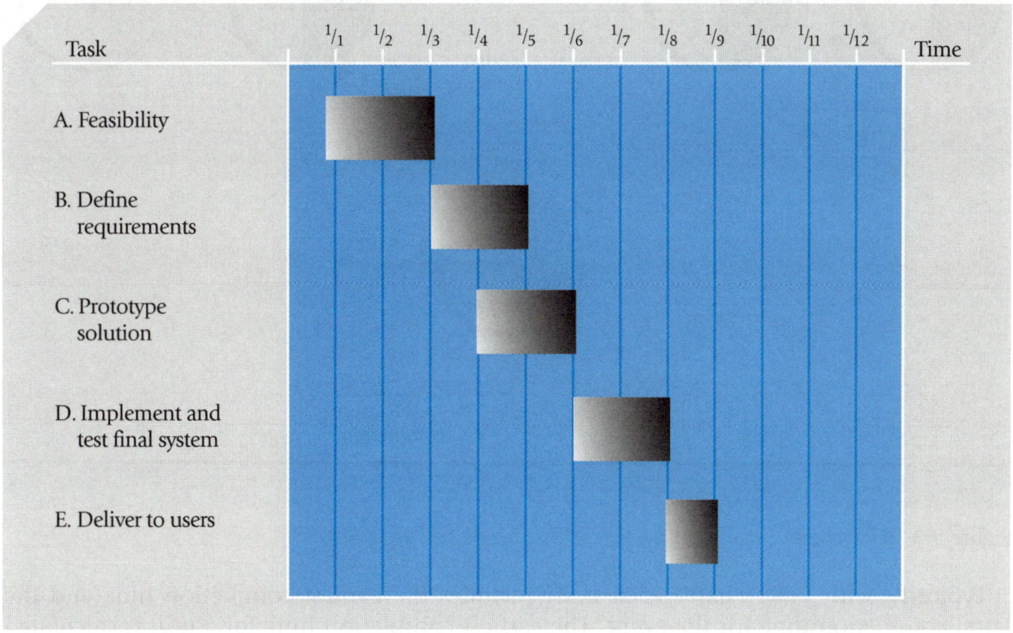

Figure 9.2 Gantt chart

A more sophisticated diagrammatic tool for specifying the complexity of a project is the **program evaluation and review technique (PERT)** (see figure 9.3). The tasks of a project are often interdependent, i.e. one task cannot start until another has been completed. The problem with Gantt charts is that they do not show these interdependencies and do not highlight the critical tasks, i.e. the tasks that have to be completed before other work can be done.

A project consists of events and tasks. A task (or activity) is a piece of work that is clearly defined and can be assigned to a person or team, such as 'gather requirements for a system' or 'install software'. An event is the stage which marks the beginning or end of a task and is represented by a node (i.e. a circle in figure 9.3). A predecessor task is a task that precedes another task (obviously, the first task in the chart does not have a predecessor task). A successor task is a task that follows a task (the last task in the network does not have a successor task).

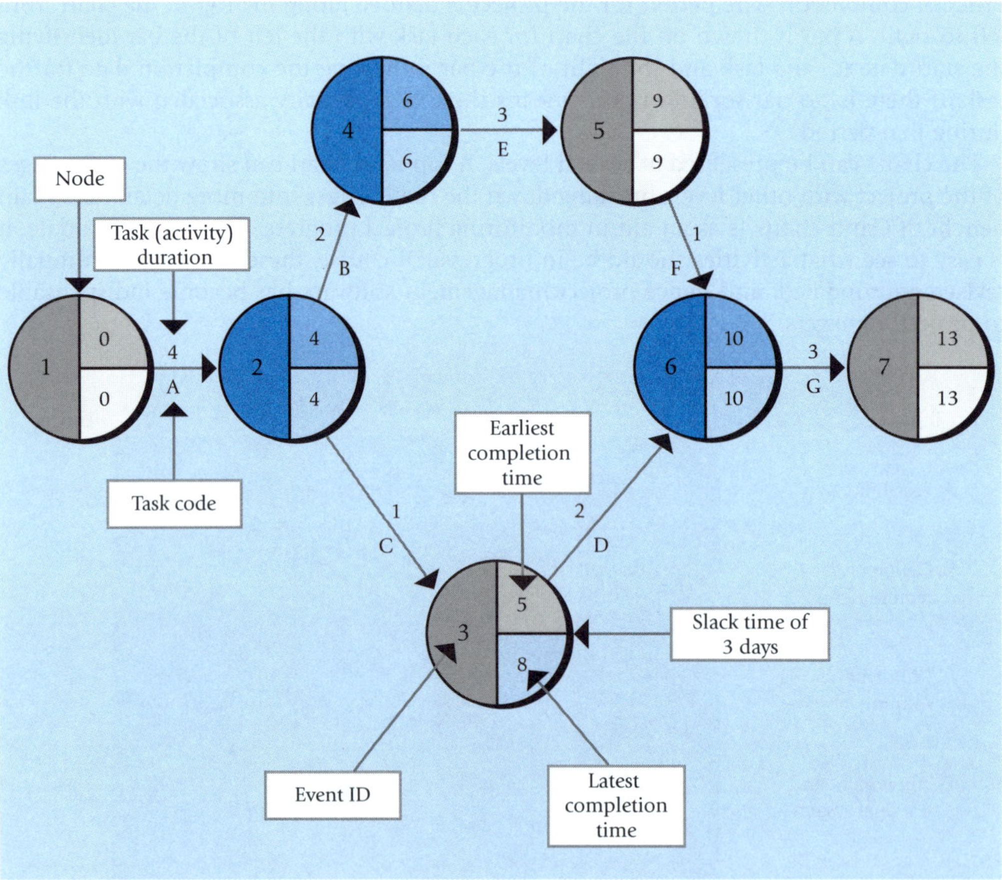

Figure 9.3 PERT chart

Typically, with PERT charts, each node includes the earliest completion time and the latest completion time for the event. The earliest completion time for a task is calculated by taking the earliest completion time for the preceding event and adding the expected duration time for the task in hand. (For example, in figure 9.3, the earliest completion time for event 3 is day 5, since the earliest completion time for event 2 is day 4 and the duration time for task C is 1 day.) The latest completion time for an event is found by taking the latest completion time for the following event and deducting the estimated duration time for the task leading to that event. (For example, for event 3, the latest completion time is calculated from event 6 which follows it — there, the latest completion time is day 10, and since task D takes 2 days, then event 3 must be completed by day 8. Note that this means that event 3 has a 'slack time' of 3 days, i.e. there are 3 days between the earliest completion time and the time the event must be finished by. Slack time is significant if tasks on that path fall behind schedule a little.)

The capability maturity model for software

The IS function should be striving to become more effective and professional in all aspects of its operations and planning. The capability maturity model for software is a useful framework for checking the progress of an IS department in becoming more proficient in software development (figure 9.4). The basic idea, although designed for software development, can be useful for examining other aspects of a department's operations.

The capability maturity model for software (CMM) was developed by the software community in association with the Software Engineering Institute at Carnegie Mellon University in the United States. It is a model that can be used for judging the sophistication or maturity of the software processes of an organisation and for identifying the key practices that are required to increase the maturity of these processes (SEI 2000).

The stages in the model are:

- *Initial.* Ad hoc processes and success depend on individual effort.
- *Repeatable.* Basic project management processes are in place to track costs, schedules and functionality. Thus earlier successes on projects with similar applications can be repeated.
- *Defined.* The software processes are standardised and documented.
- *Managed.* Detailed measures of the software process and product quality are collected. Statistics on the software quality process are gathered.
- *Optimising.* Continuous process improvement using quantitative feedback and piloting innovative ideas.

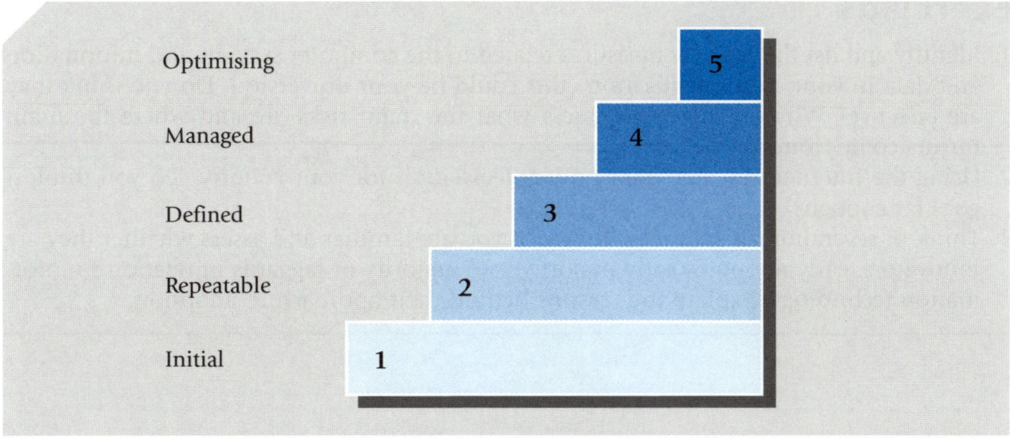

Figure 9.4 The capability maturity model (*Source:* SEI 2000)

Summary

Managing the information systems function requires breadth of knowledge and a wide range of skills. The IS manager should have one eye on the internal machinations of the organisation and the other eye on the external developments in the business world. The key points in this chapter are:

- IS management must develop good working relationships with IS professionals, users, senior management and external partners, customer groups and suppliers.
- Managing IS staff effectively is perhaps the greatest challenge facing the IS manager. Staff require challenges, flexibility and consideration of their personal and family responsibilities.
- Creativity is as much a part of the information systems profession as is problem solving.
- The day-to-day performance and effectiveness of the IS function has to be monitored, including the network, software and database systems.
- Information security is mostly about getting the basics right day in and day out.
- Techniques such as Gantt and PERT charts can help monitor project performance.

Questions

1. Explain the main groups of people with whom IS management should develop good relationships.
2. What is meant by managing system performance?
3. What types of security issues need to be covered in relation to the Internet?
4. What are some examples of physical security measures?
5. When an IS project is running over its projected time, what are the likely causes and potential remedies?
6. How can Gantt and PERT charts help in managing IS projects?
7. In your opinion, is organisational politics always likely to have a negative influence on IS development projects?

Exercises

1. Identify and list the security measures related to the computer systems and information and data in your own organisation (this could be your university). Do you think they are effective? Why or why not? Assess what the main risks are and where the main threats come from.
2. Using the Internet, research data privacy legislation for your country. Do you think it goes far enough?
3. Think of several organisations with which you are familiar and assess whether they are innovators, early adopters, early majority, late majority or laggards in relation to information technology. Explain the reasons behind their approach to adoption.

CASE STUDY A nightmare project

One day the boss called me into her office and offered me the leadership of a high-profile internal IS project. At first I was rather pleased, but as I found out more about the project I wondered whether it is such a good idea to accept it. The boss gave me some background to the project.

'It is a good opportunity to prove your project management expertise,' she said. 'However, there are a number of problems related to the project. In fact, the project should have started a while back. It failed to get off the ground because of a dispute between the two user departments — finance and marketing. Both felt they should be responsible for it, and because of clashing personalities the matter just got worse. There is, as you are probably aware, a history of conflict between the two departments.'

'Who will be the main users of the system?' I asked.

'The users of the system will be from marketing, but the information produced by the system will also be of use to finance and they will want to query the data,' she said.

'Before we go any further,' I said, 'can I ask what happened to Gerry? He was managing the project, wasn't he?'

'Gerry is off work with stress and won't be back for a while, but it is not all due to managing this project, so don't worry too much,' she replied. 'The project is really very high profile and is, in fact, critical to the company's financial success. Even the CEO has told the two departments to get on with it and sort out the problems. I know that if the project doesn't get moving, he'll be knocking on my door asking for an explanation.'

I accepted the project position and was provided with a project update, which is summarised below, together with some of my own thoughts from personal observations.

- The finance and marketing departments have each now assigned someone to the project to define the business requirements. Although the two people are experts in their own domains and appear to get on well together, the key user has not been identified. In fact, both department managers still want to blame each other if anything goes wrong. At this point no other resources have been allocated to the project.
- I have been told that the system should be completed by the end of the year. But that is only 4 months away, and it seems impossible to have the system up and running in such a short time.
- I still have a number of concerns — will I still have to oversee the maintenance of System Alpha which I have been looking after for the past year? This takes about 10 hours per week to attend to but the work is spread over every day of the week. Will my planned leave later this month have to be postponed?
- The new project looks to involve the development of new software. It will also affect existing systems and databases. A large number of screens will have to be updated so there is considerable interface work to be done.

(*continued*)

- The team allocated to the project consists of:
  - two analysts who seem competent and appear willing to do some programming if required; their knowledge of systems development techniques is acceptable; both are motivated and work hard
  - a junior programmer who is enthusiastic but lacks the ability to work independently and so will need close supervision
  - a contract programmer who was taken on a number of months ago to work on a different project; he has some ability but appears unmotivated due to uncertainties with his contract; could be a real problem and a threat to the project if his attitude gets worse.
- Overall, my guess is that the project can be completed successfully but I need extra resources. Any advice would be appreciated.

QUESTIONS

1. What do you consider to be the major issues related to the project?
2. Can the project be made a success?
3. What action should be taken and what recommendations should be made?
4. Was I foolish for taking the project on?

References

Bartol, K.M., Martin, D.C., Tein, M.H. & Matthews, G.W. 1998, *Management: A Pacific Rim Focus*, 2nd edn, McGraw-Hill, Sydney.

Briney, A. 2000, 'Security focused', *Information Security*, September, www.infosecurity mag.com/pdfs/2000survey.pdf [accessed June 2001].

Connolly, P.J. 2000, 'Security starts from within', *Information Age*, October/November 2000, pp. 12–15.

Grover, V., Lederer, A.L. & Sabherwal, R. 1988, 'Recognising the politics of MIS', *Information and Management*, vol. 14, pp. 145–56.

Hirschheim, R. & Newman, M. 1991, 'Symbolism and information systems development: Myth, metaphor and magic', *Information Systems Research*, vol. 2, no. 1, pp. 29–62.

Hofstede, G. 1991, *Culture and Organisations: Software of the Mind*, McGraw-Hill, London.

Jasperson, J., Carte, T.A., Saunders, C.S., Butler, B.S., Croes, H.J.P. & Zheng, W. 2002, 'Power and information technology research: A metatriangulation review', *MIS Quarterly*, vol. 26, no. 4, pp. 397–459.

Limerick, D., Cunnington, B. & Crowther, F. 1998, *Managing the New Organisation*, Business and Professional Publishing, Warriewood, NSW.

McKenna, R. 1999, *New Management*, Irwin/McGraw-Hill, Sydney.

Myers, M.D., & Tan, F. 2002, 'Beyond models of national culture in information systems research', *Journal of Global Information Management*, vol. 10, no. 1, pp. 24–32.

Pfeffer, J. 1981, *Power in Organisations*, Pitman, London.

SEI 2000, 'Capability maturity model for software', Software Engineering Institute, Carnegie Mellon University, August 2000, www.sei.cmu.edu/cmm/cmm.sum/html (accessed June 2001).

Thompson, P. & McHugh, D. 1995, *Work Organizations: A Critical Introduction*, Macmillan, New York.

Vecchio, R., Hearn, G. & Southey, G. 1997, *Organisational Behaviour*, Harcourt Brace, Sydney.

Walsham, G. 2002, 'Cross-cultural software production and use: A structurational analysis', *MIS Quarterly*, vol. 26, no. 4, pp. 359–80.

Chapter 10

E-business

LEARNING OBJECTIVES

After reading this chapter, you should be able to:

- explain the features of the Internet that have created so much business potential
- understand the role of strategy in e-business and how an opportunistic approach to e-business can be effective
- understand the components of business models and where e-business can be used effectively
- explain how e-marketplaces are changing supply chains
- describe and explain a range of e-business concepts relating to planning and strategy.

10

Introduction

The growth of e-business has had a profound influence on many aspects of business. As a consequence this chapter examines e-business strategies and techniques to effectively take advantage of the opportunities provided by the Internet.

E-business is the use of the Internet and related technologies and services in business. It encompasses e-commerce, which is generally viewed in a narrower sense as the marketing, selling and buying of products and services via the Internet. E-business therefore is a term that includes such things as relationship-building between suppliers and consumers, information provision and after-sales service. If organisations explore the broader dimensions of e-business, they are more likely to tap into a greater amount of the potential provided by the Internet. This chapter examines the world of e-business. It discusses its evolution, effective e-business models and the development of e-strategies. Web development and design issues are covered in chapter 11.

E-business opportunities

The Internet is having a profound effect on the business world for several reasons.

- It is very accessible. A web site can sell goods and services around the clock, 365 days of the year (this is sometimes shortened to 24/7/52, meaning 24 hours a day, seven days a week, 52 weeks a year).
- It is convenient. People can access the Internet from home, work or even while they are on the move by using their mobile phone or a palmtop or laptop computer. Accessing the Internet while on the move is known as m-commerce (mobile e-commerce).
- The number of people worldwide with access to the Internet is increasing. Although there is some difficulty in trying to estimate accurately the number of Internet users, it is clear that it is a very large market which will increase in size. A large market provides companies with a great opportunity to sell their products or services.
- The global reach of the Internet provides an opportunity for companies to market their products and services internationally. Many companies that once thought only about servicing local customers are now selling products and services to customers from other countries. The Internet has contributed greatly to the trend of globalisation. This means that companies have to think in terms of global markets rather than national boundaries. In fact, the Internet has created a type of global marketplace where buyers and sellers can be matched, irrespective of national boundaries.
- There are significant cost savings for businesses in providing information, products and services over the Internet. Something as simple as putting the company's annual report online can create substantial savings on the costs of printing and mailing.
- Consumers can do some comparison shopping on the Internet as it is relatively easy and quick to visit comparable web sites to check prices and models.
- The Internet can link buyers directly with sellers. This factor can change entire industry supply chains by cutting out companies which act as intermediaries. For example, a wholesaler may bypass retailers and sell directly to consumers via the Internet.

The impact of the Internet on business is radical and far-reaching. To be effective, however, companies cannot simply transfer their current business operations to the Web — they need to redefine their business model and strategy, reinvent business processes, change corporate culture and improve relationships with customers and suppliers.

The Internet has the potential to change the nature of work in organisations. Employees can:

- work from home and access and input company data and information through the Internet
- cooperate in virtual teams and use the Internet and email to communicate and share information
- be part of decentralised organisations, since the Internet provides a rich medium for communicating and sharing knowledge.

[**Key concept:** Some technologies, albeit rarely, create a business revolution.]

Consumers are changing in that they are more educated and discerning. Increasingly, they require a high level of customisation in products and services, many of which become obsolete very quickly. Companies should take into account the changing profile of consumers if they are to be effective in their marketing.

E-business has a number of advantages to offer organisations, such as:

- reducing costs by streamlining processes
- increasing income by adding revenue sources
- improving customer service by providing more and better quality information and greater convenience
- increasing innovation by sharing ideas
- improving information and knowledge management through the use of intranets.

Although few organisations would dispute that e-business provides real opportunities for businesses, such opportunities can be realised only by developing and implementing effective strategies.

[**Key concept:** Business and information technology are merging to the extent that in many cases you can't do business without the technology.]

Types of systems

Web-based systems can be classified according to whether they are intended for customers, suppliers or business partners, or for employees of the company (see figure 10.1). These are briefly explained in this section and are elaborated on later in the chapter.

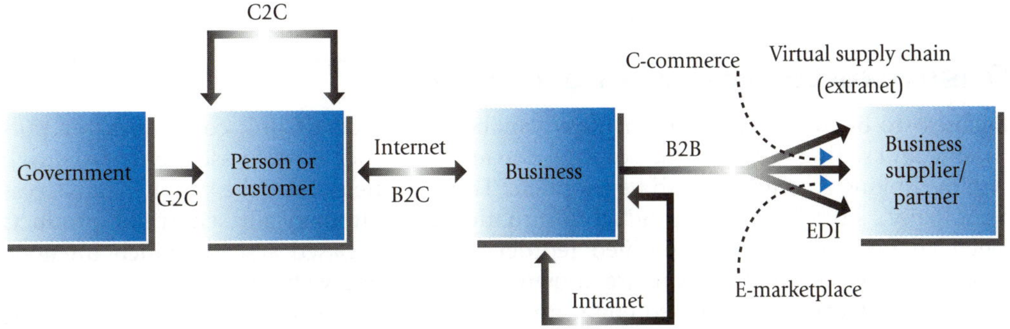

Figure 10.1 Types of e-business

Business-to-consumer e-business

Web systems developed for customers are used for **business-to-consumer (B2C) e-business**. There are various aspects of B2C e-business that can be exploited by companies:

- *Product or service information.* The Internet can be used to help a potential customer make a purchasing decision by providing information on products and services.
- *Purchasing facility.* A web site can be developed to include a transaction facility for purchasing and paying for products and services.
- *After-sales service.* After-sales service relates to all the forms of service that can be provided once the customer has made a purchase. It can include answering enquiries about faulty products and information on how to best use the product.
- *Marketing data.* Information can be gathered from customers and potential customers to create customer profiles which can be used in marketing and product development.
- *Business partnerships.* Companies can provide links to other web sites and so recommend particular products or services that are complementary to their own. For example, a hotel may include a link to a taxi service which, in turn, includes a link back to the hotel.
- *Brand image and public relations.* The Internet can be used to promote the brand image of a company and thereby increase awareness with consumers of their products or services. Some companies provide more general information about the organisation to keep the public informed about their strategies and values. For example, a mining company can inform the public about its environmental policies or a fast-food company may explain how it is involved in community projects.
- *Investor information.* Providing information on the company's financial performance is of interest to investors and may include the facility to download annual reports and company press releases.

Consumer-to-consumer e-business

A company can act as an intermediary and set up an electronic marketplace to facilitate consumers selling to other consumers. An example is eBay (www.ebay.com). The intermediary can make money through advertising, commission on the sales or subscriptions to the site.

Business-to-business e-business

Business-to-business (B2B) e-business can be developed to link companies for purchasing and selling products and services. The term 'extranet' is often used to describe web systems linking a company with its suppliers. Through the system, the supplier can access a company's stock levels and product information and automatically send more products when an item is below its specified reorder level. Web-based systems which integrate suppliers down the supply chain are known as 'virtual supply chain systems'.

E-marketplaces are web-based environments where suppliers are matched with buyers for the sale of products, services and specialised equipment. They are open exchanges which are challenging many of the fixed virtual supply chain systems.

Electronic data interchange is the sale of goods and services online, typically on proprietary networks rather than on the Web. For example, travel agencies subscribe to various reservation systems which allow the booking of airline seats and hotel rooms. These systems are not directly available to customers.

Collaborative commerce (c-commerce) refers to online collaboration between business partners. Data, information and ideas may be exchanged as part of the collaboration.

IS in action

Reducing paper invoices

Fisher Scientific is a UK-based company, manufacturing its own Fisherbrand chemicals and distributing laboratory products from around 3000 suppliers. Its web and paper catalogues offer more than 80 000 products to about 40 000 customers around the world.

Fisher Scientific receives approximately 85 000 invoices each year. In the past, for each invoice, a member of the accounts payable department had to open the envelope manually, check the details were correct, enter data into the accounting system and then file the invoice. Fisher was keen to reduce the time and paperwork and therefore the cost of this process as well as improve its filing of the invoices.

The company was keen to adopt electronic invoicing. An open technology platform, OB10 by Open Business Exchange, was chosen. The system translates electronic invoice formats between different systems, so an invoice received in any format is automatically put into the correct format for the company's accounting information system. Although the system would rely on suppliers sending invoices electronically, it would not require the installation of proprietary software or infrastructure changes and would ultimately save them money. Fisher Scientific and Open Business Exchange worked closely with Fisher's suppliers to win support for the system.

With strong initial uptake of the system, Fisher expected the majority of its invoices to be received electronically within 12 months of its introduction. The company has already noticed improved levels of efficiency within the accounts payable department. It estimated that it could save up to 80% of the cost of manually handling each invoice.

Fisher's case highlights the effectiveness of the Web for reducing costs and improving efficiency. Systems that operate among organisations need a high level of participation and support. Therefore the involvement of partners and communication with them in the development process is important.

Source: information from www.fisher.co.uk/ebusiness/casestudy2.htm (accessed 9 September 2003); www.obexchange.com/Docs/Fisher%20Case%20Study.pdf (accessed 10 September 2003).

Intranets

Hypertext systems designed for the employees of a company are known as intranets. One of their main uses is as a document management system for an organisation. Intranets can be used for a range of purposes, including:

- accessing information in databases
- accessing company manuals and documents
- providing information on the latest company initiatives
- processing internal data and information
- internal sales and purchasing
- communicating company guidelines and policies
- advertising employment opportunities within the organisation
- internal promotion of activities and events
- contact details of employees including email addresses and telephone numbers.

Government-to-citizen e-business

Governments at federal, state and local levels are increasingly interacting with citizens via the Web. This mode of e-business is discussed later in this chapter.

E-business as a strategic driver

In chapter 8 a number of IS strategic approaches were covered and the importance of strategic thinking overall was stressed. It was mentioned that IS/IT can be, in certain situations, a strategic driver of the business. The e-business area has numerous examples of this in practice. However, there are some dangers with this approach. Traditional IS planning emphasises a top-down approach. In this model, the corporate strategy defines the business goals and these determine which technologies should or should not be chosen (see figure 10.2). These methods are well documented (see chapter 8).

A criticism of the 'traditional' approach is that it is not opportunistic enough. Because the business environment is rapidly changing, it is difficult to predict a long time in advance. Strategic approaches generally take at least a medium-term perspective. However, the more detailed the strategy, the less scope there is to take advantage of new opportunities if and when they arise.

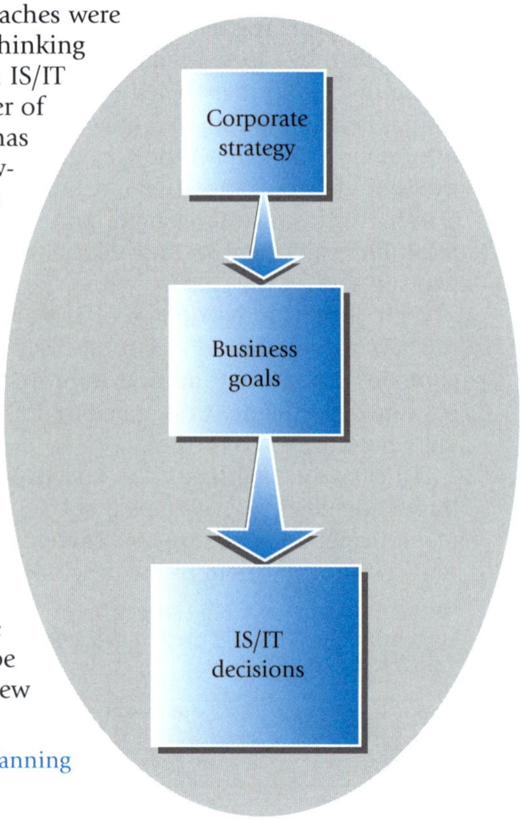

Figure 10.2 Strategy-driver IS/IT planning

Many technological or information systems innovations can have such an impact on businesses that companies which adopt the technology or technique early can gain a competitive advantage — this can, with careful management, become a sustainable advantage. Hence, scanning the technological environment and adopting new, appropriate technology can be seen as a strategy in its own right. This can be described as an IS/IT-driven approach (see figure 10.3).

The Web is an example of a technology for which other uses have evolved *after* it has been initially adopted in organisations. There are many other cases of this happening in the information systems field. It appears to go completely against the grain as far as previous IS/IT strategies are concerned, since it can be seen as a bottom-up rather than a top-down approach — i.e. the technology is adopted, uses are found for it, and then this affects the business goals and strategy, which change accordingly. The approach is more opportunistic and flexible than previous approaches and realises the profound impact IT can have.

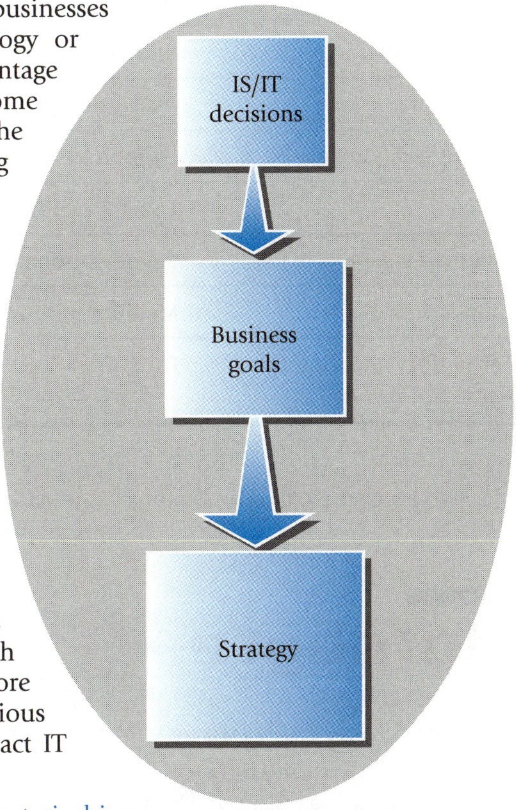

Figure 10.3 IS/IT as a strategic driver

Of course, there are several dangers with this approach. Some might argue that it is high risk and hence likely to have high failure rates. For example, what happens if a technology is adopted but is never properly made use of? Dot.com businesses make use of the Web (a form of technology) as their main business advantage, yet many commentators suggest this explains the high failure rates. Although it is higher risk, for those who do succeed there are phenomenal advantages. As a whole, the approach is certainly more experimental, but if the outlays are minimised then risk is also minimised while still allowing for many benefits.

An IT-driven approach does not abandon planning and strategic thinking altogether. Rather, there is a shift in emphasis from strategic to opportunistic approaches (see table 10.1). This may be considered a more effective way to operate in a rapidly changing environment and relevant for the digital world where new business concepts and technologies are emerging on a regular basis.

■ **Reflection question 1:** How do the strategic and opportunistic approaches discussed apply to your personal use of information systems and technology?

TABLE 10.1 Strategy-driven versus technology-driven approaches

Characteristics	Strategy-driven	Technology-driven
Key feature	Planned	Opportunistic
Role of technology	Support system emphasis	Business driver
Risk	Low to medium	Medium to high
Rationality approach	Highly rational	Live with uncertainty
Gains (period)	Medium to long term	Short to medium term
Technology adoption (see figure 9.1, p. 244)	Early majority	Innovators, early adopters

[**Key concept:** The business environment is changing constantly and planning methods should adapt to new conditions.]

Infobyte

Build on the community of use!

A starting point for the effective adoption and use of e-business is to examine 'communities of use'. The term 'community of use' refers to a group whose members work together in some way by exchanging data/information, transacting or communicating. The processes and communication within the community of use can be facilitated and improved by web technologies. A business cluster, for example, would already exchange data/information and communicate and collaborate. Improved processes via the Web are likely to speed up communication and efficiency of data/information exchange.

E-business models

The growth of electronic business has generated many references to the concept of **business models**. In particular, researchers and practitioners have proposed that e-business has been responsible for the emergence of new forms of business models and that these models are the driving force in the 'new economy'.

The following is an analysis of business models with the aim of classifying the Internet's contribution to business.

Web-site functionality

A number of researchers have tried to classify e-business models by examining web-site functionality. These classifications and 'models' abound in the literature and typically include such types as the advertising model, the online brochure and transaction-based systems.

One simple classification of e-business models is as follows (Telstra 1998):

- the electronic brochure — products and services are simply displayed on the Internet, and purchases are transacted through conventional means such as by phone, fax or in person
- the electronic brochure plus ordering system — in addition to brochure information, the customer may order over the Internet, but has to pay by conventional means
- the electronic brochure, ordering system plus payment system — in addition to the above facilities, this allows the customer to pay over the Internet.

Classifications of web-site functionality provide descriptions of systems which vary in complexity. The simplest ones, such as the poster/brochure model, provide general basic information about the product or service in an online brochure (Lawrence et al. 2000). Highly complex models such as Craig Settles' 3.5.7 model are multifunctional and provide marketing information as well as purchasing capabilities. Settles' 3.5.7 model (Settles 1997) refers to 'three steps to a better focus' (these steps present the case that the Internet is mainly a communications tool rather than a sales channel), 'five-dimensional strategy' (companies evaluate the financial impact of five online strategic options and use these options to develop an online business strategy) and 'seven-point tactical guide' (seven tactical areas to focus thinking and maximise a web site's capabilities).

In relation to e-business models, the question often asked is 'Where is the revenue stream?' The revenue may come from selling products, from commission in a brokerage system, or from selling advertising space. Of course, not all e-business systems create a revenue stream, but may still affect the bottom-line by attracting new customers to the offline channel, or by keeping customers informed and therefore improving customer retention rates offline.

Organisational structure

Organisational structure is a component of a business model. The structure should facilitate the implementation of the business objectives. Flatter network organisational structures are put forward as being able to respond more quickly to change than more hierarchical structures. Communication technologies can be instrumental in facilitating newer organisational forms.

Organisational management

Management approaches are another aspect of business models. They range from cautious, bureaucratic approaches, where the emphasis is on accountability and procedures, to highly innovative and entrepreneurial environments which require a style that is more encouraging and tolerant of risk. Management styles are certainly influenced by the culture of the organisation. In network organisations (explained in chapter 9), for example, executives guide ideas through the network, most of the routine functions are outsourced, and power is seen as an attribute of value-adding capability rather than position. Management is seen as a key facilitator for getting new initiatives off the ground and for encouraging innovation. Companies wishing to engage in e-business need to consider how they can incorporate an effective management culture.

Other business model components

There are other relevant components of business models, such as:

- *Distribution channel* — this considers how the product or service is distributed to customers. For example, software can be distributed through retail outlets on CDs or can be downloaded from a web site.
- *Partnerships and alliances* — an organisation could be totally independent or engage in partnerships or alliances with other organisations.
- *Marketing approach* — the marketing function can be viewed as a separate component of the business model.
- *Revenue stream* — a company may have single or multiple revenue streams.

The human resource model and the IS/IT function can also be viewed as significant components of a business model.

Effective e-business models

For a business model to be effective it must consider most, if not all, components (see figure 10.4). Considering simply one aspect of the model, such as marketing or organisational structure, will not create an effective e-business model.

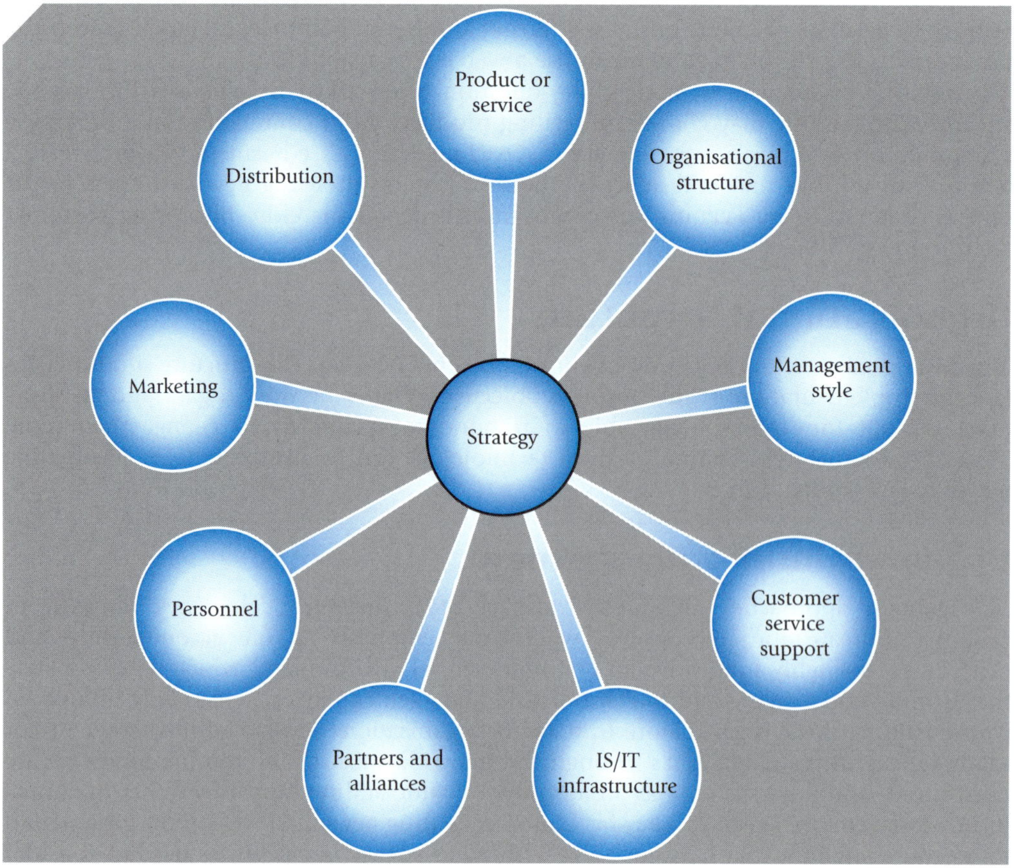

Figure 10.4 Key components of a business model

Some definitions of 'business model' emphasise the economic basis of the idea. Others take a broader view according to three main features, which are presented below (*Australian eBusiness Guide* 2001).

- *Business configuration.* This covers how the business works. It addresses which activities the business performs and whether they are outsourced.
- *Value proposition.* This defines how the business benefits customers. The business must have a competitive advantage in relation to its services or products.
- *Revenue model.* This explains how the business generates revenue.

E-business strategies

The Internet can be used to implement a range of business strategies. The last section looked at various business model components and how they can be tailored to the e-business paradigm. In this section, e-business strategies are examined in detail.

Marketing and advertising on the Web

The Web can be used for brand-name marketing, and for providing sales information, product catalogues, and product or service announcements. Marketing systems, just like retailing systems, require considerable planning and support. Many strategies and techniques can be used to market via the Internet and many are unique to the Web in that they have no offline equivalent. The Web has a number of unique attributes: all customers can be accessed and informed at once; large amounts of information can be communicated cheaply; users can interact with the system; and information can be personalised very easily. Personalisation of information involves taking into account what a customer has accessed or bought previously and then changing what is presented on the web pages to be more relevant. This is different from customisation, which is the process whereby a user sets preferences at a site, such as selecting categories of information to be displayed on a search engine.

The Web can be used strategically to capture an increased share of a particular market segment. Some companies are aggressively marketing via the Web with advertisements at leading Internet sites. For example, some credit card companies have chosen to advertise at sites that attract young people in the hope that they can tap into new markets.

Email marketing is now an important technique in marketing. Databases of email addresses are set up, but to be effective among the plethora of emails people receive, the email header and the content of the email need to grab people's attention. The better examples of marketing via the Internet make good use of the interactivity of the medium and the facility to allow users to exchange information with other users. The development of online communities provides an example of the real potential of the Internet for marketing (see chapter 11).

Retailing on the Web

Transaction-based online shopping systems which allow customers to buy various products and services over the Internet are now commonplace. Many companies use this approach to supplement their traditional retailing channels. It provides a convenient service for consumers who can order products at a time and place of their choosing. For companies, this model is not as straightforward as it might first appear since the web application should be preceded by a strategic plan and accompanied by a transaction support infrastructure. Such systems need to effectively deal with payments, ideally link to corporate database systems, and provide customer service support.

Beyond a basic retail model, the Web can be used in innovative ways to retail products and services. For instance, Internet auctions can provide an alternative to offline approaches. Retail auction sites generally require a large number of visitors to generate the level of competition needed to sell products and services in a cost-effective manner for the company. The method can be used as a way of selling slow-moving stock and attracting general interest in the web site. **Online auctions** have been used for selling airline seats, cars and even cases of wine. **Reverse auctions** are where the customer makes an offer for a product, and the seller decides whether to accept it.

IS in action

eBay

eBay (www.ebay.com) is the world's largest online trading community. eBay started as a company in 1995, and has grown to be a well-known marketplace for the sale of both goods and services, mainly for individuals and small businesses. The eBay site (see figure 10.5) is the Web's most popular e-marketplace by user numbers and, when measured by total user minutes spent at the site, is the most popular shopping destination on the Internet.

Figure 10.5 eBay's web site. Reproduced with the permission of eBay Inc. © eBay Inc. All rights reserved.

eBay's mission is basically to help people trade anything they wish. These people include collectors, hobbyists, dealers, unique-item seekers, bargain hunters, opportunistic sellers and browsers. Items that are sold include cars, jewellery, musical instruments, photographic equipment, computers, furniture and sporting goods. The total value of goods sold per year runs into billions of dollars. Sales can be conducted on a local, national and international basis.

eBay's site now combines traditional auction-style trading and fixed-price trading. To put in a bid for an item, the prospective buyer must first register at the site, then put in a maximum bid for the item and wait to see if the bid is accepted. For the seller there are two basic charges: (1) an insertion fee for putting an item up for sale through eBay, and (2) a final value fee at the end of the auction which is generally in the range of 1.25% to 5% of the final sale price.

Source: information from eBay Inc.'s web site, http://pages.ebay.com/community/aboutebay/overview/index.html (accessed September 2003).

A particularly successful form of web retailing (**e-tailing**) has been in the area of digital goods. Software, for example, is easy to download from the Internet, and downloadable music is a major issue in the music industry. Similarly, research reports and magazines can easily be sent to subscribers over the Internet. Even providing access to the Web in different ways from different situations can be a strategy, and, of course, this is where m-commerce (mobile commerce) makes an impact.

Although highly innovative web sites gain media attention, more traditional products and services can use the Internet just as effectively. Many business owners thought that the Internet was suited only to businesses with certain characteristics, yet selling groceries over the Web has caught on in some parts of the world. In fact, selling groceries over the Internet provides an interesting retail case, because there has been a common assumption that it is the high-value low-weight goods which are better suited to retailing online because of their cost-effective distribution and high returns. However, many supermarket chains feel the need to experiment with online sales so that they can build up e-business expertise and perhaps, in the future, turn it into a profitable exercise.

Reflection question 2: What do you think are some of the problems associated with selling groceries online?

Selling services on the Web

Some argue that all Internet-based marketing can be seen as part of broader services marketing. This is because data, convenience, empowerment and time savings are largely intangible and services in general are viewed as being more intangible than physical products. On the Web it is more difficult to distinguish between products and services since e-business is about service or a retailing event. Services can be stand-alone or they can be bundled with products to make them appear more tangible.

The Web has a number of strengths in relation to service delivery. For example, on the Web there is reduced time dependency since the service receiver and the service deliverer do not need to meet physically. Services can be consistently delivered over the Web compared with retail outlets where much can depend on the knowledge or approach used by staff providing the service. The web site also has the advantage of delivering a consistent image and brand to all customers.

The nature of the consumer experience varies with the Web. For example, a consumer buying a service in a store can ask for a demonstration first, but on the Web the purchase is often made before the product or service is fully evaluated.

There are still issues in relation to the marketing and sale of services on the Web. It is difficult to replicate the personal touch of a shop assistant, although some web sites have assistants answering questions online. Customer care is difficult to replicate. In some cases the consumer has more control on the Web and typically might not feel the same pressure to buy that might be felt in a store with a shop assistant.

Customer service and support on the Web

The Web can be used to improve customer service and support in a cost-effective manner. The consumer goes through several stages of decision-making before buying a product, which may involve one or several enquiries. The process typically involves researching product features and prices. Once the product has been purchased, then the customer may experience difficulties which need to be sorted out. It makes sense therefore for many organisations to use the Web where possible for these functions. Web-based customer service enquiry and support systems typically reduce the cost per enquiry to 20% or less compared with traditional telephone enquiries. For the customer, the main benefit is the convenience of being able to get support and service at a time and place of their own choosing.

The Web can be used for providing after-sales support in the form of extra information on how to use or care for a product. Software patches or updates can be downloaded in a cheap and efficient manner, so the Web acts as a distribution channel for customer support. Online chat systems can be used where the customer base is large enough so that customers can help one another.

Customers or potential customers can make enquiries via the Web and receive personalised replies. Airlines, for example, can have systems for frequent flier points which the user can query easily rather than telephoning a customer service centre.

A company can provide information and interactive applications to improve customer relationships and service. The Tax Office, for example, can provide information on completing tax returns, or a bank can provide information on the types of accounts it offers. Collaborative e-business has emerged to meet the growing demand for real-time customer care. Other terms that are used to cover the same area include 'customer interaction software', '1-to-1 consumer intimacy' and 'web-based call centres'. Some people argue that the Web is very impersonal, and this is a barrier to attracting more buying customers, but online chat, for example, can be used to provide a real-time, personal interaction (see chapter 11 for more information).

The Internet is ideal for public relations campaigns. Information can be presented in different ways and has a longer life than advertisements in newspapers and on television. However, in a cluttered environment such as the Web, effort must be made to stand out from the crowd. The important factor is to target the desired audience. Tactics have to be used to attract interest in the web site or the email. This may require using key words, catchy titles or, on occasion, even outrageousness.

IS in action

Reaching new markets

Many companies struggle to differentiate themselves from the competition. This often means that it is difficult to break into new markets and be noticed. ERT (Scotland) Ltd is a well-established marine environmental monitoring and consultancy company, employing nineteen staff.

ERT wanted to use e-business to differentiate it from its larger competitors and help it target new markets internationally. The company used an e-business management consultant to formulate and implement a new e-business strategy.

The strategy was designed to exploit weaknesses in the competition's approaches. The response involved redefining ERT's brand image. A new web site was developed to allow ERT to manage its web content and share documents with clients via an extranet. Systems were put in place to monitor the effectiveness of ERT's online and offline marketing, and the results were fed back into the revisions of the web site. Search engine marketing was used to target the intended international audience while minimising the cost to the company per enquiry.

Source: information from www.quickredfox.co.uk/ert.htm (accessed 10 September 2003).

Environmental scanning

The Web can be used for **environmental scanning**. This concept uses the Internet to gain information on market trends and the strategies of competitors. Companies have performed environmental scanning, either formally or informally, for many years. In some cases, specialist staff are employed to investigate trends in the marketplace and to check what competitors are doing so that this information can be fed back into product or service development. In other cases, environmental scanning is outsourced to market research companies. The Web is a cost-effective tool for environmental scanning in that it provides access to a wealth of information on trends and the competitive environment (see table 10.2).

TABLE 10.2 Environmental scanning on the Web

Advantages	Disadvantages
Cost-effective	The Web is unstructured
Can be done internally within the organisation	Content is not always reliable
Most competitors have web sites	Can be very time-consuming

■ **Reflection question 3:** What are other advantages and disadvantages of environmental scanning via the Web?

Business-to-business e-business

Many organisations are moving into using business-to-business electronic commerce in their supply and purchasing chains. As the drive towards a unified e-business effort continues, it is anticipated that significant changes will take place within these organisations. The changes will affect organisational structure, management approaches, business models, staffing levels and responsibilities, and relationships with customers and suppliers.

The nature of business with suppliers and customers is changing with the increasing use of supply chain software linked with Internet technology, with the goal of virtual end-to-end supply chain management or virtual supply chain management (VSCM). For example, Solectron, a manufacturer in the electronics industry, through its Internet-based supply chain system has reduced the time taken to produce a prototype from 10 days to 24 hours mainly as a result of the improved exchange of data between suppliers and customers. For many suppliers, e-business projects are externally driven. Although there is no disputing the technical difficulties for suppliers involved in integrating back-end transaction systems, data warehouses, manufacturing and inventory tracking systems with web applications, some believe that the *organisational issues* are more difficult to overcome. These issues include changing management and organisational culture, and engendering trust between companies. Companies must be confident in their suppliers so as to allow supply chains to open up to partners, and thereby providing increased visibility into the company.

IS in action

Small business sense

Dinghy Solutions is a small business that has successfully embraced e-business. Dinghy Solutions runs a sailing school in Sydney and sells sailing accessories and boats. The company started five years ago as a one-man outfit and now employs around ten people.

The company had a very successful start with e-business: its revenue tripled after it introduced its web site. Although Dinghy Solutions has invested only a few thousand dollars in its web site over the past three years, it has returned tens of thousands of dollars in increased revenue and reduced costs.

Dinghy Solutions has used the Internet to increase market opportunity, reduce costs and provide superior customer service. The owner of the business built the web site himself and spends an hour a day updating it — time that was once spent writing print newsletters, producing print catalogues and answering customer enquiries.

The Internet provides a way for Dinghy Solutions to increase its market reach. Promoting the web site is of course important, so Dinghy Solutions includes its web address — www.dinghysolutions.com.au — on business cards and stationery, and arranged for links to appear on the web sites of sailing associations and clubs. Potential and existing customers can learn more about, and interact with, the business online. The company has also made sales to international customers who would otherwise have been beyond its marketing reach.

Cost reductions have been the biggest benefit of using the Web. The web site has enabled the company to reduce its $20 000 annual advertising and print catalogue budget to less than $5000 — partly because its print advertisements are generally simpler and smaller because they can simply refer customers to additional information found on the web site. Staff time is also saved by referring customer enquiries to the web site when the information they require is available there.

On the flip side of that, the web site has freed up staff time so that they can spend more time with those customers requiring face-to-face or personal service for more complicated matters. Convenience is a big selling point for customers. Colour images of the products are used, and orders and payment can be made online.

Source: information from www-8.ibm.com/businesscenter/au/casestudies/dinghysolutions.html (accessed 9 September 2003); and http://smallbusiness.ninemsn.com.au/smallbusiness/technology/story_653.asp (accessed 10 September 2003).

E-marketplaces

Many of the virtual supply chains that have been implemented are relatively fixed since companies are fully integrated with their suppliers (see figure 10.6). Other developments on the Web are creating opportunities for marketplace relationships between companies. Some are suggesting that the Web will be increasingly used for transient supplier relationships between traders with little or no pre-established relationship in e-marketplace arrangements (see figure 10.7).

Indeed, e-marketplace trading is likely to threaten the more fixed forms of virtual supply chains. These types of opportunities bring not only potential benefits but also difficult issues relating to trust and risk. The rapid emergence of e-marketplaces is creating trading hubs where suppliers are matched with buyers for specialised equipment, products and services. Some companies want to be the owner of the dominant trading hub for their industry but know that if they become too dominant they will deter many other companies from becoming involved.

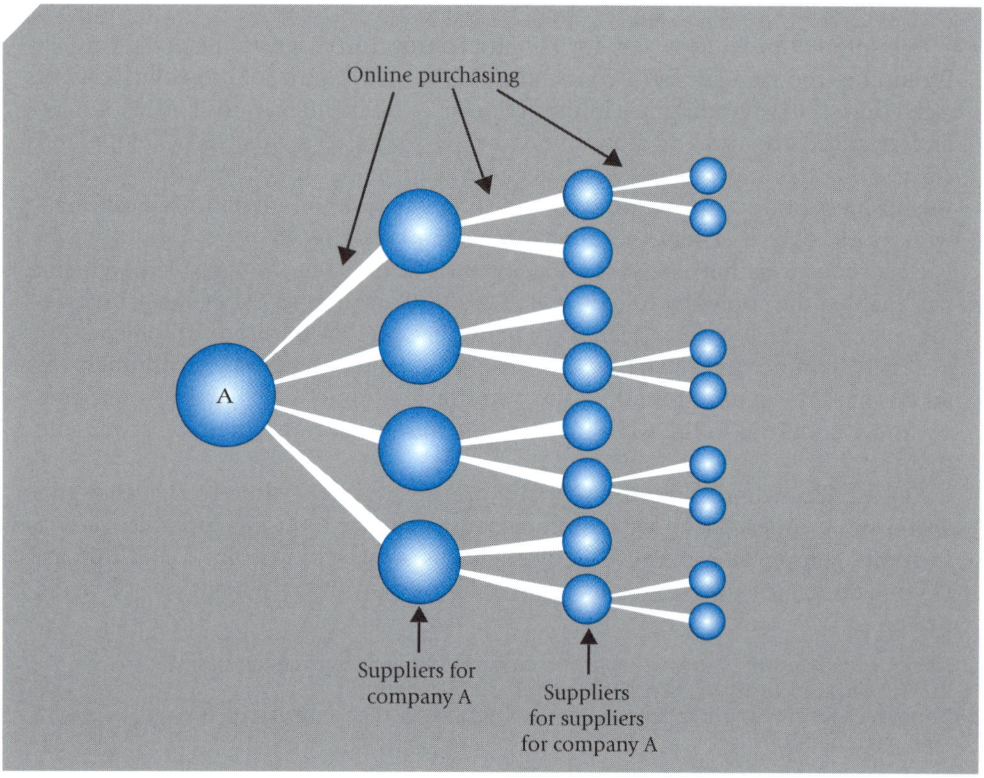

Figure 10.6 Virtual supply chain

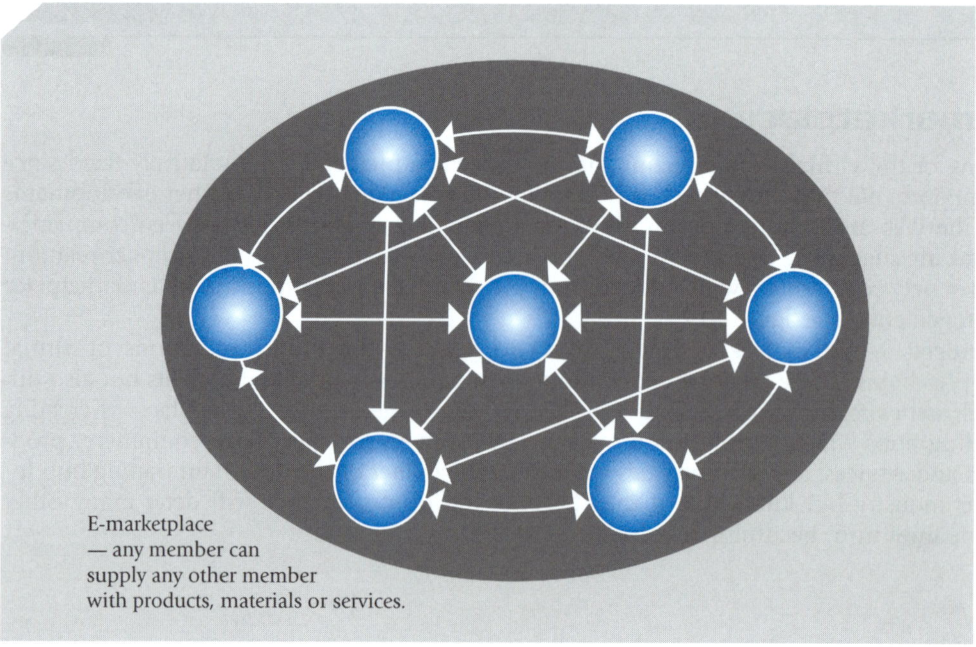

Figure 10.7 E-marketplaces

E-marketplaces can be classified in numerous ways. The vertical (sector-based) and horizontal (across sectors) classification is widely referred to, but there are other factors used to classify them:

- *vertical/horizontal* — according to industry sector
- *geographic coverage* — whether the market is national, regional or global
- *size of companies involved* — e-marketplaces are thought of as being used by large companies but small companies can create e-marketplaces
- *operating model*
  - the laissez-faire model provides information from the seller for the buyer but does not support negotiation between buyer and seller
  - the mediated operating model makes the marketplace an active intermediary between buyers and sellers, supporting transactions through the marketplace
- *delivery model*
  - the stand-alone model is not part of an application; it is an independent entity accessed directly by users where transactions may or may not occur online
  - the embedded delivery model is embedded within an application or sets of applications; users can take advantage of the integrated features this provides but transactions must occur online
- *private versus public* — private e-marketplaces restrict users and accessibility, whereas public marketplaces are potentially available to any company.

There are many examples of electronic marketplaces. Quadrem.com is a major e-marketplace for mining, minerals and metals operating on a global basis with most of the major mining companies involved. Covisint.com is the e-marketplace for the automotive industry, operating on a global level.

There are many success factors in the development and sustainability of an electronic marketplace:

- *Technology infrastructure.* This includes the compatibility of the software with other software systems and its reliability and performance with large numbers of members.
- *Transaction administration system.* E-marketplace software should handle payments and contracts effectively, as well as the general management of membership services.
- *Income stream.* There are several models relating to how the e-marketplace makes money. These include membership subscriptions and commission on trades or other marketplace services.
- *Participants.* A major issue for e-marketplaces is whether they have a sufficient number of members for viability. It is generally thought that it is better to draw existing customers and suppliers in rather than rely on new participants.
- *Fulfils participant needs.* An e-marketplace that fulfils the needs of the participants will be successful. Therefore it should be tailored to participant requirements and add value to the process.
- *Competitive advantage.* In this type of arrangement, gaining a competitive advantage by becoming the leader of the marketplace gives rise to a sustainable advantage.
- *Relationship management.* The issue of relationships and, in particular, developing and maintaining trust between the participants of the marketplace is important.
- *Security.* Security in relation to financial transactions and in the confidentiality of information must be achieved.
- *Level of independence.* Whether the e-marketplace is neutral in that the owners of the marketplace are not participants is a factor which many people consider important.

Perhaps the most critical factor for success is the minimum number of participants required by an e-marketplace to make it effective. This is an important topic since in some industry sectors there are many e-marketplaces coexisting. Another key issue is how the e-marketplace can generate sufficient and sustainable revenue. A major issue is the need for the marketplace to match participant requirements in relation to specialist or customised information.

Problems associated with e-marketplaces

A number of problems have been highlighted in relation to e-marketplaces. The most frequently mentioned problem is the plethora of e-marketplaces and the likely lack of a sufficient number of participants:

- too many e-marketplaces and so some suffer from a lack of participants
- lack of revenue due to lack of participants or viable income streams
- security in relation to payments and confidentiality of information
- technical and administrative performance of the e-marketplace
- legal issues relating to contract handling
- lack of strategy.

Benefits associated with e-marketplaces

The main benefits reported in the literature on e-marketplaces relate to savings for both buyers and sellers and exposure to new customers:

- cost savings in selling
- savings in purchasing
- speed selling/purchasing
- exposure to new customers (global reach)
- convenience for users
- transparency to users, since a marketplace (by definition) is an open environment
- better quality of product/service (global reach)
- reduced need for office space
- fewer resources required for performing transactions, making it ecologically sound
- greater choice of products and services for buyers
- better quality information on products/services.

Infobyte

E-marketplace software

Ariba Inc. is a leading solutions provider in the business-to-business e-commerce sector. It specialises in enterprise spend management software, which aims to help companies achieve savings in procurement. It uses an integrated perspective of a company's spending to drive down costs. Systems include an integrated strategy development model for outlining the spending strategy, an analysis model that coordinates category management, procurement compliance, operational effectiveness and supplier performance. Other modules include sourcing, procurement and supplier management. Aribas's clients include such major companies as Unilever, BMW, ABN, AMRO, Chevron, Cisco Systems and Hewlett-Packard.

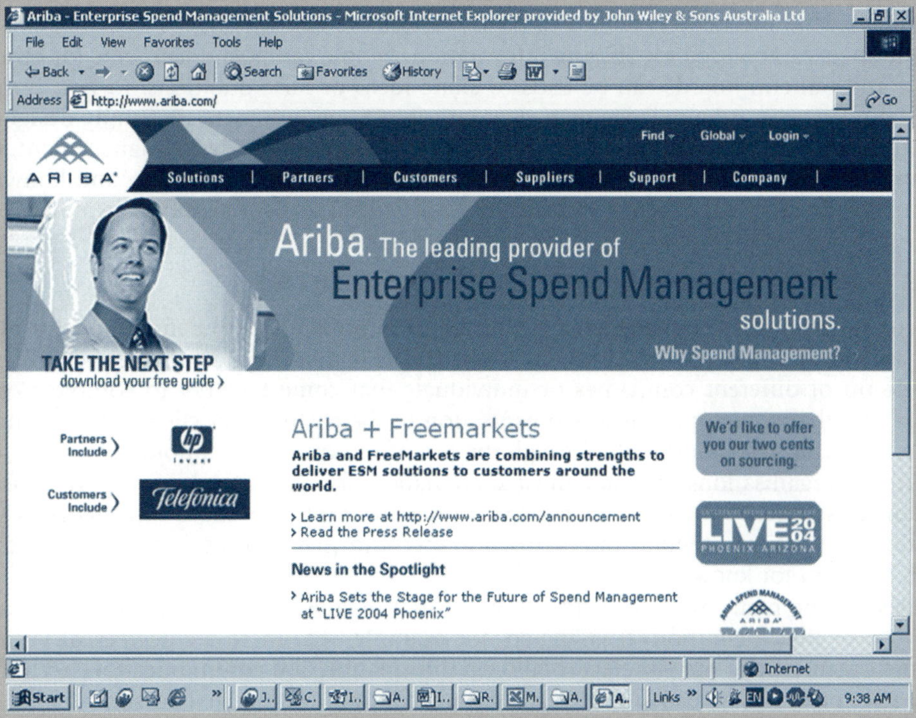

Figure 10.8 The web site of e-marketplace software vendor Ariba (*Source:* Ariba 2004)

Government-to-citizen e-business

Web-based systems have the potential to change radically the way governments interact with citizens. For many government agencies the problems of introducing new approaches are not technical but organisational. Traditionally, government agencies have been slow to change, and so cultural changes are required to adopt e-business effectively.

Governments adopt e-business for a number of purposes. A primary reason is to improve access to information. Brochures, leaflets and documents can be published online. Many governments have introduced portals to provide a central entry point to government-related information. Services can also be made available online, and citizens can have the convenience of paying bills from home. Some local governments have introduced community-based portals that are developed and maintained by the citizens themselves to keep one another informed about activities and events.

Intra-organisational systems

Intranets are being used for a range of organisational applications that are revolutionising internal communication and information processing. As document management systems, intranets provide a cost-effective method of presenting documents that incorporate policies, procedures and organisational initiatives. Transaction and query systems can be developed for many internal functions such as IT support systems, internal purchasing, raising orders, and matters related to payroll and leave entitlements.

Intranets can be used for sharing information. People can post documents for others to read and bulletin boards can be used to share ideas or raise questions. In fact, intranets are being viewed as knowledge management tools. Many intranets are simply designed to capture and present data and information, but for effective knowledge management, more than this is required. Techniques for capturing and sharing information and knowledge that provide an environment conducive to knowledge transfer need to be explored.

Virtual organisations and dot.coms

There are a number of characteristics that are commonly used to define the term **virtual organisation**. A key feature of virtual corporations is that they form structures which are made up of different companies or individuals that come together to complete certain tasks and therefore appear as one organisation to the customer or client. They communicate, cooperate and coordinate through the use of information technology.

Virtual organisations or teams must share data, information and knowledge. This type of organisational structure is typically formed to explicitly share knowledge. Organisational web sites, whether Internet or intranet, can play a strategic role in providing a rich medium for knowledge communication.

Despite the many articles written about virtual organisations, there is still some ambiguity over their definition. It is argued, for example, that there are degrees of virtuality. Some organisations may interact totally via information and communications technology whereas others may also include face-to-face communication. It is assumed in the literature that virtual organisations need to be flexible to cope with a variety of tasks and locations. However, there are varying degrees of flexibility and it is a relative concept. Trust is often viewed as an important characteristic of virtual organisations, but some studies conclude that it is no more significant in virtual organisations than it is in non-virtual organisations (Staples & Ratnasingham 1998).

A commonly proposed characteristic of virtual enterprises is that they operate with some informality and with a flatter management structure than the traditional hierarchies found in many bureaucratic organisations. Ahuja and Carley (1998) suggest that this is an oversimplification of the management approaches required in virtual environments. They argue that the management approach (hierarchical/centralised or flatter/decentralised) should depend on the task or the project being undertaken.

The Internet or intranet applications of a virtual enterprise require careful thought and consideration just as with non-virtual organisations. Indeed, due to the heavy emphasis on the use of communications technology in virtual organisations and the geographically distributed nature of these organisations, it could be assumed that their web sites would be even more strategically significant.

Virtual organisations are often confused with **dot.com** companies. A dot.com is usually taken to mean a company which exists entirely on the Web and has no real offline equivalent. It does not have to be an amalgamation of independent entities that come together to deliver a product or service. In practice, though, many dot.coms rely on other companies for functions such as distribution of the product.

One of the best known online retail companies is Amazon.com, the bookseller. It has the features and characteristics of a dot.com. Many other similar companies exist on the Web, even if only for a short time.

Infobyte

Local or global?

E-business has provided companies with the opportunity to market products and services globally. The general perception is that trading internationally is just an extension of trading locally. However, a number of issues need to be addressed in order to take advantage of the opportunities. A major issue is how staff deal with customers or suppliers of a different culture. Research is highlighting the fact that cultural differences are important (Walsham 2002). Some managers might have global business aspirations but not be cosmopolitan in outlook! In other words, they lack real understanding of the cultural differences and their implications.

[**Key concept:** For many technologies, their uses developed over time, sometimes long after their initial introduction. The same can be said for the Web — many uses for this technology are still evolving.]

Strategic concepts related to e-business

A number of important concepts related to e-business need to be kept in mind. In this section creative destruction, channel conflict, disintermediation and global markets are discussed.

Creative destruction

Radical transformation sometimes cannot take place without the replacement of certain parts of the business. Traditionally, in the business world, the emphasis has been placed on adding new business directions to current operations. However, in today's competitive environment it may be impossible to develop a radically transformed business without destroying some aspects of the existing business. This process has been termed **creative destruction**. For example, the Web strategy and existing business goals may be in conflict or be competing and therefore difficult to maintain.

[**Key concept:** In times of change and opportunities, a business may not be able to do everything but should identify the opportunities with the greatest potential.]

Channel conflict

There are numerous accounts of retail companies across business sectors experiencing some form of e-channel conflict and competition. **Channel conflict** arises when the competition between channels has an adverse effect on the cooperation between channel members.

A number of strategies have been observed and classified to deal with channel conflict. These strategies are considered, on the whole, quite defensive:

- limitation of electronic sales to customers not served through conventional channels
- electronic sales of products not offered through conventional channels
- electronic sales of a limited product selection
- maintaining prices at least equal to conventional retail prices
- selling through hybrid intermediaries
- promoting and supporting conventional retailers.

However, there are complementary factors at work in the relationship between offline and online business components:

- increased customer awareness of a product type
- increased brand awareness built up over years
- improved trust because of offline presence
- customers view a transaction as less risky as the company is established offline
- supplementary support from offline operations for online operations
- coverage of diverse customer preferences.

Disintermediation

Besides performing a competitive analysis, organisations should assess the threat of disintermediation. Due to the ease with which suppliers of products and services can market and sell directly to consumers, those companies that act as intermediaries in the distribution chain risk being bypassed. This has disastrous consequences for the intermediaries and is termed **disintermediation**. The businesses that are most at risk of disintermediation are those that do not significantly add value to the products and services they are distributing.

Intermediaries add value to the sales chain by creating a space where the parties to the business transaction can meet and where the search costs are reduced. For example, an online broker provides insurance quotes from a number of insurance companies for potential consumers. The web site provides convenience for the consumer since a range of quotes can be obtained in one visit to the site. **Reintermediation**, as the term suggests, is all about intermediaries repositioning themselves on the Web.

[**Key concept:** Some technologies actually cause a restructuring of industry sectors.]

Global strategy

The growth of the Internet has created a large global market. Some companies are able to take advantage of the global opportunities provided by the Internet. National borders, time-zone differences and the cost of advertising in remote areas become less of a problem. The flexibility provided by the Web means that a one-person operation can develop a global strategy and implement it in a cost-effective way. A global strategy needs to consider the differences in culture, language and distribution mechanisms. The Web can be used to gather information or find products and services from suppliers to cut costs or provide a stimulus for improvement. A small environmental protection consultancy, for example, could use the Web to find suitable projects and research grants. Their expertise may be in demand worldwide, but they may have been applying for projects within a restricted geographic domain only, because the print publications they use as a source of information are locally or nationally oriented. Through the Web, however, the company can apply for projects on a global basis.

Although many companies are considered global entities, there is no generally accepted understanding of what makes a business successful globally. Companies that have managed to sustain a competitive advantage globally have certain characteristics. Deloitte Touche Tohmatsu and the World Economics Forum have developed the Globalization Framework as a tool to evaluate global companies (Deloitte Touche Tohmatsu 2000). The framework has six areas that can be applied when developing a global Internet commerce strategy.

- *Governance and responsibility.* The directors need to be knowledgeable about the regions they are to market to. The company should disclose data and information so that it is readily accessible to other countries and the ethical standards of the organisation need to be understood by employees worldwide.
- *Strategy and planning.* Projects need to be given the go-ahead according to their potential to create value for shareholders, customers and employees. The company should have the ability to develop alliances with other companies in foreign regions and the world should be seen as a single economic and operating entity.
- *Marketing and service.* Marketing should be on a global basis and attempt to develop a global brand, but it should take into account local needs.
- *Operations and technology.* The company should source materials from the most cost-effective supplier. Core processes should be standardised yet allow for specialisation at the local level. The Web can play a leading a role in the technological infrastructure by improving the supply chain management systems and in the marketing and retailing of services and products.
- *Research and development.* Researchers require information about global markets, and knowledge sharing should be encouraged. This again can be facilitated by Web technology which can also be used to develop strategic partnerships across the world.
- *Organisation and human resource management.* Staff should be moved to geographical locations where they can both disseminate knowledge and absorb it.

Summary

E-business has made a huge impact on the business world. Although many of the rules of business are the same, there are many new lessons to be learned when doing business on the Internet. The key points in this chapter are:

- The Internet is available 24/7/52, has created a global marketplace, and provides companies with many opportunities to increase revenue and reduce costs.
- Although strategy is still important in e-business, opportunistic IT-driven approaches can provide a competitive advantage.
- E-business models can be used to market and sell products, support customers and deal with suppliers.

- E-marketplaces are revolutionising the way companies acquire products and services from suppliers.
- The Web may create the threat of disintermediation for some companies that add little value to the product or service, but it also provides opportunities for reintermediation where convenience or choice, for example, are provided for the customer.

Questions

1. Provide three examples of how a web site can reduce costs for a company.
2. Business-to-consumer e-business covers a range of service types, such as providing product or service information. Explain others forms of business-to-consumer e-business.
3. Explain the advantages for organisations that take an IT-driven approach in relation to the Internet.
4. What is meant by virtual supply chain management (VSCM)? How do you expect VSCM to affect an organisation?
5. What are the advantages of trading via an e-marketplace?
6. What is meant by the term 'business model' and what are its components?
7. Explain five key ways e-business can affect an organisation.
8. What is a virtual organisation?
9. How effective is the Web for conducting environmental scanning?
10. Briefly explain each of the following terms in relation to e-business: channel conflict, creative destruction and globalisation.

Exercises

1. Margaret River Winery (MRW) is a family-run winery in the south-west of Western Australia. It employs all four members of the Jimson family: Stan and Ella, their son Paul and daughter Samantha. Paul has suggested that MRW really needs to become more efficient and should put in place strategies 'to make some real money'. Stan says that they are doing pretty well as they are. About 10% of their total sales are made at the winery to tourists. The rest of the wine is sold to a wine wholesaler for distribution throughout Australia.

   Ella feels that the family work too hard and that they should sell the business and finance Paul and Samantha through university. Samantha, however, enjoys selling wine to the tourists in the cellar bar they constructed a few years ago.

   Stan is concerned that the large wineries on the busy road attract much of the passing tourist trade and, although they are situated in an attractive location, they are not attracting enough customers. Paul says they should not worry about this as it is a small percentage of their potential trade. He has friends at university who have suggested to him that MRW should use the Web to promote and sell the wines. They have limited capital resources, but Stan says it is worth considering if it means they can compete with those big companies down the road that have no passion about their wines. Samantha says she could acquire some web development skills if there is a need as there are no web development companies in the south-west.

   What do you suggest they do in relation to e-business?

2. The Automobile Club (AC) has fifteen offices which operate as travel agencies throughout Australia. At present they have a web site to promote special offers but they have no transaction facilities. The senior staff of AC have become disillusioned with their web site and e-business, since the web site doesn't seem to be making an impact on the business as a whole. You have been called in to act as an e-business consultant and provide advice.

   Provide an industry overview, competitor analysis and broad recommendations or options for the company to consider in relation to its use of the Web.
3. On the basis of the theory of selling products and services on the Web in the chapter, list a number of questions to determine the reasons why someone would buy over the Web. Ask at least eight people what their reasons were for buying products or services over the Web. Does it all come down to cost?

CASE STUDY Manchester Airport's web strategy

Manchester Airport hosts about 18 million passengers per year, making it one of the UK's busiest airports. The customers include a relatively high percentage of business travellers along with recreational travellers on scheduled and charter airlines.

The airport had a web site but not a clearly defined web strategy. The airport saw the potential of the Internet to implement a simple document publishing system and for the development of a major customer-focused web presence, and to integrate partners' systems to provide services to customers.

In essence the airport wanted to develop online services that would generate income and ultimately increase profitability. In addition, it was thought that the web site should offer local residents information in relation to the ways in which the airport might affect them as one way to maintain and improve community relations.

Manchester Airport has adopted a 'Smartsource' methodology for acquiring partner organisations to provide skills that the airport does not possess internally. The airport was aware that it did not have internal expertise in web development so it would need to seek an outside partner to design, develop and maintain its web presence.

As the airport has complex relationships with the companies that operate within its boundaries it was clear that the business objectives of the airport would need to be handled sensitively in order to maintain the high level of rapport enjoyed between all parties.

The airport considered the web site to be fundamentally important so it decided it should host the system. The web site had to integrate with existing systems, such as customer relationship management (CRM) database and messaging systems, along with the platforms used by partners and suppliers. The preferred approach was to have a fully integrated system under the Manchester Airport brand.

(*continued*)

An underlying principle was to make use of existing technology as much as possible. Also the solution had to fit wherever possible with existing skill sets in the organisation. The airport decided to pick the technical infrastructure requirements, leaving the supplier to design and build the solution.

The airport required a solution developer with the technical expertise to design and develop a fully functional web site that was integrated with backend systems. The web developer also had to be qualified to act as a one-stop-shop partner who would assume full responsibility for the design, building and installation of the web site, able to provide 24/7/52 operational support, capable of understanding the airport's business, and able to communicate and work with all airport staff.

The company chosen, from a shortlist of four, was based about 10 kilometres from the airport, met all of the airport's selection criteria and was very comfortable working closely with non-technical staff.

The first stage of the web site provided up-to-the-minute details of arrivals and departures similar to those shown in the passenger lounges at the airport. This reduced the number of phone calls enquiring about the timing of flights. The web site provided the facility to book scheduled flights and hotel accommodation. Rather than develop a new system it was decided to integrate with the already-available Telme.com online travel booking service. This integration was designed in a seamless way.

In order to use many of the services supplied on the site, users must register online. These data are then utilised whenever a service is requested. If the customer wishes to book a flight via Telme.com, the airport's own CRM system feeds information into the Telme system, receives data in response and then passes it to the user as appropriate. A significant amount of effort was expended to ensure that the functioning of the web site met the real-world requirements of users by involving them in the testing process.

The second phase of the operation was targeted to exploit the new web presence and the online Manchester Airport brand. The second-phase offerings included the ability for customers to:

- preorder duty-free products online
- reserve airport car parking spaces
- book charter flights and package holidays
- preorder foreign currency.

The web site receives up to 500 000 hits per day. The benefits of the e-business systems are many. Passengers are feeling more comfortable with the airport as a result of the web site since they can understand the layout, parking, shopping and currency exchange facilities before they leave home. Local community residents can be informed of developments at the airport, which helps community relations. Through the online shopping and ordering systems, income and profits are increasing. Finally, the airport has received substantially increased revenue from car parking. Before the new web site an outside company had sole control of the parking, and the airport received only 5% of revenue. Via online booking, 90% of the revenue now comes to the airport.

Overall, the main lessons learned from their experiences are: exploit the experience of employees; work closely with the real end-users and work with suppliers in a partnership fashion.

From an e-business perspective the system is successful because it provides what the users want in a convenient manner. Travellers require timely and accurate data, and the new web applications provide them.

Source: adapted from www-3.ibm.com/software/success/cssdb.nsf/CS/AKLR-5K4QJQ?OpenDocument&Site=webappsrv
www.kmpassociates.com/kmpinternet/web/site/flashsite

QUESTIONS

1. Identify the key business objectives related to the airport's e-business initiatives.
2. Who was involved in the web development team? Did the choice of parties involved conform to good practice principles explained in this chapter?
3. Classify the main benefits of the new web site.
4. Visit the web site of Manchester Airport (www.manairport.co.uk) and write a 250-word review of the site.
5. How do you see the site evolving in the future?

References

Ahuja, M.K. & Carley, K.M. 1998, 'Network structure in virtual organisations', *JCMC*, vol. 3, no. 4.

Ariba 2004, www.ariba.com (accessed May 2004).

Australian eBusiness Guide 2001, CCH Press, Sydney.

Deloitte Touche Tohmatsu 2000, 'Globalization diagnostic', www.deloitte.com/davos/global.html (accessed March 2001).

Lawrence, E., Corbitt, B., Tidwell, A., Fisher, J. & Lawrence, J.R. 2000, *Internet Commerce: Digital Models for Business*, 2nd edn, John Wiley & Sons, Brisbane.

Settles, C. 1997, 'The 3.5.7 for maximising your business online', available www.successful.com/357artic.html (accessed June 2001).

Staples, D.S. & Ratnasingham, P. 1998, 'Trust: The panacea of virtual management', *Proceedings of the International Conference on Information Systems*, pp. 128–46.

Telstra 1998, *Small Business Index — Special Report*, p. 32; see also http://telstra.com/business/RunYourBusiness/Technology/InternetMarketing.asp (accessed June 2001).

Walsham, G. 2002, 'Cross-cultural software production and use: A structurational analysis', *MIS Quarterly*, vol. 26, no. 4, pp. 359–80.

Chapter 11

Web commerce development

LEARNING OBJECTIVES

After reading this chapter, you should be able to:

- describe the characteristics of web applications
- understand the various web technologies and web-authoring tools
- explain how the scope and complexity of web projects affect development
- understand the types of users of web systems
- describe the critical issues in web-site design
- understand how to attract visitors to web sites
- explain how to measure the effectiveness of web sites.

11

Introduction

Web site development is an area of information systems in its own right. It incorporates the analysis of requirements, design, implementation and, of course, the issue of evolution and updating. Web site projects can vary significantly in scope and complexity. There is a lot of pressure to design and implement a web site well the first time since a problematic web site is likely to lose customers. Chapter 10 examined the strategies behind e-business. In this chapter, we look in some detail at the issues surrounding the development of web sites.

Characteristics of web applications

Web applications are systems developed for the web environment. Although web applications have some similar characteristics to other types of information systems, they also have certain unique characteristics. This is largely due to the demands put on web applications from being directly accessible by customers and suppliers. Some of the main characteristics of web applications are described below.

Web sites often evolve from simple beginnings to become multifunctional in nature. Common functions include providing information to users or customers, developing relationships with customers, enabling customers to perform transactions, and documenting management systems for internal users (intranet). The multifunctionality of many systems forces organisations to work across traditional departmental boundaries. A customer focus epitomised by the question 'how do we meet the customer's needs?' requires an integrated effort from sales, marketing, customer service and IS. This requires a high degree of collaboration, which means that traditional organisational boundaries are de-emphasised.

Teams made up of different business representatives may not be adequate for developing web applications, especially if they are led by an information systems person. The problems associated with representative teams are that members do not speak the same language and have different goals and expectations. The teams that are required for web applications development need to have a business focus and be led by a 'producer' figure who has expertise in the technical, marketing and business aspects of the organisation. The analogy of a film production team is useful, as such teams have one goal in mind but manage diverse skills and tasks in the process. Large web project teams can include:

- a project leader who coordinates the team and project
- systems analysts who gather requirements for the web site
- web designers
- graphic designers who do detailed designs of logos and icons
- content providers who provide the information content for the site
- technical developers
- web editors who ensure the content is correct and that links work
- web marketing specialists who build the marketing techniques into the site
- representative users/customers who make sure the system is acceptable and fulfils the requirements.

■ **Reflection question 1:** Which role do you think there is the greatest demand for?

Due to the multifunctionality of many web sites, there are often diverse groups of stakeholders. Stakeholders can include people both within the organisation and outside it. Internal stakeholders may be specialised categories of employees and external stakeholders may be current customers or key suppliers. These stakeholder groups can live locally, interstate or overseas. Overseas users may have a different cultural and linguistic background and this may have to be considered in web application development. As a result, responsibility for the web site within the organisation can be ambiguous, and the overall management of the web strategy may be given little consideration.

The content and functionality of web sites change through time. Because of this the notion of project completion is inappropriate. Even the standard six-monthly update reviews used with traditional IS applications may be unsuitable for managing the rapid amount of change required. Web sites can be viewed as organic systems that are continually adapting to their environment. Some components of sites flourish under certain conditions, but other components become redundant and wither away. Systems can start off as intranets and go on to develop an Internet or extranet component, and others start off as Internets and develop an intranet component.

[**Key concept:** Evolutionary development approaches dominate in e-commerce.]

History of the Internet

The Internet began in the mid-1960s as a US Defense Department network called ARPAnet. It was an experimental network designed specifically to withstand various forms of attack on communications lines. In the ARPAnet model, communication always occurred between a source and destination computer. To send a message, the data was put into a packet of data called an 'Internet protocol packet' and addressed. The computers, not the network, were given the responsibility of ensuring that the communication was completed. The approach worked on the premise that the network itself was unreliable and open to attack. In the early 1980s, universities began to use the Internet as an inexpensive and convenient method for communicating. The Internet expanded rapidly with improvements in the telecommunications infrastructure and its use by commercial organisations.

The World Wide Web (also referred to as the Web and WWW) is a network of information sites. The sites are created using hypertext which is the method of linking information and screens that allow simple navigation and linking together of sources of information. Even though the Web is expanding rapidly, it is largely an unorganised and unstructured web of information available on servers throughout the world.

The Web was first developed in 1989 at the European Laboratory for Particle Physics (CERN) in Geneva and has grown to be a huge number of information repositories today. The success of the Web owes much to the simplicity of hypertext, a type of 'point and click' interface which was used earlier in Apple Computer's hypercard system.

Web technologies

There are various web technologies that you need to have some understanding of, including browsers, search engines, hypertext, web addresses and m-commerce.

Browsers

The World Wide Web can be accessed by software applications known as **browsers**, such as Netscape Navigator and Microsoft Internet Explorer. The browser allows the user to input a uniform resource locator (URL), i.e. the web-site address. A connection is made to the remote computer (using that URL) and the HTML code is returned to the client and formatted as a page using the HTML within the browser. Browsers make temporary copies of the page in an area of memory called the 'cache'. These pages are used when the user clicks the 'back' button, which saves accessing the pages over the Internet again. Web browsers are becoming more sophisticated in terms of the operations they support. Below are some typical facilities supported by web browsers:

- retrieving web pages
- navigating through web pages
- searching facilities based on key words
- accessing web pages by inputting the URL
- retrieving previously viewed web pages
- saving web pages
- printing web pages
- using email
- constructing web pages.

Search engines

The browser does not do the searching on the Internet but uses search engines. **Search engines** are software systems located at web sites that collect and order information from the Internet. Examples of search engines include Google, AltaVista, Yahoo! and Excite. Different search engines work on different principles and will often retrieve different 'finds'. However, most tend to list key words and headings on the screen with the information's location in a hypertext link that can be selected to take the user to that site. Some search engines are general, and others are more specialised, either geographically (focus on a country) or in terms of subject matter. Meta-search engines are systems that use more than one search engine in the search process. Accessing six or ten search engines within one search is clearly an effective way of searching.

■ **Reflection question 2:** Which search engine do you use? Why?

Hypertext and hyperlinks

Web pages can be linked using **hyperlinks**. Hyperlinks are a method of navigating the Web. The hyperlink can be a word or words or a picture or area within a page. Words that are hyperlinks are typically highlighted in some way and, once clicked, take the user to another page. Hypertext markup language (HTML) is a language for developing hypertext documents that can be viewed in a browser. The transmission of documents on the Web is handled by the hypertext transfer protocol.

HTTP

Hypertext transfer protocol (HTTP) is the web communications protocol, and handles the transfer of data over the Internet. When a client opens a connection to a web server, an HTTP header is sent which contains a command to, for example, get or input data. The server transmits a message back to the client which includes the format of the data being returned. This allows the browser to display different types of data such as text, images and HTML.

Web sites

Related web pages located together on a computer or the Internet are known as a web site. Universities, for example, typically have web sites that run into thousands of pages. (For example, check out Edith Cowan University's web site at www.ecu.edu.au.) Of course, the organisation and management of such large sites is complex and time-consuming.

Web addresses

Web sites must have a unique address to avoid clashes and ambiguity for those accessing the data. The address is composed of several pieces of information and known as the **uniform resource locator**. The URL is composed of the protocol, the server and the path of the file or web page, e.g. http://www.looksmart.com.au. In this example, the letters 'http' stand for hypertext transfer protocol, and 'www.looksmart.com.au' is the server address, which also includes the type of organisation (in this case, 'com' stands for *commercial*) and the country where it is located (in this example, 'au' denotes Australia).

Examples of Internet address codes are shown below:

biz	businesses
com	commercial institutions
edu	educational institutions
gov	government organisations
net	networks
uk	United Kingdom
nz	New Zealand
jp	Japan
ca	Canada

The United States does not have a country abbreviation, e.g. http://www.ibm.com/.

M-commerce

'M-commerce' means mobile commerce, and it has become a key feature of the e-commerce landscape. The term is used to describe activity involving transactions with monetary value conducted via a mobile phone or personal digital assistant that connects with or includes phone technology. The transaction could be for intangible goods, such as information in digital format sent to the mobile device, or it could involve physical goods that are bought via a mobile phone. A further distinction in mobile transactions is between remote transactions and point-of-sale transactions.

A significant amount of mobile commerce is related to the purchase of different types of digital content for the mobile phone itself. These include: ringing tones, screen savers, wallpapers, games, music and video clips.

Mobile commerce is convenient and easy to use. Hence new applications that are too difficult to use are unlikely to be successful. They should build on existing ways of working and then add mobile value. The benefits of m-commerce are immediate access and delivery of service, flexibility, personalisation, location awareness or better customer service (see, for example, www.forum.nokia.com).

IS in action

Library in your pocket

Have you ever wondered how doctors remember every condition and treatment when consulting with a patient? Now they don't have to because they can carry around a library of proven procedures and practices in their pocket.

Evidence-based medical guidelines (EBM) contain up-to-date information covering the diagnosis and treatment of diseases and conditions that the general physician might come across. It began as a paper-based product, produced by Duodecim Medical Publications, which was converted into electronic format available via the Internet or as a CD-ROM. This meant that access to a computer or laptop was needed, which could be difficult when answers were needed immediately at a patient's bedside.

Mobile applications provided the solution. By using technology supplied by Nokia and a Symbian operating system, detailed medical information is at the physician's fingertips 24/7. The EBM guidelines are supplied preloaded on to the Nokia Communicator's 64 Mb memory card, and updates can be downloaded over the network from Duodecim.

The work spent converting the EBM guidelines in hard copy to electronic format had forced the developers to consider the contents and define it more simply and in terms of functionality and usability on the screen. This experience proved invaluable when converting to the smaller-sized Communicator screen.

Opening directly to the main menu, a search needs only the first few letters of a term to begin, and the results are prioritised into primary and secondary documents. Clinical data is provided as bullets or numbered steps. Previously searched terms are saved so they can be returned to quickly. There are no complex menus or screens, and search results are quick to skim and easy to read. It is a fast and easy resource to access at the medical practitioner's fingertips.

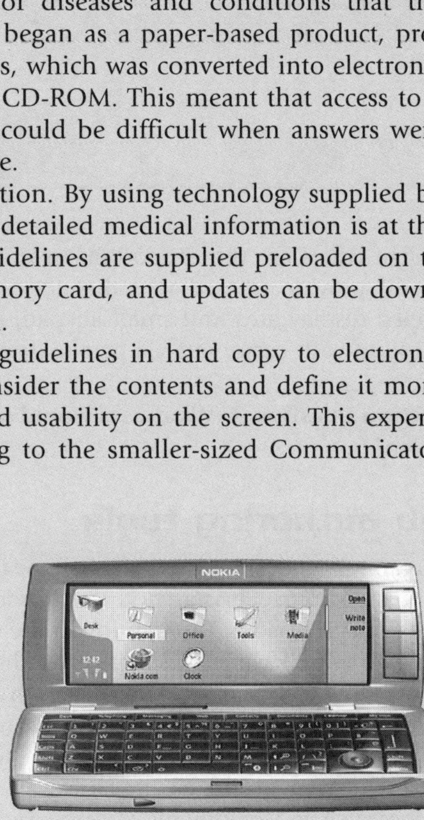

Figure 11.1

Source: adapted from www.nokia.com/downloads/solutions/business/Duodecim_final.pdf (accessed October 2003).

[**Key concept:** The trend for systems is to provide greater flexibility of access.]

Infobyte

So what are the uses of m-commerce?

Person to person — voice communications, video calls.
Person to machine — personal banking, personal shopping, Internet access, voice-activated services.
Machine to person — intelligent home monitoring, information services, entertainment services.
Machine to machine — remote telemetry, electronic wallet, toll systems, car telematics.

Design issues are very important in m-commerce. It is important to pick applications that will provide immediate value to customers. For example, mobile phones have a restricted display area and small keypad, so it is important to focus content. Loyalty can be built up with customers via personalised services.

- **Reflection question 3:** What uses would you make of a mobile phone that could access the Web?

Web authoring tools

An organisation developing a web site or intranet needs to consider which web authoring tool or tools to use. It is a good idea to decide on one as a standard for the organisation for three main reasons: (1) training in the web authoring package can be focused, (2) supporting one package is easier from a help and advice perspective, and (3) licensing arrangements will be eased and may even be more cost-effective.

Hypertext markup language has become the language of the Internet and is used for describing web pages to web browsers. A text editor can be used to develop HTML files in the HTML command language. However, most people developing web sites use software packages such as Macromedia Dreamweaver or Microsoft's Frontpage. These packages provide a graphical environment for page development which is a better option for people without programming skills since they have a WYSIWYG ('what you see is what you get') interface. HTML is based on standard generalised markup language (SGML). SGML is a system of rules for describing the treatment and use of documents. HTML, in fact, is a specialised subset of SGML. However, professional developers often use a variety of scripting and programming languages to add extra functionality to the systems. Some of the main scripting and programming languages used on the Internet are described below.

XML

HTML is not sophisticated enough to deal with all the demands of e-business today. **XML**, which stands for extensible markup language, is a simplified version of SGML. XML allows the display of text and data in a browser as HTML does, but it is also a flexible way of creating common information formats and sharing *both* the format and the data on the Web, intranets and elsewhere. In other words, where HTML describes the content of a web page only in terms of how it is to be displayed and interacted with, XML describes the content in terms of what data is being described and hence provides meta-data and a way of structuring data. XML documents are associated with their own information contexts. This means document tags can be defined that have meanings within that context. This provides a powerful environment for document management since XML could define the document type, its use and other features that would be helpful in structuring the information space. A benefit of XML is that it allows data to be shared between different applications because the tags relate to the function and identity of the data rather than anything application-specific.

Web client programming languages

Web pages can have scripts (VBScript, JScript or JavaScript) or Java applets embedded in them, and these are then executed on the client machine once the page has downloaded. These scripts and applets add interactivity to the web pages and perform specialised functions such as data validation on data input into forms. In addition, they take some of the processing burden off the web server.

The importance of Java

Java is a programming language which can be used to develop programs which can be embedded in web pages to add extra functionality such as animation and forms. Much media attention has surrounded the Java programming language, because (1) Sun Microsystems (the company that developed Java) has to compete in the same environment as Microsoft, so to get noticed there has to be a concerted promotion of the product, and (2) Java is a sound language that has a number of innovative features.

Sun Microsystems developed a language called Oak that was used for consumer electronic devices. This language was small, reliable and architecture-independent. The developers realised that, with the rise of the Internet, there was a need for an architecture-neutral language, hence the development of Java from Oak.

Java is described as 'a simple, object-oriented, distributed, interpreted, robust, secure, architecture-neutral, portable, high-performance, multi-threaded and dynamic language' (Sun Microsystems 2004). Although this description might seem too good to be true, Java does have a number of excellent attributes for being used on the Internet. Java is an interpreted language but is also compiled first into byte-code. This means that a Java program can be downloaded and interpreted by a browser whatever the operating system or hardware (as long as the Java interpreter is available). This is possible because the device-dependent features of the program are loaded in at runtime. This makes Java programs or **Java applets** (graphical Java programs) very portable between machines, hence the phrase 'write once, run anywhere', often used with Java.

[**Key concept:** Technical programming is just as important as ever.]

Assessing the feasibility of adopting web commerce

Feasibility is about assessing whether the proposed project is viable. Viability is normally assessed in terms of the costs and benefits attached to the development of the application. Generally, the benefits, which are quantified financially, should outweigh the costs of developing and running the system. A time scale of three to five years can be used to examine the feasibility, since much of the cost of a system is incurred early in its life whereas the benefits are more evenly spread throughout the life of the system.

The costs are typically such things as staff time, hired expertise, equipment and programmer time. The benefits are increased orders, less cost per transaction processed, more information, better quality information, increased staff satisfaction and improved customer satisfaction.

It is difficult to develop a cost–benefit analysis until full details of the system are ascertained. Hence, a relatively fast feasibility assessment should be conducted at the start of the planning and strategy development stage, and further assessment should be made periodically. A feasibility study should also be carried out for each component of the web development.

Some organisations view their web commerce initiatives as an investment in the future. Rather than taking a typical cost–benefit analysis perspective where future benefits are estimated, the main benefit is seen as providing scope and choice for future business directions. This perspective assumes that a company that has stepped into the web commerce arena is in a better position to take advantage of new opportunities that arise in the area than a company that is watching from the sidelines.

[**Key concept:** Feasibility is a moving target.]

Project complexity and scope

A web development project can vary in scope from setting up an entire web site for a large organisation, to developing a component of a large web site, to developing a small web site of limited functionality. These are very different types of projects which vary greatly in complexity. Such complexity depends on a number of factors:

- *The scope of the project.* The scope of a project usually refers to the functionality of a system. A system could have a narrow, well-defined scope in that it might deal only with customer enquiries, or it may be broader in scope and cover a wider range of customer service options.
- *The size of the project.* This can be measured in many ways, such as the number of functions, the number of sites and the volume of information.
- *The number of users and range of users.* As the number of users increases so, too, can the complexity of the system. A larger number of users often means more time spent consulting users to determine requirements for the system. The organisational dynamics of work groups often increases the complexity of systems. Work groups form social and political entities which cannot be ignored when developing information systems.
- *The geographic distribution of users.* The geographic distribution of users has an effect in several ways. The communications hardware and software infrastructure becomes more complex as data is sent across several sites. If users are internationally dispersed, there may be linguistic and cultural differences which will affect the design process.
- *The type (complexity) of functionality required in the system.* The complexity of a web-site application can be characterised by general functionality and applies equally to an intranet and the Internet:
  - Static document publishing systems — these are often used for intranet applications to put company manuals and documentation on the Web and to provide

information to customers. They are relatively simple systems because they are not connected to databases although they can be multimedia systems that include text, graphics, video and animations.
  - Dynamic web applications — these are more sophisticated interactive systems. They include forms for input of customer details which are then stored in a simple database or file. Querying facilities, e.g. to find staff telephone extension numbers, may also be present.
  - Complex web applications — these types of systems provide a fully interactive interface which connects to one or several databases. They can complete transactions such as adding, amending or deleting. Examples include allowing suppliers access to inventory control systems, and allowing customers to make purchases which automatically update the order entry and stock control systems.
- *The stage of evolution of the overall web site.* If there are no web applications in the organisation, the project will involve work at a strategic level to define the goals of the system. On the other hand, if the site is relatively mature and working well, then later projects will be additions that will not usually require the same broad planning phases, although some strategic planning will still be required.
- *The amount of expertise within the organisation.* The less expertise there is for any IS project within an organisation, the higher the risk associated with the project. Expertise can save a great amount of time as it improves the chances of completing tasks correctly, working appropriately, using suitable tools, estimating better and so on. If expertise does not exist within the organisation, the expertise has to be brought into the organisation from outside. This can alleviate some of the problems but adds complexity since the organisation has to source suitable consultants or vendors and assess their performance.
- *The number of interfaces with other systems.* The more connections with other systems, the more complex the development and testing process.
- *The strategic/critical nature of the project.* If the project is critical to the organisation, e.g. if it is costing a large amount of money or the system it connects to is part of the core business system(s), then the consequences of failure will be significant. In such cases, the project could influence corporate profits, and/or influence relationships with customers and suppliers.

There are several strategies that can be used by a company when developing a new web site. It is unlikely, unless the site is small, that the whole site will be designed and implemented in one project cycle. A major issue in web-site development is defining responsibility for both the development and maintenance of sections of the web site. Responsibility for development of the web site may be taken by a team working centrally. In other situations each organisational unit may have its own team. An issue that needs to be resolved therefore is the overall development strategy and the level of responsibility given to organisational units. The key web-site development alternatives are:

- plan the entire site and strictly regulate its distributed development
- plan the core of the site (outsourcing or in-house) and make no further changes
- plan the core of the site and let user departments develop their own neighbourhoods
- plan the core of the site and loosely regulate the development of the rest of the site
- allow unregulated development of the entire site (not recommended)
- plan the entire site, develop the core and then incrementally develop the rest of the site.

Defining the users

Many different groups of people interact with web sites. Understanding their characteristics and the roles these groups play helps define the requirements for a web application. The more detail that can be added to the development of user profiles, the more likely the completed system will be of use. For example, there may be many types of customers who interact with a business. Understanding how they differ should go a long way to understanding how their needs can be served.

Surfers

The Web is an environment where people stumble on a web site without any intention of making a purchase. They may simply be browsing, which is similar to window shopping in a shopping centre. This type of user will just pass through quickly if the site is not appealing or easy to navigate. If the site is memorable, they may return at a later date to look again or even make a purchase. Increasingly, people are more focused in their use of the Web. They are less likely to surf and are more likely to be using the Web with a specific objective in mind.

Buyers

These people come to the site to make a purchase. They have some knowledge about the item required. A clear, well-designed system will help the customer complete the transaction.

Member and non-member customers

In some organisations, customers must be members. This may give them special privileges or discounts which are not open to non-members. Non-members must complete an application form and apply for membership.

Dissatisfied customers

There should be some way for customers to make a complaint. This can be done by providing customer service contact details on the web site.

Recipients

The person who buys the goods may not be the same person as the one who receives the goods. This must be taken into account in the information system.

Suppliers

Suppliers may access an extranet to determine which products require supplying.

Internal users

There are many people within an organisation that interact with the web site. There are systems developers such as the analyst who defines the requirements of the system. Designers decide on the layout and design features of the system. There are content specialists who provide the text for the system. There are those who have the technical expertise to implement the system. If the system is connected to corporate databases, then the database administrator will interact with the web interface. Customer service representatives will also interact with the Internet, as well as marketing and sales staff. Senior management will be involved more in developing the web-site strategy. If there is an intranet available, then anyone in the company may use the system.

[**Key concept:** Know your users.]

■ **Reflection question 4:** Which type(s) of user are you?

Working with different cultures and languages

If the product or service is to be promoted to people of different linguistic backgrounds, then translations of web content should be provided. Tourism-related sites, in particular those intended to appeal to overseas tourists, should provide at least translations into the languages of the targeted nationalities. For example, the Australian National Tourism Site, a site aimed at tourists visiting Australia (www.australia.com), has translations into a number of languages, including Japanese. The developers may also have to consider alternative languages for local residents who cannot read the national language.

Although the Internet may appear to be making the world a 'global village', there are still many cultural differences between people of different nationalities. Religious, economic, political, legislative and social differences dictate what is and what is not appropriate web content.

Muslim countries usually have certain expectations in terms of how women are portrayed in advertisements. For many years, the French restricted travel advertising, believing it had a negative impact on their domestic tourism revenue. There can be restrictions on advertising with an overt or covert political message. Some countries restrict the advertising of tobacco.

Web accessibility issues

Web accessibility design issues have been highlighted in relation to the disabled (Sellitto & Wenn 2000). The general perception was that the Web was accessible by all but this is not strictly true as a number of high-profile web sites have been identified as not catering to people with various disabilities, such as physical, visual, hearing and cognitive or neurological disabilities.

There is a range of design features which can be built into web sites to help people with disabilities, such as:

- captioned (transcripts) audio files for people with hearing problems
- voice output of all text for the vision-impaired, and descriptions of graphics files so they, too, can be voice-output — the layout of text is very important, because the text reader must follow a logical flow; tables are especially problematical in relation to this feature
- control of colour settings and styles for people who are colour-blind
- keyboard equivalents for mouse-driven commands, to avoid repetitive stress injury from constantly clicking a mouse
- magnification tools to aid readability, and avoidance of scrolling text
- use of clear and simple language for those with cognitive disabilities, and consistent design and navigation options.

Many national governments have Disability Discrimination Acts which cover issues related to the design of web sites, and the World Wide Web Consortium (W3C) is keen to promote the design of accessible web sites for the disabled.

IS in action

World Wide Web Consortium

The World Wide Web Consortium (W3C) was created in 1994 and now has more than 400 member organisations from around the world. The mission of W3C is to promote interoperability and an open forum discussion on issues related to the Web's development. In particular, W3C has three long-term goals:

- *Universal access*: to work towards the Web being accessible to all sections of the community by taking into account differences in culture, education, ability, material resources and physical limitations
- *Semantic Web*: to work towards a software environment that helps users to make the best use of the resources available on the Web
- *Web of trust*: to play a role in guiding the Web's development from a legal, commercial and social perspective.

W3C activities are organised into groups:

- working groups for technical developments
- interest groups for more general work
- coordination groups for communication among related groups.

The work of the Consortium breaks down into four main areas:

- *Architecture Domain* — for examining issues related to the underlying technologies of the Web
- *Interaction Domain* — specialises in improving user interaction with the Web
- *Technology and Society Domain* — focuses on developing the Web infrastructure to solve social, legal and public policy concerns
- *Web Accessibility Initiative* (WAI) — examines accessibility (for people with disabilities) of the Web through five main areas of work: technology, guidelines, tools, education and outreach, and research and development.

Source: information from www.w3.org (accessed February 2004).

Design issues for web commerce

Designing a web commerce system involves more than just developing web pages with appropriate content. Today, organisations are using the Web as a unifying portal to tie their disparate corporate systems together. In a sense, the organisational expectations in relation to IT have not changed. They are to develop flexible systems that help the organisation by improving productivity. Hence, the development of web systems is an opportunity to examine the entire IT/IS infrastructure to determine how and where improvements can be made.

Developing a web site in an organisation involves decisions related to the hardware and software for the client machines and web server. If the system is to perform transactions which access the corporate databases, then an applications server and database server will be needed. The design of the site's pages requires making decisions on the design framework, the navigation mechanism and the detailed layout of pages.

Evolution of web-site designs

The conventions used in the design of web sites have undergone considerable evolution over the Web's brief history. Early web-site designs were characterised by a simplistic functionality. They tended to have text across the full width of the screen and in continuous paragraphs on one page. Often, they had been constructed by technical people with the main aim being to convey a simple message.

Later design approaches took advantage of extensions to HTML. Images and graphics replaced some of the text and the pages were organised in simple hierarchies. (If you surf the Web you will find many of these so-called first- and second-generation sites.)

Effective design

Design is a multifaceted concept with harmony and balance at its core. Design of web sites has evolved to ensure better usability and functionality. Technical features are not the overriding factors. Design is evident in the structure of a web site, in the navigation mechanisms, the metaphors used and the detailed design and layout of each page.

Designing effective web interfaces is both an art and a science. It is an art because a certain amount of creativity is required to develop web systems which are functional yet aesthetically pleasing to look at and work with. There are times when fashion and fun play a vital role in the design; a scientific, engineered or more purely rational approach would not achieve the same level of success. However, people process and interpret information according to cognitive principles, and adhering to these helps a designer to develop systems that communicate effectively. So a more scientific or engineered approach provides a strong underlying set of principles that can serve as a framework for design.

Human–computer interaction (HCI) is an important field within the IS/IT disciplines. It involves the theory and practice of how users interact with computer systems. It draws on cognitive psychology for principles of how people interpret information. Designing systems according to these principles generally leads to systems which have a higher level of usability.

Research in cognitive psychology tells us that in most situations people are easily cognitively overloaded. For example, people find it difficult to remember much more than seven, plus or minus two, chunks of information. These could be instructions or digits or key words. Hence, designers should not expect users to remember a great deal of information or data from one web page to another, but should have this information repeated on each screen if it is important. The brain processes information serially. This means that developing systems which have competing features is likely to distract the user from acquiring necessary information. Generally speaking, therefore, simplicity of design and layout is desirable for improving the degree of information communicated.

The designer works with web pages that are displayed in a browser. Each web page provides a design space where text, graphics, animations and images can be arranged to maximum effect.

Layout

Space can be used on a web page to separate features, whether text or graphics, and thereby communicate meaning and relevance without using lines or borders that would add to the cognitive load on the user (see figure 11.2). The techniques of using space and position in design are evident, of course, in newspapers, magazines and books. Using space wisely creates a design that is both simple and effective.

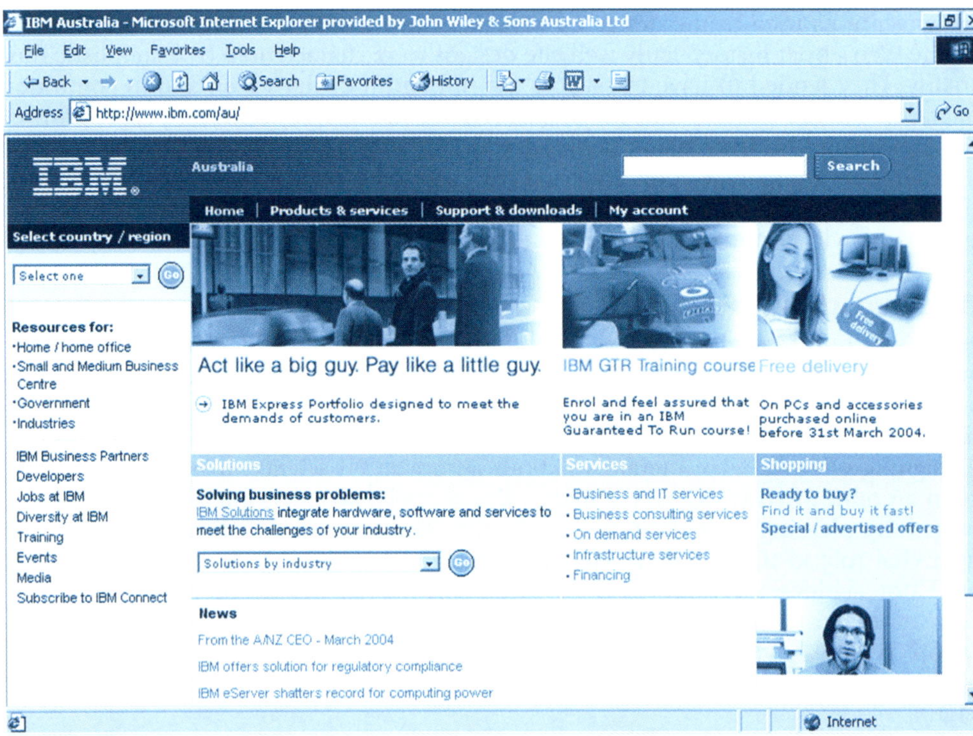

Figure 11.2 IBM's Australian home page showing plenty of white space (*Source*: www.ibm.com.au)

Consistency

Consistency is an easy principle to understand but one which is often forgotten. Consistency relates to the uniform application of terms or key words, the use of icons and graphics, the position of web page features such as menu items, the use of colour and so on. The designer should work out a design strategy along with the details and stick to it. Users will then find it easier to navigate around the web site.

Flow of content

People are used to reading from top to bottom and from left to right. What does this mean for web designers? It is important to know how text should be arranged on the web page for ease of reading. For example, examine the two sets of sentences in figure 11.3. The text on the right is definitely quicker and easier to read with its top-to-bottom and left-to-right orientation.

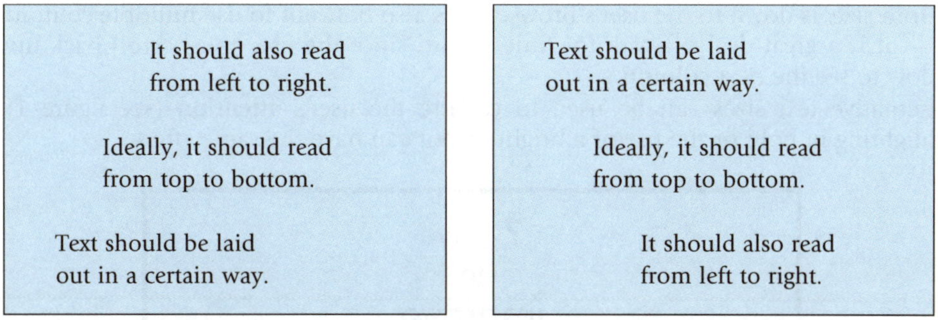

Figure 11.3 Text top-to-bottom and left-to-right principles

The desire to create distinctive web sites has led many developers to ignore cognitive principles. The resulting applications are then often distinctive for the wrong reasons.

Zoning

Browser windows or screens can be divided up into zones. These are areas of the screen which are used for certain functions. For example, figure 11.2 shows zones for the menu, advertisements and title, and the bulk of the screen area for displaying other information. There are many different zone layouts that can be used to great effect. The main advantage of zoning is that all pages will have a similar structure and hence provide a consistent framework for the designer and the user.

Grouping

Logically related items should be grouped together. In this respect, proximity conveys meaning. This applies to links, icons and menu items, for example.

Text

The size of the text denotes its significance. For example, the heading for a web page is usually larger than the other text on the page. A problem for designers is that HTML is so limited in terms of text sizes and fonts. An additional problem associated with headings in HTML is that they leave too much space below. Hence, many designers use a text heading that has been created in a graphics package and saved as a GIF file. Headings can then be developed along the lines of a logo and their effect can contribute to the image branding of the site.

Subheadings can also be developed as GIFs or can be left in bold with no space following. Two levels of headings are usually enough for most designs — if you need another level, you should go to another page.

Horizontal lines in any form to separate areas of the web page should be avoided as they simply add to the cognitive load without conveying useful information. A blank line space is preferable in most cases.

Margins are effective for making the text stand out on the page. Tables are used to do this as there is no margin function in HTML. The first column of the table is left blank and so creates the margin effect.

One of the main design problems with many web sites is that the text is often difficult to read. This is because the text is either too small or in the wrong font. Long lines of text on a screen make reading difficult for the user. Approximately ten to twelve words per line is a suitable line length to aim for, although much of the control, in terms of window size and font size, is down to the user's browser. It is also best not to use multiple columns of text — it is a great deal of work for little reward since the user must scroll back up the window to see the next column.

Alternative text sizes can be used to capture the user's attention (see figure 11.4). Highlighting in bold or the use of a bright colour can have the same effect.

7 ways
to
improve
your
GRADES

Figure 11.4 Varying text size and font to attract attention

Colour

Inexperienced designers often make the mistake of designing web pages using many different colours. It results in what is known as the 'Christmas-tree effect'. Good design does not rely primarily on the use of different colours. Usually, it is better to design originally in black and white to focus on layout and other features — the colour can be built in where needed afterwards. When more than four or five colours are used in any web page there is a tendency to increase the cognitive load on the user. A colour scheme should be chosen that adds value to the design but that does not become the overriding feature.

Certain combinations of colours go well together; others contrast and are not aesthetically pleasing to the eye. Blue and dull white go together well but purple and blue do not. Background and foreground colours need to be carefully chosen so that the text is easy to read. The background should not be too bright, such as a bright white, because it can strain the eye, but a dull white is a common background since black text shows up well against it. Readability is the key to good presentation.

■ **Reflection question 5:** What are some considerations for designing for people with some form of colour blindness?

IS in action

Groceries from Green Hills

Picking up an assortment of specialty, international gourmet and high-quality fresh foods without fighting queues or paying delivery fees can be simple. Residents in the Central New York area can visit the Green Hills Grocery online store (www.greenhills.com) then collect the order when it is convenient, as quickly as three hours after choosing the groceries.

The brands and products offered by the online store are arranged into different categories just like aisles in a real store. In addition, customers can search for or request any item they can't find. All the selected items are compiled into a shopping list for review. The shopping list becomes a master list and is saved for the next time the customer visits the online store.

The customer can add special notes and instructions to the shopping list; for example, how they would like the items chosen or any substitutions they would accept if a product was unavailable. Customers can select from advertised specials by clicking the 'This week's ad' button and choosing which items to add to the shopping list.

Green Hills Grocery store uses MyWebGrocer.com to host the infrastructure, provide the software and manage the databases behind the shopping service.

Source: adapted from www.mywebgrocer.com/news_01-23-03_GreenHills.htm (accessed October 2003).

Graphics and use of icons

Icons are used extensively in web-page design because they can incorporate and convey a lot of information. The designer can use location (on the screen), colour, space between icons, and the size, interior and shape of icons to convey information to the user.

There are some problems and challenges documented with iconic systems. Not all tasks can be easily represented by an icon. Ideally, the purpose of an icon should be obvious from its graphics. Searching, for example, is an action which is somewhat difficult to design an icon for — some software packages use a torch for this function. When a large number of functions are represented in iconic form, users may find it difficult to differentiate between the icons.

Metaphors

Metaphors have played a significant role in software design. Metaphors help people understand and experience a concept in terms of another. In the software world, the desktop metaphor has been the most notable. Metaphors can be used at various levels of the interface. They can be a unifying model for the entire design or used at the icon level. Some people liken a web site to visiting a library or an art gallery — or a restaurant, e.g. think about the equivalents of smelling the aromas, waiting for a table and so on.

Navigation

A web site is an information space divided into pages. The designer must provide a mechanism for navigating around the web space. Hyperlinks are used to move from one page to another — they are normally placed as menu items or on icons. Key words in the text can also be hyperlinks to connect to a page somewhere in the system. In a large web site with many pages, these links form a complex network of paths.

[**Key concept:** Systems are for people — design them accordingly.]

Form design

A form consists of questions or prompts and text input boxes (see figure 11.5). Designing an effective form involves:

- logically sequencing questions and input boxes
- using meaningful prompts or questions
- avoiding jargon and abbreviations
- aligning prompts and input boxes for ease of data entry
- providing the facility to make corrections and cancellations
- providing access to help facilities to provide information to complete the form
- having correctly sized input boxes to view data
- minimising keyboard input as much as possible
- using dropdown lists for restricted options
- providing validation of input
- providing informative error messages
- grouping related input boxes.

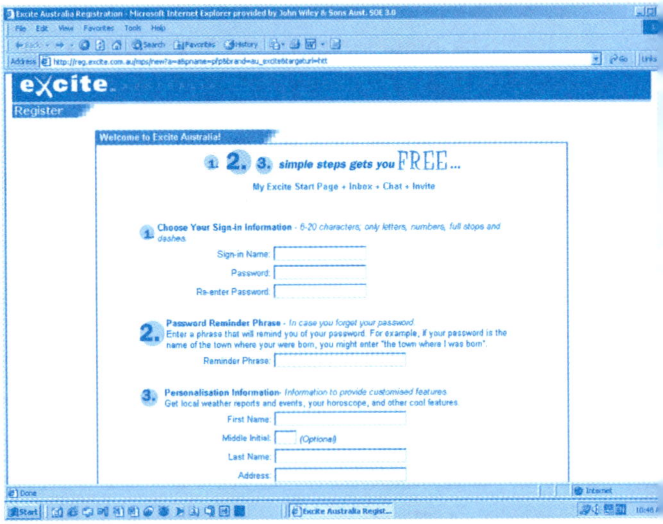

Figure 11.5 A form (*Source:* www.iselect.com.au)

Input boxes should be left-aligned and text can be displayed above the text input box or to the left and aligned right (preferably) or left. (If text prompts are aligned left, however, there may be large gaps between the text prompt and the input box.)

Infobyte

A little usability goes a long way

Many companies view usability testing as too expensive and too time-consuming. In fact many companies still don't involve systematic usability methods to help improve their designs. Jakob Nielsen, an expert in usability design, reports: 'On average, best practice calls for spending 10% of a design budget on usability. That's a cheap way to ensure that you spend the remaining 90% correctly, rather than blow your budget on an unworkable design.'

A key benefit of having user-driven designs is that time and money don't have to be wasted on functions and features that users don't need.

Source: adapted from www.useit.com/alertbox/20030908.html (accessed 25 November 2003).

Techniques for marketing and attracting visitors to sites

There are numerous ways to attract visitors to a web site. The site should:

- have a clear strategy and aim
- have a clear and easy-to-use design
- contain creative and memorable features
- be relevant, with recent content
- be registered with search engines
- be promoted offline
- have a relevant and easy-to-remember domain name
- have online events, such as chatting with a celebrity
- give something away, such as a gift or simply useful information.

To make the experience of visiting the web site more personal, other techniques include developing an online community and moving to interactive functionality.

Online communities

Online communities are real-time online forums where people can communicate and exchange information. They use online chat, publishing tools to gather and share information, message boards and email, and generally emphasise a high level of interactivity. The interactions may be between the users themselves or between the company and the users. Online communities form a business model in their own right. They provide a framework for integrating content, communication and business and usually fulfil social and business objectives. Communities can be based around any common interest, such as geography, age, providing support (e.g. Cancer Society) or activities (e.g. professional activities, sports).

There are five key attributes that distinguish an Internet community from other online ventures (Rockwell 1998):

- *Community members.* The community members are the people who visit the site and feel part of the community. People choose to be members and are not compelled to take part. The members have something in common but membership may be short-lived. Members of the community feel a sense of ownership and contribute in various ways to the community by providing information, and chatting and posting to discussion groups. In this way, the members create the community.
- *Community organisers.* The community requires an organiser who is responsible for the virtual space in terms of growth and maintenance. The owner needs a sponsor who will invest in the community for a reasonable time span.
- *Guiding principles.* Rules and guidelines must be used to make sure that the purpose(s) of the community is upheld in the running of the community. Some examples of guiding principles are tolerance of alternative opinions, a clear statement of moral expectations, and what is considered to be the focus of the community.
- *Institutional benefits.* There should be clear institutional benefits for building the community. Intranets can be developed to foster a sense of community and sharing or Internets can be used to create a loyal customer base.

- *Interactivity.* The richer the media space, the more scope there is for developing a vibrant community. The easier the system is to use, the lower the barrier is in terms of entry to the community.

Community building is not suited to every company and product. For example, a soccer club with a large supporter base may find it worthwhile to develop an online community, because through it they could enhance their image, and advertise merchandise, club games, etc. But a consulting company is not likely to want its clients to chat to one another — they may swap information on fees paid and what they got (or didn't get) for their money.

■ **Reflection question 6:** Are you part of any online community? What is its purpose?

Online customer interaction

The impersonality of many web sites is proving a barrier to more customers purchasing over the Web. Customers get confused by web-site options, and frequently have questions about a product or service. Frequently asked questions (FAQS) on web pages are helpful to a point but are still impersonal. Bulletin boards can provide a more customer-focused perspective, but can be a rambling mess of comments unless moderated properly by the company. Of course, potential customers can always email their enquiry, but by the time a reply is sent, potential customers may have changed their mind.

The trend in online sales in particular is to move to a more personal experience with the use of specialist software to manage the interaction between a sales assistant and a customer. This includes the management of email enquiries so that customers get a response within a reasonable time, the one-to-one chat sessions with customers and, with some packages, a web video link with the customer.

Infobyte

Information architecture or graphic design?

Some believe that too much emphasis has been put on graphic design in the web design process. Rather than graphic design, web content management consultant Gerry McGovern believes the emphasis should be put on information architecture with graphic design playing a support role. The reasons for this are as follows. Graphic design deals with visual images whereas the Web is generally a literate medium. That is to say that the Web is mainly about presenting information in text format. The attention-getting techniques used in graphic design should not be the fundamental premise of the design of web pages. If a web site is viewed as a channel to present information (text), then different approaches are required and ones that specifically require the information to be structured.

Source: adapted from www.gerrymcgovern.com (accessed October 2003).

Building trust online

In electronic commerce, transactions frequently take place between parties that have never physically met. Trust has always been a significant factor in doing business and is regarded as just as important in online business. Although trust is a complex concept to define, three sources of trust have been identified as being important in business (Ba & Pavlou 2002). The first is familiarity, which relates to repeated interaction between parties. The second is calculativeness, which is based on an assessment of the costs and benefits to the other party of cheating. Third is values, which are related to aspects of the organisational culture that convey trustworthiness and goodwill. There are two types of trust: benevolence and credibility. The former relates to a genuine interest in the other party, even under adverse conditions. The latter relates to a belief in a party's honesty, reliability and competence. The credibility type of trust is generally viewed as being more applicable to online business (Ba & Pavlou 2002).

How can trust be improved through web-site design? A number of ideas have been proposed to try to improve the perception of the trustworthiness of e-business sites:

- Refer to the offline business if there is one as this adds credibility to the online business. It will reassure the customer that the business is established.
- Develop a level of quality in the web site that conveys commitment. Mistakes in content or out-of-date content will dent confidence and trust.
- Develop a strong brand design that will enhance the level of trust.
- Aim to get repeat business as familiarity will improve levels of trust and improve credibility.
- Try to include recommendations from high-profile customers and satisfied customers as they will add to the credibility of the web site and help develop trust.
- Make sure offline deliveries are carried out effectively.
- Include statements about the company's commitment to quality.

Infobyte

Measuring the quality of a web site

An instrument for ascertaining the perception of web-site quality by customers has been developed by Barnes and Vidgen (2002). It is called WebQual. WebQual assesses e-business web-site quality on a seven-point scale. It assess the site in relation to usability, information quality and service interaction quality. For example, under 'Usability' it asks users whether they find the site easy to navigate and easy to use, along with several other questions. Under 'Service Interaction', users are asked whether they feel that their personal information is secure, and so on (Barnes & Vidgen 2002; Vidgen et al. 2003).

Measuring the effectiveness of the web site

Measuring the effectiveness of a web site is often overlooked, because so much effort has gone into the analysis and development of the site that there may be little energy or enthusiasm left, once it is up and running, to properly evaluate its effectiveness. In addition, the evaluation may be postponed because of the argument that the site is quickly evolving, so there is little point in evaluating now. Of course, there is never an ideal point to evaluate the effectiveness of the system but it should still be done.

The site's effectiveness should be evaluated because it is an investment of organisational resources and should not be treated differently from any other resource. Evaluations should be completed periodically as the site develops and matures. Useful information should be fed back into the development and evolution process. A good time to perform a review of the effectiveness of the site is three months and six months after it has gone online — this should be enough time to identify any immediate problems with the system. Further reviews can be conducted on a six-monthly basis or as necessary.

Senior management should be involved in the reviews to determine if the requirements that were detailed early in the project are being met by the web site. It is quite possible that the requirements may change over several months of development. These need to be discussed and, if viewed as critical, should be built into the system as early as it is feasible to do so.

Web efficiency variables that can be used in determining the overall efficiency of the web site include:

- number of hits on the site (visitors)
- number of active visitors (visitors who interact with the site)
- number of purchases
- number of repurchases (people who purchase repeatedly).

If there are only a small number of users accessing the site then it may not be the site in particular that is at fault but rather how it is being advertised and promoted. This may be rectified by registering the site URL with all the major search engines, by advertising on other sites, and by promoting the site by more traditional methods such as putting the URL on company stationery and business cards.

Using basic statistics such as the number of hits is a very limited way of evaluating a site. A more business-centric approach is needed rather than a technical one that relies on hits and views. For example, Northwest Airlines in the United States aims to sell as many tickets online as possible. The advantage of selling tickets online is that they are 50% cheaper per transaction to process than through traditional methods. So the most important measurement for Northwest Airlines is the number of bookings made through the Web. A second important statistic is the number of enquiries handled through the site, as every enquiry handled in this way is cheaper to deal with compared with telephone calls made to a call centre. Northwest is mostly concerned with increasing revenue and reducing costs and so its measurement statistics reflect this.

Another variable is the percentage of visitors to a site who actually make a purchase. Simply attracting visitors may not actually do a business much good in the long run. The site needs to be improved to handle large numbers of visitors, but there is a cost for that, and unless there is a payback it may be a poor business investment. The site has to be designed to attract the right type of person, ideally a person who is likely to make a purchase or interact with the site in some cost-saving way for the organisation.

Some organisations that have nothing to sell directly via the Web, such as those involved in publishing, can monitor how long people stay at the site. They can try to measure whether the person is actively engaged with the content and whether they return to the site. Employment recruitment sites can monitor the number of enquiries made through the site and the number of applications for jobs that are made. Companies can review the effectiveness of the site from the perspective of how much revenue is generated from advertising, if that is part of their objectives.

Interviews and questionnaires can be used to obtain feedback from internal and external users of the site. The results can provide information on the problems users face, what they like about the site and whether the design features are easy to use.

Some of the benefits of a web site may be very difficult to quantify, such as improved public relations. Surveys can be conducted to determine what effect the site is having in such areas. This may mean that external research companies are used if the expertise to conduct professional surveys does not exist within the organisation. A company's site can also be compared with other companies' sites for functionality, design effectiveness and level of innovation. Therefore, considerably more work has to be put into obtaining information on intangible benefits compared with finding out how many new orders have come in online.

Summary

Designing effective web sites is a complex task that requires a range of skills. Attracting visitors to a site requires the site to be easy to navigate, aesthetically appealing, and to engage the user as much as possible. The key points in this chapter are:

- The external focus of many web applications has created a whole new set of issues for systems developers.
- The complexity of web-site development depends on factors such as the amount of functionality required and the level of integration with other corporate systems.
- Effective web-site design requires structure, and good use of space, text, colour and graphics.
- Web-site designers need to consider how they can develop trust with their customers.
- Online communities, chat and voice over Internet protocol are ways of attracting visitors to a web site.
- Measuring the effectiveness of a web site relies on a number of methods beyond a simple 'hit rate'.

Questions

1. Explain the various roles involved in a large web project development team.
2. Develop five general design guidelines for using text on web pages.
3. What factors affect the scope and complexity of web-development projects?
4. Explain the role of search engines.
5. What are the key strengths of Java?
6. What is meant by the term 'm-commerce'?
7. Why is it important for organisations to integrate their web applications with other corporate applications?

8. List the ten most important ways of measuring the effectiveness of an e-commerce project. Separate them into methods of evaluating web sites and the e-commerce project as a whole.
9. How can online community members be encouraged to feel a sense of ownership and belonging?
10. How can trust be developed through the design of a web site?

Exercises

1. You have just taken up a position with a company as the e-commerce strategist. The CEO is under the impression that developing web applications is just the same as developing typical information systems. Outline what is new about web development and how it differs from developing information systems in the past.
2. Develop ten key design guidelines for web-site design. Evaluate three web sites using your guidelines.
3. Find two web sites that incorporate online communities. Analyse the sites and explain why you think they work as online communities. Use the characteristics of an effective online community discussed earlier in the chapter as a guide.

CASE STUDY Food Concepts Inc.

Food Concepts Inc. is a company that designs and produces food merchandiser equipment and provides training, brand development of food and other services for the foodservice industry.

The company started in 1991 and now employs thirteen people generating $US2 million of annual sales. The head office is in the USA with a regional office in New Zealand. The establishment of a web presence began when Brad Duesler, president of Food Concepts Inc., mentioned that he would like to establish an Internet presence to Stephan Spencer, president of Netconcepts LLC (www.netconcepts.com), at a social meeting.

Things soon started to happen with a more formal meeting being arranged to discuss what Duesler wanted from an Internet presence. He was eager to expand his business by letting current and potential clients see the full range of products and services offered. His initial thought was an online brochure, which would be easy to update and provide more accurate, timely information to users. He had also thought of producing and selling a CD-ROM directory based on the company's database of branded foods, restaurants and other foodservice businesses.

There was concern about the effectiveness of having only an online brochure. The brochure approach might attract users once, but return visits would be less likely. Something to encourage users to return to the site regularly was needed. This usually involves changing 'users' into 'participants'.

It was decided to look at the possibility of using the brand directory as a basis for the web site. A similar idea is used by INX International Ink Co., which has a corporate site and a sponsored site, PrinterSpace (www.printerspace.com), providing resources for printers and those involved in printing services. PrinterSpace is vendor-neutral and has developed into an online community. This service has encouraged 'users' to become 'participants' and helped to build the reputation of the sponsoring company, thereby establishing it as an expert in its field.

Return on invested capital is a long-term objective. The company sees the establishment of an Internet presence as an investment in the future and anticipates that the sites will be self-supporting. (It was decided to have two sites.) The benefits of web commerce are difficult to measure, but cost considerations are still important. Selling the brand directory in hard-copy format would realise immediate revenue for the company. The choice of using the directory as the foundation for the web site will delay a measurable return on the directory until advertisement space could be sold in the future. However, limits and goals had to be established for the Internet project in order to protect the company's bottom line. The objective of the web sites became 'to increase industry awareness resulting in tangible sales and margin growth of at least 10% in the first year, which should cover the capital investment cost of the online initiative'.

Duesler looked at web sites over the next few weeks. He got some more ideas of what he would like on the company's sites and how he would like them to operate. It was important that the sites should load quickly and provide relevant information and easy navigation. The function of the sites became clearer. The brand directory would offer to connect retail chains and large employers, running or intending to open food courts, with potential food vendors and brands. To grow the site it was proposed to invite food brands and service providers to list products and post photographs on the directory. The corporate site would offer a complete listing of the products and services available from Food Concepts Inc.

Domain names were checked for availability, and several likely names were bought. All these would link to the corporate site or the brand directory site to make finding the sites as easy as possible for potential clients. Eventually foodpros.com was chosen as the name for the brand directory site and foodconcepts.net for the corporate site.

Advertising the sites and getting users involved are important tasks. To attract the attention and participation of the vendors listed in the directory they will be invited to review and amend their entries, even add artwork if they want to. An added benefit would be to help iron out early any bugs in the database system. Attending trade fairs, issuing press releases and printing web site and email addresses on all stationery would help gain a wider awareness.

The analysis phase of the development lasted about three months, and then the detailed design work began. The complexity of the project became more apparent as all the details to be included in the database had to be considered along with the objectives of the sites. It was obvious that decisions made during the design process would affect all areas of the business. Economic factors had been considered to some extent, but now more detailed costs could be determined. Other areas to feel a major impact from decisions being made were tactical and maintenance.

(*continued*)

Duesler was the main driver of the project, but all the company was involved. The staff became involved in the design process; they knew the company, its policies and procedures and the image it wanted to promote. This also helped to cut costs to some extent. Even though Netconcepts was helping to design the system, it became apparent that the company would need a web manager to head the Internet development. The office manager was appointed to this position, to be assisted by Duesler.

Design of the database was a major project and had to consider such things as which fields to include, which could be left empty, searching, sorting, input and security. The more the sites were capable of, the higher the cost would be. Duesler remained convinced that getting the company on to the Internet was a jump in the right direction and would give it a competitive edge. He sees the web sites as global trade shows and would partly fund the sites from money set aside for a trade show. The initial cost was US$36 000, and the design allowed for the sites to grow.

Two months down the track the FoodPros site was posted in a trial version. It was particularly important to clearly identify the site as a work in progress, so a banner headline notified users of the fact and advertised future features of the site. Duesler invited a couple of companies listed in the brand directory to trial the site, comment on functionality and ease of use, and add or amend their information. The site continued to expand with new features being added daily.

After a month the sites were up and running. They list 610 brands and 670 suppliers, a discussion forum, book reviews and an example ad. There is some discussion of enhancing the graphics, but loading speed, information content and simplicity of design are more important. A few companies from the trade show visited the brand directory to update their information before the direct mail invitations were sent to each vendor. Suggestions from vendors were received and could be implemented immediately if needed so that initial teething problems could be solved.

The final versions of the sites were up and running a couple of months later. They incorporated a chat room and bulletin board and a book listing with the intention to include book reviews.

A secure extranet helps the company manage web projects, budgets and priorities in real-time. Up-to-date reports on web-site usage, traffic patterns and rankings in the search engines contribute in many areas of analysis for the company.

Duesler is still excited about the opportunities of the Internet and is sure that it is only going to grow in the future. Having a store in the right position on the e-superhighway is going to be a great advantage.

Source: adapted from www.netconcepts.com/news/InBusiness_Article.php (accessed October 2003)

QUESTIONS

1. Summarise the aims of the two web sites.
2. What are the key design features of Food Concepts' web sites?
3. Where were employees involved in the development of the web sites?
4. What form did offline promotion of the web sites take?

References

Ba, S. & Pavlou, D.A. 2002, 'Evidence of the effect of trust-building technology in electronic markets: Price premiums and buyer behaviour', *MIS Quarterly*, vol. 26, no. 3, pp. 243–68.

Barnes, S. & Vidgen, R. 2002, 'An integrative approach to the assessment of e-commerce quality', *Journal of Electronic Commerce Research*, vol. 3, no. 3, pp. 114–27.

Rockwell, B. 1998, *Using the Web to Compete in a Global Marketplace*, John Wiley & Sons, New York.

Sellitto, C. & Wenn, A. 2000, 'Business web sites: Simple guidelines and practice for checking if a site conforms to emerging standards', *Proceedings of the First International Web Conference*, Fremantle, Australia (CD-ROM).

Sun Microsystems 2004, 'The Java language: An overview', available at http://java.sun.com/docs/overviews/java/java-overview-1.html (accessed February 2004).

Vidgen, R., Avison, D., Wood, B. & Wood-Harper, T. 2003, *Developing Web Information Systems*, Butterworth-Heinemann, Oxford.

Chapter 12

Personal productivity with information systems

LEARNING OBJECTIVES

After reading this chapter, you should be able to:

- describe the skills required to be a knowledge worker in the knowledge economy
- suggest ways of being more creative in the use of digital technology
- explain what is meant by 'information overload' and discuss methods and techniques for coping with it
- explain the effective use of electronic mail
- discuss the ethical issues related to using information systems.
- understand the concept of ergonomic design in relation to information systems

12

Introduction

Most of this book has looked at the impact of information systems and information technology at the organisational level, which has been very significant. Interestingly, at the individual level, information systems don't seem to have been as widely adopted as personal productivity approaches. Certainly, many people use word processors, spreadsheets and databases on a daily basis as part of work and study. These are part of the personal productivity toolset but are not in themselves an integrated personal information system. Many people say that they are suffering from information overload but use only very rudimentary methods and techniques for coping with personal information on a daily basis. The aim of this chapter is to examine where and how IS/IT can be used to improve personal productivity and how to effectively engage in a lifelong association with information systems.

Many of the methods and techniques discussed earlier in the book can be used to some extent on a personal level.

Skills needed in the knowledge economy

The agricultural age was characterised by the majority of people working in some capacity related to the land. The industrial age saw a large percentage of people move to the cities to work in factories. The post-industrial age is characterised by a large percentage of people working in service industries such as the financial sector, hospitality, tourism, and professions such as accounting and information systems. The post-industrial age can also be termed the **information age** since many people work in office environments and to a large extent buy, process and sell information of one kind or another. This is frequently referred to as the knowledge economy.

Certain skills are essential for operating effectively in the knowledge economy. These skills must be developed to an acceptable standard according to:

- an employer's expectations — these can be seen in job advertisements
- a school or tertiary institution's requirements — these are tested by assignments and examinations
- the standards expected by professional bodies — these are stipulated in the various membership grades.

In the past, the emphasis in education was on memorising many facts. Today, we have access to a vast amount of data and information, too much to spend time memorising it all. Information can go out of date so rapidly it seems pointless memorising a mass of facts on a regular basis. A certain body of knowledge and facts is required for people to operate as professionals, but a range of general transferable skills is much more significant today, since we can access facts as and when they are needed.

It is worthwhile examining these knowledge economy skills and how information systems are involved. Note that they are basically transferable skills which can be applied to any profession or discipline.

Research and information-gathering

Research skills involve the ability to find relevant information for decision-making purposes. The data or information may come from a variety of sources:

- *Internet*. The Internet provides an increasing wealth of information sources. There are online magazines, journals and newspapers. In addition, most of the large IT companies provide information about their products and often have case studies which can be downloaded. Reliable sources of information on the Web are professional organisations which have an image and reputation to maintain and therefore something to lose if they provide unreliable or incorrect information which would tarnish their reputation. However, remember that companies use the Web to promote their products and so the weaknesses or limitations of their products or services are unlikely to be presented in any detail.
- *Libraries*. Libraries provide information in books, magazines and journals and in paper or digital format. Libraries use information systems to provide search and query facilities to their catalogues. Many libraries now have remote access via modems and subscribe to online databases of journals and magazines which can be downloaded to your own local machine. This means, of course, that you can do your research or information-gathering without leaving home or your office.
- *Friends and work colleagues*. A less formal way of gathering information and conducting research is to use a network of people. This may involve face-to-face meetings, or communication by telephone, email or chat group. This type of information gathering through networks may not be objective, but it is often useful for highlighting strategic or important issues.
- *Associations and societies*. Professional organisations such as computer societies provide information via magazines, journals, and meetings of special-interest groups such as computer security and e-commerce.

Reflection question 1: Where do you get most of your information from for assignments?

Planning

Planning is a skill which can be greatly enhanced with information systems and information technology. Planning is the ability to break a task down into components and estimate the time needed for each one. It also requires an understanding of the resources required to complete the task and how these can be effectively applied to the project. Planning requires the ability to take a high-level view of matters, to see the 'big picture'.

Processing information

It is hard to imagine processing data and information these days without the aid of computer technology. There is no shortage of information and data available in the information age and a major factor determining success is how we filter, process and analyse that data. Processing data and information involves:

- extracting and filtering relevant data
- defining relationships between data sets
- analysing data, both numerical and text
- summarising data and information
- adding, updating and amending data and information.

Our ability to use information systems greatly affects our ability to process information. Unfortunately, many people receive little or no formal training in the use of information systems for personal productivity.

Presenting information and data has become an important part of most knowledge economy occupations. IT is essential for preparing high-quality reports and presentations that use graphics and charts to summarise data.

Creativity and problem solving

With the range of business opportunities available in a rapidly changing world, the ability to produce innovative ideas and solutions is now very important. New technologies provide opportunities for innovation in organisations. However, it is not just the ability to foresee the implications of a technology's impact on a business sector that is important but also how to effectively instil it in the organisation.

Many problems in organisations are a result of lack of information, poor-quality information, irrelevant information or too much information. Information systems can be used in various ways to solve these problems.

Communication

Communication skills are always rated as important in surveys of employers' expectations and requirements. In some ways, communication has become a more complex skill since there are more channels to use to communicate in business in the information age:

- telephone
- telephone conference
- mail
- fax
- face-to-face meeting
- presentation to a group
- electronic mail
- bulletin boards
- web pages
- video-conference
- reports
- memorandums.

IS in action

Women in information technology?

Do you think of IT workers as nerdy, geeky and introverted?

Some people do, according to research by Julie Fisher (2003) of Monash University. She says this is part of the reason women are not considering or continuing careers in information technology. And often, if young women are confident enough to disregard these types of preconceptions and actually study IT, once they enter the workforce they are soon disillusioned.

The majority of women employed in the Australian IT industry are still on lower pay than their male counterparts. A female IT worker may get 10 to 20% less than a male colleague. There is a suggestion that this is the result of an entrenched gender bias in a male-dominated sector.

(*continued*)

The participation rate for women in the IT industry is less than half the rate of all other industry sectors. Figures from the Australian Census (1996–2001) show that there have been small rises in the number of women working as computing professionals, software designers, systems managers and information technology managers, while the number of women participating as technical support, applications and analyst programmers and computer systems auditors is declining. The UK and North American IT industries are in a similar position to the Australian industry.

The move of labour-intensive IT needs, such as programming and hardware development, to countries with low labour costs reduces the perceived 'technical' aspects of the industry in other countries. This could change the way some people feel about working in the Australian IT industry as customer focus and interpersonal skills become more important. However, effort will have to be put into promoting the image of the computer professional and ensuring equality.

Source: information from Fisher (2003), 'Are we really serious about having women in IT?', *Information Age,* June/July, pp. 31–4.

Teamwork skills

The ability to work as part of a team is a valuable skill. Knowing how to reach a consensus, when to lead the group, and when and how to listen are all part of team skills. The communication between group members in today's business world relies heavily on communication technologies.

[**Key concept:** People with excellent transferable skills will always be in demand.]

Infobyte

Teenagers change the world

Young people are changing the way they live and play and the world in which they live. Children aged 7 to 16 have more purchasing power than ever before and increasingly influence the way the household dollar is spent. They are able to adapt technological tools such as computers, the Internet and phones to define their own environment.

New technologies are quickly picked up by this affluent group, who are demanding that technology fits into their lifestyle. Digital channels are being used for communication, interaction and entertainment. The tools have to be usable, customisable and affordable, or they are quickly dropped in favour of those that are.

Teenagers are the 'agents of change' in the digital world, where manufacturers and marketers try to satisfy their demands. Faster computer processors, smaller and more technologically advanced phones and interactive web sites are just a few of their growing demands.

Source: information from 'Agents of change. Teenagers: Mobile lifestyles trends', Spero Communications Ltd, November 2003.

Using personal information systems and technology

Do you view information systems and information technology in a positive or negative light? When was the last time you adopted a new information system or new piece of information technology on a personal level?

As a professional in the knowledge economy, you will need to develop a lifelong association with information systems. To a large extent, the success of this relationship depends on your mental attitude or mindset. Consider the following attitudes to information systems and IT:

- *It's just not me.* This view is held by people who feel that they are not 'technical', and is a particular mindset which acts as a barrier to adoption. Information systems are not necessarily technical systems, as have been discussed throughout this book, but rather social systems of which there is a technical component.
- *I'll adopt it when it gets more reliable.* The problem with this attitude is that someone somewhere will always point out a weakness with a certain technology no matter how long it has been in use. The lesson to learn from this is don't wait for the systems to be perfect before using them.
- *Computer rage syndrome.* Some people get very frustrated when using systems because they expect to be highly productive straight away. In this respect they have unrealistic expectations and may become very frustrated. Even experienced users often work on the basis that the system will run perfectly all the time and are frustrated when it doesn't. Always remember that throwing your computer out of the window will set you back in several ways!
- *I'll use it when I have to.* Rather than being a laggard, be a leader and get the benefit of the systems and technology from the start.
- *I'm developing a lifelong association with IS/IT.* This attitude takes the view that IS/IT are integral to the information age.

Although the last perspective is perhaps a more helpful one in terms of using IS/IT on a daily basis, it lacks a certain energy. It is interesting to reassess on a regular basis how you can work more productively with IS/IT on a personal level. There are two sides to using computer systems productively. The first is using systems creatively and the second is using systems as a problem-solving tool. These two rely on using both the left and right sides of the brain.

Left-brain thinking is related more to verbal and deductive thinking (logic) skills. Right-brain thinking is related more to visual and inductive thinking (intuition) (Edwards 1979). You may associate computer systems with the more rational and logical side of the brain required for problem solving in organisations. However, to use IS creatively on a personal level, you need a certain amount of creativity and to draw on the right side of the brain. The following discusses some ways to improve your use of information systems and technology.

Go digital early

Try to capture as much work as possible early in digital format. In other words, don't spend hours creating detailed plans or writing out material on paper first. Transfer your thoughts and ideas as early as possible to the computer. Once the ideas are in digital format you will be able to improve them and see them evolve. It also means that you become more skilled with the technology by using it as a planning and thinking tool. Handheld computers are especially useful for this way of working because you can capture ideas as they arise. Palmtop computers boot up almost immediately since the operating system is held in ROM. The boot-up time therefore does not act as a barrier to capturing thoughts digitally.

Cognitive maps or mindmaps can be used to map your information space (see figure 12.1).

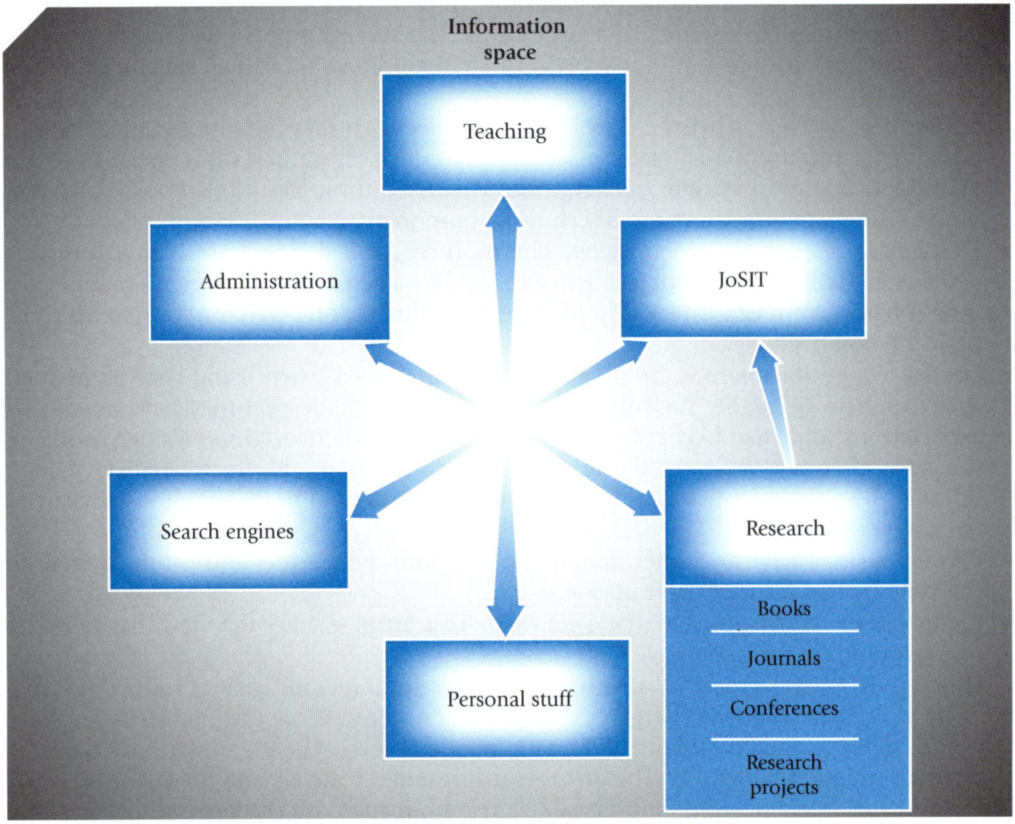

Figure 12.1 Mindmap of author's information space

One author's information space includes the following:

- university administration
- *Journal of Systems and Information Technology* (*JoSIT*)
- personal stuff
- search engines
- research
- conferences
- journals
- teaching.

These have been incorporated into a series of web pages which map the author's information space. Each feature is a hyperlink. Bookmarks in your browser can be used in a similar way but they lack the spatial and media richness that can be built up by developing your own information-space web site.

Think multimedia

Don't think only about text when thinking about information systems — think multimedia. Look for ways to build an information and media-rich approach in whatever you are doing. Start or expand your database of graphics and photographs and PowerPoint designs, for example. Work as though you expect to be using the same tools, albeit improved ones, in five years time. You will change your perspective on whether it is worthwhile creating the information infrastructure for yourself.

Learn from the environment

How do professionals keep up to date these days in such a rapidly changing environment? One way is to learn from the environment itself. IT programs on television, the IT section in the newspaper and certain web sites all provide relevant information. The cost of IT is no longer prohibitive, so now you can adopt a technology and learn on the job, rather than thinking that you need to be an expert in that tool before you adopt it. This is rather like getting a new computer game and playing until you are an expert, never having read the instructions.

Set goals and experiment

At some point you have to experiment with certain technologies. You need to set a goal of using some technology and becoming proficient with it. Voice-recognition software, for example, allows your computer to understand your speech patterns and pronunciations, saving you the trouble of typing text into documents. The software, especially inexpensive versions, is not faultless, but it has potential when you train it properly. Your short-term goal could be to investigate and trial this type of software for its potential for personal productivity gains.

[**Key concept:** You do not need to take a course for everything — most IS professionals gain much of their knowledge from the environment.]

Information overload and personal information systems

Information overload is a real problem for many information economy workers. Few people have an effective personal information system; in fact, it seems that organisational information systems are way ahead of personal information systems in quality and levels of adoption.

The problem in most organisations is not lack of information but too much. Email is one of the main culprits, together with the plethora of reports, meetings, telephone messages and professional journals.

Think how easy it is to contribute to information overload for other people. You have attended a seminar which captured your imagination; back at your desk you build a web site related to the materials and themes of the seminar. You then email everyone in your organisation with a review of the seminar and the URL for your web site. You are creating the information equivalent of landfill.

What can be done about information overload? The major problem is the inability of organisations to admit that it is a problem. When a manager's time is spent in meetings every day of every week there is little time to reflect, organise or just be productive. The same is true of answering a couple of hundred emails each day — if each email takes, on average, a minute or two to answer, then there is little time left to do any work. Most occupations are not meant to have internal messaging as their main feature. In many organisations this has got out of hand, but admitting that it is a problem signals disorganisation on a personal level. However, a professional must recognise that there may be a problem, decide what the critical success factors are, and determine the role that internal messaging plays.

[**Key concept:** Information access has improved significantly in recent years — most people in professional occupations receive too much irrelevant information.]

Infobyte

The real cost of information overload

- 38% of managers waste a substantial amount of time trying to locate the right information.
- 43% of managers think decisions are delayed as a result of having too much information.
- 47% say the collection of information for decision-making distracts them from their main job responsibilities.
- Two out of three managers state that tension with work colleagues and loss of job satisfaction arise because of stress associated with information overload.
- 49% of managers work late either often or very frequently or take work home as a result of having to deal with too much information.
- 61% of managers report that their social activities are cancelled in order to deal with excessive information (Albrecht 2001).

■ **Reflection question 2:** Can you think of any other contributors to information overload?

Partly due to the concept of customer service, including the notion of treating staff as internal customers, many employees have become victims of the 'do it now syndrome'. Hence, every enquiry, whether by email, phone or letter, must be dealt with immediately.

In this approach, the technology is used to make the employee accessible at all times, in many cases even when at home. The trouble with this approach, however, is that the interruption created by breaking off one task to attend to the enquiry or email has a major impact on productivity. It is not simply the time involved in doing the task — it is also the time taken to get one's thought processes back to where they were before the interruption.

To be effective with information on a personal level requires the adoption of procedures which become a habit. Consider the following suggestions:

- *Batching.* A general principle is to batch (group together) the enquiries and use the technology to advantage rather than be controlled by the technology. For example, you may decide to answer email messages at the start and end of the day rather than throughout the day. The same can be done with voicemail messages.
- *Use of email.* If possible, check your email once or twice a day rather than continually breaking off work when emails arrive. If you subscribe to mail group lists which are no longer of interest, then unsubscribe. (It is always wise to save the instructions on how to do so.) The fewer emails you have, the more you will feel you are in control of the situation and able to respond to them. File emails in folders rather than keeping them in your inbox. Systems are available to filter unwanted email messages — these work by specifying certain key words.
- *Use meetings efficiently.* Make a careful note of each meeting you have attended in the last month. Ask yourself whether every meeting was relevant or whether someone else could have attended in your place. Was the meeting carefully planned and chaired to keep within time constraints? If not, then suggest that this be done in the future. Meetings incur expenses for any organisation, including time for the actual meeting, preparation time, travel to and from, food and drinks, and opportunity costs (what could have been accomplished if people had not been at the meeting).
- *Become outcome-focused.* Identify what is really important in your work and focus on this. Make any communication related to this issue a priority and leave the other things until later.
- *Develop support structures.* There is only so much work one person can get through. Develop a support structure which can share the workload.
- *Know what to keep.* In deciding whether to file a piece of paper or throw it away, ask yourself the following questions:
  - Does it require any action? If not, throw it away.
  - Does it exist elsewhere? If it does, throw it away.
  - Is it recent enough to be useful? If not, throw it away.
  - Do I understand the contents? If not, throw it away.

  If you are still seriously in doubt, ask yourself what is the worst possible thing that could happen if you didn't have this information. If you can live with the answer, then throw the information away.
- *Develop personal information systems.* A key feature of a support structure should be your personal information system.

Developing a personal information system

Examine how you accomplish the regular tasks you are faced with. Decide if there is a pattern to how you work or solve problems. If you spend time reinventing processes related to completing tasks, invest some time in documenting how they are completed. In this respect you are defining your own methodologies for getting things done. As well as being a reference point for you each time you complete a similar task, you can pass on the methodology to others and so delegate or share the workload.

The innovation cycle explained in chapter 9 (see figure 9.1, p. 244) can be used on a personal level. Be more creative and innovative with technology and information systems rather than one of the last to adopt new methods and approaches. In doing so, you will become skilled in the technology, and early adoption will become a habit.

Consider using personal productivity tools. A personal data assistant (PDA) is a handheld computer that allows you to store, access and organise information (see figure 12.2). Most PDAs are either Windows-based or work on a Palm operating system. PDAs can be screen-based or keyboard-based, or both.

Basic PDAs allow you to store and retrieve addresses and phone numbers, maintain a calendar, and create to-do lists and notes. More sophisticated PDAs can run word processing, spreadsheet, money manager, and electronic book-reading programs, and also provide email and Internet access. Some PDAs come with all these programs included. Most PDAs can exchange information with a desktop or laptop computer, although you may need additional accessories.

- *Convenience and portability.* The small size and light weight of a palmtop mean that it isn't difficult to carry. Notebook or laptop computers are comparatively heavy and a burden to carry around. Palmtops or handheld computers can be used for accessing email and the Internet. Because they are small, compact systems, the batteries last for a relatively long time before they need recharging.
- *Speed of boot-up.* The operating system is stored in ROM, which means that a palmtop is very quick to boot up. The delay of booting-up a notebook computer can become a barrier if all you want to do is add a name and address to a database of contacts.
- *Software compatibility.* On the more sophisticated palmtop computers, the software is often a cut-down version of the software used on desktop machines. This means that you don't have to learn new instructions and operating procedures.

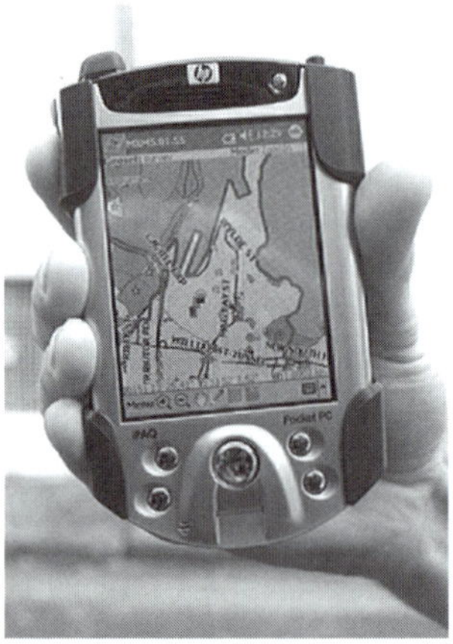

Figure 12.2 Palmtop computer

- *Transferring data.* You can transfer files between your palmtop and desktop machines and set options to synchronise mail messages, contacts, appointments and tasks with your other machine. This allows you to update data in one place only — your other systems will be updated from that location.

[**Key concept:** Take many of the principles used in organisational information systems and apply them at the individual level.]

Electronic mail

Electronic mail (email) has been fully embraced by the business world in just a few short years. There are a large number of electronic mail packages that can be used for sending messages over the Internet. It is not the purpose here to explore individual packages but rather to describe their common features. It is worth considering how electronic mail compares with other forms of communication (see table 12.1).

TABLE 12.1 Comparison of various methods of communication

	Method of communication				
Feature	**Mail**	**Fax**	**Email**	**Face to face**	**Telephone**
Speed	Low	High	Moderate to high	Slow	High
Cost	Low to moderate	Low	Low	High	Moderate
Accountability	High	High	Moderate	Moderate	Low
Conferencing	One-way	No	All groups	All groups	Small groups
Ease of duplication	Moderate	Moderate	High	Low	Low
Synchronised	No	No	No	Yes	Yes
Security	Moderate	Low	Moderate	Moderate	Moderate
Richness	Low	Low	Low	High	Moderate to high
Formality	High	Low	Low to moderate	High	Moderate

Speed

In evaluating speed it is important to consider the time it takes to transmit/deliver the communication and the delay time before it is read. The communication process can be broken down into compose, transmit, receive and read. For example, a letter takes time to write, is posted, received and then read. There could be a considerable delay before the letter is read even though the letter was efficiently delivered.

In terms of speed, telephone and fax are quick to send, although there may be several aborted attempts with the telephone to actually speak to the intended person. Face-to-face communication has the added problem of getting two or more people together at the same time, which can be time-consuming and expensive. Mail, sometimes referred to as snail-mail, is slow but reasonably inexpensive. Email is fast to transmit but may involve some delay before it is read, especially if the recipient is away or does not regularly check email. If people check their email at specific regular times, the more effective it is as a form of communication and in some cases can be more effective than the telephone as the message can be read, reread and thought about before a response is made.

One of the main problems with telephone communication is that the people involved must be synchronised, i.e. both people must be on the telephone at the same time. Email and traditional mail are asynchronous, i.e. the recipient does not need to be present when the communication is sent or delivered. This is especially useful where large distances and different time zones are involved.

Cost

The cost of sending email is so low that in many organisations it has become overused and has added to information overload. Other forms of communication generally have a much higher and more obvious cost associated with them.

[**Key concept:** The low cost of sending email has meant that it is overused in many organisations.]

Accountability

Accountability may be an important issue in communications, especially in business where the expectation is usually one of formality and accountability, although there are occasions when people are more casual. Hence, formality and accountability are closely related. Due to the fact that written (typed) letters have been the accepted form of business communication for many years, other forms of communication may appear less formal and, as a result, hold the senders and recipients less accountable as a consequence. Some people may prefer face-to-face contact with a formal handshake as part of a business deal but it might be legally difficult to prove. Although email may appear to be a very informal form of communication it could be used as evidence in a court of law. Therefore people must not underestimate the accountability associated with the content of email.

Conferencing

Sometimes group communication is needed. The telephone is effective for group conferencing but only for small groups. Fax and mail are poor for conferencing, and face-to-face conferencing is more expensive. Email is fast and effective when dealing with groups of people as the same message can be posted to a large group simultaneously.

Security

Security, like accountability, is an important issue in business. There are many occasions when the communication is private and confidential. Letters can be lost in the mail or opened by others and so qualify as being poor in terms of security. Telephone conversations can be overheard or tapped, but on the whole are moderately secure. Face-to-face communication has a number of security problems but is moderately secure as long as basic precautions are taken and people are trustworthy. The problem with faxes is that they are frequently left by the fax machine for other people to read. Email is relatively secure and private as long as basic security measures are adhered to, such as using a good password system and not leaving the machine with the email package open and unattended.

Infobyte

Email interruption

The constant flow of emails is costing you valuable time and energy. Every time you break off from a task to read or respond to emails and return to your original task your mind is doing mental acrobatics. These mind-switching activities take time to complete, and interruptions to your thoughts can be devastating. Have you ever had an idea, been distracted, and then not been able to remember your great idea?

It has been estimated to take 64 seconds to recover from reading an email and get back to the original task. This is less than the recovery time from a telephone call (15 minutes if involved in a creative task), but the volume of email can be substantially greater than the volume of telephone calls.

The way you handle incoming mail is important. Turn off the automatic alert for incoming mail to avoid distractions, and set aside convenient times during the day to deal with email. If you can't do this, set your email application to check for mail less frequently. Also remember everyone else has this problem, so don't send general emails or reply-to-all; target your recipient and your message.

Source: information from T. Jackson, R. Dawson and D. Wilson (2003), 'Understanding email interaction increases organizational productivity', *Communications of the ACM*, August, vol. 36, no. 8.

Personal and professional ethics

Ethics in relation to the workplace is now a major issue for most professions including information systems. Nobody is above the law, so any illegal act should be reported by an IS professional. However, there are many acts on a personal or organisational level which may be legal but are still considered unethical.

For example, you are concerned about a system which you have been involved in developing. Although you are not aware of any immediate bugs in the system, you feel that standards and testing have been underplayed, but your boss, the project leader, wants to deliver the project on time. What do you do?

Defining what is ethical is not always so easy. **Ethical behaviour** is decent, fair, good, honest or moral behaviour. Ethical standards are framed by the society in which a person lives and works. But professionals are bound also by legal standards. For example, an IS professional sends an email criticising someone without being aware of all the facts. This email is printed out and left in a tray next to the printer for all to see. This is not only unethical behaviour, but it could be considered an act of defamation, and the email may be used as evidence in court.

[**Key concept:** Ethical behaviour never goes out of fashion!]

IS in action

IT governance

IT governance has gained more importance as technology has become a critical part of business success. There has been a tendency to think of IT as a way to align business processes without considering how to include it in the corporate governance of the business. This has led to each department, manager or individual developing their own objectives without considering the corporate governance strategy. Ethical improprieties have led to calls for more stringent corporate governance and, as technology pervades most areas of a business, IT governance should be a top priority.

IT governance is described by the IT Governance Institute as 'an integral part of enterprise governance and consists of the leadership and organisational structures and processes that ensure that the organisation's IT sustains and extends the organisation's strategies and objectives' (ITGI 2003, p. 10). Getting every area of the business to work together requires communication between individuals and departments and requires frequent contact with, and from, the IT department. Executives from all departments should be involved in corporate governance committees and support IT governance activities within business units. This will get everyone involved in IT issues and ensure the development of an effective IT governance structure.

There are several corporate governance models that can be used to incorporate IT, such as Control Objectives for Information and related Technology (CoBIT). These can form the basis for developing the IT governance policy within an enterprise.

Management issues associated with IT governance are:

- *Strategic alignment:* requiring planned and purposeful management processes to align business with collaborative solutions.
- *Value delivery:* supporting the organisation by optimising expenses and proving the value of IT.
- *Risk management:* managing operational and system risks, which means safeguarding IT assets and disaster recovery.
- *Resource management:* optimising knowledge and infrastructure including people, applications, data, technology and facilities.
- *Performance measurement:* tracking IT projects and monitoring services by using the balanced scorecard approach.

IT governance is a complex area, but it must be included in the corporate governance of any entity that uses IT, not left to each department or business unit.

Source: information from Ron Exler, 'IT governance frameworks', *CIO Magazine*, www2.cio.com/analyst/report1559.html (accessed March 2004).

IS in action

British Computer Society Code of Conduct

The Code of Conduct of the British Computer Society governs personal conduct and covers the following areas:

- the public interest
- duty to the profession
- professional competence and integrity
- duty to relevant authority.

Some of the key points are:

The public interest

1 You shall carry out work or study with due care and diligence in accordance with the relevant authority's requirements, and the interests of system users. If your professional judgement is overruled, you shall indicate the likely risks and consequences.

—The crux of the issue here, familiar to all professionals in whatever field, is the potential conflict between full and committed compliance with the relevant authority's wishes, and the independent and considered exercise of your judgement.

—If your judgement is overruled, you are encouraged to seek advice and guidance from a peer or colleague on how best to respond....

Duty to relevant authority

7 You shall avoid any situation that may give rise to a conflict of interest between you and your relevant authority. You shall make full and immediate disclosure to them if any conflict is likely to occur or be seen by a third party as likely to occur....

9 You shall not misrepresent or withhold information on the performance of products, systems or services, or take advantage of the lack of relevant knowledge or inexperience of others....

Duty to the profession

11 You shall act with integrity in your relationships with all members of the BCS and with members of other professions with whom you work in a professional capacity.

12 You shall have due regard for the possible consequences of your statements on others. You shall not make any public statement in your professional capacity unless you are properly qualified and, where appropriate, authorised to do so. You shall not purport to represent the BCS unless authorised to do so.

—The offering of an opinion in public, holding oneself out to be an expert in the subject in question, is a major personal responsibility and should not be undertaken lightly.

—To give an opinion that subsequently proves ill founded is a disservice to the profession, and the BCS....

(continued)

Professional competence and integrity

14 You shall seek to upgrade your professional knowledge and skill, and shall maintain awareness of technological developments, procedures and standards which are relevant to your field, and encourage your subordinates to do likewise. . . .

17 You shall accept professional responsibility for your work and for the work of colleagues who are defined in a given context as working under your supervision. . . .

Source: extracted from the British Computer Society, 'Code of Conduct', Version 2.0, 5 September 2001, www.bcs.org.uk (accessed March 2004). Reproduced with the permission of the British Computer Society.

Ergonomics

Most people have heard of the word **ergonomics**. It is used in many situations including advertisements for kitchens, computers and many other everyday objects.

According to the UK Ergonomics Society (www.ergonomics.org.uk), a definition of the term is:

> Ergonomics is about fit: the fit between people, the things they do, the objects they use and the environments they work, travel and play in. If good fit is achieved, the stresses on people are reduced. They are more comfortable, they can do things more quickly and easily, and they make fewer mistakes.

The 'fit' takes into account not just the physical factors but also psychological and other factors. In some countries, ergonomics is referred to as 'human factors'.

Poor ergonomic design can result in increased error rates and physical fatigue and, in the long term, physical problems. Ergonomics is especially relevant to the office environment and to using computers. One aspect of ergonomics is inclusive design where products are designed with, for example, older and disabled users in mind.

Information design or the way we use information is another important area of human factors. The design of signs, symbols and instructions is part of information design. This includes the design of computer software interfaces to make them easier and more effective to use.

■ **Reflection question 3:** Does your current working situation rate highly ergonomically?

Physical and psychological issues are key areas of concern related to ergonomics and information systems.

Physical issues

Repetitive strain injury (RSI) is caused by the inflammation of muscles, nerves or tendons. In extreme cases the problem can lead to permanent tissue damage. RSI is caused by many repetitions of the same activity, maintaining a static posture for too long, and failing to take short breaks. Use of the keyboard over prolonged periods is a reported cause of RSI.

Arm and neck problems can be a result of badly designed workstations where the user has to reach too far or twist awkwardly in the process of working. These problems can be alleviated by relaxing while working, taking breaks and changing tasks frequently. It is best to have the keyboard positioned right under your hands with your elbows bent at 90 degrees. The backrest of your chair should support the hollow of your back.

Eye strain can be caused by focusing on the screen for prolonged periods without taking breaks. The user should also look away from the screen from time to time and focus on distant objects briefly.

Psychological issues

Badly designed systems can lead to poor productivity and hence dissatisfaction in general. In extreme cases, this can cause stress and lead to periods off work. The safety and welfare of staff is an important issue — the work environment should be conducive to high-quality work.

A poorly designed interface can lead to an increase in errors being input into the systems, increased search time when looking for information on the screen and wasted time working through poor software navigation systems.

[**Key concept:** Ergonomic design pays in the long run.]

Infobyte

Workplace layout

Symptoms of musculoskeletal disorders (MSDs) are common among workers in office environments. These symptoms most commonly occur in the neck, lower arms, wrists and shoulders. To alleviate these problems, workstation design and layout should be considered. In particular, the placement of the keyboard and mouse and posture while sitting at the workstation should be reviewed.

Some questions that could help you find the best layout of your work area include:

- Is my seat the right height?
- Where is the best place to position my work?
- Do I need a footrest?
- How high should my bench be?
- What should be the angle of my seat?
- How far should I reach?

The physical layout of your workplace can lead to increased stress levels, especially if you work near noisy equipment or use hazardous materials. Workplace design also includes such things as air temperature, lighting and ventilation.

Summary

Organisational information systems are flourishing but many people are drowning in a sea of information. This chapter has discussed some issues related to being more effective on a personal level with information systems.

The key points in this chapter are:

- The main transferable skills required to be a knowledge worker in the knowledge economy are related to gathering information, processing and organising information and communicating information.
- It is important to have the right mindset to take advantage of digital technology — be in it for the long term.
- Using digital technology requires new approaches to working including getting data into digital format as soon as possible.
- Information overload results from having access to too much information, especially at an individual level. It can be dealt with by having strategies to manage email and by developing a personal information system.
- Computer societies have developed codes of conduct to guide their members in the ethical use of information systems.
- An ergonomically designed system can reduce the potential of physical and psychological problems directly attributed to working with computer systems.

Questions

1. What skills are required by workers in the knowledge economy?
2. Why is it important to have a positive outlook in relation to the use of information technology?
3. Is information overload likely to lead to stress? Why?
4. List and explain five ways to reduce information overload.
5. Suggest ways to manage emails effectively.
6. What techniques and methods can be used as part of a personal information system?
7. What types of injuries can occur through using badly designed workstations?
8. Explain why ethical behaviour is an important issue for information systems professionals.

Exercises

1. Develop a short questionnaire for use in your class to find out the extent to which information overload is a problem. From where do the problems arise — e.g. email, telephone, meetings, paper handouts, computer files? Determine how seriously the issue affects people's lives and their effectiveness as students or employees. Analyse the data obtained and use charts to illustrate your findings.
2. In a group of four, share ideas on how to deal with the issue of information overload. List your key recommendations. As a class share your ideas and rank the best suggestions in a list of 'Top ten ways to combat information overload'.
3. Compare the codes of conduct or codes of ethics of two computer societies (for example, the British Computer Society and the Australian Computer Society). These are typically available on the Web.

CASE STUDY Mandy's information overload

Mandy recently graduated from university with an accounting degree and landed what appeared to be a great job with a major accounting company. This is her first permanent job, as all her other jobs as a student involved working as a casual in supermarkets or fast-food outlets. After Mandy's first few months in the job she feels overwhelmed by the sheer volume of information that she has to deal with and feels that if it doesn't get any better she might have to quit the job.

Mandy receives a lot of emails from colleagues. There are some days when she gets fifty or so emails, and she cannot read them all and still get on with her work. Many of the emails have attachments that could be of use some time in the future. Mandy usually tries to be efficient by answering the emails as soon as they arrive. However, this causes an interruption to her work and stops her getting on with the task in hand. Overall she is very frustrated by the feeling of being overwhelmed. A few weeks earlier Mandy started to take more work home with her since there were fewer interruptions in the evening and at weekends. This has meant she now has more time for answering emails during the day. In addition, Mandy gave her work email address to friends and relatives, and she thinks this might have been a mistake.

The files on Mandy's office computer are not well organised, and she frequently spends a lot of time trying to find documents. She would like to know the best way for organising files on her hard disk.

Mandy has a computer at home connected to the Internet. It was bought when she was a first-year student to help with her studies. It is now three years old, and it is a bit slow to work on. Mandy is not sure whether she should buy another computer. Maybe a scanner would be useful also.

When Mandy takes work home in the evenings and at weekends she will often work on the computer. On many occasions she has forgotten to take a copy of the computer files back to work with her, and so the additional effort the evening before has been in vain.

Last weekend, she saw a Palmtop computer advertised in a magazine. She wonders whether it would be a worthwhile investment. Maybe she could use her mobile phone to access her emails.

While at work Mandy is passed a lot of forms and paperwork. They are now piling up on her desk and are adding to the feeling of being overwhelmed. Mandy has examined how her colleagues work in an attempt to find a role model. John started work at the same time as Mandy, and he too looks very disorganised. In fact, he has been reprimanded for missing a couple of recent meetings. He said that he completely forgot about them. He looks very stressed most of the time. Margaret on the other hand is completely organised. There isn't a paper on her desk, and she never looks stressed at all. Mandy asked her for advice. Margaret replied that these things are important:

- Refuse as much work as you can get away with. Always tell the boss that you have too much work to do in the hope he doesn't give you any more.
- Keep everything computerised. Throw away most paper copies of documents.

(*continued*)

- Never take work home — this is fatal!
- Send more emails than you receive. There is a politics to communication, and it makes it look as if you are always thinking about work even if you aren't.

Mandy thinks that she has little to learn from either John or Margaret.

Mandy is not finding her new job enjoyable because now there is no time to socialise with friends or even go to the gym. Maybe working in a shop would be better; at least she could have a social life.

QUESTIONS

1. What are the main problem areas that Mandy is faced with?
2. What can Mandy do to manage more effectively the information she is getting? Explain your answer in relation to the techniques, methods and information technology tools that can be used.
3. Does Mandy have the right attitude towards technology and information systems? Why or why not?
4. Explain what skills Mandy needs to develop to become more efficient in her handling of information.
5. Have you experienced anything in common with Mandy? Did you manage to overcome it? How?

References

Albrecht, K. 2001, 'The true information survival skills', *Training and Development*, February, pp. 24–30.

Edwards, B. 1979, *Drawing on the Right Side of the Brain*, J.P. Tarcher, Los Angeles.

IT Governance Institute 2003, 'Board briefing on IT governance', 2nd edn, www.itgi.org (accessed 15 March 2004).

ActiveX controls
software segments that are automatically downloaded with a web page to the client machine.

allocated cost centre
a situation in which IS costs are allocated to internal clients, which entails internal accounting and budget transfers.

alternative solutions phase
a phase in the systems development lifecycle when alternative solutions to the problem or potential systems are defined.

application program interface (API)
the toolbars and menus that are used to access software application functions. Ideally, APIs should be obvious and easy to use and standardised over a range of software.

application service provider (ASP)
a third party which provides developmental expertise in, and access to, large customisable software packages for businesses (usually small–medium enterprises). In some instances, the software manufacturer may assume the ASP role.

applications software
software which performs specific, non-systems related functions for users.

arithmetic and logic unit (ALU)
that part of a microprocessor which carries out arithmetic and logical functions.

artificial intelligence (AI)
a system which mimics human expertise, either generally or more usually in a specific field of endeavour such as fault diagnosis.

assembly language
second-generation, low-level programming language which uses mnemonic instructions.

authentication
deals with proving the identity of a person.

backbone network (BN)
a network which connects everything on the same site including other networks. Its main purpose is to provide interconnection.

back-ups
copies of data and software.

bandwidth
the difference in cycles per second (Hz) between the highest and lowest frequencies on a channel. It is the measure of a channel's ability to carry information. The bandwidth of the telephone system is around 3.3 kHz.

baseband
transmission of a signal in its original form, i.e. unaltered by modulation. Baseband transmission is digital, most often using direct current.

batch
a style of system operation in which transactions are grouped together (batched) for later processing.

batch systems
systems which store up transaction data for processing at a later time.

Bluetooth
a mobile wireless communication standard for low-cost short-range wireless communications between static and mobile PCs, mobile telephones and peripheral devices. Bluetooth was developed by a consortium which includes IBM and Intel, and allows the development of personal area networks (PANs).

broadband
an alternative name for analog transmission.

browser
software used to display web pages.

bus
the part of the system or motherboard that performs interconnection between the onboard components.

business-to-business e-business
e-business that deals with procurement between businesses.

business-to-consumer e-business
e-business that deals with supplying information, products or services to customers.

business engineering (BE)
a term which is more inclusive than business process re-engineering since it adopts a 'big picture' perspective on business activities.

business-level strategy
plans developed at a business level within an organisation where the business operates independently.

business model
the features and characteristics of a business that describe how a business operates.

business process re-engineering
redesigning business processes to achieve improvements in performance measures.

byte
measure of storage capacity, 8 binary digits.

cache
part of RAM set aside to be accessed as though it is disk, thus increasing performance. Data related to previous accesses are fetched into the cache on the off-chance that they might be needed. Some processors also have an internal cache to speed access to RAM.

cellular digital packet data (CDPD)
a specification for wireless access to the Internet and other public packet-switched networks. Usage may be point-to-point or multicast, and is usually offered at 19.2 Kbps.

central processor unit (CPU)
the microprocessor installed on a motherboard.

channel conflict
the issues and problems that arise from having multiple sales channels.

chief executive officer (CEO)
the most senior manager in an organisation responsible for all decisions made by the board of directors.

chief information officer (CIO)
the manager responsible for the information systems and strategy of an organisation.

chief technology officer (CTO)
responsible for keeping abreast of technology and the market, briefing other staff and outlining plans whereby the business could take advantage of the new technology within its existing IS framework in a cost-effective manner.

class
a template from which to create objects defining the data values and methods or functions that can be performed on the data.

collaborative commerce
the online exchange of ideas, data and information between business partners.

competitive strategic analysis
examination of the competition in the business environment to gain an advantage or advantages.

compiler
a translation program which translates the source code of a high-level language into a form which the processor can execute. Compilers are large programs which translate all of the program in one go. A compiler is only resident in RAM during the translation process and is specific to a particular hardware platform.

complex instruction-set chip (CISC)
the type of processor most often used in PCs; it has an extensive and versatile instruction set.

componentisation
a trend in many software systems whereby a large package is divided into functional modules that can be implemented or ignored as required.

compromising information integrity
a possible result of a virus attack on data files, whereby records such as financial statements may be modified.

computer-aided software engineering (CASE)
software tools to help in the development of systems through providing diagrammatic facilities for modelling the system and managing the process.

consumer-to-consumer e-business
consumers interact over the Web via an intermediary organisation.

control unit (CU)
that part of a processor responsible for coordinating/managing the execution of instructions.

corporate-level strategy
the highest level of strategy, which is developed by the most senior people in

the business, concerning long-term goals and objectives for the entire organisation.

creative destruction
closing or discontinuing part of a business to make way for more productive ventures.

custom software
software developed to meet a person's or organisation's specific needs, as opposed to buying packaged software.

customer relationship management (CRM)
the practice of using information systems such as enterprise resource planning and extended enterprise resource planning to manage all aspects of dealings with clients and customers.

customisable software
a software package which can be adapted to meet specific needs. This work is often carried out by integrators and value-added resellers.

database
a single central repository for corporate data together with a management system that allows data organisation, retrieval, update and analysis to be performed.

database administrator (DBA)
person who exercises control over the use of the database, manages the data and metadata and is responsible for the day-to-day running of the database and its security.

database management system (DBMS)
software that allows users to store, retrieve and update data in a database. It also allows the database adminstrator to control accounts, and structure and organise the data.

data-flow diagrams (DFDs)
a diagrammatic technique that models the processes in an organisation.

datamart
a smaller and more specialised version of a data warehouse in which archived and organised data may be analysed for relationships and trends.

data mining
the process of trawling through archived and processed data for useful information.

data modelling
a method of organising and documenting a system's data. Used in the early stages of database design.

data (or project) dictionary
a database of data and information gathered during the systems development process.

data privacy
concerned mainly with protecting the rights of the individual in terms of privacy.

data warehouse
a large collection of data categorised by information type rather than application origin. Data warehouses are equipped with online analytical processing tools for multidimensional analysis.

decision support system (DSS)
software that helps managers make decisions by modelling various scenarios. The data used can come from many sources including a data warehouse.

decision table
a technique to explain complex process logic in a tabular format.

denial of service
a malicious program that renders part of a system unusable.

dense wave division multiplexing (DWDM)
a type of frequency division multiplexing for optical fibre. Currently, up to forty 10 Gbps channels can be obtained on the same fibre and it is predicted that speeds will rise to a total of 25 terabits (trillion) without the need for new fibre.

digital audio tape (DAT)
serial access format used for data archival.

disclosure of information
occurs when a malicious program sends information about a system back to the program's originator.

disintermediation
process whereby intermediaries are bypassed in the sales chain.

divisional information officers (DIOs)
similar to a chief information officer but with responsibility for a specific business area rather than the entire enterprise. DIOs are found in distributed IS organisations.

dot.com
a company that exists entirely on the Web and has no real offline equivalent.

e-business
use of the Internet and related technologies and services in business.

e cycle
part of the machine cycle concerned with the execution of instructions.

electronic data interchange (EDI)
sale of goods and services online, typically on proprietary networks.

e-marketplaces
web-based environments where suppliers are matched with buyers for the sale of products, services and specialised equipment.

encryption
a method of changing the text in a file by using a coding system. It can be used when a file is transmitted over the Internet.

enterprise application integration (EAI)
a method of working which ignores lower level compatibility problems caused by hardware and data formats and focuses instead on achieving integration at the application level.

enterprise resource planning (ERP)
applying materials requirements planning concepts to almost every facet of business operation, including finance, accounting, marketing, human resource management. ERP is usually the province of large companies using large modular software suites which allow the business to be fully integrated.

entity relationship diagram (ERD)
a diagrammatic style of data modelling that shows the relationships between the data in a business.

environmental scanning
gathering data on trends and competitors from various sources.

eraseable programmable read-only memory (EPROM)
ROM chips that can be programmed, erased and reprogrammed.

ergonomics
the study of the engineering aspects of the relationship between human workers and their working environment.

e-tailing
online retailing.

ethical behaviour
decent, fair, good, honest or moral behaviour.

executive information system (EIS)
a very high level business information system to support management and decision-making. Data may come from inside or outside the organisation. EISs may be linked to data warehouses.

expansion slots
spaces left on the motherboard to allow expansion cards to be fitted to add extra functionality to the system, e.g. a fax/modem card.

expert system
a system which mimics human expertise in a well-defined application area.

extended enterprise resource planning (EERP)
an ERP system which incorporates elements of electronic (often web-based) commerce in addition to supply chain management and customer relationship management.

fail soft
ability of a system to detect component failures and temporarily modify its processing to prevent irretrievable loss of data or equipment.

fast circuit switching
a hybrid scheme which combines the best of circuit and packet switch systems. The access time is very low and dependable and transmission is synchronous. It is more complicated than other methods but gives excellent performance.

fat client
a PC in a client–server network which stores and runs most of its own applications software. Fat clients are more expensive and difficult to manage than thin clients.

feasibility phase
phase in the systems development lifecycle that seeks to determine if a project is worthwhile, i.e. if the benefits outweigh the costs.

FireWire
newer standard high-speed PC port.

firmware
ROM chips (a chip with software already installed).

flash memory
semi-stable storage eraseable programmable read-only memory on a card, faster but more expensive than a hard drive and of much lower capacity. Widely used in handhelds, mobile telephones and digital cameras.

flexible manufacturing system (FMS)
computer-operated manufacturing tools which can carry out a wide range of processes instead of the older, highly specialised dedicated machinery. FMSs can be set up economically for short production runs, reducing product cycle times.

floating point operations per second (FLOPS)
measure of processor performance or, more specifically, the ability of the processor to perform mathematical functions.

forward engineering
the process of deriving a new system following requirements analysis, specification and design.

fourth-generation language (4GL)
a non-procedural language. A user formulating a request does not need to specify exactly how that request is to be carried out by the computer. 4GLs are easier to use than procedural languages and are often found in applications such as databases.

frequency division multiplexing (FDM)
a method for sharing the use of a communication medium by allocating different frequency bands to different users, thus creating multiple simultaneous channels. Used in analog transmission systems.

function-level strategy
deals with plans at the functional level of a business, such as marketing, information systems and finance.

Gantt chart
a form of bar chart that shows the activities of a project and the amount of time each activity will take.

general ledger system
a transaction processing system for recording basic financial data. Most of an organisation's transaction processing systems would be tied into a general ledger system somehow.

geosynchronous earth orbit (GEO)
the so-called Clarke orbit in which satellites orbit the Earth at a height of 35 680 km above the equator.

gigabyte
approximately 1 trillion bytes.

gigahertz
a measure of system clock speed, one trillion cycles per second.

government-to-citizen e-business
governments interacting with citizens via the Web.

graphical user interface (GUI)
an interface which allows the user to interact with the system without the need to resort to inputting commands in text format. Windows 2000 provides a GUI.

group decision support system (GDSS)
networked hardware and software that allows work groups to collaborate on brainstorming and decision-making processes. Eliminating human interaction and allowing anonymity sometimes improves the quality and speed of outcomes.

groupware
hardware and software which support document creation, management and communications for work groups. Combined with intelligent agents, groupware improves productivity and facilitates systems integration.

guard band
gaps (wasted bandwidth) between the frequencies allocated to users in radio and microwave analog systems to prevent transmissions interfering with each other. In digital systems, the need for guard bands is minimal, making more effective use of bandwidth.

hierarchical database
a system of database organisation in which data are shown as a logical hierarchy, a series of parent and child nodes. Hierarchical views can model

one-to-many relationships very well and deliver excellent performance when used as intended. However, for ad hoc or complex queries, performance is poor due to vastly increased search space.

high-level language
a third-generation procedural language (3GL). 3GLs are closer to natural language than machine code or assembly languages, and usually incorporate some elements of structure which allow subprogram units to be reused in other programs. 3GLs allow programs to be moved from one computer to another and recompiled for use on that machine.

horizontal software
software which is general purpose and widely used throughout business, such as word processing and spreadsheet software.

hub
junction boxes which connect computers with the network. These are usually broadcast devices and may also be called concentrators, multi-station access units or transceivers. Hubs simplify the process of cabling and make it easier to relocate and add computers to the network.

human–computer interaction (HCI)
the theory and practice of how users interact with computer systems.

hyperlinks
a method of navigating through the Web. They are clickable text, icons or graphics which link to other web pages or other parts of the same web page.

hypertext markup language (HTML)
the language of the Internet used for describing web pages to web browsers.

hypertext transfer protocol (HTTP)
the Web communications protocol; handles the transfer of data over the Internet.

i cycle
instruction cycle, the half of the machine cycle in which instructions are fetched and translated.

implementation
stage in the systems development lifecycle when the system is physically built and put in place.

information age
period and societies characterised by a large percentage of people working with information and information systems.

information architecture
defines the data, processes, information, organisational network and stakeholders in information systems; explains information technology trends and opportunities; defines the technology needed to support the aims of the organisation.

information economy
the exchange and sale of information and knowledge and related services.

information overload
a syndrome related to receiving too much information to process.

information security policy
a document detailing the strategies, methods and techniques related to information security.

information systems methodology
a collection of philosophies, phases, procedures, rules, techniques, tools, documentation, management and training for developers of information systems.

integrated circuits
system of electronic manufacture in which previously separate components are reduced in size and integrated into a modular sub-assembly.

integrated package
a single software package which performs several functions, e.g. database, spreadsheet and word processing. Integrated packages are more limited in functionality than software suites.

integrators
third parties who provide systems solutions by combining hardware and software from different sources and adapting them to meet the client's needs.

intelligent agent (IA)
a software entity that carries out tasks for users in an intelligent and autonomous way, e.g. an IA might search the Web for the cheapest air fares for a particular journey.

interpreter
a translation program similar to a compiler except that it translates a program line by line and is permanently in RAM at run-time. Interpreter programs run more slowly than compiled code.

IS planning
the development of medium- and long-range plans for IT and IS in an organisation.

Java
an object-oriented programming language that can be embedded in web pages to add extra functionality, such as animation.

Java applet
small graphical Java program.

joint application design (JAD)
intensive workshops with key personnel and a skilled facilitator with the aim of capturing the essential requirements for a system in as short a time frame as possible.

just-in-time (JIT) delivery
the practice of reducing stock on hand by having suppliers deliver materials as they are required. This makes available capital that would have been tied up in stock on hand and reduces direct overheads.

kilobyte
approximately 1000 bytes.

knowledge economy
characterised by the buying and selling of knowledge, information and data.

knowledge management
the process of creating, storing, managing, accessing and sharing tactic and explicit knowledge within the organisation.

legacy systems
older information systems that need to be incorporated into the present IS environment because it is uneconomical to redevelop them.

light-emitting diode (LED)
used in computer displays, as warning lights or as signalling devices for multimode optical fibres.

LINUX
a PC version of UNIX developed in 1991 by Linus Torvalds; the source code was made freely available, encouraging software developers to produce applications for it. It has the potential to be a serious competitor to Microsoft Windows.

liquid crystal displays (LCDs)
devices used to display screen output in laptops and handheld devices.

low earth orbit (LEO)
for satellites at a height of 640–1600 km. Launch costs are much lower than for other orbits and because the distances involved are much less, both satellites and users can use less powerful signals. However, due to the frequently changing position of the satellites, more satellites are needed for global communications.

lower computer-aided software engineering (CASE) tools
concentrate on the later stages of the systems development lifecycle (implementation and maintenance).

machine code
first-generation procedural code in binary form. Has no structure and the code produced is specific to a particular processor.

machine cycle
the cycle that a processor goes through in the execution of instructions.

mainframe
large, centralised computer for corporate use.

maintenance
stage in a system's lifecycle when the system requires amendments and updating.

materials as needed (MAN)
a system similar to just-in-time delivery, but it delivers supplies when and where they are actually needed.

materials requirements planning (MRP)
a precursor to enterprise resource planning in which the manufacture supply chain is intelligently managed to yield greater efficiencies and cost-effectiveness.

m-commerce
mobile e-commerce, i.e. accessing the Web for business from a mobile phone.

medium earth orbit (MEO)
for satellites used for communications and earth resource mapping. Medium

earth orbits are inclined to the equator at a height of around 9600 km. The overcrowded geosynchronous earth orbit (GEO), shorter delay time and cheaper costs make MEO an attractive option for many applications.

megabyte
approximately 1 million bytes.

megahertz
measure of system clock speed, one million cycles per second.

metadata
data about data; data structures, relationships, methods of data organisation and access are defined. Usually used in a database context.

methodology
an approach to solving a problem.

metropolitan area network (MAN)
a network which interconnects local area networks and provides gateway services to wide area networks over a citywide area.

millions of instructions per second (MIPS)
measure of processor performance.

mission statement
expands the vision statement to state the broad objectives of the business.

mobile agent
an intelligent agent which 'moves' around in a network to carry out its tasks. By carrying out work at source, it reduces the load on networks. Mobile agents are slow to catch on because of security and portability problems.

modulation
the process whereby an electromagnetic wave's amplitude, frequency or phase is changed in order to transmit information. The characteristics of a carrier wave are changed by another 'modulating' waveform.

Moore's law
the rule of thumb which notes that the cost-effectiveness of microprocessor devices increases by a factor of 2 every 18 months or so.

motherboard
also known as systemboard, the main circuit board in a PC holding the central processing unit, random access memory, read-only memory, etc.

multimedia interfaces
interfaces that include graphics, text, audio and video.

network administrator/manager
person with responsibility for the day-to-day running of all corporate networks, overseeing accounts etc.

network database
system of database organisation that expresses relationships between data nodes by making connections between them. This can be fairly flexible but link management limits its use in complex databases.

network interface card (NIC)
a PC card which handles the interface between the computer and the network. It converts the computer's parallel logic into network serial logic and vice versa, and carries out signalling.

network structure
a flatter organisational distributed form that relies on communication technologies with decentralised decision-making.

non-procedural languages
languages in which users input a request without needing to specify how that request is to be met. For example, when retrieving records from a database, a user might request the names and contact details of all employees earning more than $70 000. The user would not need to specify file names and precise locations, or how the the search should be carried out.

object modelling
defining objects, along with their relationships to other objects, for the system being developed.

object-oriented development
systems development methodology which focuses on the use of objects and their reuse as a fundamental design feature.

object-oriented programming (OOP)
a system of programming in which data and executable code are packaged together to form an object. These objects can be used as templates to develop new objects, and objects can be copied and reused as

needed. Object-oriented programming favours rapid applications development.

online analytical processing (OLAP)
set of multidimensional analytical tools for use in datamarts and data warehouses. They allow hidden trends and relationships to be discovered.

online auctions
where an online company, often a broker, takes the highest bid for a product or service.

online communities
real-time online forums where people who have something in common can communicate and exchange information.

open systems
systems which use software which is not proprietary but which is in the public domain. Often used to refer to products which are proprietary but are available for any industry-standard platform.

operational management
management of daily activities in an organisation.

optical fibre
hair-thin glass strands used to carry information at high speed. Most fibres are multimode but the fastest fibres are monomode.

order-entry systems
a transaction processing system which can accept data from a variety of sources and produce the required billing information.

organic light-emitting diodes (OLEDs)
newer technology for lightweight, high-definition screen displays which may replace liquid crystal displays.

organisational structure
the administrative and decision-making mechanisms within an organisation.

outsourcing
transferring responsibility for some area of a business to an outside source.

paradigm
the basic framework of a discipline, language/jargon, protocols, systems of thinking etc. Hence paradigm shift caused by new technology.

personal area network (PAN)
a small (one room) network of a PC and associated devices or a one-person network providing mobile network services over a short range. PANs usually (though not exclusively) make use of mobile communications.

personal data assistant (PDA)
small palmtop or handheld PC or smart organiser for individual use.

pervasive networking
communications and networking which are virtually everywhere. As communications continue to improve, it is possible to offload the burden of computing from desktop and handheld machines to the network; in short, the network becomes the computer.

pixel
the smallest addressable point on a display screen.

point of sale (POS) systems
a transaction processing system which gathers transaction data at the point of sale, often using direct data entry via bar codes. Frequently seen in supermarkets.

Porter's competitive forces model
emphasises five competitive forces to analyse the competition within an industry.

primary storage
on-board memory which may be subdivided into random access memory and read-only memory.

procedural language
a third-generation high-level programming language, close to natural language, in which users must specify exactly what must be done and how it must be done.

process models
models of the systems that define the processes or actions within an organisation.

profit centre
a method of charging out for IS services that makes no distinction between internal and external clients. This tends to increase prices and increase the likelihood of outsourcing parts of the IS function.

program evaluation and review technique (PERT)
a sophisticated diagrammatic tool for specifying the complexity of a project.

programmable ROM (PROM)
ROM chip that can be programmed.

programmer
a person who produces software according to a given specification.

project architect/applications development manager
monitors and helps coordinate all software development activity with an emphasis on reducing duplication and enforcing standards.

project dictionary
see data dictionary.

PROM blaster
device used to embed software into chips.

proprietary systems
systems in which the hardware and/or software are specific to their suppliers, making flexibility and adaptability difficult.

protocol
the rules which govern the exchange of information within a network. They say how communication is to be established, what to do in case of an error etc.

prototype
a system that is part of a solution developed to obtain feedback from users and make for a more interactive development cycle.

quantum computer
a computer which offers a theoretical alternative to conventional computing which would give very high performance and small size. No quantum computer has yet been built, although low-level switching devices have been constructed.

random access memory (RAM)
chips on the motherboard which store programs and data so that the central processing unit can access them.

rapid application development (RAD)
combines prototyping, computer-aided software engineering and joint application design in an iterative cycle until the users and developers are satisfied with the system designs.

read-only memory (ROM)
chips on the motherboard which have instructions embedded in them, e.g. for starting the system, carrying out diagnostics.

real-time systems
systems which process transactions as soon as they are received.

reduced instruction-set chip (RISC)
a type of chip which is optimised for a number of instructions. Complex instructions are rendered by combining simple instructions. RISC technology is used in workstations and Apple computers and is usually faster than CISC technology.

redundant arrays of inexpensive disks (RAIDs)
method of improving system reliability and disk access speeds by distributing and sometimes replicating data over several disks instead of one.

refresh
when a screen display changes, it is said to be refreshed. The higher the refresh rate, the less the screen appears to flicker.

reintermediation
process whereby intermediaries reposition themselves on the Web.

relational database
system of database organisation that groups data into relations or tables. Data are accessed using relationships between and within tables.

request for proposal (RFP)
an invitation to a vendor to prepare a bid for the supply of goods and/or services.

reservation system
a transaction processing system which allows users to reserve hotel rooms, book air travel etc.

resolution
the clarity of a monitor determined by the total number of pixels and the density of pixels on the screen.

return on investment (ROI)
a measure of cost-effectiveness; more formally, the ratio of generated income divided by outgoing costs.

reverse auctions
where the customer makes an offer for a product stating how much they are prepared to pay, and the seller decides whether to accept it.

reverse engineering
the practice of deriving specifications for software (and often firmware) from an existing, frequently undocumented, system.

router
a device which can interconnect similar and dissimilar local area networks and similar wide area networks. Routers have a high degree of software intelligence and can choose the best route for communication when there are multiple paths. They can also handle several message streams, enabling (for example) several simultaneous Internet connections to be managed.

search engines
software systems located at web sites that collect and order information from the Internet.

single inline memory modules (SIMMs)
subassembly of memory chips affixed to the motherboard.

small–medium enterprise (SME)
most businesses are assumed to be small if they employ 19 or fewer people; the number required for a medium-sized enterprise is widely accepted to be fewer than 650. Changes in technology and economics have led to an increase in the number of SMEs worldwide.

soft systems methodology (SSM)
a people-centred methodology for defining the problem and requirements of a system.

software crisis
a term used in the 1970s when it was realised that the demand for software was increasing exponentially while the supply of software developers was increasing only linearly. This shortfall limited the amount of software that could be supplied.

software suite
a set of separate programs which may be purchased individually or as a bundle and which can work together and share information. Microsoft Office is a well-known example.

solutions architect
a person who elicits information and knowledge requirements throughout the organisation, consolidates and rationalises those needs and then provides infrastructure-based solutions. Solutions architects are especially useful in enterprise resource planning.

strategic alliances
links or associations between organisations that provide a strategic advantage.

strategic driver
a force that enables the business to improve in relation to competitors.

strategic plan
a map of actions to be taken that has been developed from the strategy.

strategy
the planning and directing of actions to achieve overall objectives.

structured English
a restricted English technique to clearly explain an organisational procedure.

supply chain management (SCM)
the practice of linking one's suppliers into core business processes. This usually involves the use of information systems to improve linkages between supplier and customer to facilitate ordering, payment and delivery.

switch
connects two or more network segments that use the same protocol, or individual users within the same network segment. Since switches provide synchronous communication and allow all ports to be in use at the same time, they make much more efficient use of bandwidth than hubs and allow applications such as video-conferencing.

SWOT analysis
an assessment of the strengths, weaknesses, environmental opportunities of and threats to an organisation.

system unit
the main box of a PC containing the motherboard, hard drive, DVD etc.; does not include the monitor, mouse, keyboard or peripheral devices.

systemboard
another term for motherboard.

systems analyst/business analyst
often the graduate entry position into the IS industry. Involved with every aspect of

the systems development lifecycle with the exception of programming.

systems conversion
phase in the systems development lifecycle when the system is handed over to the users.

systems design
phase in the systems development lifecycle when the features of the proposed system are defined in detail.

systems development
process of developing or building information systems.

systems development lifecycle (SDLC)
a framework for developing information systems. Consists of the classical phases of analysis, design, implementation and maintenance; provides a logical and structured approach for building systems.

systems manager/operations manager
the person responsible for the entire day-to-day running of the IS division from an operational perspective.

systems software
software which controls the underlying resources of the computer, manages file systems, drives devices etc. and which provides a convenient interface between the user and the hardware. Microsoft Windows is a well-known example.

telecommuter
person who works away from the company, at home or on the road, and who uses communications technology to access corporate systems.

testing
the stage in developing systems when components, such as software, are checked for correctness and reliability.

thin client
a PC in a client–server network which downloads most of its application software from a server as required. Thin clients are cheaper and easier to manage than fat clients.

time division multiplexing (TDM)
a system of 'turn taking' to control the use of a communication medium. Transmitting parties are given a time slot during which they have exclusive use of the medium. It is most common in (but not exclusive to) digital transmission systems.

transaction
a group of instructions that are grouped together for atomic execution, i.e. the entire group of instructions either executes or does not — there are no half measures.

transaction processing system (TPS)
a system which executes transactions in a reliable manner and records their details.

turnkey system
an off-the-shelf ready-to-roll system for a particular industry segment, such as the restaurant trade.

unallocated cost centre
a system of accounting in which the IS function is considered to be an organisational cost. The IS manager often receives a one-line budget for the financial year and no further budget transfers or charges are made.

uniform resource locator (URL)
a web site address.

universal serial bus (USB)
a newer PC port standard which is much faster than older serial and parallel ports. It is used for webcams, flash memory, scanners and other applications which require a high transfer rate.

UNIX
an older example of system software which is well established and available for most computer platforms. Its PC derivative, LINUX, is much less demanding in terms of hardware requirements than products such as Windows. UNIX is an open system in that the source code is available to anyone who wishes to develop programs for the UNIX (or LINUX) platform, in contrast to systems such as Windows which are proprietary.

upper computer-aided software engineering (CASE) tools
CASE tools that focus on the early stages of the systems development lifecycle, especially the analysis and design phases.

value-added reseller (VAR)
a person or company that takes an existing software product and adds extra

functionality to it in order to increase its value to a client. Many software companies have a list of approved VARs.

value chain analysis
examination of the business as an input–output chain.

vertical software
software that is targeted to a particular function or narrow market sector in business, i.e. software that could not be widely used, as word processing software is.

very large scale integration (VLSI)
refers to microchips having millions of components on the same piece of silicon, a vast improvement on the previous integrated circuit technology.

virtual local area network (VLAN)
a system in which intelligent switches replace hubs. The switches are used to create network segments which may be managed independently if required. The attached computers and devices may be 'moved' from one segment to another using software; no physical movement or recabling is needed. This in turn allows staff to be assigned to different project teams and work groups easily. It may be thought of as a network within a network.

virtual organisation
structures that are made up of different companies or individuals that come together to complete certain tasks.

virtual private networks (VPNs)
include both public and private resources. A company can lease a bundle of circuits and configure the VPN on a needs basis so that some traffic flows over the public carrier and some on the private network. Like a virtual local area network, it may be thought of as a network within a network.

virtuoso programmer
a specialist and highly talented programmer. For example, such people may rewrite critical portions of software in order to improve the performance of a system.

virus infection
in this context it means a software program designed to damage or infect other files or consume system resources.

vision statement
a definition of the main purpose of the business.

voice over Internet protocol (VoIP)
a way to converse via an Internet connection, even while browsing web pages.

Von Neumann machine
the architecture used by most modern computers; relies on a single processor and data and programs being stored in RAM.

web manager/administrator
person who manages web sites. Often controls the company intranet and performs web site design.

wrapper engineering
'wrapping' old systems in newer, more friendly systems, thus providing a more convenient interface to users and other systems.

XML (extensible markup language)
allows the display of text and data in a browser like HTML but also provides a context and a structure for creating a knowledge structure.

Index

C

J

K

S

T

U